T0323811

"This latest book from global expert Henry Wang is another example of his absolutely detailed and inspiring knowledge of the critical issues in relation to this topic. Henry makes it clear what the challenges and opportunities are. He has expounded these in a body of work that leaves the reader so much better informed."

Simon Haigh, BA *(Hons Law Dunelm)*, *MBA, GAICD, FAIM;*
Managing Director & International Lawyer, Leading International
Executive Coach and Global Growth Strategist

"Another pearl released to the world; Author Henry Wang puts forth the critical place we are in the world with climate issues. Henry is a world renowned and respected voice for the issues in this great book and his perspective is on-point and relevant."

H.E. Ambassador Terry Earthwind Nichols, *Chairman,*
Evolutionary Healer, LLC, Leading International Executive Coach
and Keynote Speaker

The Roadmap for Sustainable Business and Net Zero Carbon Emission

What does sustainable business and net zero carbon emission mean for businesses globally? How should companies globally transform into sustainable businesses with net zero carbon emissions? This book unpacks the institutional, organisational and management challenges in pursuing sustainable business and carbon neutrality for businesses.

In this book, Henry K. H. Wang, an internationally recognised Climate and Business expert, provides real-life cases across different countries and business sectors. He outlines potential policy implications and strategy options for companies to consider in their transitions to sustainable business practices. He also explores important new global developments in smart cities, green transport and carbon solutions, and how the adoption of sustainable finance and green investments can accelerate business transformation.

This book will appeal to anyone interested to learn more about the successful planning and execution of sustainable business and net zero carbon neutrality transformations.

Henry K. H. Wang is an international advisor, author and speaker with extensive high-level business experience. He is President of Gate International and a former director of both Shell China and SABIC in Riyadh. He is a Fellow of the Royal Society of Arts (FRSA) and Fellow of Institute of Chemical Engineering. He has been invited to join the G20/B20 Taskforces and Action Councils to advise Global Leaders. He is also a board member of the London University SOAS SCI Advisory Board and China Carbon Forum Advisory Board. He has published five books as well as over 100 papers and speeches.

The Roadmap for Sustainable Business and Net Zero Carbon Emission

Henry K. H. Wang

Routledge
Taylor & Francis Group

LONDON AND NEW YORK

Designed cover image: © Getty Images

First published 2023
by Routledge
4 Park Square, Milton Park, Abingdon, Oxon OX14 4RN

and by Routledge
605 Third Avenue, New York, NY 10158

Routledge is an imprint of the Taylor & Francis Group, an informa business

British Library Cataloguing-in-Publication Data
A catalogue record for this book is available from the British Library

Library of Congress Cataloging-in-Publication Data
Names: Wang, Henry K. H., author.
Title: The roadmap for sustainable business and net zero carbon emission / Henry K. H. Wang.
Description: New York, NY: Routledge, 2023. | Includes bibliographical references and index. |
Identifiers: LCCN 2022050676 (print) | LCCN 2022050677 (ebook) |
ISBN 9780367695712 (hardback) | ISBN 9780367695699 (paperback) |
ISBN 9781003142348 (ebook)
Subjects: LCSH: Industrial management—Environmental aspects. |
Corporations—Environmental aspects. | Social responsibility of business. | Carbon dioxide mitigation.
Classification: LCC HD30.255.W346 2023 (print) |
LCC HD30.255 (ebook) | DDC 658.4/08—dc23/eng/20221024
LC record available at https://lccn.loc.gov/2022050676
LC ebook record available at https://lccn.loc.gov/2022050677

ISBN: 9780367695712 (hbk)
ISBN: 9780367695699 (pbk)
ISBN: 9781003142348 (ebk)

DOI: 10.4324/9781003142348

Typeset in Goudy
by codeMantra

Contents

Author's Notes

This book is based on the author's research, literature surveys, high-level business experiences and learnings accumulated over some 40 plus years of successful international businesses globally. He has worked as senior executive and international advisor, author and speaker plus as director and board member of leading companies. He has also been invited to advise various leading universities, international institutions and companies.

The views expressed in this book are results of the research insights, personal learnings and high-level business experiences of the author. This book represents a contribution by the author, as part of his global corporate social responsibilities together with his services to support the development of future thought leaders plus outstanding professionals from various countries globally. We hope that this book would also help executives and professional practitioners as well as academics, researchers and students.

Preface

This new book aims to provide a holistic overview of the institutional, organisational and management challenges that underpin various successful roadmaps for various companies globally to adopt in their urgent transformations to become sustainable businesses with net zero carbon emissions and to achieve their carbon neutrality targets.

Sustainable business development and net zero carbon emissions/carbon neutrality are currently an urgent topic for governments, companies, non-governmental organisations (NGOs) and universities globally. Companies face rising pressure from governments globally to transform into sustainable businesses and to achieve their net zero carbon emissions and carbon neutrality targets, so as to meet Paris Agreement commitments. There is also strong rising pressure from international stakeholders, shareholders, investors, NGOs and public interest groups. This is matched by growing demands for full disclosure and transparency from businesses on their new business strategies and plans.

Industrialisation and rising fossil-fuel consumption globally have resulted in rising emissions and pollution. This has led to global warming and worsening environmental pollution in many countries. Significant international pressure is being applied to reduce emissions and mitigate the worst impacts of climate change. Many countries are promoting clean energy transitions by raising renewable energy usage and reducing fossil-fuel consumption. Leading countries are also actively developing new net zero carbon neutrality pathways as part of their Paris Agreement commitments, and local governments are also enacting new climate and carbon policies that companies will have to comply with. In the face of fierce competition and the changing business landscape, developing good new corporate strategies and business plans will be essential to support the successful transformation of various companies into long-term sustainable businesses with net zero carbon emissions.

This new book will address these latest developments and their key strategic challenges and opportunities. The important interlinking roles of governments, international agencies, businesses and individuals will be addressed. Potential new policy implications and strategic options for companies to consider in their sustainable business and net zero carbon emission plus carbon neutrality transformations globally will be addressed. High-level international business examples and case studies are also included, as will reference sources from leading universities, international agencies and taskforces that the author has been invited to work with or advise.

Each chapter will include the key underlying challenges together with potential new strategies and approaches along with international examples and case studies. It will also provide practical and theoretical perspectives with a relevant up-to-date commercial business context so as to help international business executives and professionals better understand the challenges in developing their roadmap for sustainable business and net zero carbon emission plus carbon neutrality globally. The book will also help academics, researchers and students in their research on the various roadmaps for sustainable business and net zero carbon emission plus carbon neutrality, with a situational and contextual bound nature.

The book will also cover and include relevant international high-level country and business case examples based on the author's extensive international experience and involvements, for example, G20/B20 International Taskforces and Action Councils plus the advisory boards of leading global universities. There will be extensive use of relevant international examples and case studies to compare strategies and progress across different countries and multinational businesses. These should help the readers, practitioners, executives, students and academic staff to gain valuable first-hand insights into businesses that normally do not disclose this information. The book will also cite extensive secondary works by experts globally whilst building on existing knowledge in these important fields.

The roadmaps for sustainable business and net zero carbon emission plus carbon neutrality developments are important topics of rising global interest. Looking ahead, there should be attractive opportunities to provide regular updates to the book or new editions, so as to keep pace with the fast-growing changes, plus new policy and business developments globally.

Henry K. H. Wang is an international advisor, author and speaker with extensive high-level business experience globally. He is President of Gate International Ltd. plus a former director of Shell China and then SABIC in Riyadh. He has held various board roles in public companies and joint ventures globally. He has been invited to advise leading universities, international institutions and companies globally. He is invited to speak regularly at international conferences and media interviews. Leading universities and business schools globally frequently invite him to speak and lecture.

He is a Fellow of the Royal Society of Arts (FRSA) and a Fellow of Institute of Chemical Engineering, UK. He has been invited to join the London University SOAS SCI Advisory Board and the University College London China Advisory Board. He has been invited to join the UK Climate Change Committee Working Group and the Imperial College London Grantham Institute of Climate Change Stakeholder Committee plus the China Carbon Forum Advisory Board. He was a former Vice Chairman of the OECD Business Energy & Environment Committee, plus a former Vice President of the EU & British Chambers of Commerce of China. He is a graduate of Imperial College London and University College London. He has also undertaken advanced management courses at Wharton and Tsinghua.

He has published five books plus over 100 papers and speeches globally. The books included "Climate Change and Clean Energy Management" in 2019, "Renewable Energy Management in Emerging Economies" in 2020, "Successful Business Dealings & Management with China Oil, Gas & Chemical Giants" in 2014, "Energy Markets in Emerging Economies: Strategies for Growth" in 2017 and "Business Negotiations in China: Strategy, Planning and Management" in 2018. His negotiation management paper was selected as one of the Top Five UK Management Papers of the Year 2015 and published by UK Chartered Management Institute globally. He is also undertaking voluntary charity work in leadership, climate and sustainable developments globally.

Acknowledgements

I like to acknowledge the valuable inputs, support and encouragement that I have received from many senior executives, thought leaders and key stakeholders in top universities and business schools globally on this book.

My sincere thanks to Taylor & Francis Routledge who commissioned and published this book. I like to thank all the editorial, production and marketing staff who have contributed to the successful design, editing, copywriting, typesetting, proof-reading, publication and marketing of this book.

I would also like to thank the leading international institutions, universities and companies globally who have invited me to advise, speak and work with them on climate change, clean energy and sustainable developments. The keen interest from the international taskforce members, university staff and students plus various professionals globally has motivated me to write this book so as to share my experience and research with professionals, executives, academics and students globally.

I sincerely like to thank my late wife and two wonderful children plus my family for all their great support, love, understanding and encouragement which are much appreciated and treasured everyday. I also like to thank my mother, sisters and their families plus my close friends globally for their valuable advice and support. Their strong support and encouragement have been essential to keep me going on to complete the book with the large amounts of personal time and efforts required for the extensive research, writing and editing.

I would like to dedicate this book to my dear elderly mother whose love and support I very much value and appreciate.

Abbreviations

ACIA	ASEAN Comprehensive Investment Agreement
ADB	Asian Development Bank
AIIB	Asia Infrastructure Investment Bank
AMAC	Asset Management Association of China
ASEAN	Association of South East Asia Nations
ASW	ASEAN Single Window
B2C	Business-to-Consumer
BCM	Billion Cubic Meters
BDS	Big Data System
BECCU	Bio-Energy Carbon Capture Utilisation
BP	British Petroleum
BPD	Barrels Per Day
BRI	Belt and Road Initiative China
C40	C40 Global City Alliance
CAGR	Cumulative Annual Growth Rates
CASS	Chinese Academy of Social Science
CBRC	China Banking Regulatory Commission
CCAA	China Certification & Accreditation Agency (CNCA)
CCC	Committee on Climate Change UK (CCC)
CCER	Chinese Certified Emission Reductions or CCERs
CCPC	Chinese Communist Party Congress
cCR	Carbon Climate Registry (cCR)
CCR	Continuous Catalytic Reformers
CCS	Carbon Capture Storage
CCSU	Carbon Capture Storage Utilisation
CCU	Carbon Capture Utilisation
CDM	Clean Development Mechanism
CEO	Chief Executive Officer
CETS	Carbon Emission Trading Scheme
CF	Cubic Feet

CFO	Chief Finance Officer
CIETAC	China International Economic & Trade Arbitration Commission
CIF	Co-Investment Fund
CJV	Contractual Joint Venture
CNCA	The Chinese Certification and Accreditation Agency
CNODC	China National Oil and Gas Exploration and Development Corporation
CNOOC	China National Offshore Oil Corp
CNPC	China National Petroleum Corp
CM	Cubic Meters
CMI	Confederation of Management Institute UK
CMPY	Cubic Meters Per Year
CNPC	China National Petroleum Corporation
CO2	Carbon Dioxide
COP	Conference of the Parties
COP26	Conference of the Parties 26th Summit in Glasgow in Nov 2021
CPCIF	China Petroleum and Chemical Industry Federation
CPEIA	China Petroleum & Petroleum Equipment Industry Association
CSO	Combined Sewer Overflows
CSP	Concentrated Solar Power
CSR	Corporate Social Responsibility
CSRC	China Securities Regulatory Commission
CTO	Chief Technology Officer
DICP	Dalian Institute of Chemical Physics
DNL	Dalian National Laboratory for Clean Energy
DoS	Denial-of-Service
E&P	Exploration & Production
ECFA	Economic Cooperation Framework Agreement
EDF	Environmental Defence Fund
EGS	Enhanced Geothermal Systems
EIA	Environment Impact Assessment
EIA USA	Energy Information Administration of USA
EJV	Equity Joint Venture
EOR	Enhanced Oil Recovery
EPA	Environmental Protection Agency
EPB	Environmental Protection Bureau
EPC	Engineering, Procurement and Construction
ESG	Environment, Social and Governance (ESG)
ETS	Emission Trading Scheme

EV	Electric Vehicles
FAME	Fatty Acid Methyl Ester
FDI	Foreign Direct Investment
FIT	Feed-In Tariff
FORESEA	Funding for Ocean Renewable Energy through Strategic European Action project
FTA	Free Trade Agreement
FTZ	Free Trade Zones
FYP	Five Year Plans of China
GDP	Gross Domestic Products
GFANZ	Glasgow Financial Alliance for Net Zero (GFANZ)
GFC	Green Finance Committee (GFC) of the China Society for Finance and Banking
GFI	Green Finance Initiative UK
GHG	Green House Gases
GM	General Manager
GM	Genetically Modifications
GTL	Gas to Liquid
GVC	Green Venture Capital
GW	Giga watts
GWP	GHG Global Warming Potential
HKEX	Hong Kong Stock Exchange
HR	Human Resources
IBP	Integrated Business Planning
ICBC	Commercial and Industrial Bank of China
ICE	Internal Combustion Engines
IEA	International Energy Agency
IEFS	Integrated Food Energy Systems
IFC	International Finance Corporation
IFRS	International Financial Reporting Standards Foundations (IFRS)
IMF	International Monetary Fund
INDC	Intended Nationally Determined Contributions
INRM	Integrated Natural Resource Management
IOC	International Oil Company
IOT	Internet of Things
IPM	Integrated Pest Management
ISO	International Organization for Standardization
ISSB	International Sustainability Standards Board
JV	Joint Ventures
KPI	Key Performance Indicators
KBPD	Thousand or Kilo Barrels Per Day

KTPA	Thousand or Kilo Metric Tons Per Annum
LCOE	Levelized Cost of Electricity
LNG	Liquefied Natural Gas
LPG	Liquefied Petroleum Gas
LTO	Light Tight Oil
M&A	Merger and Acquisition
MEE	PRC China's Ministry of Ecology and Environment (MEE)
MENA	Middle East and North Africa
MEP	Ministry of Environmental Protection of China
MBPD	Million Metric Barrels Per Day
MLR	Ministry of Land and Resources of China
MTPA	Million Metric Tonnes Per Annum
MNC	Multi-National Company
MOFCOM	Ministry of Commerce of China
MOU	Memorandum of Understanding
MSW	Municipal Solid Wastes
MTG	Methanol to Gasoline
MTO	Methanol to Olefin
MTO+OCP	Methanol to Olefin + Olefin Cracking Process
NAFMII	National Association of Financial Market Institutional Investors China
NDC	Nationally Determined Contributions
NDRC	National Development Reform Commission of China
NELP	New Exploration Licensing Policy of India
NGL	Natural Gas Liquids
NOC	National Oil Company
NPC	National People's Congress of China
NPM	Non-Pesticidal Management
NSIDC	National Snow & Ice Data Centre
NSSF	National Social Security Fund China
NTB	Non-Tariff Barriers
OE	Oil Equivalent
OECD	Organisation of Economic Cooperation & Development
OPEC	Organisation Petroleum Exporting Countries
PAR	Project Application Report
PBOC	People Bank Of China
PHEV	Partial Hybrid Electric Vehicle
PDO	Petroleum Development Oman
PE	Poly-Ethylene
PMI	Purchasing Managers Index
PNG	Papua New Guinea
PP	Poly-Propylene

PPA	Power Purchase Agreements
PRC	People's Republic of China
Q&A	Questions & Answers
QP	Qatar Petroleum
REC	Renewable Energy Certificates
REDD	Reducing Emissions from Deforestation and forest Degradation
RFP	Request for Proposals (RFP)
RFS	Renewable Fuel Standard
SABIC	Saudi Arabia Basic Industries Company
SAFE	State Administration for Foreign Exchange
SAIC	State Administration for Industry and Commerce
SASAC	State Assets Supervision and Administration Commission
SAT	State Administration for Taxation
SAT	Soil Aquifer Treatment
SCEPC	State Council Environmental Protection Committee
SDG	Sustainable Development Goals UN
SECEP	Sinochem Energy Conservation & Environmental Protection Co. Ltd.
SECURE	Social Economic and Cultural Upliftment in Rural Communities India
SEEC	Saudi Arabia Energy Efficiency Centre
SFJV	Sino-Foreign Joint Venture
SG&A	Selling, General, and Administrative costs
SIA	Social Impact Assessment
SIPC	Sinopec International Petroleum Exploration & Production Corp.
SME	Small Medium Enterprise
SMTO	Sinopec Methanol to Olefin Process
SNG	Synthetic Natural Gas
SOE	State-Owned Enterprise
SPA	Sale & Purchase Agreements
SPC	Singapore Petroleum Company
SPR	Strategic Petroleum Reserves
SRI	Systems of Rice Intensification
SSE	Shanghai Stock Exchange
SST	Sea Surface Temperature
TCF	Trillion Cubic Feet
TCFD	Task Force on Climate Finance Disclosure
TCM	Trillion Cubic Meters
TES	Thermal Energy System
TPA	Tonnes Per Annum

TPD	Tonnes Per Day
TPP	Trans Pacific Partnerships by USA
UN	United Nations
UNCHE	United Nations Conference on the Human Environment
UNGC	United Nation Global Compact
UNIPCC	United Nation International Panel on Climate Change
UN PRI	UN Principles for Responsible Investment
USEPA	United States Environmental Protection Agency
VBM	Value-Based Management
VC	Venture Capital
VR	Virtual Reality
VW	Volkswagen Group
WEO	World Energy Outlooks
WOFE	Wholly Owned Foreign Enterprise
WTO	World Trade Organisation
WWF	World Wide Life Fund
Yoy	Year on Year growth
ZEV	Zero Emission Vehicles
%	Percent or Percentage

1

Impacts of Climate Change on Sustainable Business

吃得苦中苦，方为人上人

chī dé kǔ zhōng kǔ, fāng wéi rén shàng rén

A person who can endure hardships, will become a better person
No pains, no gains.

Climate Change and Sustainability Definitions

Climate change and sustainability are two key areas that are receiving a lot of attention from scientists, companies and governments globally. Literature surveys and research have highlighted that there are different ways of defining climate change and sustainability management in addition to explaining what they involve and their key implications globally (Wang, Climate Change and Clean Energy Management, Routledge UK 2019).

Climate change is usually defined as the significant, long-term changes in the global climate conditions, such as temperature or rainfalls, in different regions in the world. These climate changes are usually caused by major, long-term variations in the key global weather conditions. The changes in global and regional climate patterns have been particularly apparent and important from the middle of the 20th century onwards. Climate changes have also been largely attributed to causing the global warming and the global greenhouse effects (NASA, What is Climate Change, 2014).

It is important to note the differences between weather and climate. Weather is generally referred to as short-term changes which involved various weather conditions such as rainfalls, temperatures, humidity, in addition to wind speeds and directions for a specific region or a city. Weather conditions can generally vary greatly from hour to hour and day to day. The climate of a region or city is normally its weather conditions averaged over many years.

DOI: 10.4324/9781003142348-1

The climate of a city or region on the Earth will generally only change very slowly. Climate changes have normally led to changes in the typical or average weather of a region or city over a long period. A good example is the changes in a region's average annual rainfall over months or seasons. Climate change is also the cumulative changes in the Earth's overall climate conditions. Good international examples include the changes in the Earth's average temperature and typical precipitation patterns.

The global climate is usually more than the "average" of the climates of specific cities or places. The worldwide systematic connectivity of the global climate systems has contributed to making climate changes impacts to be felt globally. Climate changes have led to higher global temperatures and global warming in addition to more frequent climate-induced extreme weather incidents. These have significant impacts on the daily life of populations and cities around the world.

Global warming is usually defined as the rise of global temperatures resulting from the global greenhouse effects. The global greenhouse effect is usually defined as the process whereby the major GHG emissions, including carbon dioxide (CO2), methane, etc., are impacting the Earth's climate and environment. These GHGs are being generated by various human activities, such as industrial and transport activities. GHG emissions into the Earth's atmosphere have caused serious damage to the ozone layer. The ozone layer has been helping to absorb or re-emit the heat being radiated from the sun and various regions on the Earth. These have resulted in the trapping of various heat emissions which led to rising global temperatures and global warming around the world (NRDC, Global Warming, 2016).

Global warming has resulted in slow increases in the average temperature of the Earth's atmosphere. This is due to the fact that the rising GHG concentrations in the atmosphere have been trapping increasing amounts of the heat energy striking the Earth from the sun and heat emissions from different regions globally. These trapped heat energies have not been able to be dissipated fast enough back into space, and these have then resulted in global warming.

It is important to know that the Earth's atmosphere has been acting like a giant greenhouse which has been capturing the sun's heat for many years. These have helped to create the right temperatures to support the emergence of different life forms, including humans, on the Earth. Without the Earth's atmospheric greenhouse effect, the Earth would become very cold. Scientists have estimated that the temperatures could fall by over 30°C on the Earth which would make many regions uninhabitable. On the other hand, GHG emissions starting after the industrial revolution have also led to serious global warming.

Climate change and GHG emissions have led to the temperatures around the world going up faster now than at any other times before in history.

GHGs are major contributors to global warming. GHGs are commonly defined as various gasses that have been emitted into the atmosphere which could absorb various infrared radiation and heat emissions. These GHGs are major contributors to the increased global warming resulting from climate changes globally. The key GHGs would normally include methane, CO2, Chloro Fluoro Carbon (CFC), etc.

Environment and sustainable development management have become important parts of climate change management by countries, companies and cities globally. Environment and sustainability have first become integral parts of the global climate change discussions at the world's first Earth Summit in Rio in 1992. There were no universally agreed definitions on what environment and sustainability really entailed. There were many different views on what these would involve.

The original definition of sustainable development, which is still the most often quoted definition, came from the UN Bruntland commission which stated that "Sustainable Development is development that meets the needs of the present without compromising the ability of future generations to meet their own needs" (UN Bruntland Commission Report 1987).

Another good definition of environment and sustainable development is by the World Commission on Environment and Development. It is expressed as "A process of change in which the exploitation of resources, the direction of investments, the orientation of technological development and institutional change are all in harmony and enhance both current and future potentials to meet human needs and aspirations".

In practice, many leading international and state companies globally have been developing new environmental and sustainable development strategies as an integral part of their corporate strategy. Global experience has shown that companies cannot just add environment and sustainable development to their list of things for corporate action, but they must integrate these into their core strategy. Many leading international companies have developed detailed environment and sustainable development strategies to support the long-term growth of their business globally. These sustainable development strategies would normally aim to pursue simultaneously the three sustainable development pillars which should include healthy environment, economic prosperity and social justice. Global experience has shown that these three sustainable development pillars should be pursued simultaneously to ensure the sustainable well-being of current and future generations. More details on sustainable business developments and strategy management will be given in Chapters 2 and 5 of this book.

Climate Change and Global Warming Overviews

Climate change and global warming have serious implications on global developments. Industrialisation and fossil fuel consumptions have contributed to significant rises in GHG emissions and global warming. Global CO_2 level has risen from 357 parts per million (ppm) in 1993 to 405.5 ppm in 2019. In 2020, despite the global Covid pandemic, the global average amount of CO_2 hit a new record high of 412.5 ppm. Looking ahead, the global CO_2 levels are expected to increase further as global GHG emissions exceed the capacities of natural links to absorb them on the Earth. Understanding the natural balance and time lags is fundamental in addressing the problems and identifying why carbon neutrality by 2050–2060 should be important global targets (UN WMO, State of the Climate Global Report, 2019).

Climate change in addition to excessive CO_2 and various GHG emissions have resulted in high temperature rises globally. These have also caused rising number of climate-induced extreme weather incidents globally. These have included flooding of coastal cities, heavier rainfalls, stronger hurricanes, droughts, etc. These have resulted in major negative social and economic impacts on various countries and cities globally.

Countries and companies globally are coming to realise that climate change and global warming are likely to be two of the biggest threats to their future sustainable business growths and developments. Many countries and companies are actively developing their new sustainability plans and net zero strategies in addition to climate change net zero pathways to meet their Paris Agreement commitments. They will need to link their climate action plans together with their plans for economic recoveries and Build Back Better post Covid. They will also need to develop suitable carbon neutrality and net zero decarbonisation strategies for their key industrial and service sectors so as to reduce their emissions inline with their Paris Agreement commitments and to improve their climate resilience (IEA, Global Energy & CO_2 Report, 2019).

Climate changes and global warming have led to large-scale, long-term changes in the Earth's weather patterns and rises in its average temperatures. The Earth's climate systems have been constantly changing over the last 4.55 billion years. After the last ice age which ended about 11,000 years ago on the Earth, the global averaged temperature has been relatively stable at about 14°C. However, in recent years, meteorologists from different countries globally have noticed some significant changes in the Earth's temperature profiles and measurements. These have shown that the average temperatures of the Earth have been increasing steadily due to global warming. Scientists have also noticed that the rates of climate changes are still rising with various industrial and human activities. These have been shown to have contributed directly to accelerating the rates of climate changes and global warming worldwide. These global climate changes have resulted in many regions around the world suffering severe weather conditions and rising climate-induced extreme weather incidents. In addition, climate changes have also created conditions which are difficult for many plants, insects and animal species which have not been able to adapt or evolve fast enough to cope with the fast-changing climate conditions.

Looking ahead, leading climate institutions have predicted further significant growths in global emissions due to rising industrialisation and population growths. Looking ahead to 2100, scientists have forecasted that global CO2 emissions could further rise alarmingly by over 60% when compared with the CO2 emission levels in 2010. Looking ahead to 2050, the emissions from the developed countries are forecasted to be reduced to about 15% of global emissions, which is half of their 30% share in 2010. On the other hand, the CO2 emissions from developing countries globally are forecasted to increase significantly by 2050. These increases are likely generated by their forecasted higher economic growths and industrialisation rates (MIT USA, MIT Climate Action, 2017).

It is also expected that CO2 emissions from fossil fuels usages globally will continue to remain as the largest sources of GHG emissions. Other GHG emissions and non-fossil energy sources of CO2 usages will likely account for almost 33% of total global GHG emissions by 2100. The emissions from the electricity generation and transportation sectors will likely account for over half, about 51%, of the global CO2 emissions from fossil fuel uses. This would represent a slight decrease from their 56% emission levels recorded in 2010.

Looking ahead, experts have forecasted that fossil fuels may still account for about 30–50% of primary energy usages around the world, depending on the global decarbonisation efforts. This is in spite of the rapid growths in renewable and clean energies globally. Within the fossil fuel primary energy mix, there will be a strong shift away from coal and oil to cleaner fuels, such as natural gas and nuclear energy in addition to renewables. The natural gas share in the primary energy mix in most countries globally is expected to increase strongly. The rising natural gas consumptions have resulted from the new energy transition policies introduced by different governments to promote clean fuel usages and to reduce GHG emissions as part of their Paris Agreement commitments.

The continued rises in global temperatures are likely to cause more climate-induced severe weather events, including hurricanes, extreme precipitation, sea-level rises, ocean acidification, etc. Global mean surface temperatures have risen by 1°C already. Looking ahead to 2050, it is forecasted to further increase by a range of 1.9–2.6°C. Looking ahead to 2100, the global mean surface temperatures are forecasted to rise even further by a range of 2.8–5.2°C, if little joint global actions would be undertaken to achieve the IPCC 1.5°C aspiration target. By 2050, the mean precipitation or rainfalls are expected to increase by a range of 4–5.5%. Looking ahead to 2100, it is expected to further rise to 7–11.5% as a result of the continued rising climate change impacts globally.

Global warming has also resulted in serious melting of the polar ice caps and various glaciers globally. These accelerated ice melting incidents are expected to continue to increase globally. Looking ahead to 2100, many glaciers around the world are expected to vanish and no longer exist by the end of the century. These will cause serious negative impacts on the local biosystem and communities in addition to contribute to global sea-level rise.

Looking ahead, ocean levels globally are expected to rise further. The thermal expansions of the oceans due to higher global temperatures in addition to the accelerated melting of the ice sheets and glaciers are forecasted to add a further 0.15–0.25 m rises in sea levels by 2050 globally. Looking ahead to 2100, the global sea levels are forecasted to rise further by 0.30–0.5 m due to worsening climate changes and global warming. These large international sea-level rises are expected to lead to more frequent flooding incidents globally together with increased flooding risks for many coastal cities and Pacific islands across the world.

Looking ahead, both climate change and global warming are seen to be two of the biggest threats to future sustainable human existence on the Earth. The late famous physicist Stephen Hawking and other leading scientists globally have all warned of potentially very serious climate change tipping points coming up globally. Leading scientists have forecasted that if the world would go beyond these climate tipping points, then the negative effects of global warming and climate change that we have been observing would become more serious and the damages sustained would then become irreversible. Climate scientists have warned that we are now globally very close to the climate tipping points in addition to the damages that have been caused internationally by global warming could become permanent and irreversible. The UN's Intergovernmental Panel on Climate Change (UNIPCC) has also highlighted the potential serious risk of hitting the climate change tipping points as global warming continues with rising global temperatures. Hence, there are urgent needs for joint global actions to control climate change and reduce global warming before these serious climate tipping points are exceeded (BBC, Stephen Hawking's warnings, What he predicted for the future, 2018).

G20 and B20 experts globally have studied in detail the negative economic and physical impacts of climate change globally. They have shown that climate change is one of the most pressing global issues with drastic impacts on the G20 countries and other countries around the world. Climate risks are already impacting human lives, natural resources, biodiversity and physical assets in many harmful ways. Extreme climate-induced crises, including droughts, floods, rising sea levels, infrastructure damages, in addition to consequent economic damages and losses of human lives, are already realities of climate change and global warming. Global climate studies and scientific data have clearly shown that these serious climate impacts and risks will continue to increase. Negative impacts by extreme climate incidents will continue growing in a non-linear manner and will affect all countries globally. Without a joint global course for climate correction actions, experts have forecasted that the global GDP could potentially drop by 30% or more by 2100. In addition, the total human life losses and deaths, relating to outdoor air pollution and other climate catastrophes, could exceed 4 million annually worldwide. These are very serious climate impacts globally and joint global climate actions are required urgently (B20, Energy, Sustainability & Climate Taskforce White Paper, KSA 2020).

Global Climate Change Impacts and Risks Updates

The various climate change impacts and risks have been researched and studied extensively by UNIPCC experts together with climate scientists globally. Since the first UNIPCC reports, the evidence on climate change and global warming has become stronger. The results have shown conclusively that global warming is rising. Dangerous extreme climate-induced incidents are getting more frequent, including flooding, droughts, wide fires, etc. These are increasingly impacting nature, cities and people's lives everywhere. The extent and magnitude of negative climate change impacts globally are shown to be larger than estimated in previous assessments. These are causing severe impacts and widespread disruptions in nature and in society in addition to in rural and urban areas. These are reducing our ability to grow nutritious food or provide enough clean drinking water. These are seriously affecting people's health and well-being and damaging livelihoods globally. The negative impacts of climate change are affecting billions of people in many countries globally.

Since the Fifth IPCC Assessment Report was first published in 2014, a wider range of negative impacts can be directly attributed to climate change based on the research and work by climate scientists globally. These assessments have shown that climate changes are causing many negative impacts globally. A serious international example is that the rising temperatures and extreme weather conditions are driving plants and animals on land and in the ocean to leave their normal breeding grounds so as to migrate towards the poles, to higher altitudes or to the deeper ocean waters. Many species are reaching their biological limits in their ability to adapt to climate changes. Many species that cannot adjust or move fast enough are at serious risk of extinction or have been driven to extinction already. As a result, climate change is negatively affecting biodiversity globally (UNIPCC, Fifth Climate Assessment Report, 2014).

There have also been adverse climate change impacts on the natural distribution of plants and animals across the globe. A good international example is that the timings of key biological events such as the breeding or flowering seasons have been altering fast due to global warming. These trends are affecting biodiversity and various food chains globally. In many cases, these are reducing the ability of nature to provide balance and the essential environment for various species to survive. These have adverse impacts on coastal protection, food supply or biodiversity.

Climate change is also changing temperature and rainfall patterns in addition to generating extreme weather incidents. These have also increased the frequency and spread of dangerous diseases in wildlife, agriculture and people globally. There have also been more wide fires globally with lengthening wildfire seasons. The areas and regions affected by wide fires are rising around the world. Serious wide fires have been recorded in the USA, Australia and many other regions. The latest research also shows that these wide fires are causing serious damage to the Earth's ozone layer.

Climate change has also intensified droughts globally. Roughly half of the world's population have experienced severe water shortages at some points during the year. These are in part due to climate change and extreme events such as extreme heat and droughts. Drought conditions have become more frequent in many regions, especially in Africa. These have negatively affected agriculture, food production and hydro-power generation from hydroelectric power plants, etc.

Climate change has also serious impacts on cities and urban areas globally. People living in cities nowadays are facing higher risks of heat stress, poor air quality, rising pollution, wildfires, lack of water supplies, food shortages, etc.

Climate change is also affecting global supply chains, transport networks and other critical infrastructures. There are leading to serious supply disruptions, which, in turn, are leading to shortages of food and other valuable commodities globally.

Globally, climate change is also increasingly causing injuries, illness, malnutrition, etc. These are posing serious threats to physical and mental health in addition to well-being, and even deaths. Global warming is also making hot areas even hotter globally. This is drastically reducing the time that people can spend outside. This means that some outdoor workers cannot work the required hours and thus will earn less.

Climate change impacts are expected to intensify with rising global warming. It is also an established fact that they are interacting with multiple other societal and environmental challenges. These include growing world population, unsustainable consumption, rapidly increasing number of people living in cities, significant inequality, continuing poverty, land degradation, biodiversity loss due to land-use change, ocean pollution, overfishing and habitat destruction, a global pandemic, etc. Experts have warned that when global trends intersect, they can reinforce the negative impacts of each other. These intensifying risks and negative impacts are also disapportionately affecting the poor and most vulnerable populations the hardest around the Earth.

Global Climate Studies and Reports Highlights

The latest UNIPCC reports have provided various new data and insights on climate impacts, vulnerability and adaptation. The joint research and studies by experts globally have confirmed that climate change is adversely affecting nature, people's lives and infrastructures globally. The dangerous and pervasive impacts by climate change and global warming are increasingly evident in every region and country globally. These serious negative climate impacts are having serious negative implications on all countries globally and posing major threats to future international sustainable development (UNIPCC, Sixth Assessment Report WG1, Aug 2021).

These UNIPCC reports have confirmed unequivocally that the rising climate change impacts, such as more extreme heatwaves, floods, droughts, wildfires, etc., are endangering people's health, safety, jobs and livelihoods globally. The UNIPCC has been working on the Sixth Assessment Report which consists of three Working Group contributions and a Synthesis Report. The Working Group I contribution was finalised in August 2021, and the Working Group II contribution was published in February 2022 (UNIPCC, Sixth Assessment Report WG2, Feb 2022).

This research, from the world's top climate scientists, has shown that the world will face unavoidable multiple climate hazards over the next few decades with rising global warming and extreme weather incidents resulting from climate change. The weather extremes that are already being experienced globally are exposing millions of people around the world to acute food and water insecurity in addition to shortages, especially in Africa, Asia, Latin America, etc.

Cities globally are at particular risks from climate change impacts. More than half of the world's population are currently living in various urban cities globally. Climate change is affecting different aspects of city lives, including public health, livelihoods and homes. City energy and transport systems in addition to other critical city infrastructure are also being increasingly affected by extreme weather incidents. These include heatwaves, storms, drought, flooding, rising sea levels and other serious negative climate impacts.

These scientific findings have made clear the important imperative and urgent need to improve the systemic climate resilience of cities globally to cope with the worsening climate impacts and consequences that are now unavoidable. In parallel, cities and countries have to accelerate their clean energy transitions and emission reductions as part of their Paris Agreement commitments.

Scientists have forecasted that unless GHG emissions globally are cut at faster rates than various governments are currently planning to, then climate-driven damage will worsen rapidly and parts of the planet may become increasingly uninhabitable. The UN Climate Change High-Level Champions globally have launched at COP26 a flagship campaign, "Race to Resilience and Race to Zero". These are vehicles for tackling the twin objectives of mobilising businesses, investors, cities and regions to set and implement robust targets for global climate actions in the 2020s.

The UNIPCC reports have provided good scientific confirmations on many of the key climate concerns and issues. These reports have addressed and presented latest results for the most up-to-date physical understanding of the climate system and climate changes. The reports confirmed that climate change has been unequivocally caused by human activities globally. The reports also warned that these will bring about irreversible damage if countries and governments globally do not act immediately. The key findings by the global climate experts are summarised below (UNIPCC, Sixth Climate Change Reports, 2021/2022).

Human influence on damage to the global climate system is now described as unequivocal, as stated in the latest IPCC reports. These are a marked clear change and confirmation on the previous results of only "clear" in earlier IPCC reports (IPCC, 2013). These new confirmations are based on the latest climate research and data collected globally.

Looking ahead, scientists have predicted that within the next two decades, global temperatures are likely to rise by more than 1.5°C above pre-industrial levels. These will seriously breach the ambitions of the Paris Agreement. Extreme weather incidents induced by climate change will become more frequent globally. These will include more frequent wildfires, droughts, flooding, typhoons, hurricanes, etc. These extreme weather incidents will then lead to increased mortality rates in addition to damage to various cities and communities around the world.

Climate change has led to rising global warming with increased temperatures across the surface of the Earth. These have resulted in rising ocean thermal expansion and warming globally. These have, in turn, accounted for 50% of the sea-level rise globally during the period of 1971–2018. In addition, global warming has led to a fourfold increase in the speed of polar ice sheet melting and losses over the past decade.

Radiative forcing, which causes the accumulation of additional energy in the climate systems, has also been shown to have increased by 19% globally. This has been measured by climate scientists globally, and comparisons have been made with results from previous IPCC reports. These rises in radiative forcing have been caused mostly by human and industrial activities globally. These are contributing to rising global warming and more extreme climate incidents globally.

Extreme climate incidents, including droughts and floods, have been found to be occurring more frequently. Looking ahead, experts have forecasted that these extreme weather incidents are going to be occurring more frequently globally. These will then result in greater international climate damage, with serious negative impacts on societies and cities in addition to their populations and communities globally.

Experts advised that no country in the world will be immune to the direct and indirect climate change consequences. Scientists have forecasted that more frequent extreme climate incidents, including extreme heat and heavy precipitation, will be affecting all countries globally. Flooding will become more widespread globally. These are due to more frequent storm surges and heavy rainfall in addition to rising sea levels and polar ice melting.

Wildfires are becoming more intense and more frequent globally. Experts have forecasted that more wide fire incidents will continue growing worldwide as a result of climate change and land-use changes. These are in line with forecasts from the UN Environment Programme. Extreme wide fires are causing devastating impacts to people, biodiversity and ecosystems in many countries. These wide fires have also been found to exacerbate climate change by releasing additional GHG emissions. The latest climate research has also shown that the wildfires are causing additional higher amounts of particulates and GHG emissions which are causing serious damage to the ozone layer of the Earth. These are damaging the Earth's ozone layer and reversing the healing of the ozone layer that has been achieved in the last ten years by stopping the use of CFCs globally (MIT, Study reveals chemical link between wildfire smoke & ozone depletion, MIT, USA Feb 2022).

Global fossil subsidy surveys have also shown that some counties in the world have been spending at least US$1.8 trillion a year, or 2% of their GDP, on various fossil subsidies. These are resulting in higher GHG emissions which are driving the destruction of nature and species extinction. Research from the UNIPCC B Team and Business for Nature has shown that these have included subsidies for fossil fuel and various hydrocarbon industries in addition to associated services. They have shown that the fossil fuels, agriculture and water industries have received more than 80% of all environmentally harmful subsidies per year globally.

The UNIPCC AR6 Climate Change 2021 Report, The Physical Science Basis, was published globally in 2021. It reported that scientists have forecasted that the world is likely set to pass 1.5°C warming by 2040 with the current emission projections. It showed that human and industrial activities are driving up global warming and extreme climate-induced incidents. Worsening climate change and global warming have meant that the world is getting closer to irreversible tipping points. Methane emissions have also been shown to be an important GHG in accelerating climate change and global warming (UNIPCC, AR6 Climate Change 2021 Report: The Physical Science Basis, US 2021).

The key conclusions of the latest UNIPCC assessment reports have shown that global warming of the climate systems around the world is unequivocal since the 1950s. Many of the observed climate changes and associated damage are unprecedented over the past decades. The atmospheric concentrations of various GHGs, including CO2, methane and nitrous oxide, have increased to higher levels that are unprecedented in the last 800,000 years. Human influences and industrial impacts on the global climate system are very clear. It is extremely likely that various human activities and industrial influences have been the dominant causes of global warming between 1951 and to date.

The latest UNIPCC Sixth Assessment Reports in 2022 have looked in more detail at the various causes, impacts and potential solutions to climate change. These reports have given the clearest indications to date of how climate change and global warming are affecting all living things on the Earth (UN IPCC, Sixth Climate Assessment Report, 2022).

These UN reports have shown that the climate impacts globally are way worse than previously thought. Good examples of global climate damage include the melting of the Greenland ice sheet, the destruction of coral reefs, flooding, droughts, biodiversity damage, etc. These climate-related impacts are now hitting the world more heavily and quickly than what climate scientists have previously found.

The latest UNIPCC Sixth Climate Mitigation Report published in April 2022 reported that globally, GHG emissions have been rising continuously over the past decade. Global CO_2 emissions reached 59 gigatonnes of CO_2equivalent (GtCO2e) in 2019. This is roughly 12% higher than the CO_2 emissions in 2010 and 54% greater than those in 1990. However, there are some signs of progress in GHG emission reductions. A good international example is that the annual rate of GHG emission growth has declined from an average of 2.1% between 2000 and 2009 to 1.3% between 2010 and 2019 (UNIPCC, Sixth Climate Mitigation Report, US Apr 2022).

However, the UNIPCC has reported that the global efforts to mitigate climate change and to reduce emissions have remained far off-track. A good international example is that even if all countries are to achieve their most recent national climate commitments (NDCs), the gaps between global GHG emissions and the levels associated with limiting warming to 1.5°C would still be some 19–26 GtCO2e in 2030. This is equivalent to more than the emissions from USA and China combined in 2018. While some countries have announced new or enhanced NDCs since the UNIPCC's cut-off date, these pledges are still not ambitious enough to close the emission gaps.

The latest UNIPCC reports have also made clear that around 40% of the world's population is highly vulnerable to the negative impacts of climate change. A good international example is that in Africa around 30% of all the maize growing areas will likely become unusable and go out of production due to climate change. For beans, experts have forecasted that around 50% of all the bean growing areas will become unusable and go out of production based on the current emission trajectories. These will have serious negative impacts on global food production and supplies. These, in turn, will cause serious food shortages and widespread famines in different countries globally. Experts have also forecasted that there are certain parts of the world, particularly in Africa, which will become uninhabitable due to climate impacts. A good country example is that the long serious drought in Somalia has resulted in thousands of families being displaced from their homes, leading to some serious climate refugee problems in Africa and Europe. At the same time, livestock and farming losses have been huge and these are leading to food shortages and famines.

Climate losses and damages of developing countries have been serious, and these are supported with good scientific data. For several years, developing countries have been trying to get developed nations to consider the idea of loss and damage seriously. Loss and damage are generally defined as those impacts of climate change that can't be adapted to by developing countries. A good loss and damage example is the slow onset of sea-level rises globally which are affecting many coastal cities in both developing and developed countries.

These loss and damage concepts have been very controversial in global climate negotiations. A key reason is that these are linked to the long-term historical responsibilities for carbon emissions. Richer developed countries are worried about potential future climate lawsuits from developing countries. In addition, they are also worried about being forced to pay damages for current and future climate losses and damages that they are perceived to have contributed to. A good international example is that at COP26 in Glasgow, political progress on the issue of loss and damage was stalled when the USA and EU blocked a dedicated funding facility for climate loss and damage. The UNIPCC has clearly stated in their latest reports that the observed impacts of climate change include widespread adverse impacts in addition to related losses and damages to nature and people. These endorsements by the UNIPCC and climate experts are likely to give loss and damage a major boost in future climate talks and for suitable solutions to be developed.

The latest IPCC reports also warned that technology is not a silver bullet. According to the UNIPCC, the use of some new technologies which are designed to limit warming or reduce CO_2 emissions could also make matters worse rather than better. A good technology example is that there are serious worries that some new technologies and machines that are designed to absorb CO_2 from the air directly could also trigger the release of more greenhouse warming gasses.

Planting trees is seen as a good nature solution to climate change. However, UNIPCC experts have cautioned that planting trees in the wrong places could also do more harm than good. Scientists have warned that when CO_2 is removed from the atmosphere, there could also be a rebound effect from the other chemical elements and processes in the carbon cycle, including photosynthesis, sedimentation, etc. The various oceans and the land reservoirs in different countries could experience out-gassing effects. So, some of the CO_2 that is removed from the atmosphere will be returned to the atmosphere. There are delicate balances in the carbon cycle globally which will need to be considered carefully when implementing various new carbon reduction technologies.

Cities have important roles to play in climate change and mitigation. Major cities globally are hotspots for climate impacts. These cities can also offer good opportunities to avoid the worst impacts of warming. A good international example is that many cities and municipal governments globally are implementing new regulations and policies to promote clean energy transition in addition to the use of renewable energy, greener transport and green buildings. These should help to reduce the negative climate impacts on millions of urban residents. Another good city example is that major cities like Lagos in Nigeria are hotspots for climate impacts, but they can also become the beacons of hope for climate improvement. The UNIPCC experts have highlighted clearly that major cities of the world will be key places for climate mobilisation and mitigation. In particular, many vulnerable people are located in major cities and coastal cities. So, these are good priority action areas where governments and countries globally begin to mobilise and improve urban climate resilience.

The UNIPCC has also warned that the small window available for global climate actions is closing fast. There are bleak assessments of the serious negative climate impacts both now and in the future. However, climate scientists have remained convinced that the worst climate impacts can be averted if we all act in time globally. The UNIPCC has forecasted that the window for climate action will likely last for a short time for the rest of this decade till 2030. The UNIPCC has warned that any further delays in concerted joint global climate actions will contribute to the world missing a brief and rapidly closing window to improve and secure a live-able future. If the world can cut emissions drastically and significantly boost spending on climate mitigation and adaptation, then these should help to reduce and avoid some serious climate disasters. These climate mitigation actions should include investments on new green energy, promoting new electric cars in addition to investing in green education and robust health systems, etc. In addition, just transitions and social justice improvement should help people in different countries to better cope with the negative impacts of climate change and rising temperatures. Investing in nature will also be a bulwark against the worst impacts of climate change. The UNIPCC has called for 30–50% of the world to be conserved. Details of the various climate improvements and actions will be discussed later in the chapter and other chapters of this book.

Highlights and Analysis of Global Climate Disasters

Globally, the number of extreme weather incidents and weather-related disasters has skyrocketed over the past half-century. These have caused serious damages and economic losses in various developed and developing countries globally. Improved early warning systems have meant that there have been fewer human deaths, but the economic and social damages have been serious. A good international example is the better early warning systems for typhoons which have helped the government climate offices and observatories in various countries in Asia to give better early typhoon warnings to their local communities. These have helped to reduce typhoon damage to various cities and societies. However, climate change has also increased the frequencies of typhoons and extended the typhoon season.

A report from the UN's World Meteorological Organisation (WMO) has examined global mortality and economic losses resulting from extreme climate incidents between 1970 and 2019. The results showed that these climate disasters have increased by fivefold during that period. These increases have been driven largely by climate change and global warming. Experts are warning that a warming planet will mean that these rising climate disaster global trends will continue and could even accelerate further. The number of extreme climate incidents is increasing globally. Experts have warned that these will become more frequent and severe in many parts of the world due to climate change and global warming.

A good international example is that in total, there have been more than 11,000 climate disasters attributed to these hazards globally since 1970. These climate disasters have caused more than 2 million deaths and some US$3.64 trillion in economic losses in addition to serious damage to societies and communities globally.

A serious extreme weather incident example is Hurricane Ida, which slammed into the US Gulf Coast and killed at least four people apart from serious weather damage. The negative economic costs and damages of Hurricane Ida may be higher than Hurricane Katrina. Luckily, improved early warning systems, prevention and protection measures had ensured that Ida had caused only a fraction of the casualties of the giant hurricanes that had devastated the same areas previously.

Hurricane Katrina, which killed more than 1,800 people and destroyed large parts of New Orleans, USA, had been considered by many to be one of the costliest extreme climate incidents and weather-related disasters. It had led to nearly US$164 billion in economic losses together with widespread damage to local communities and populations.

Global surveys have shown that on average, a climate disaster linked to weather, climate and water extremes has been occurring every single day over the past 50 years. The report showed that these climate disasters have on average killed 115 people and caused US$202 million in daily losses globally. Scientists have also shown that more than 91% of the deaths have occurred in developing countries from these extreme climate disasters.

Droughts have been shown to be responsible for the largest losses of human life during the period. Global survey results have shown that widespread droughts alone have accounted for some 650,000 deaths globally. On the other hand, extreme storms have left over 577,000 people dead. Floods have meanwhile killed nearly 59,000 people over the past 50 years, and extreme temperatures have killed close to 56,000 globally.

On a positive note, the WMO report has found that even as the number of extreme climate incidents and climate-related disasters have ballooned over the past half-century, the number of associated deaths has declined nearly threefold. The human death tolls have fallen from over 50,000 deaths each year in the 1970s to fewer than 20,000 in the 2010s. A good international example is that in the period between 1970 and 1980, the reported deaths were on average about 170 related deaths per day. In the 1990s, the daily average deaths had fallen to 90, and then to 40 in the 2010s. The dramatic improvements in early warning systems have been shown to contribute to achieving these significant drops in deaths from climate disasters and extreme climate incidents globally.

The UN WMO has warned that much more work remains to be done, as only half of the agency's 193 member states globally are currently housing the life-saving multi-hazard early warning systems. It has also cautioned that severe gaps remained in weather and hydrological observing networks globally, especially in Africa and parts of Latin America in addition to in Pacific and Caribbean island states.

Economic losses from climate-induced incidents are rising globally. The reported losses from 2010 to 2019 have been estimated to be costing some US$383 million per day. These are seven times more than the US$49 million in average daily losses in the 1970s. Seven of the costliest 10 disasters in the past 50 years have happened since Hurricane Katrina hit in 2005. Three of these serious climate incidents have taken place in 2017 alone. These have included Hurricane Harvey, which caused nearly US$97 billion in damage, followed by Maria at close to US$70 billion and Irma at almost US$60 billion.

Globally, many different countries and communities are feeling the serious impacts from various climate disasters. The economic toll and damage globally are staggering. A good international example is that the likely cumulative costs for the ten worst climate disasters in 2021 have been estimated to be a massive U$170 billion globally. This is the sixth time since 2011 that the bill for natural disasters has exceeded $100 billion globally (Mckinsey, Climate hazards are getting worse. Our study reveals which countries are the most vulnerable, US Jan 2022).

Looking ahead, extreme climate incidents and severe storms are likely to grow more frequently and will also affect places where they have previously been rare. A good climate example is that hurricanes have typically formed in low-latitude regions near the equator. However, the latest studies have shown that hurricanes and tropical storms are increasingly migrating to mid-latitude areas closer to both poles with rising global warming. These will then extend the hurricanes and tropical storm vulnerable regions to cover some of the world's most populous cities, including New York City, London, Toyko, etc. Even with the most optimistic 1.5°C of global warming scenario, scientists have estimated that nearly one in four people worldwide will be experiencing the serious negative impacts of extreme weather incidents and severe climate hazards.

Global warming and rising extreme climate incidents will make life harder for huge portions of the global population. Scientists have warned that extreme climate incidents will also disproportionately affect people in the lower-income areas and developing countries. While climate mitigation and adaptation measures will be key to lessening the risk, much of the global warming that is projected to occur over the next decade is already "locked in" because of past emissions. Scientists have shared their work that has shown that even in the moderate global warming scenarios, severe climate hazards will likely become much more common in many countries globally.

Hence, it is very important for governments and countries across the world to implement the appropriate climate warning and mitigation measures to safeguard their communities and cities. Around the world, leaders should develop new climate policies and net zero plans to reduce emissions and to build up climate resilience in the face of more severe weather incidents. A good international climate disaster case study on wildfires is given below with international examples:

International Wildfires Climate Disaster Case Study

Climate change has resulted in an increased number of extreme weather incidents in different countries globally. One serious type of climate disaster is the increased occurrence of wildfires in many countries globally, including USA, Europe, Australia, etc.

The Australian wildfires in 2019 and 2020 have been massive climate disasters. It was shocking how far and fast they spread, in addition to for how long and powerfully they burned. The devastating Australian "Black Summer" wildfires blazed across more than 43 million acres of land across different regions in Australia. These wildfires have led to serious damage to many local communities and settlements. The fires have also led to serious biodiversity damage, including the death or displacement of nearly 3 billion animals. The wildfires have also caused over 1 million tonnes of smoke, soot and particles to be emitted into the atmosphere. Scientific measurements have shown that these wildfire emissions have reached up to 35 km above the Earth's surface. Scientists have found that these emissions are equivalent to comparable emissions from an erupting volcano (MIT, Study reveals chemical link between wildfire smoke & ozone depletion, MIT, USA Feb 2022).

Scientific research has now shown that wildfires can eject massive quantities of various GHG and particulates into the atmosphere. These emissions also include a cocktail of chemical emissions that can produce ozone downwind. Ozone is an important GHG, third in line behind CO2 and methane. The study has found that the extreme climate-induced wildfires may have unexpected negative impacts on the atmospheric chemistry globally. The smokes from increasingly severe wildfires have been found to invade the stratosphere and can potentially erode the ozone layer of the Earth. Volatile organic compounds (VOCs) that are present in the wildfire smoke can also photochemically react with nitrogen oxides when exposed to sunlight. These reactions can then form chemical smog, which can be very harmful to human lungs.

Atmospheric chemists have found that the smoke from wildfires can set off chemical reactions in the stratosphere that can contribute to the destruction of the ozone layer. This will then reduce the ability of the ozone layer to shield the Earth from incoming ultraviolet radiation. Scientists have also found that, shortly after the Australia wildfires subsided, there were sharp drops in the nitrogen dioxide concentrations in the stratosphere. This is the first step in a chemical cascade that is known to end in ozone depletion. Researchers have found that these sharp drops in nitrogen dioxide directly correlate with the amount of smoke that the wildfires have released into the stratosphere. They have estimated that these smoke-induced chemical reactions can deplete the column of ozone by 1% globally.

Putting this in context, scientists have highlighted that the international phase-out of ozone-depleting gasses, such as CFC, under a previous worldwide agreement to stop their production, has led to about a 1% ozone recovery from earlier ozone decreases over the past ten years. This will mean that the recent wildfires can potentially eliminate and cancel out all these hard-won gains on the repair of the ozone layer from CFC damage. If future wildfires grow stronger and more frequent, then the ozone layer could be damaged even more. The global ozone layer recovery will then be delayed even more by many years.

Scientists are predicting that rising climate change could lead to increased frequency of extreme weather incidents, including wildfires, typhoons, etc. The Australian wildfires look like the biggest events so far. However, as the world continues to warm, there is every reason to think that these wildfires will become more frequent and more intense. This is another serious wakeup call, just as the Antarctic ozone hole was, in the sense of showing how bad things could actually become in future, if no immediate international climate mitigation actions are taken.

Massive wildfires have also been known to generate pyrocumulonimbus, which are towering clouds of smoke that can reach into the stratosphere. This is the layer of the atmosphere that lies between about 15 and 50 km above the Earth's surface. The smoke from Australia's wildfires had been found to reach well into the stratosphere, as high as 35 km.

Scientists have found that the accumulated wildfire smoke can also warm up parts of the stratosphere by as much as 2°C, which could persist for some six months. The study has also found that ozone destruction has occurred in the Southern Hemisphere following these fires. Smokes from the fires could have depleted ozone through a chemistry similar to volcanic aerosols. Major volcanic eruptions can also reach into the stratosphere. The particles in these eruptions can destroy ozone through a series of chemical reactions. As the particles form in the atmosphere, they gather moisture on their surfaces. Once wet, the particles can react with circulating chemicals in the stratosphere. A good chemical example is dinitrogen pentoxide, which will react with the particles in the wildfire smokes to form nitric acid. Normally, dinitrogen pentoxide will react with the sun to form various nitrogen species, including nitrogen dioxide, a compound that binds with chlorine-containing chemicals in the stratosphere. When volcanic smoke converts dinitrogen pentoxide into nitric acid, nitrogen dioxide drops. At the same time, chlorine compounds in the wildfire smoke will take another chemical path. These will be morphing into chlorine monoxide, which is the main human-made agent that will destroy ozone.

Scientists have looked at how concentrations of nitrogen dioxide in the stratosphere have changed following the Australian fires. If these concentrations dropped significantly, it would signal that wildfire smoke can deplete ozone through the same chemical reactions as some volcanic eruptions. The team looked into measurement observations of nitrogen dioxide that have been taken by three independent satellites which have been surveying the Southern Hemisphere for varying lengths of time. They compared each satellite's records in the months and years leading up to and following the Australian wildfires. All three satellite measurement records have shown significant drops in nitrogen dioxide after the Australian wildfires. In one satellite's record, the drop represented a record low among observations spanning the last 20 years. Scientists have also calculated that the nitrogen dioxide decrease was a direct chemical effect of the fires' smoke. They have used atmospheric simulations that use a global, three-dimensional model that simulates hundreds of chemical reactions in the atmosphere, from the surface on up through the stratosphere. These have confirmed the serious wildfires' damaging impacts on the Earth's atmosphere and ozone layer.

New Global Climate Policies and Actions

The rising magnitudes of climate change and global warming have increased the likelihood of severe climate incidents, with pervasive and damaging impacts. A first step towards adaptation to future climate change is reducing the vulnerability and exposure to climate variability. The overall risks of climate change impacts can be reduced by limiting the rates and magnitudes of climate change.

New climate policies and net zero plans are urgently needed globally. Without new policies to mitigate climate change, the climate scientist projections have suggested an increase in global mean temperature in 2100 of 3.7–4.8°C, relative to pre-industrial levels. The current trajectory of global annual and cumulative emissions of GHGs is not consistent with the widely discussed UNIPCC goals of limiting global warming at 1.5–2°C above the pre-industrial level. Pledges made as part of the new COP26 Glasgow Climate Pact and Paris Agreement in addition to other climate agreements are broadly consistent with other cost-effective scenarios. These are estimated to give a likely chance of limiting global warming by 2100, to below 3°C only, relative to pre-industrial levels. It is important for the future COP27 meeting to discuss and develop concrete international measures to limit global warming by 2100, to below 1.5°C, relative to pre-industrial levels.

It is important that various countries and governments globally should urgently implement appropriate new climate policies and actions to mitigate climate change that are in line with their Paris Agreement commitments. Climate change risks and impacts can be reduced, within limits, if humans and nature adapt to the changing conditions. The scale and scope of joint international actions to reduce climate risks by adaptation need to increase much more urgently. Citizens in different countries, together with various climate and social climate movements, have been campaigning various governments to urgently implement new climate policies in addition to mitigation and adaptation actions.

The UNIPCC Working Group II Climate Report has identified large gaps between the ongoing efforts and the adaptation needed to cope with current levels of warming. The scale of the climate challenges also varies greatly in different regions and countries globally. The report has also highlighted that the effectiveness of available adaptation options will decrease with each incremental rise of global warming. Successful climate adaptations require more urgent, ambitious and accelerated actions globally. If there are quicker and further emissions reductions, then there may be more scope for people and nature to adapt to climate change globally.

The UNIPCC Climate Reports have discussed some potential new climate solutions. They have highlighted the importance of fundamental changes in society while simultaneously conserving, restoring and safeguarding nature in order to meet the Paris Agreement targets and the Sustainable Development Goals (SDGs). It is now clear that minor, marginal, reactive or incremental changes would not be sufficient. In addition to technological and economic changes, shifts in most aspects of society will be required to overcome limits to adaptation, build resilience and reduce climate risk to tolerable levels. These actions should also include just transitions with inclusive, equitable and just developments that will help to achieve societal goals without leaving anyone behind. The strong and interdependent relationships between climate, nature and people are fundamental to reaching these goals. These important requirements have been emphasised more strongly in the latest UNIPCC Working Group II Climate Report than in previous IPCC assessments.

The scientific work globally has shown that a healthy planet is fundamental to securing a sustainable and live-able future for all people on the Earth. This is why the needs of climate, nature and local communities have to be considered together and prioritised in the decision making and planning by different countries, governments and companies globally. Many countries and organisations have been developing new policies and implementing actions to combat climate changes. Some important international examples are summarised below.

The Global Wind Energy Council has shown that clean wind renewable energy can help countries and governments to accelerate their green economic recovery and form a bedrock for sustainable economic growth. The benefits of wind energy can extend beyond clean power to other important benefits. These can include sustainable job creation, public health cost savings, water consumption savings, capital injection in local value chains, etc.

The World Council of Churches and other international faith organisations are pressing the international financial sector to adopt stricter moral standards to address climate change that would steer their financial assets and investments away from the fossil fuel sectors, especially coal.

According to the Clean Cities Campaign analysis of 36 cities, European cities will need to make significant improvements in order to achieve zero-emission mobility by 2030. It has found that more local decarbonisation measures in addition to better data and monitoring are required.

International Renewable Energy Association (IRENA), in partnership with the African Development Bank, has published a new report highlighting the opportunities and challenges facing Africa in the renewable energy transition and the pathway to a renewables-based energy system.

At the World Sustainable Development Summit, UN Climate Change Executive Secretary Patricia Espinosa underlined the critical role of the multilateral process in climate change agreements. They have stated that multilateralism remains "the world's vehicle for addressing climate change".

The latest UNIPCC Climate Mitigation report, published in April 2022, has made it clear that holding global temperature rise to 1.5°C is still possible, but only if we act immediately globally. Various countries around the world will need to act urgently so as achieve peak GHG emissions before 2025. Then, we should act urgently to nearly halve the global GHG emissions by 2030. We should then reach net zero CO2 emissions around mid-century, say by 2050–2060, while ensuring just and equitable transitions globally. With escalating risks from droughts, floods, wildfires and other disastrous effects of climate change, these are deadlines that all countries and organisations should work jointly together to achieve urgently (UNIPCC, Sixth Climate Change Mitigation Report, US Apr 2022).

More details of the various new climate actions and policies being developed and implemented by different countries and organisations globally will be addressed in the different chapters of this book with international examples and case studies.

2

Sustainable Business Transformation Developments

十年树木, 百年树人

shí nián shù mù, bǎi nián shù rén

Ten years for a sapling to grow into a tree & a hundred year to develop enterprises. Good wine takes time to mature.

Definitions of Sustainable Businesses

There are many different definitions of what a sustainable business is and what it covers. One good definition is that a sustainable business is an enterprise that has minimal negative impacts plus potentially positive effects on the key areas of environment, society and economy. In simple terms, sustainable businesses will strive to meet the triple bottom lines of environment, society and economy in all their businesses. Leading sustainable businesses are globally incorporating the appropriate environmental, social and governance (ESG) standards, as part of their core corporate standards and business strategies.

In general, a business is defined and described as being a sustainable and green business or company if it matches four key criteria. A sustainable business should incorporate the key principles of sustainability into each of its business decisions. It should supply environmentally friendly products or services which will replace demands for non-green products and/or services. A sustainable company is greener than other traditional companies and competitions. A sustainable company will also make an enduring commitment to strict environmental principles in all of its business principles and operations globally.

A sustainable business has also been defined as an organisation that participates in environmentally friendly or green activities. It should also ensure that all its processes, products and manufacturing activities adequately address current environmental concerns whilst maintaining sustainable profit levels.

DOI: 10.4324/9781003142348-2

Another good definition is that a sustainable business is a business that meets the needs of the present world without compromising the ability of future generations to meet their own needs. A good business example is that a sustainable business will adopt a process of assessing how to design future products that will take advantage of the current environmental situations plus future requirements.

The Brundtland Report has emphasised that sustainability and sustainable development will include the three-legged pillars of people, planet and profit (PPP). Sustainable businesses should develop all their business models and supply chains to balance all these three key sustainable development requirements through the triple-bottom-lines concept. Sustainable companies will also use sustainable development and sustainable distribution to positively affect the environment, business growth and the society.

Sustainable developments and sustainability net zero plans within a sustainable business organisation can help to create values for customers, investors and the environment. A sustainable business must meet customer needs whilst, at the same time, treating the environment well. A sustainable company will also adopt strong stakeholder engagement and balancing. A sustainable company will develop joint win-win solutions for the company and stakeholders using a good structural approach. Good sustainable company approaches include the concepts of Sustainable Enterprise Excellence (SEE) and Sustainable Business Model (SBM). Another is the adoption of the important concepts of responsible investment and growth.

Sustainability has sometimes been confused with corporate social responsibility (CSR), though the two are not the same. The notion of 'time' distinguishes sustainability or sustainable development from CSR and other similar concepts. Whilst CSR and sustainability are not the same, they are strongly related to each other. The company management will have to consider the important interlinkages and implications between CSR and sustainability carefully in their business planning and operations.

New green sustainable business developments have also been seen by many globally as a possible mediator of global economic-environmental relationships. A good international business example is that the proliferation of new green sustainable businesses should help to diversify the economy of different countries and contribute to the creation of new green employments globally.

The definition of new green jobs can be different and ambiguous in various countries. It is generally agreed that new green jobs are created by new green business startups and businesses. Good international green job examples include the new green jobs that are linked to the new clean energy and renewables projects that are being implemented in different countries as part of their clean energy transitions. These will contribute to the reduction of greenhouse gas (GHG) emissions plus promote clean energy transition from fossil fuels to clean renewable energy sources.

The various green sustainable businesses and companies can be seen not only as generators of green energy, but also as producers of new materialities. These will include new green materials and technologies, new green jobs and green services, all of which are resulting from the sustainable development and sustainability net zero activities by these sustainable businesses.

A good international example is the accelerated implementation of renewable and clean energy globally as part of the clean energy transition from fossil fuel to clean energy sources. The International Renewable Energy Association (IRENA) has estimated that the clean energy transition and renewable energy growth in recent years globally have already helped to create more than 10 million new green jobs in different countries globally, including China, India, USA, EU, etc. (IRENA, Renewable Report, 2018).

In summary, environment, sustainable development and sustainability management have become important parts of climate change management by companies globally. Environment and sustainability have first become an integral part of the global climate change discussions at the world's first Earth Summit in Rio in 1992. There was no universally agreed definition on what environment and sustainability really entailed. There were many different views on what these would involve. The original definition of sustainable development, which is still the most often quoted definition, came from the UN Bruntland Commission which stated that "Sustainable Development is development that meets the needs of the present without compromising the ability of future generations to meet their own needs" (UN Bruntland Commission Report 1987).

Another very good definition of environment and sustainable development is by the World Commission on Environment and Development. It is defined as "A process of change in which the exploitation of resources, the direction of investments, the orientation of technological development and institutional change are all in harmony and enhance both current and future potential to meet human needs and aspirations" (Wang, Climate Change and Clean Energy Management 2019).

In practice, many leading international and state companies have been developing sustainable development and new sustainability net zero strategies as an integral part of their corporate mission and strategy planning. Global experience has shown that companies cannot just add these to their list of corporate actions. The best corporate practices have shown that they must integrate sustainable development and sustainability net zero strategies into their core corporate mission and strategy. Many leading international companies have developed detailed sustainable development and sustainability net zero strategies to support the sustainable growth of their businesses globally. These sustainable strategies will normally aim to pursue simultaneously the three key sustainable development pillars: healthy environment, economic prosperity and social justice. Global experience has shown that these three sustainable development pillars should be pursued simultaneously by sustainable businesses globally so as to ensure the sustainable well-being of current and future generations. More details of the transformation and development of sustainable businesses together with international examples and case studies will be provided below.

Global Sustainable Businesses Developments

The international COP26 meeting held in Glasgow in November 2021 has highlighted the urgent need for businesses globally to accelerate their sustainable business transformation and net zero plan developments. The urgent need for global climate actions to go from transformations and commitments to actions and reality will involve the entire global economy and all stakeholders. Joint climate actions globally will not reach the necessary speed and scale without leaders from businesses, investors, cities and civil societies encouraging their governments and countries to keep raising their climate ambitions (COP26 President Alok Sharma, COP26 Climate speech, Chatham House UK 2022).

Global climate studies by the United Nations Framework Convention on Climate Change (UNFCC) and other distinguished scientists have enabled international business leaders plus government leaders to have better understandings of the serious financial damage and economic costs of taking no actions on climate change. They have also a better understanding of the need for urgent actions. A good international business example is the Deloitte survey in the end of 2021 of international business executives, among whom over 97% said that their companies had already been negatively impacted by climate change. According to Deloitte's 2022 CxO Sustainability Report, over half of the business leaders have said that they have experienced serious climate impacts on their business operations. The rising number of business executives who are seeing the world is reaching a climate tipping point plus agreeing with the urgent need to respond to the climate crisis has also jumped to 79% in late 2021, from 59% in early 2021 within just a short eight-month period. The Deloitte survey has found that only two-thirds of international executives have said that their organisations had shifted to using more sustainable materials and improving their energy efficiency (Deloitte, 2022 CxO Sustainability Report, UK 2022).

Climate action failures have been named as the number one risk cited by different leaders in business, government and civil society in the World Economic Forum's 2022 Global Risks Perception Survey. This was followed by serious concerns about extreme weather incidents caused by climate change, and then biodiversity loss. However, there is still a serious disconnect between the perceived risks that international business leaders are seeing and the actions that they are taking. These highlight the urgent need for action by businesses on their sustainable business transformation and developments (WEF, 2022 Global Risks Perception Survey, Switzerland Jan 2022).

COP26 has also highlighted the need for sustainable businesses and their business leaders globally to bridge this disconnect with new climate targets and priority actions in follow-up to the COP26 meeting. These include keeping the aspired temperature rise limit of 1.5°C within reach by setting new sustainability net zero plans. These are in line with their Paris Agreement commitments to achieve carbon neutrality by 2050–2060 globally. In addition, the emission reduction targets for 2030 will also need to be strengthened by different countries and companies globally. Green finance for climate adaptation plus discussions on loss and damage for developing countries will also need to be accelerated.

In general, the major directions for sustainable business developments globally have been driven by new government policy and regulation, global ESG developments, customer and public pressures plus the latest international climate agreements, including the Paris Agreement and the Glasgow Climate Pact.

Some stakeholders and non-governmental organisations (NGOs) have voiced some concerns if "sustainable businesses" can be realised in practice. However, business experiences globally have shown that it is possible for businesses to improve their sustainability plus reduce their impacts on the environment and lower their GHG emissions whilst continuing as successful profitable businesses. COP26 has highlighted that sustainable business developments with realistic sustainability net zero plans will be one of the key requirements for sustainable businesses globally in the future. We shall discuss in depth which international sustainable companies are leading the way and what we can learn from their best practices later in this chapter with international examples and case studies.

There are many different ways that companies can become more sustainable businesses. These include implementing the SBMs, adopting more stringent

ESG standards and reporting, developing new net zero plans, reducing waste and improving recycling, preventing pollution and minimising emissions, adopting clean energy and phasing out fossil fuels, conserving water and reducing leakages, adopting green sourcing in their procurements, reducing their GHG emissions, planting more trees, using sustainable materials, making their products greener and more sustainable, adopting green office practices, adopting sustainable business travel policies, etc. Details of the various sustainable business best practices will be discussed more in this chapter with international examples and case studies below.

Sustainable Business Model Developments

The SBM is an important international business principle for sustainable business developments globally. Global experience has shown that investors can earn more money plus a company can boost its profitability and bottom lines by making the business more sustainable. The reasons for these positive returns include reduced business costs, improved innovative strategies, improved reputation, new customers who value sustainable products, etc. These important factors will all help to contribute to the rising success and profitability of sustainable businesses globally.

In general, the SBM will include three key elements. The first part covers the clear communication and management of the company's sustainable value propositions and business activities to all its stakeholders. The second element is for the company to consider how it can create its sustainable business plans better and how to deliver these values successfully. The third element is how the sustainable business will capture economic values whilst maintaining or regenerating its natural, social and economic capital.

Sustainable business experience globally has shown that sustainable growths are the realistically attainable growths that a company will be able to achieve and maintain sustainably. These include growing sustainably and not running into problems with their stakeholders and customers. A business that grows too quickly may find that it will be difficult to fund its fast growth sustainably. A business that grows too slowly may also find its business stagnating.

Experience globally has shown that sustainable businesses can provide services or products that are both profitable and environmentally friendly. Corporations that actively plan with climate change and new net zero plans in their minds have been shown to be able to secure higher return on investment (ROI) than other companies that do not adopt sustainable business practices. Globally, there are a growing body of business performance results and experience that are showing that companies that are adopting sustainability initiatives can help to create more sustainable profits and generate new business opportunities. There are substantial values to be gained by companies from adopting sustainability-related targets and practices. These include reducing emission and pollutions, adopting green sourcing and raw materials, reducing waste, improving recycling, etc.

Sustainable businesses have also been shown to be able to fit in better with sustainable communities globally. The five key principles for sustainable communities globally include enhancing live-ability, creating opportunities for economic prosperity, fostering environmental responsibility, embracing design excellence and demonstrating visionary leadership and strong governance.

Characteristics of a Sustainable Business and Organisation

Global experiences have shown that sustainable businesses generally share some key common business features and characteristics. These key characteristics are summarised below.

It is important to set appropriate corporate sustainability goals and targets in sustainable businesses. Strategy experts across the world have highlighted that setting meaningful and measurable goals is very important for business success.

ESG and governance priorities should be led by the board and CEO. Global experiences have shown that it is important for the top management, including the board and CEO, to lead the company's sustainability ESG plans and strategies. This will set the right priorities for the rest of the corporation and staff to follow.

It is important to adopt sustainable technologies across their operations and value chains. These include accelerating clean energy transitions by reducing fossil fuels to adopting more clean renewable energy sources and technologies.

It is important to develop eco-friendly product brands for sustainable business developments. Experience globally has shown that customers globally are favouring more eco-friendly brands over other brands which are un-eco-friendly. So, adopting eco-friendly brands can help to generate more positive customer receptions which should help to raise the company revenues and sales.

Fairtrade is an increasing important consideration from the point of view of customers and stakeholders globally. A good international consumer example is that customers globally are asking if the clothes and food that they are buying are from fairtrade suppliers. One way for sustainable businesses to show that their products are made ethically is by adopting the various international fairtrade certifications. These include the Global Organic Textile Standard and Fairtrade labels, etc.

Sustainable companies have also been adopting self-enforced sustainability codes plus voluntary inspections on trade and environmental issues. A good international drinks example is that many international drinks manufacturers increasingly use drinks bottles and containers that are made from recycled materials. These have forced the international chemical and plastic companies to increase their plastic and chemical recycling globally.

Transparency is an important characteristic of sustainable companies globally. Global CSR experience has shown that customers globally are moving strongly from the past 'believe me concept' to the new 'show me concept'. In simple terms, customers and stakeholders globally will no longer just believe what a company is saying. Instead, they are demanding companies to become more transparent and show clear evidence of what they are claiming.

Global experiences have shown that sustainable developments and sustainability practices will help to improve company performance, enhance the quality of lives, protect the ecosystems and preserve natural resources for future generations. Going green and sustainable is not only beneficial for companies and organisations globally. These will also help to maximise benefits for societies and consumers. A focus on sustainability will also help to attract top-quality talents and retain the right employees for the company. It will also help to attract and build a broader, more loyal customer base. Research by leading business schools globally has shown that sustainable businesses can generate greater financial gains than their unsustainable counterparts. These will be discussed in depth later in this chapter with international examples and case studies.

Global ESG Standards Implementation in Sustainable Organisations

Business organisations and companies globally are increasingly incorporating the ESG framework in their investment analyses and business processes as well as in their annual reporting. Many countries, governments and stock exchanges globally have also introduced new ESG policies and regulations that are requiring their publicly listed companies to adopt the international ESG framework plus also provide ESG reports together with their financial reporting annually.

The ESG standards are a non-financial assessment framework for business performance and the work environment. It is designed to evaluate the performance of companies in three key areas: Environment, Social and Governance. The ESG framework is also a key part of the PRI (Principles of Responsible

Investments) global requirements. These ESG and PRI requirements have been considered to be the most important historical steps for strengthening the relationship between the investor, the environment, society and governance aspects globally. They are also associated with the funding programmes for UN projects linked with the UN Sustainable Development Goals (SDGs), which were launched in 2015.

The ESG framework has gained so much importance recently because of the strong drives by various key governments, stock markets, regulators and businesses globally. The key ESG developments globally are summarised below with international examples and case studies:

Many leading countries, governments and stock exchanges globally have included mandatory ESG requirements in their new regulations and requirements. ESG reporting is now an integral part of international corporate, banking and financing reporting and evaluations. Leading publicly listed companies have to adopt the latest ESG standards plus prepare and publish their ESG reports annually. These ESG reports are being reviewed by the regulators, investors and various financial institutions. Hence, the ESG reports will have important impacts on the performance, financing plus future investments and growth of sustainable businesses globally.

A good international example of ESG regulatory requirements is that EU countries have imposed mandatory ESG disclosure requirements on their publicly listed firms for ESG performance and reporting. These EU mandates have also been accompanied by the EU's wide-reaching Non-Financial Reporting Directive, which has been effective since 2018 (EU Directive 2014/95/EU, Brussel 2018).

The new ESG requirements are generally considered by many governments, companies and stakeholders globally to be important requirements for sustainable business developments globally. These are considered by many to be the appropriate steps to improve the comprehensive assessment of businesses and for the management of sustainable enterprises. ESG should improve the business governance systems and standards of various companies globally. ESG should also help to reduce administrative corruption in various countries globally. ESG should also help to improve the performance of the top management, including the Board and CEOs, as they will now be accountable for their ESG framework plus the company's ESG performance and reports. It should also improve empowerment and delegations in various sustainable businesses as part of their ESG plans and strategies.

ESG reports have also helped to improve the ability of investors, banks and stakeholders to develop better assessments and evaluation of risk-adjusted returns from various leading sustainable companies. A good international ESG financial example is that many investment banks and investor groups are now actively reviewing the ESG reports of various companies as part of their financing and credit analysis. Responsible investors globally are also reviewing various companies' ESG reports. They are also raising serious searching questions to company CEOs, on their ESG report, at various company AGMs globally. These are helping to put more pressure on company CEOs and top managements globally to improve their ESG systems, reporting and performance.

However, many stakeholders globally have also voiced serious concerns that the current accounting and reporting standards for ESG are not adequate and will need improvement. Corporate reporting of ESG factors has generally been considered to be in its infancy compared to the traditional financial reporting. The World Economic Forum's Stakeholder Capitalism Metrics work has sought to tackle the plethora of ESG reporting standards. The work is seen as a good stepping stone for companies to use now.

The G20 Finance Ministers have also voiced similar concerns on urgent improvements to the ESG framework and reporting. G20 has commissioned the TCFD, Taskforce on Climate Financial Disclosure, to develop the new TCFD framework to help to improve ESG reporting by companies and banks globally.

These international pushes are helping to build a momentum towards the development of new global methodologies and solutions under the newly created International Sustainability Standards Board (ISSB). These international developments will help to improve the global standardisation of ESG and TCFD data, reporting and ratings across different companies and countries globally. There should also be room for developing various future approaches with continuous improvement. These new developments will allow governments, stakeholders and investors to be able to better evaluate and compare companies and portfolios across a core set of metrics on a more transparent and fair basis globally.

Investors collectively have some of the greatest power to hold companies and their management accountable. A good international example is that various Responsible Investor Groups are increasing using their power to push company boards and management for better sustainable performances and practices. They are increasingly questioning companies and organisations on details of their ESG reports and are demanding concrete improvement.

At the same time, there are also strong needs to streamline what can be considered as sustainable investments or financial products. The CFA Institute has recently found that almost 80% of practitioners surveyed believe that there is a real need to improve standards around ESG investment and financial products, so as to mitigate 'greenwashing'. This is something that regulators around the world are already looking at closely. Experts are forecasting that there will undoubtedly be more new measures that will be developed and rolled out on these important areas in the near future.

There is also some way to go when it comes to developing the supply side of sustainable financing and investing. Financial innovations such as green bonds, green loans and sustainability linked loans (SLL) have proliferated in recent years. There is currently much room for improvement plus new opportunities for innovation and standardisation on these various financial instruments.

Finally, many leading governments and regulators globally share the common understanding that their interventions are needed to really improve the markets plus improve sustainable performance and reporting. Some critics have argued that sustainable investing is a dangerous distraction from effective climate change fixes such as a carbon tax, or a price on carbon. However, the majority of international investors and stakeholders are pushing for more continuous improvements in these areas by governments, regulators and companies globally. These should help to lead to more improvements in sustainable company performance, improved returns and better governance globally.

Sustainable Business Practices and Transformations

The COP26 Climate meeting held in Glasgow in November 2021 has made both sustainability and net zero developments important core principles for businesses and business leaders globally. The global momentum has shifted positively, with leading businesses and CEOs globally making public commitments for their companies to achieving sustainability net zero and carbon neutrality targets as the norm. These are generally viewed as positive developments by international businesses and their top management leaders.

As COP26 delegates concluded their climate negotiations, it was clear that the climate commitments launched in Glasgow will reshape the global agenda for international businesses. There are high hopes that post-COP26, businesses globally will be undertaking various follow-up actions so that they can deliver their new sustainability net zero plans with concrete actions to meet their COP26 and Paris Agreement commitments.

During COP26, the various public, private and cross-sector pledges have signalled that the major new global focus is toward net zero and to achieve carbon neutrality. Business executives globally are expecting that there will be an acceleration of climate actions across the real economy globally. These will cover all levels, including the system level, throughout industries, and across different business organisations globally (Mckinsey; COP26 made net zero a core principle for business. Here's how leaders can act, USA November 12, 2021).

As a result, the current demands for new sustainability net zero plans and business solutions are huge from businesses and companies globally. Many businesses are actively developing their new sustainability net zero strategies and carbon neutrality plans as part of their COP26 and Paris Agreement commitments.

Many believe that these new net zero and carbon neutrality commitments by international companies will help to improve the international supply chains, market mechanisms, financing models, etc. These should also promote relevant business solutions and structures that will be required to achieve the world's decarbonisation pathway and carbon neutrality targets. For sustainable businesses globally, these conditions should create new opportunities to innovate and to develop new coordinated climate actions by industry peers, value-chain partners, capital providers and policy makers. It should be noted that these actions may also introduce additional risks, for instance, some key commodity prices may spike with higher demands. A good international example is the rising prices for rare earth minerals which are in big demand for EV and battery manufacturing globally.

The public commitments by many international businesses to systemic changes to achieve net zero and carbon neutrality have meant that these principles are now some of the top guiding principles for sustainable businesses globally. In the follow-up to COP26, there have been many discussions about whether the climate commitments that were made at COP26 will imply that there will be temperature increases of greater than 1.5°C by 2100. This is an important international temperature target, as proposed by UN's Intergovernmental Panel on Climate Change (UNIPCC). It will help to show how much more must be done to cut emissions globally so as to minimise global warming. For business executives globally, it is important to realise that, post-COP26, the global focus of many countries and governments is converging on the 1.5°C aspiration target proposed by the UNIPCC. The sustainability net zero imperative for businesses globally is no longer in question. Instead, the sustainability net zero imperative has become a new key objective and organising principle for sustainable business globally.

Many of the net zero commitments made at COP26 in Glasgow had emerged from international coalitions or alliances of the various stakeholders. These include many governments, financial institutions, companies, multilateral organisations and other key stakeholders. These coalitions with international stakeholder participation should help to solve many climate systemic problems globally. These should also help to shift the entire operating contexts for companies globally to achieve their green transitions, which is more of a reality.

A good international shipping example is that the transition to clean shipping will require customers to push for more shipping services with clean shipping fuels rather than continue using current shipping practices with the traditional fossil fuels. The shipping and fuel companies globally will have to respond accordingly. They will need to invest in new shipping vessels which can run on new clean zero-emission fuels. These, in turn, will push the international oil and gas companies plus the shipping fuel producers to produce more new clean shipping fuels rather than the tradition fossil bunker fuels. Investment banks and financial institution will have to provide more green finance capital for developing these green shipping projects and endeavours. When all these green business activities are coordinated, they should ensure they make the global transition to green shipping with new clean fuels more of a reality.

Globally, CEOs can also get ahead of and get involved in these various global green transformations by joining different international coalitions that are existing now. Good international business coalition examples include the Mission Possible Partnership plus the new commitments from various leading financial institutions globally to form the Glasgow Financial Alliance for Net Zero (GFANZ) at COP26.

Looking ahead, CEOs who see new pressing and unmet needs for cross-sector net zero efforts may wish to organise other new international coalitions. They might also choose to engage and lobby the public sector and governments collectively in setting new policies and rules that will favour a more orderly net zero transition.

With these opportunities and risks in mind, plus to meet their COP26 commitments, international businesses should focus on some key business areas and fundamentals which should help executives to develop effective new sustainability strategies and new net zero plans for the next few years. These will be described in more detail below with international examples and case studies.

Corporate Sustainability Net Zero Pledges and Plans

Global business experiences have shown that leading companies can gain significant business advantages from translating their net zero pledges into new realistic net zero plans with concrete actions. In practice, corporate net zero commitments are currently running ahead of companies' own plans to meet them. Relatively few businesses have yet to make clear, detailed sustainability strategies and net zero plans with concrete action on how they will achieve net zero and carbon neutrality by a certain target date. These will be the priority focus areas for international business leaders to concentrate on now. It is important for business leaders to realise that their investors, customers, regulators and key stakeholders are all expecting them to do this and to deliver on these new plans in the foreseeable future.

A good international country example is that the former UK Chancellor of the Exchequer Rishi Sunak had reiterated in his keynote speech at COP26 in 2021, that the UK Treasury will be requiring all UK-listed companies to develop and release their new sustainability net zero plans by 2023. Many expect that it will only be a matter of time before all governments and regulators from other countries globally will be enacting similar mandatory requirements on all the listed and private companies globally.

International experience has shown that sustainable businesses which have put convincing sustainability strategy and net zero plans in place can distinguish their companies positively from their peers and competitors. The basis of global competition has clearly changed post-COP26. There is now a good business premium on sound net zero planning and execution by businesses globally. A good international business example is when BP announced its new net zero plans, which were well received by the public, its investors and shareholders. These positive receptions have resulted in BP's share price rising in the London Stock Exchange.

Global business experience has shown that new corporate sustainability strategy and net zero plans will vary in their specifics. In general, the well-formed corporate sustainability strategy and net zero plans will feature certain common key elements as summarised below:

There should be clear new corporate emission targets for Scope 1, 2 and 3 emissions. These new emission targets should include long-term targets, as well as near-term goals for 2025 and 2030. These emission targets should also be aligned with science-based mitigation trajectories or sector-specific trajectories from credible authorities.

There should be a clear strategic view of the climate risks and new opportunities for each part of the company's business portfolio. These should cover both competitive dynamics and environmental exposures.

There should be detailed assessments on the transition capital and financial spendings that will be required to reduce emissions. These should include rectifications and investments that will be required to improve existing emissions-intensive assets. There should also be a credible plan and stance on the use of high-quality carbon credits and carbon offsets by companies.

There should be a good detailed programme to build up the necessary corporate capabilities to monitor external business conditions plus to make sound decisions and update the company's plans when required. In addition, there should be good regular monitoring of the impacts after implementing the plans so as to decide if any additional follow-up or remedial actions will be required.

It should be recognised that the new corporate sustainability strategy and net zero plans will take time to prepare. However, international business conditions are also changing quickly. So, companies should not wait too long to act. Most companies can make no-regrets moves even whilst they are drawing up their detailed long-term agendas and plans. Companies should start with straightforward moves that are sure to generate values. A good business example will be for companies to invest in energy efficiency improvements across their business operations. These should help to save energy and fuel consumption plus reduce emissions.

Good communication and explaining the company's new plans well to key stakeholders and consumers will also be very important. Sustainable business leaders should develop good investor relations and external-engagement programmes. These should help to put the companies on the front foot by explaining how they see the future, what they are doing now and what they will do next. These should help the key stakeholders and investors to become more engaged and to support the company's new sustainability strategy and net zero plans.

Sustainable Company Financing and Investments

Sustainable financing and green investment are growing fast in different countries globally. These are critical for supporting the growth of sustainable businesses and green projects. Financial institutions, investment banks and markets are recognising the new sustainable finance opportunities and green investment opportunities. They are working with sustainable business companies to help them to raise their sustainable financing requirements and to meet their green investment needs. A good international green finance example is the exponential growth of green bond markets in many financial centres, including London, New York, Hong Kong, etc.

Financial institutions globally have also been active in their drives to develop new sustainability strategies and new net zero plans. A good international finance example is that at COP26, the GFANZ brought together more than 450 international financial institutions. They collectively represented about US$130 trillion of financial assets globally. This is significant as it accounted for 40% of the global total. These international financial institutions have promised to work together to align their financial and investment portfolios with the new carbon neutrality requirements and the net zero goals agreed at COP26.

To put these in perspective, expert analysis has shown that successful global clean energy transitions and achieving net zero carbon neutrality goals will require some US$150 trillion of capital spending. Experts have also highlighted that two-thirds of the new climate finance and green investment capital will need to be in developing economies; the other one-third of the green investments will be needed in developed countries. The GFANZ pact is a good start on the global commitment to meet the high climate finance and green investment capital financing requirements. Looking ahead, far more green investment capital and climate financing will be needed as different countries around the world urgently pursue their various clean energy transitions and carbon neutrality net zero targets.

Deploying sufficient green capital quickly enough to achieve the new net zero and carbon neutrality targets will be a major challenge for all sustainable businesses globally. At a system level, sustainable businesses should focus on scaling suitable capital markets and financial institutions which will support channelling green investments and climate financing money into their various sustainable net zero investments. These will include energy efficiency improvements, clean renewable energy projects, decarbonisation plus climate adaptation and mitigation projects. Sustainable businesses will also need to scale other international sources, including the voluntary carbon markets, multilateral development banks, developing country platforms, various futures markets for green commodities, etc.

At the sustainable company level, corporate leaders, CEOs, CFOs and CIOs will need to work hard to raise suitable green investment capital and climate financing for their various green investments. These will include decarbonisation, emission reduction, clean energy transition, climate adaptation, mitigation projects, etc. Sustainable business leaders will also have to focus on building and transforming their existing businesses to serve the new growing markets internationally for new zero-emission goods and services.

Traditional companies which are currently owning carbon-intensive assets, including fossil fuels and coal assets, will need to work actively to transform these into new low carbon assets with well-developed plans and strategies. They will need to work with various financial institutions to secure suitable green investment funds to retrofit or retire these assets responsibly. Sustainable business should, in some extreme business situations, also consider divesting off or shutting down their most carbon-intensive assets as part of their new carbon neutrality net zero plans.

Sustainable Company Sourcing and Procurement

Sustainable company sourcing and procurement are fast growth sectors for sustainable businesses and suppliers globally. Sustainable businesses are recognising the attractive financial and commercial benefits of securing green materials and suppliers. These should help to improve business performances plus help to mitigate potential risks amidst global shortages and price volatility. Extreme weather incidents and pandemics in various countries globally are also posing serious climate-related threats to global supply chains now and in the years ahead. A good international example is that the COVID-19 pandemic and extreme weather incidents in the USA, from 2020 to 2022, have led to serious disruptions in their supply chains, logistics and ports, especially on the US West Coast.

There are also emerging green sourcing concerns that can create serious potential risks for many sustainable businesses. One main international business concern is that as the global demands increase for new green materials and suppliers with low emissions intensity, their production capacities globally may not be able to expand quickly enough to keep pace with the rising demands, at least in the near term. A good international supply example is that expert analysis has shown that the global shortage of suitable high-quality iron ore could potentially constrain the production of new green zero-emission steel in many places. These green steel supply constraints can have serious impacts on sustainable businesses globally, especially for electric car EV manufacturers, etc.

Another serious concern of sustainable businesses globally is the potential shortfalls in the supply of suitable climate technologies. A good international example is in the new zero-emission trucks sector. A recent truck report from Road Freight Zero, which is a cross-industry coalition that is part of the Mission Possible Partnership, and McKinsey has indicated that the projected growth in sales of zero-emission trucks in Europe will not be enough to help the EU road-freight sector onto a 1.5°C pathway (Mckinsey, Road Freight Zero, Zero-Emission Trucks Report, EU 2021).

Executives of sustainable businesses globally will need to consider these serious supply and sourcing constraints in their business planning and strategy formulation. They will need to prepare well for potential tightening in green material supplies and for upward pressure in their supply costs. Potential solutions include locking in future green suppliers and materials early now if they can. A good international example is that some sustainable businesses are formulating new purchasing contracts which are locking in critical green materials and commodity supplies, such as green steel. It may also be possible for sustainable businesses to hedge the gap in prices between conventional materials and new green zero-emission substitutes. This will require sustainable businesses to work innovatively with suitable investment banks or traders with the appropriate international trading and hedging capabilities that a few companies outside the financial sector may possess.

Traditional businesses and makers of steel, cement and other raw materials should recognise the growing demands for new green zero-emission goods globally, and these may be important new green business opportunities for them. Smart sustainable suppliers should consider transforming their traditional businesses into sustainable businesses by decarbonising their currently installed plants and assets. These green modifications and revamps will take significant green capital, as well as suitable green technology and time. In their sustainable business transformations, these companies should also consider other interim ways of satisfying their customers' demands for green sustainable materials and goods. One stop-gap approach may involve securing high-integrity carbon credits from nature-based projects globally.

Sustainable Company Disclosures and Reporting

Sustainable businesses globally will have to adopt and abide by the new sustainable business reporting requirements that are being introduced by various governments and regulators globally. A good international ESG example is that all publicly listed companies will have to develop rigorous sustainability measurements plus ESG disclosures and reports that will comply with the latest ESG requirements and standards in many countries globally. Many governments and leading stock markets globally, including the New York, London and Hong Kong stock exchanges, have introduced stringent ESG requirements.

Financial institutions and banks are also asking companies to disclose more information about their exposures to climate risks and their climate action plans, as part of their financing and credit rating work. Many companies have so far only disclosed the minimum required information. Global experience has shown that it will be beneficial for sustainable businesses to give more detailed reports on their ESG and climate performance in a more transparent manner. These are necessary to meet the expectations of various governments, regulators, investors and shareholders. Looking ahead, governments and regulators are planning to introduce more stringent ESG reporting plus more rigorous sustainability climate risk financial reporting, such as TCFD. More details on these developments are being given in the ESG and green finance sections of this book with international examples and case studies.

Sustainable Company Digitalisations

Leading sustainable companies' experience globally has suggested that digital transformation will be an important aspect of sustainability management.

A good international digital example is that distributed sensing and computing technologies have lent themselves well to sustainable value-chain management. These are particularly valuable in monitoring various emissions and helping to lower these emissions. At each point in a sustainable company's value chain, good accurate digital measurements of the actual emissions should lead the company, suppliers and business partners towards better understanding of what are the various emission sources that will help them to reducing their emissions further. Digital systems for tracking and tracing goods should also help to reveal where emissions are concentrated so that companies can take appropriate steps and actions to reduce these emissions.

Digital technologies can also have powerful applications within various sustainable companies' operations, such as manufacturing and sourcing. Global research has shown that digital transformations can boost the sustainability performance in the majority of sustainable companies globally.

Sustainable Company Climate Resilience

Sustainable investments in climate resilience can help to better protect people and companies from various physical climate hazards and extreme weather incidents. Climate change and global warming have led to more frequent extreme weather incidents with serious physical consequences plus damages to communities and residents.

The Sixth Assessment Report of the UNIPCC had concluded that climate changes and global warming have and will lead to very serious impacts on communities and companies globally. In addition, the multiple climate-modelling efforts based on current COP26 pledges have suggested that continued emissions globally will likely lead to more rising global warming, with the global temperatures rising to more than 1.5°C to above pre-industrial levels.

The various physical damages and hazards posed by climate change have serious humanitarian and economic impacts. A good international example is that experts have found, in a scenario-based climate analysis for the Race to Resilience campaign led by the UN High-Level Climate Champions, that in a future 2.0°C temperature rise world, roughly a billion more people would be exposed to climate hazards than in a 1.5°C world. In another climate scenario where 1.5°C of warming occurs, by 2030 almost half of the world's population could be exposed to serious climate hazards, including heat stress, drought, flood or water shortage. In addition, the lower income developing countries, in comparison with the higher income developed countries, will have larger shares of their population more likely to be exposed to at least one climate hazard (Mckinsey, COP26 made net zero a core principle for business, USA Nov 2021).

Companies globally will likely experience more frequent business and operational disruptions as the physical risks from climate hazards increase in future. By building greater resilience, sustainable companies can improve their ability to maintain business continuity amidst these rising climate risks. This should be a source of confidence and competitive advantage for sustainable companies globally. A good international example is that experts have estimated that downstream electronics companies globally could lose up to a third of their annual revenues if their supplies of chips were disrupted for five months due to extreme climate incidents, such as typhoons, hurricanes, flooding, etc.

Sustainable Company Business Travel Developments

Making business travels more sustainable will not only benefit the environment but also benefit each sustainable company positively. By reducing the needs to travel, sustainable companies can cut down on their travel and hotel costs significantly plus also reduce their corporate carbon dioxide (CO_2) emissions and footprints.

Sustainable business travels include managing all the different modes of travel by company staff, which will help to limit the impacts that business travel has on the planet. One way is to encourage employees to take alternative green transportation instead of flying, such as rail or public transport, etc. Air travels can account for as much as 10–25% of the CO_2 footprint of international companies. Offering alternative, greener, ways of business travel, such as train or public transport, is one way to reduce CO_2 emissions from business travel.

A good recent international green travel example is that some of the leaders and ministers attending the COP26 meeting in Glasgow have chosen to travel to the COP26 Conference in Glasgow by rail instead of by air, so as to reduce their carbon footprints. International media have reported that these green travel news reports have received favourable public comments globally.

With the COVID-19 pandemic, online video and zoom conferencing tools have also become very popular and widely available. So, companies can reduce the need to travel by their staff by encouraging and hosting more video or zoom conferences. Video conferencing has been shown to positively improve PPP in some positive ways. Video conferencing can also help people and staff to improve their work-life balance. In addition, it helps to protect the planet by reducing the corporate CO_2 emissions with less business travel. It can also improve corporate profits by a reduction in the business travel costs, less wasted time and lower hotel costs.

Companies can also help to reduce and offset CO_2 emissions as part of their new net zero plans. Businesses can invest in CO_2 reduction projects, such as planting trees or buying carbon credits. They can also encourage employees to buy their flight tickets from sustainable flight agencies, which helps to offset a flight's CO_2 emissions for free.

COP26 has highlighted that the global momentum has shifted towards companies being required to achieve carbon neutrality by agreed timelines, such as 2050, plus meeting their new net zero targets. These are providing sustainable businesses with important new priorities, missions and goals. The transition to net zero will be complicated and needs lots of efforts. Sustainable companies have to develop good new net zero plans and sustainable strategies. These should be well planned so the transition will be relatively orderly, rather than punctuated by sudden, unexpected shifts. The basis of competition will change as stakeholders, investors and customers globally are increasing favouring and rewarding sustainable companies that exhibit high levels of preparedness and commitment to sustainability plus achieving carbon neutrality and net zero goals.

Sustainable Company Office Buildings

Leading sustainable businesses globally have been improving the sustainability of their office buildings and warehouses globally. International experiences have shown that there are several essential elements that sustainable companies have to focus on to make their offices and buildings more sustainable.

One key area that sustainable companies should focus on is to improve the energy efficiency and insulation of their offices and buildings. Sustainable offices should have enough insulation as most buildings are currently built with an insufficient amount of insulation. Improved insulation should help to reduce energy losses and improve energy efficiency. These will help to reduce fuel uses and lower emissions.

Sustainable offices should also use the building's thermal mass to the best effect. Sustainable office should make best use of natural lights. These will help to reduce lighting and electricity energy uses and costs. Sustainable offices should also choose to use green, recycled and sustainable materials as much as possible.

Sustainable Company Investments Performance and Outlooks

Sustainable finance and green investments are growing fast globally. Sustainability-aligned investing has been growing fast globally. International surveys have shown that international companies had taken in a record amount of US$859 billion in sustainable investments in 2021. This included a record amount of US$481.8 billion in green bonds, which have helped to raise money for specific environmental projects in different countries.

Looking ahead, the level of sustainable finance and green investments is set to grow significantly. A good international example is that the total value of global ESG investments is projected to be on track to rise and exceed US$50 trillion by 2025. This will account for more than a third of all global investments, according to a recent analysis by Bloomberg. Looking ahead, Bloomberg has also estimated that by 2025, more than US$53 trillion could be invested globally in sustainability funds and portfolios (Bloomberg, ESG Investment Study, 2021).

There is also growing international pressure on sustainable company and green investments. In a stark message in the wake of COP26, more than half of the stakeholders and consumers across 17 markets have expressed their strong belief that investors and financial services companies have an obligation to help to improve the environment and they should be doing more than now.

Investors and stakeholders globally are also pushing for greater scrutiny of the sustainable finance and green investment sectors in various countries globally. Many investors are concerned by their performance in comparison to other traditional investments. In addition, there are rising concerns about the possibility of greenwashing by some companies and funds. Many have suggested that strong and more uniform definitions of sustainable investment and ESG products are urgently needed globally (WEF, How to address sustainable investment backlash and improve ESG reporting, WEF Switzerland Dec 2021).

Sustainable finance and responsible investing have undergone some important evolutions in their rapid growth in recent years. A few decades ago, sustainable investment started as a somewhat basic ethical assessment of business and financial investment activities. These have grown significantly with the recent focus on climate change and sustainability globally. Sustainable finance and green investments have now evolved into a more thorough integration of ESG factors via various quantitative and qualitative assessments.

These developments have been evolving in line with the rising global requirements to measure more precisely the key business risks that may have adverse societal or environmental consequences. There are particular concerns on those business risks which could adversely affect the financial results and business performance of leading companies globally. It should also be noted that these should also help to identify new green business and new sustainable investment opportunities. A good international financial example is the emergence of various new sustainable investment financial products and instruments, such as ESG-specialised exchange traded funds (ETFs) and green bonds, etc.

However, there has been some international scepticism regarding sustainable investing and various so-called sustainable financial products. Leading regulators globally, such as the USA's Securities Exchange Commission (SEC), the UK's Financial Conduct Authority (FCA) and the European Commission (EC), have started to pay close attention to the claims and construction of various so-called green sustainable financial products. There are also some critics claiming that sustainable investing has to be more closely regulated.

Sustainable investing can cover a range of activities, from putting cash into green energy projects, or to investing in sustainable companies which demonstrate social values such as social inclusion or good governance. A good international example of recent sustainable company board development is the push to improve the gender diversity and equity of some boards globally. Many leading international companies have improved the gender equity and diversity of their boards by appointing more qualified women directors on their boards.

Sustainable finance and green investment have important roles to play in the global clean energy transition. In addition, large amounts of sustainable finance will be required to support companies and countries achieving their various carbon neutrality goals and net zero targets. A good international financial example is the sustainable investments by both public and private money into new carbon neutrality projects. This includes the EU Green Deal Investment Plan which aims to raise US$1.14 trillion to help pay for the costs of achieving the Europe net zero climate change emissions targets by 2050 (WEF, What is sustainable finance, WEF Switzerland Jan 2022).

To ensure that sustainable investments will deliver on their promises, various global accounting bodies are working together to push for new global standards. A good international standards example is that the International Financial Reporting Standards Foundation (IFRSF) has set up the ISSB to come up with new rules to validate the sustainability performance claims by various companies globally. These should help to improve global transparency and standards.

As well as helping to improve the planet plus making society fairer and more inclusive, evidence is also mounting that sustainable businesses and green investments can actually offer higher returns for investors. A recent sustainable investment study was conducted for Fidelity, the international asset manager. The study tracked the performance of a range of ESG investments worldwide between 1970 and 2014. The results showed that half of these sustainable investments have outperformed the international financial markets. However, a minority of the sustainable investment, some 11%, have also shown negative performance relative to the markets (Fidelity, ESG Investment Study, UK 2021).

Another international sustainable investment analysis has been conducted by BlackRock, which is the world's biggest asset management company. Their study has shown that during the height of the COVID-19 pandemic in 2020, more than eight out of ten sustainable investment funds have performed better than other share portfolios that are not based on ESG criteria. It is also interesting to note that, as well as paying higher dividends to shareholders, sustainable companies which have high ESG ratings have also enjoyed stronger increases in their share prices in the past five years (BlackRock, ESG Company Study, 2020).

These sustainable investment international studies and their results are important because most stock market investments are being made by international financial institutions, such as pension funds and mutual funds. In the USA, 80% of the listed equity in leading companies is being held by pension or financial organisations which are looking after pensions or investors' money. These institutional investors and pension fund trustees have strong focuses on sustainable investment performance as part of their fiduciary duty to act in the best financial interest of their investors and pensioners.

In practice, the rising returns on sustainable investments and assets has meant that trustees no longer have to sacrifice sustainability for profit and returns. The World Economic Forum's Transformational Investment report has cited the good example of New Zealand's State Pension Fund. The trustees of the New Zealand State Pension Fund have argued that climate change and global warming has posed serious risks to their ability to fund their pension investments and commitments. So, they have decided to switch to a new sustainable finance and responsible investment strategy. As a result, their pension fund has outperformed other comparable investments by 1.24% a year since its inception in 2003. In monetary terms, this has represented a total positive increase or difference of US$7.24 billion (NZD10.65 billion). These are very good news and positive returns for their investors and pensioners in New Zealand.

Global experience and analysis have also shown that there are many good reasons for ESG-friendly investments doing better than other conventional investments. The key reasons and explanations for their outperformance are summarised below with international examples:

One key factor is the rapidly changing investors' and customers' attitudes. A recent study in the USA has found that two-thirds of the consumers of all ages prefer to buy from sustainable and ethical companies that share their high values. Amongst millennials, who are people aged between 18 and 34, that figure had risen higher to 83%. Global studies have shown that consumers are four to six times more likely to buy from a company or brand with strong corporate purposes and values which they endorse. These often include high sustainability and ethical standards. If a company does something that the consumers and stakeholders disagree with, then three-quarters have said that they would stop buying from that brand and they will also encourage others to do the same. These are strong drivers and incentives for companies to become more sustainable. Their sustainability transformation should help to promote more sales and returns from sustainable products that are preferred by customers globally.

Carbon-intensive industries, such as coal, oil and gas, are also finding it increasingly harder and more expensive to raise capital. The reason is that leading international lenders and investment banks are placing more scrutiny on their investments plus which company they will work with. A good international investment example is the announcement by some leading international investment banks that they will not be providing financing and funding for fossil coal projects in selected countries.

In contrast, sustainable companies are more likely to have easier access to financing globally. Sustainable businesses are likely to enjoy more benefits, including more likely to win future contracts, save more costs, have less regulation concerns, retain their best people and avoid losing money on old carbon-intensive processes. These important drivers and factors should all contribute positively to the performance and financial results of sustainable companies globally.

Sustainable Company Business Case Studies

Many leading corporations and companies globally are actively developing themselves into international sustainable companies. They are actively developing their sustainability strategy and new net zero plans in line with their Paris Agreement and COP26 commitments. These sustainability developments are helping them to develop their business and to be sustainable globally. Some of the key developments by some leading international sustainable companies in different sectors are summarised below with the following case studies of some leading international sustainable companies in different sectors:

TomTom Sustainable Tech Company Case Study 1

TomTom is one of the best-known eco-friendly sustainable company and brands globally. They have started with a simple corporate mission to make digital navigation accessible for everyone globally in both the developed and developing countries. TomTom was founded in 1991, and their portable navigation aids are currently helping millions of drivers around the world. The first

TomTom sat nav has become one of the fastest selling consumer technology devices in history.

Today, TomTom is one of the leading independent sustainable geolocation technology specialist companies globally. Their sustainable products include maps for automated driving, navigation software for top car brands, maps APIs for leading tech companies and traffic data for all. They are actively developing new sustainable digital technologies which are aiming at minimising road accidents, lowering emissions and reducing traffic congestions globally. Working together with their international customers and partners, they aspire to reshape the future of mobility and create a world that will move better together.

At TomTom, corporate responsibility is not an afterthought or about checking a box. They are guided by their strong corporate mission and desire to create a better world. Their sustainable values and vision come through in their sustainable products and services, people and their business operations. TomTom is focusing their efforts in five key sustainability areas, including road safety, environmental impact, equality, giving back and ethical business. These are described in more detail below:

On road safety, more than 3,000 people are dying in road accidents every day globally. TomTom has been creating various new technologies that will make driving safer for both the human drivers and self-driving cars. Improved safety is one of the key benefits of using digital navigation, which will allow vehicle control to switch from human to machine or artificial intelligence (AI). A good example is that the new TomTom international digital maps for automated driving are delivering greater safety and comfort to automated driverless cars globally.

On environmental impacts, TomTom has been using their traffic insights to help people, cities, governments and businesses to move more freely. These will help to reducing the emissions from the transport and mobility sectors globally. A good example is that their digital ADAS Maps are helping one to achieve up to 5% fuel savings on various road transports globally. In addition, TomTom is looking for ways to reduce their corporate environmental and carbon footprints.

On equality, TomTom is encouraging individuality and embracing self-expression of their staff. Their corporate approach to diversity and inclusion includes diverse hiring; fair and equal growth opportunities; promotion of an inclusive work culture; and accountability to help them reach diversity targets. They believe that cultivating a true culture of diversity, inclusion and belonging, will make TomTom better inside and out. These include diversity, inclusion and promoting a sense of belonging.

On giving back, TomTom has been playing various active roles in their communities with special focus on promoting technical education, specifically for women in tech. They are aiming to help shape a new, gender-balanced generation that is equipped with in-demand skills. A good example is that after launching a successful paid-time-off volunteer programme in the Netherlands, TomTom has started to roll this initiative out globally.

On ethical business, TomTom is a data-driven company that separates itself from competition through strict data privacy practices. These are reflected throughout the organisation, products and services. They don't identify users, show ads or sell people's data. They are protecting their customers' personal data privacy with strict protocols and technologies.

The TomTom 2021 corporate responsibility report has highlighted that building a better sustainable world is core to their business. Their ESG Report 2021 has taken a closer look at how they are driving ESG practices across TomTom. Based on their five focus areas, they are committed to supporting the various UN SDGs. These include supporting the SDG goals of quality education (4), gender equality (5), and sustainable cities and communities (11). They are also supporting quality education, gender equality plus sustainable cities and community developments globally.

Patagonia Sustainable Clothing Company Case Study 2

Patagonia is one of the top sustainable clothing companies and brands globally. According to Rank a Brand, Patagonia is one of the most sustainable clothing brands globally in both the sport and outdoor sectors.

Patagonia has been striving to be an environmentally friendly sustainable business for more than 20 years. One percent of their corporate revenue is going to environmental organisations. They are also organising workshops where their customers and consumers can learn how to repair their own clothing and belongings so they do not have to throw these away. They are also encouraging sustainable business travels for all their staff. A good example is that they are organising an annual event in June, when all their employees will come together to cycle and celebrate.

In 2019, Patagonia CEO Rose Marcario announced that the outdoor clothing brand will strive to be completely CO2 neutral by 2025. Patagonia is developing their new net zero and carbon neutrality plans so they will have a fully sustainable CO2 neutral production cycle.

They are also active in clean energy transitions. They will phase out fossil fuel consumption by using clean renewable energy, including solar and wind energy. They will also comply with strict standards in terms of sustainable sourcing, sustainable production materials and the use of sustainable ethical raw materials.

The Patagonia founder has also transferred ownership of the company to a specially designed trust and an NGO. His purpose is to preserve the independence of Patagonia and ensure that all of its profits will be used to combating climate change and protecting undeveloped land around the world.

Triodos Bank Sustainable Banking Case Study 3

Triodos Bank is striving to be a sustainable international bank. They believe in adopting a new banking model, that is, sustainable ethical banking. They have been adopting the sustainable investment principle from the start of the company since 1980. A good example is that they have been using the deposits of their customers to invest in other sustainable companies which are working to create a better world. They are also providing their customers with useful sustainability tips and advice.

A good sustainable investment example is that Triodos will, instead of loaning their money to the fossil sector, invest their funds in the clean energy and renewable sectors. They believe that these are key part of their sustainable investment approaches right from the start of the company since 1980.

Tony's Chocolonely Sustainable Food Company Case Study 4

Tony's Chocolonely is one of the top sustainable food companies and brands globally. It was the Winner of the Sustainable Brand Index in 2019.

Tony's Chocolonely is a Dutch company that focuses on making the cocoa industry more fairtrade and free from slave labour work. A good example is that they have been calculating the true social cost of their chocolate bar, including all negative social impacts together with impacts on the environment, like child labour or CO2 emissions, etc.

In addition to working on having positive social impacts, Tony's Chocolonely is also working on limiting their environmental impacts. According to Rank a Brand, they do not use palm oil in their products. In addition, they are implementing various measures to offset and reduce their GHG emissions. They are measuring the various climate impacts of their activities so they can better control and reduce these emissions.

They are also collaborating with Justdiggit on land restoration. Justdiggit is an NGO that focuses on restoring landscapes and regreening dry lands in Africa. These should have positive impacts on the environment, climate and land uses globally.

3
International Policy Developments on Climate Change

求人不如求己

Qiú rén bù rú qiú jǐ

It is better to rely on yourself rather than depend on the help from others.
If you want things to be done well, then do it yourself.

Global Climate Policy Overviews

The global impacts by climate change and global warming are accelerating and affecting all countries. Many countries are introducing new climate policies and regulations to mitigate these serious climate impacts and to reduce their emissions in line with their Paris Agreement commitments.

The International Energy Authority (IEA) has shown that the energy-related carbon dioxide ($CO2$) emissions have seriously contributed to the large majority of global greenhouse gas (GHG) emissions to date. These have led to rising global temperatures and global warming. These, in turn, have led to a rising number of extreme weather incidents induced by climate changes which have caused serious damages and economic losses. As a result, many countries have been introducing new climate policies to reduce their emissions. A good international example is that many governments have enacted new clean energy transition policies to transform their energy mixes by reducing fossil fuel consumptions and promoting clean energy sources. These should reduce their GHG emissions and help the countries to meet their Paris Agreement commitments.

However, there are various serious climate challenges and hurdles. Experts have forecasted that even if all the countries were able to meet their emission goals as pledged under the United Nations Framework Convention on Climate Change (UNFCC), it would likely still leave the world with 13.7 billion tonnes

DOI: 10.4324/9781003142348-3

of excess CO_2 emissions. These would be equivalent to being some 60% above the CO_2 levels that would be required for the world to remain on track to meet just 2°C global temperature rise target by 2035.

Many governments and countries around the world have also recognised the importance of working together to jointly managing climate change and to reduce global warming. However, in practice, there are many difficulties in achieving effective joint climate change management. Key hurdles include some key stakeholders and companies having believed that climate management is expensive and will increase business costs plus reduce company profits. In addition, many have argued that new climate change measures would require major changes in policies and lifestyles in different countries. Some executives in the traditional business sectors, especially those in the utilities and fossil fuel sectors, have also argued that new climate change measures would create additional costs for their businesses, which would then reduce their short-term profitability (Wang, Climate Change and Clean Energy Management, Routledge UK 2019).

A good international business example is that many utilities and power generation companies will have to retrofit their fossil fuel power station with new flue gas and waste treatment facilities so as to meet the new stringent emission requirements being introduced by various governments. Many companies have been reluctant to make these extra investments in the past as they believed that these will reduce their profitability. However, they have now to recognise that these new requirements will be essential parts of their licence to continue operate sustainably in future.

Globally, many governments have been developing and introducing new clean energy transition policies to reduce their fossil fuel consumptions plus accelerate their clean energy implementation. Many countries have also introduced new carbon management policies and systems, including carbon emission trading and carbon tax systems. Businesses have to actively consider these new carbon policy requirements as part of their new climate change strategy and business planning.

A good international country carbon tax example is the new carbon tax system that has been recently introduced by the Federal Government of Canada. They have introduced a new national carbon tax system which is in line with their new climate change policies and their Paris Agreement commitments. The Federal and Provincial Governments of Canada have used the revenues generated by their new carbon tax system to fund various climate change improvements across Canada. A good example is the use of the carbon tax income as a green funding source for construction of the new green public transport system in Toronto, Ontario, Canada (Canada Global News, Climate and carbon taxes, 2018).

The UNFCC has been active in organising the international effort to monitor climate change impacts plus measuring the impacts of various climate actions by the different countries. The UNFCCC was launched at the 1992 Rio Earth Summit. It aspires to reduce the GHG emissions to a lower level, which would prevent dangerous anthropogenic interference with the Earth's climate system. It has also set voluntary GHG emissions reduction targets which the various countries have to develop individual climate action plans to meet.

After the failure of the Rio initiatives, the 191 signatories to the UNFCCC agreed to meet in Kyoto in 1997 to establish a more stringent climate change regime. The resulting Kyoto Protocol has created a global carbon credits trading system with binding GHG reductions for the various ratifying countries. Some key countries were not part of this Kyoto Protocol. Key international country examples included USA, which did not sign the Kyoto Protocol, plus China and India, both of which were exempt as developing countries (UNFCC, Kyoto Protocol Targets for the first commitment period, 2012).

In follow-up to the Kyoto Protocol, the annual Conferences of the Parties (COPs) to the Kyoto Protocol have been held almost every year in different countries. The international COP meetings have been held in different locations, including at The Hague, Cancun, Doha, etc. However, little progress has been made mainly due to the serious conflicting interests between the various countries. In 2012, the Kyoto carbon trading system was not renewed and it collapsed after the failure of the 2012 Doha COP meetings.

In 2016, the various countries met at the COP21 meetings in Paris. After long, intense and difficult climate negotiations, the various countries managed to make major advances in their climate negotiations. In the end, many countries were able to jointly sign and support the Paris Agreement. At the end of the UN COP21 climate conference in Paris in December 2015, 195 nations unanimously agreed to restrict the temperature rise to less than 2°C, or preferably 1.5°C, above the pre-industrial "baseline". This was an extraordinary international political achievement and climate agreement by the 195 countries. However, to achieve the very stretched and ambitious targets set, it would require almost a complete cessation of global CO_2 emissions by the second half of this century. This would be very difficult to achieve and would involve very difficult discussions by the various countries to agree on how to achieve these challenging targets. In the meantime, the world has crossed the important 400 ppm mark in CO_2 concentrations, which has led to more global warming plus also resulted in a global temperature rise of 1°C (UNFCCC, United Nations Framework Convention on Climate Change, Paris Agreement, 2015).

The Paris Agreement has also reaffirmed joint international commitments to reduce emissions by the 195 different countries. They have agreed to strive to achieve a 2°C warming limit target by 2100. These would include mandatory reductions by developed countries plus calls upon developing countries to contribute. They have created an international climate change fund which would be used to compensate climate change losers. They have also re-established a new Kyoto style Clean Development Mechanism (CDM) and carbon trading systems.

It is important to note that the Paris Agreement has made no provisions for agricultural emission reductions and also largely ignored the developing economies. These are important areas that would also have big implications on global climate change and global warming. More difficult work and negotiations will need to be undertaken by the various countries so as to come to some international agreements in these two important areas in future COP meetings.

The Paris Agreement has anticipated that future revisions and refinements would be required every five years. These would provide the much-needed scope for incremental policy reviews and developments at the national country levels. A practical approach to climate change policymaking should complement the Paris framework. This would provide flexibility for individual governments to facilitate the use of more incremental and adaptable policy responses. These should also better reflect the local resource endowments and socio-economic circumstances.

The UN Climate Change Conference COP26 was held in Glasgow during November 2021. It brought together 120 world leaders and over 40,000 participants from 200 countries. For two weeks, they discussed all facets of climate change, including the science, the solutions, the political will to act together on potential joint climate actions, etc. (UN Climate Action, COP26 Summary, UN US 2021).

After intensive negotiations by 200 countries over two weeks, the Glasgow Climate Pact was agreed and signed. The UN has commented that the approved texts were a compromise by the 200 countries, but the various countries have taken important steps forward on their joint efforts to mitigate climate change.

Experts have advised that the proposed cuts in global GHG emissions are still far from where they would need to be to preserve a liveable climate by the end of this century. In addition, the supports for the most vulnerable countries affected by the impacts of climate change are still falling far short. However, COP26 has produced new building blocks to advance the implementation of the Paris Agreement through actions that can get the world on a more sustainable, low-carbon pathway forward.

Highlights of the recent international COP meetings, especially COP24 and COP26, plus the different international climate agreements will be discussed in more detail in the sections below plus in different chapters of this book. The key agreements and their implications will be discussed together with international examples and case studies.

COP24 Meeting in 2018 Highlights

The COP24 meeting held in Poland in December 2018 had over 23,000 attendees from different countries. There was important sharing between the participants as well as tough climate negotiations. There were serious concerns amongst many representatives that some leading countries have not been placing sufficient priority and focus on climate change.

A good international example is that 200 Parliamentarians from different countries held an important meeting between them during a weekend in the middle of the COP. They shared their common concerns that, following the IPCC 1.5°C report, many governments have still not been doing enough to reduce their GHG emissions. They discussed various important climate change topics plus how various Parliaments in different countries can help to push for appropriate legal frameworks at their national levels so as to push various governments to meet their Paris Agreement commitments. In addition, they discussed how different Parliaments could hold their governments and politicians more accountable to implementing their required climate mitigation actions, as agreed in the Paris Agreement. A good international example is that recent international climate research has shown that less than 10% of the countries have implemented appropriate domestic legal frameworks which would be compatible with their nationally determined conditions (NDCs) to meet their Paris Agreement commitments (LSE Grantham Institute Post COP24 Forum, London Dec 2018).

After tough negotiations during COP24, the Paris Rulebook was finally agreed and delivered by the delegates. At the COP21 meeting, constructive ambiguity was used to allow countries with different views to sign up to the Paris Agreement. To reach agreement on the new Paris Rulebook, it was necessary to eliminate these ambiguities between all the countries. There were tough negotiations taking into account the various technicalities and political positions. The new Paris Rulebook that was finally agreed and adopted by all the countries comprised 133 pages together with appendixes. The agreed Paris Rulebook should help to provide a common reporting structure for all countries on their climate adaptation and mitigation action plans. This should help to build trust between countries and promote climate action. It should also help various countries to plan, implement and review their climate adaptation and mitigation actions. It might also encourage some countries to ratchet up their climate change ambitions and actions.

The agreed Rulebook contained good and detailed guidelines on the planning of climate adaptation and mitigation actions. It also provided improved ex-ante and ex-post information on the climate finances that have been pledged. It covered transparency on future climate finances. However, it was difficult for developed countries to commit to finances beyond their budget cycles. These have often been from one year to a maximum of four years.

The Rulebook also helped to strengthen environmental integrity and emission reductions reporting. The Rulebooks included specific climate and emission reporting guidelines which have been based on strict scientific basis. These should help to reduce the use of various accounting tricks that have occurred in the past.

There was one significant area which was not agreed at COP24. This was the important Article 6 on global carbon markets. The key reason was that some countries wanted a more permissive carbon market regime than other countries. This could then potentially lead to problems on double carbon accounting and standards globally. In addition, there was also some serious technical work outstanding. Hence, it was agreed by all the delegates at COP24 to postpone the carbon markets discussions by another year. This delay was preferred by all delegates rather than forcing agreement on some weak and fuzzy carbon market rules.

In addition, the Climate Finance Ministerial dialogue was good. Many of the Less Developed Countries (LDC) would need more capacity support to improve their climate finance reporting. Currently, there have not been enough trickling down to the local levels and on adaptation. The climate finance package could have been stronger and it was agreed to postpone setting up a new goal for climate finance to 2020.

One encouraging development was that most of the countries, apart from a few oil-producing countries, all agreed that it would be important to focus on meeting the new UN's Intergovernmental Panel on Climate Change (UNIPCC) target of 1.5°C rather than the current 2.0–3.5°C envelopes. This was a major global shift following the publication of the UNIPCC 1.5°C report. The UNIPCC report highlighted the negative impacts of climate change and stressed the importance of urgent international climate change actions. It was disappointing that some countries, especially some oil- and gas-producing countries, have chosen not to welcome and adopt the UNIPCC 1.5°C report due to their own specific national and economic interests. These hurdles would be major challenges for future COP meetings to deal with and to resolve.

Following the agreement of the Rulebook, countries would need to focus on improving their NDCs to get to the 1.5°C envelope rather than the previous

2.0–3.5°C envelope. The common playing field established by the Rulebook should help to make countries more willing to consider these improvements. In addition, most countries recognised that their BAU would not be sufficient to deliver the required climate actions. Looking ahead, various countries would need to discuss their improved NDCs at the 2019 climate summit. Then, they would have to meet the key requirement to deliver their new NDC updates at the planned COP meeting in 2020.

Looking ahead, it was also recognised that as countries introduce new policies to reduce their emissions these could potentially raise social licence and public acceptance issues. These problems have led to serious public protests and demonstrations in some countries. One good international example was the Yellow Vests protests in France and demonstrations in Paris about the fuel price increases proposed by the French government.

It would be important for governments to realise that their new climate policies and clean energy transition plans could disproportionately affect some social segments in their country, especially the lower-income families which might suffer some serious social hardships. Hence, appropriate Just Transition process and actions should be incorporated as an integral part of their integrated climate action plans in various countries.

The agreed Rulebook would be common for all countries. It also provided enough flexibility for developing countries taking into account their special national conditions and development status. During COP24, the LDCs pushed for a strong Rulebook taking into account their special situation and requirements.

The international LDCs comprised 47 of the poorest countries in the world. Their total population amounted to 1 billion people, but they accounted for less than 1% of the GHG emissions. These countries have already been badly impacted by various climate change impacts, including flooding, drought and plastic wastes. The LDCs have also been developing new long-term initiatives for effective climate adaptation and resilience.

In summary, COP24 was a partial technical success but there would be more work required to build momentum, especially around raising national climate ambitions and climate mitigation actions. Whilst countries have managed to agree to a lengthy 'Paris Rulebook', they also could not finalise future rules for carbon markets which they have agreed to postpone for decision by one year. More importantly, most governments have to step up development of their national climate targets and mitigation actions. The findings of the UNIPCC's 1.5°C report have shown that GHG emissions have actually risen significantly, which have raised concerns. The rules for reviewing progress against the Paris

Agreement and raising ambition in the 2020s have to be further developed, including national reviews with clear and transparent guidelines.

COP26 and Glasgow Climate Pact 2021 Highlights

The UN Climate Change Conference of Parties COP 26 meeting was held in Glasgow, UK during November 2021. It brought together 120 world leaders from 200 countries. The meeting had over 40,000 registered participants, including 22,274 party delegates plus 14.124 observers and 3.886 media representatives. For two weeks, they discussed all the different facets of climate change and its serious impacts. The discussions covered the science of climate change and the potential climate solutions. In addition, the political will to act and potential joint climate actions by different countries were also discussed (UN Climate Action, COP26 Summary, UN US 2021).

An important outcome of COP26, the Glasgow Climate Pact, was the fruit of intensive negotiations amongst almost 200 countries over the two weeks. It had involved strenuous formal and informal work and negotiations by various climate negotiators from different countries over many months, together with constant engagement both in-person and virtually for nearly two years.

The UN has said that the approved texts in the COP26 Glasgow Climate Pact were a compromise between the different countries. These have reflected the interests, the conditions, the contradictions and the state of political will in the various countries around the world today. These countries have collectively taken some important steps, but unfortunately the collective political will was not enough to overcome some deep contradictions between the different countries (UN Climate Action, COP26 Summary, UN US 2021).

The agreed COP26 Glasgow Climate Pact aims to promote and accelerate emissions reductions toward achieving the climate goals that were set in the 2015 Paris Agreement. That accord held governments worldwide responsible for emissions cuts that would keep the global temperature rises well below 2°C (3.6 degrees Fahrenheit) relative to pre-industrial times, with an aspired target of 1.5°C (2.7 degrees Fahrenheit).

Climate experts have advised that the proposed cuts in global GHG emissions from the different countries are still far from where they need to be to preserve a liveable climate. In addition, the support for the most vulnerable developing countries affected by the impacts of climate change is still falling far short. However, COP26 has produced new building blocks to further advance the implementation of the various global climate agreements, including both the Paris Agreement and the Glasgow Climate Pact. These coordinated global climate actions should get the world moving towards their carbon neutrality targets by adopting more sustainable, low-carbon pathways going forward.

The COP26 Glasgow Climate Pact aims to reduce the worst impacts of climate change. However, some key stakeholders and climate campaigners have said that these did not go far enough. The Glasgow Climate Pact is also not legally binding on the 200 countries that have signed it. It should help to set the global agenda on climate change going forward for the next decade or so.

At COP26, various key countries, in addition to agreeing to the Glasgow Climate Pact, also made important side climate deals. These included bold collective commitments to curb methane emissions, to halt and reverse forest loss, to align the finance sector with net zero by 2050, to phase out the internal combustion engine, to accelerate the phase-out of coal, to reduce international financing for fossil fuels, etc. These important new side deals to COP26 will be discussed in more detail in the various sections below in this book with international examples.

COP26 in Glasgow was also a good global platform for launching innovative sectoral partnerships and new climate fundings to support these. Their collective aims are to promote re-shaping every sector of the economy at scales necessary to promote the contribution by different key international sectors to achieve the aspired carbon neutrality and net zero goals.

At COP26, despite significant headways made on several climate fronts, the various national climate and financing commitments were found to be still far short of what will be required to come to grips with the global climate challenges. However, there were good discussions on climate loss and damages on providing further climate supports for developing countries.

The various key climate issues and actions that were discussed and agreed in the COP26 meeting and the Glasgow Climate Pact will be summarised and discussed in more detail below with international examples:

COP26 Countries Agreement of Global Climate Emergency

At COP26, over 200 countries reaffirmed the Paris Agreement goal of limiting the increases in the global average temperatures to well below 2°C above pre-industrial levels. They have also agreed to continue global efforts to pursue limiting the global temperature rise to 1.5°C above pre-industrial levels. All these countries have recognised that the global impacts of climate change will be much lower at a temperature increase of 1.5°C when compared with 2°C.

All the countries that were present at COP26 have expressed alarm and utmost concerns that human and industrial activities have already caused around 1.1°C of temperature rise to date. They also agreed that serious climate impacts and damages are already being felt in every country and region.

In COP26, all the countries agreed that they should resolve to pursue efforts to aspire to limit the global temperature increase to 1.5°C by the end of 2100. This new COP26 decision should help to give this lower global temperature rise threshold even greater emphasis than in the Paris Agreement. Unfortunately, there was not yet a firm global commitment to this lower global temperature rise threshold after intensive negotiations and lobbying at COP26.

In addition, the Glasgow Climate Pact has also asked all nations to consider further climate actions to curb their emissions by potent non-CO2 gasses, such as methane. This is an important step forward to reduce the emissions by important GHGs, in addition to CO2.

The Glasgow Climate Pact also included suitable languages, after intensive negotiations, to emphasise the global need to phase down unabated coal consumptions and to phase out fossil fuel subsidies. These marked the first time that negotiators have explicitly referenced the global clean energy transition plus the urgent need to shift away from coal and phasing out fossil fuel subsidies. Unfortunately, the intensive negotiations and strong lobbying by some countries at COP26 had meant that in the end of COP26, it was not able to reach a global agreement to stop all coal uses and to eliminate all fossil fuel subsidies in the final COP26 agreement text.

In addition, COP26 finally recognised the importance of nature and natural carbon solution for both reducing emissions and building resilience to the impacts of climate change. These were expressed both in the formal agreement text and also through a raft of initiatives that were announced on the sidelines of COP26. These announcements will be discussed in the sections below with international examples (WRI, COP26: Key Outcomes from the UN Climate Talks in Glasgow, US Nov 2021).

Recognising the international urgency of climate challenges plus the urgent need to accelerate global joint climate actions, the ministers from all over the world agreed that all the countries should meet again at the end of 2022 at the planned international COP27 meeting in Egypt. They agreed that they would try to submit their new stronger 2030 emissions reduction targets at COP27. They also planned to discuss their collective aims and actions more at COP27 to close the gap required for limiting global warming to 1.5°C (2.7 degrees F).

COP26 Countries NDC Emission Plans & Net Zero Pathways

By the end of the COP26 meeting, 151 countries have submitted their NDCs and national climate action plans. These included their new NDCs, which are their updated plans to reduce their emissions by 2030. The UNIPCC has calculated that these new NDC plans, if all achieved, should put the world on track for a 2.5°C of warming by the end of the century. This is better than the 4°C temperature rise trajectory that the world was previously on before the Paris Agreement was struck. However, the new projected temperature rise of some 2.5°C will still be extremely dangerous and damaging to global GDPs. To keep the goal of limiting the global temperature rise to 1.5°C within reach, all the countries in the world will need to act urgently together to cut the global emissions in half by the end of this decade.

In COP26, countries were also encouraged to use common timeframes for their NDCs. A good international example is that this will mean that the new NDCs that the countries will put forward in 2025 should have an end-date of 2035. In 2030, they should put forward their NDC commitments with a 2040 end-date and so on. Aligning NDC targets' dates around the five-year cycles will hopefully help spur the climate ambitions and actions in the near term. It should also facilitate a better understanding of climate progress. It should also ensure that countries should take appropriate climate actions over the same time period and keep pace with the Paris Agreement's five-year cycle to strengthen their plans.

Taking into account the different commitments by various countries to reach carbon neutrality and net zero emissions by 2050 or 2060, scientific analysis has shown that the global temperature rise could be kept to around 1.8 or 1.9°C. However, climate experts have advised that some major countries' 2030 emission targets are still too weak. These include those from Australia, China, Saudi Arabia, Brazil, Russia, etc. Experts advised that their NDCs currently do not offer credible net zero pathways to achieve their net zero targets and Paris Agreement commitments. These have shown that there are major credibility gaps between the 2.5°C-aligned 2030 targets and various nations' net zero targets. To rectify these serious problems, these countries will have to strengthen their NDCs plus their 2030 emissions reduction targets and net zero pathways so that these are at least aligned with their Paris Agreement commitments and net zero goals.

The Glasgow Climate Pact that was signed at the end of COP26 has agreed to call on all countries to revisit and strengthen their 2030 targets by the end of 2022. This should better align them with the Paris Agreement's temperature goals. It has also asked all countries that have not yet done so to submit their new NDC plus long-term net zero pathways and strategies to 2050. It has also called on all countries to aim for a just transition to net zero emissions by around mid-century. Hopefully, the new stronger NDCs with new long-term net zero strategies from different countries to be discussed at COP27 should help to better align all the net zero targets, as well as ramping up the climate ambitions.

COP26 Glasgow Climate Pact to Deepen and Accelerate Global Climate Actions

The COP26 Glasgow Climate Pact aims to reduce the worst impacts of climate change. However, some leaders and climate campaigners have said that it does not go far enough. The COP26 agreement, although not legally binding, should help to set the global agenda on climate change for the next decade.

It was agreed that all the countries should meet again at the end of 2022 at the planned COP27 meeting in Egypt. It is planned that they will then pledge further cuts to emissions of CO_2 and other GHGs which cause climate change and global warming. These should help to keep the global temperature rises to the aspired target of within 1.5C. Climate scientists have stressed that these will be urgently required to prevent a global climate catastrophe. Scientists have calculated that the current pledges made at COP26, if all achieved, will only limit global temperature rises to about 2.4°C only (BBC, A new global agreement—the Glasgow Climate Pact—was reached at the COP26 summit, Dec 2021).

The Glasgow Climate Pact signed at COP26 has called on all countries to revisit and strengthen their 2030 targets by the end of 2022, so as to better align them with the Paris Agreement's temperature goals. It has also asked all the countries that have not yet done so to submit their long-term strategies to 2050. These should aim for a just transition to net zero emissions around mid-century. Together, stronger NDCs and long-term strategies should help align the net zero and 2030 targets, as well as ramping up the climate ambitions of different countries around the world.

After hard negotiations, the COP26 Glasgow Climate Pact called on all countries to resolve to pursue efforts to aspire to limit the global temperature increase to 1.5°C. The Glasgow Climate Pact should help to give this lower aspired temperature threshold even greater emphasis than in the Paris Agreement. Diplomats and ministers managed to keep the hopes of limiting the global temperature rise to 1.5°C alive, but just barely amidst strong objections from some major countries. When the major emitters will share their new climate targets by the end of 2022 at COP27 as planned, then there should be a better idea of whether the world will be able to avoid breaching the aspired temperature threshold, and if it is breached then by how much.

Most commitments made at COP26 and other COP meetings will also have to be self-policed by the various countries. Only a few countries have made their climate pledges legally binding to date. A good international country example is the UK where they have developed and enacted the new UK Climate Law. Looking ahead, more countries should be encouraged to undertake similar actions in developing and enacting their own new national climate laws and legislations.

COP26 Global Fossil to Clean Energy Transition Agreements

In COP26, there were many discussions and debates on various aspects of the clean energy transition plus the shift from fossil fuels to clean energy sources in various countries. In one of the most contested debates and decisions in Glasgow, the countries ultimately agreed to a provision calling for a phase-down of coal power and a phase-out of inefficient fossil fuel subsidies, after much heated negotiations and debates. These two key issues had never been explicitly mentioned or decided in other UN climate talks before. However, analysis by international experts has shown that the fossil fuel sector, including coal, oil and gas, has been responsible for the bulk of GHG emissions. These have been shown to be the main drivers of climate change and global warming.

On coal, for the first time at a COP conference, there was an explicit plan to reduce the global uses of coal. The international uses of coal have been shown to be responsible for 40% of annual CO_2 emissions. However, the countries only managed to agree to a weaker commitment to 'phase down' rather than 'phase out' coal after much debate. These included a strong late intervention by both China and India. Many countries and non-governmental organisations (NGOs) have expressed their dissatisfaction that the final language on coal was significantly weakened, from 'phase-out' to 'phase-down' in the final COP26 Glasgow Climate Pact. The final compromise was consequently not as ambitious as it needs to due to different country interests. The final compromise was due to strong objections from some countries which are still heavily reliant on coal fossil power as part of their existing energy mix, especially for power generations. Hopefully stronger plans for the eventual global phase-out and elimination of coal uses can be agreed in future COP meetings.

World leaders also agreed to the phase-out of fossil subsidies that have artificially lowered the actual price of coal, oil or natural gas for consumers. However, no firm dates for the phase-out of these fossil subsidies have been set at COP26. This was due to different country interests. The international timetable to phase out fossil subsidies will require further intensive debates and negotiations in the next COP27 meeting at the end of 2022.

On a more positive note, methane was agreed to be a serious GHG problem by different countries. Methane is currently responsible for a third of human-generated global warming impacts. A new scheme to cut 30% of methane emissions globally by 2030 was agreed by more than 100 countries. The big emitters, including China, Russia and India, have not joined the new international methane deal yet. However, it is hoped that they will be joining it in the near future.

International financial organisations controlling US$130 trillion of investments and financial assets have also agreed to form the Glasgow Finance Alliance on Net Zero (GFANZ). They all agreed to support the global clean energy transition with the shift from fossil fuels to clean energy sources plus the deployment and development of clean technology, such as renewable energy sources. They also agreed to limit their future lendings and direct their future financing away from fossil fuel-burning industries. This will include stopping lending to and financing new coal projects in future.

COP26 Agreements on Climate Finance

In 2009, the rich developed countries agreed and committed to mobilise US$100 billion a year by 2020 and through 2025 to support the climate efforts in developing countries. To date, the developed countries have so far fallen short on their previous promise to deliver US$100 billion a year for developing countries. Countries at COP26 voiced regret at these shortfalls. They reaffirmed the pledge plus urged the developed countries to fully deliver on the US$100 billion goal urgently. A recent Organisation for Economic Cooperation and Development (OECD) estimate has shown that the climate finance fund reached US$79.6 billion in 2019. The COP26 outcomes made it clear that the developed countries are still expected to fulfil their agreed financing goal as soon as possible. COP26 has also stipulated that the developed countries must also report on their progress. Developed countries expressed confidence that the agreed financing target should be met in 2023.

The COP26 Glasgow Climate Pact pledged to significantly increase climate funding to help poor developing countries cope with the effects of climate change plus to promote their switch to clean energy. There is also the prospect of a new trillion-dollar-a-year climate fund from 2025. This is in follow-up to a previous pledge for richer developed countries to provide US$100 billion (£72billion) a year by 2020 that was missed.

Countries also agreed to a robust process to develop a new, larger climate finance goal to come into effect after 2025. They identified a wide range of options to ensure an inclusive and robust technical process to develop the new finance goal. This has included the need to establish an Ad Hoc Work Programme to convene technical experts and ministers to flesh out the details. The post-2025 climate finance goal is expected to be set by 2024.

COP26 also took steps to help developing countries to access good quality climate finance options. An important area is to encourage multilateral institutions to further consider the links between climate vulnerabilities and the need for concessional financial resources for developing countries. A good international example is for developing countries to access grants rather than loans so as to avoid increasing their national debt burdens.

At COP26, the countries also agreed that the various green finance and carbon budgets that will be required to achieving the Paris Agreement temperature goals are now too small and the budgets are being rapidly depleted. The ministers also agreed that developed countries should urgently deliver more resources to help the climate-vulnerable developing countries to adapt to the dangerous and costly consequences of climate change that they are suffering already. These include various negative impacts from extreme climate incidents, such as droughts, dwindling crop yields, devastating storms, flooding, etc.

Financial organisations and investment banks controlling US\$130 trillion of financial assets have agreed to form GFANZ to support future green investments in clean technology and renewable energy. They also agreed to direct their climate finance and green investments away from fossil fuel-burning industries, especially coal. This important international finance initiative is a good attempt to involve private financial companies and banks in helping various countries around the world to better meet their new carbon neutrality and net zero targets.

More international actions on climate finance and green investments will be discussed in detail in the Green Finance chapter later in this book with international examples and case studies.

COP26 Agreement to Step Up Support for Global Climate Adaptation

The COP26 Glasgow Climate Pact has pledged to significantly increase climate fundings to help poor countries to adapt to the worse effects of climate change and to promote their clean energy transitions. It also called for a doubling of international finance to support developing countries in adapting to the negative impacts of climate change and to build their climate resilience.

It is important to realise that these moves will not provide all the financial fundings that poorer countries will need. However, it should significantly increase the climate finance required for protecting vulnerable lives and livelihoods from the worst impacts of climate change. These are estimated to make up only about 25% of all the required climate finances. The other 75% will be required to support the developments and implementations of new green technologies. These will be required to promote clean energy transitions plus to reduce GHG emissions.

Developed countries have also agreed at COP26 to at least double their funding for climate adaptation by 2025. These should amount to at least US$40 billion. This is a significant milestone to address the persisting imbalance between funding for climate mitigation and adaptation efforts. Climate adaptation finance currently amounts to only a quarter of the total climate finances. These need to increase in line with the urgent requirement to adapt to the increasing negative impacts of the climate change.

The international Climate Adaptation Fund reached unprecedented levels of contributions. A good international example is the new pledges for US$356 million that represent almost three times its mobilisation target for 2022. The LDC Fund, which supports climate change adaptation in the world's least developed countries, also received a record US$413 million in new contributions. Looking ahead, more financing and money contributions will be required to help developing countries to increase their resilience to the effects of climate change. These positive developments were warmly welcomed by developing countries in COP26 at Glasgow.

The COP26 Glasgow Climate Pact also established a work programme to define the global goals on climate adaptation. These should help to identify the collective needs plus the required solutions to the climate crisis that are already affecting many countries.

Various countries have come to COP26 in Glasgow hoping to create a clear plan to develop guidance on the collective assessment of progress toward the Global Goal on Adaptation (GGA). This was a key component of the Paris Agreement which aimed to strengthen climate resilience and to reduce vulnerability to climate impacts. COP26 adopted the Glasgow-Sharm el-Sheikh work programme for the GGA. This will take place between 2022 and 2024. This will then help to improve the assessment of international progress toward the various climate adaptation goals. This should also help to promote their implementation. The countries also agreed to hold regular workshops and develop suitable methodologies to assess progress.

COP26 Agreement on Climate Loss & Damages

COP26 finally placed the critical issue of loss and damage squarely on the main global stage. Climate change is already causing devastating losses of lives and livelihoods. Some of these climate damages are unfortunately permanent and irreversible. Serious international examples have included local communities that are being wiped out on the Pacific islands due to flooding. These islands are disappearing fast beneath the rising international sea levels which have been caused by climate change and global warming. In addition, valuable water resources are drying up as a result of rising incidents of droughts in various countries, especially in Africa.

The critical issue of loss and damage was finally put on to the front and centre stage at the COP26 meeting. A number of climate-vulnerable countries advocated for COP26 to create a new international finance facility which is dedicated to loss and damage. This proposal had faced serious pushbacks by some developed nations, including the USA. After much debate, the countries landed on creating a new dialogue which would be dedicated to discussing potential international arrangements for loss and damage funding. Whilst this compromise is grossly insufficient, it does offer the appropriate space to develop possible future concrete solutions which can help to provide more progress on financing in the years ahead. This represented a first for meaningful international discussions of loss and damage at a global COP meeting.

There are also some encouraging international climate developments in various countries announced at COP26. Good international examples included the financial pledges from Scotland and Wallonia, Belgium, which were £2 million (US$2.6 million) and EUR 1 million (US$1.1 million) respectively. These financial pledges will help to address loss and damage globally. These pledges should help to cut through the various political debates and place responsibility for the finances for loss and damage firmly on the international table.

Countries also agreed to operationalise and provide fundings for the Santiago Network on Loss and Damage. This was originally established at COP25 in Madrid. At COP26, the countries agreed to catalyse appropriate technical assistance for the developing countries. These should help them to better address loss and damage in a more robust and effective manner. Looking ahead, the topic on 'Loss and Damage' is likely to be one of the key international climate issues leading up to the next COP27 summit in Egypt in 2022.

COP26 Agreement on Completing the Paris Agreement Rulebook

In COP26, countries and leaders discussed new joint agreements on the remaining issues of the so-called 'Paris Agreement Rulebook'. These included the various detailed operational details for the practical implementation of the Paris Agreement by various countries.

A good international example is the COP26 agreement on the norms relating to the global carbon markets. These will allow countries which are struggling to meet their emissions targets to purchase international carbon credits or emissions reduction credits from other nations that have already exceeded their targets. More details on the international carbon markets and trading will be discussed in the section below plus the chapter on carbon later in this book with international examples and case studies.

COP26 Carbon Markets Agreements

On the international carbon markets, countries and governments have finally agreed in COP26, after five years of international negotiations, on the appropriate new rules for the international carbon market arrangements that were covered under the Paris Agreement's Article 6.

This has been one of the most contentious international climate issues in recent years. The negotiators at COP26 have tried to balance the final agreement on the new rules by ensuring that they will not undermine international climate ambitions plus also maintaining environmental and social integrity. Ultimately, the negotiators agreed on important new international rules to avoid double-counting. Double-counting relates to more than one country potentially claiming the same emissions reductions as counting toward their own climate commitments. This new agreement is critical to make real progress on reducing carbon emissions.

Countries also decided that 5% of the international carbon proceeds must go toward funding adaptation under traditional market mechanisms, as stipulated in Article 6.4. However, it should be realised that under the bilateral trading of international carbon credits between different countries, as stipulated in Article 6.2, the contribution of funds toward climate adaptation was only strongly encouraged. This may contribute to reducing this potentially secure source of international finance for climate adaptation.

Unfortunately, countries also decided that they should allow the carry-over of old carbon credits that have been generated since 2013 under the CDM of the Kyoto Protocol, so as to help to meet the climate commitments of the Paris Agreement. At COP27, it will be crucial that negotiators put stringent guidelines in place to ensure that any of these older carbon credits which have been existing are allowed to be used and should actually represent real carbon emissions reductions and not greenwashing.

COP26 Agreement on Global Climate Transparency

In COP26, all the countries agreed to improve their climate transparency plus to submit regular information and reports about their emissions. They agreed to include relevant information on key aspects, including financial, technological and capacity-building, by using a common and standardised set of international formats. These should help to make international climate reporting more transparent, consistent and comparable. This is an important international development which will allow the global community to better monitor and hold various countries accountable for what they have said that they will do and their Paris Agreement commitments.

International negotiations were also concluded at COP26 on the Enhanced Transparency Framework. This will provide common timeframes and agreed formats for countries to regularly report on their climate progress. This is designed to build more international trust and confidence that all countries are contributing their fair shares to the global climate mitigation efforts.

Significant New Deals and Developments Outside the COP26 Negotiations

At COP26, many significant announcements and new deals have also been made outside the official COP26 negotiations during the two-week long summit. The first two days of COP26 featured over 100 high-level announcements during the "World Leaders Summit". These included a bold commitment from India to reach net zero emissions by 2070 that is backed up with near-term targets together with ambitious renewable energy targets for 2030.

On methane, 109 countries have signed up to the new Global Methane Pledge announced at COP26. They agreed to jointly slash methane emissions by 30% by 2030.

On forests, there was a new pledge by 141 countries to halt and reverse forest loss and land degradation by 2030. This was backed up by U$18 billion in green finance funding. This included U$1.7 billion of funding dedicated to supporting indigenous peoples.

In addition, the UK announced the Glasgow Breakthroughs. This is a set of global targets which are meant to dramatically accelerate the innovation and use of clean technologies in five emissions-heavy sectors. These sectors include power, road transport, steel, hydrogen and agriculture.

On coal, a group of 46 countries, including the UK, Canada, Poland and Vietnam, have made joint commitments to phase out domestic coal uses in future.

A further 29 countries, including the UK, Canada, Germany and Italy, have committed to end new direct international public support for unabated fossil fuel uses by the end of 2022. They also agreed to redirect their fundings to promote clean energy growths.

The Beyond Oil and Gas Alliance was announced at COP26. It is led by Costa Rica and Denmark. The other core members include France, Greenland, Ireland, Quebec, Sweden, Wales, etc. They have jointly pledged to end new licencing rounds for oil and gas exploration and productions in their countries. They have also agreed on an international timetable with an end-date that is aligned with the Paris Agreement objectives.

Efforts were also made to scale up international solar investment with the launch of a new Solar Investment Action Agenda by the World Resources Institute (WRI), the International Solar Alliance (ISA) and Bloomberg Philanthropies. They will be identifying new high-impact opportunities to speed up solar investments. These should help countries to achieve the ISA's goal of mobilising US$1 trillion in solar investments by 2030.

The USA became the 15th nation to join the High-Level Panel for a Sustainable Ocean Economy. This panel commits all its members to sustainably manage 100% each of their countries' national waters and oceans.

Various non-state actors, including leading investors, businesses, cities and subnational regions, also joined new collective action initiatives aimed at driving green economic transformation at COP26. A good international business example is that over 2,000 companies have committed at COP26 to develop science-based targets for reducing their emissions.

New international guidance for companies to set credible net zero corporate targets was released just ahead of the COP26 meeting. The guidance for robust target-setting for net zero claims in the international finance sector is still under development.

The new GFANZ was formed at COP26. Over 400 international financial firms which control over US$130 trillion in financial assets have committed to support future green investments and to align their portfolios with net zero goals by 2030. The new GFANZ made clear that banks, asset managers and asset owners are now fully recognising the business case for climate action. They have also recognised the significant risks of investing in the high-carbon, polluting traditional industries. They agreed to take appropriate steps to limit or stop future investments in the fossil sector, especially coal. The key challenge is for these institutions now to scale up their actions, at the pace and scale necessary. They should develop new science-based net zero pathways plus set intermediate corporate targets which align with their net zero goals and produce transparent reports on their net zero progress.

Over 1,000 cities and local governments joined the Cities Race to Zero to promote new international climate actions to limit the global temperature rise to 1.5°C. In addition, around 41 cities, 34 countries and 11 major automakers agreed to work toward selling only zero-emission vehicles ZEV by 2040, and by no later than 2035 in leading international markets.

The UN announced that in order to help hold businesses and others to be more accountable for achieving their net zero goals, they will be creating a new high-level international UN expert group which will establish clear international standards to measure and assess these commitments.

Overall, there were many significant new climate deals and announcements outside of the COP26 negotiations and the Glasgow Climate Pact. These should help to generate major positive impacts globally when they are implemented. The new key international deals and announcements are described in greater detail below.

COP26 Forests New Deal

At COP26, 137 countries took a landmark step forward by jointly committing to halting and reversing the forest losses plus land degradation in their countries by 2030. Their important pledge is backed up by U$12 billion in public funding and U$7.2 billion in private green funding. In addition, CEOs from more than 30 international financial institutions with over US$8.7 trillion of global assets were also committed to eliminating their future lending to and to stopping financing investments in activities which are linked to deforestation.

Leaders from more than 100 countries also collectively promised to stop deforestation by 2030. These 100 countries covered about 85% of the world's forests. Forests are now seen as a vital natural carbon solution as trees can absorb vast amounts of CO2. It is important to realise that similar previous forest initiatives have not been successful in stopped deforestation. This new initiative is better funded. In addition, there is greater international recognition of the importance of forests. However, it's unclear how this international pledge will be policed and monitored.

COP26 Methane New Deal

Methane is one of the most potent GHGs globally and is responsible for a third of the current global warming generated by various human and industrial activities. In COP26, 103 countries, including 15 major emitters, have signed up to the new Global Methane Pledge.

They agreed collectively to aim to limit global methane emissions by 30% by 2030, as compared to the 2020 levels. However, it is a pity that some of the major methane-emitting countries, including China, Russia and India, have decided not to join the Global Methane Pledge yet. It is hoped that these countries will join the Global Methane Pledge in future COP meetings. This should help to contribute to the international efforts in reducing methane emissions.

COP26 Green Cars & Clean Fuel Developments

The road transport sector is currently accounting for about 10% of the global GHG emissions. Accelerating the decarbonisation of the transport sector is vitally important for reducing global emissions and lowering global warming.

New zero-emission cars, including electric vehicles (EV), and new clean fuels are important key areas to reduce global emissions. At COP26, over 30 countries, six major vehicle manufacturers and other actors, including major cities, have set out their determination for all new car and van sales to be zero-emission vehicles by 2040 globally and by 2035 in some leading international markets.

At COP26, global leaders also agreed to phase out their various current subsidies for fossil fuels. These fossil subsidies have artificially lowered the market price of coal, oil or natural gas in some markets. However, no firm dates have yet been set for final phase-out of the fossil subsidies due to different country interests. The details of the global phase-out, including timetables and target dates for different countries, will need to be discussed more at the next COP27 meeting. The elimination of these fossil fuel subsidies in different countries should help to reduce emission plus promote electric vehicles and zero-emission vehicle use plus clean fuel developments.

International financial organisations and banks, controlling US$130 trillion of assets, have agreed to support future green investments in clean technology, renewable energy, EV, new zero-emission vehicles, clean fuel developments, etc.

COP26 Coal Reduction Plans

Coal is responsible for 40% of annual CO_2 emissions globally. At COP26, for the first time at an international COP conference, there were discussions in COP26 of a new explicit agreement and an international plan to reduce the use of coal. However, there were heavy debates and negotiations amongst the countries. In the end, all the countries can only reach an agreement to a weaker commitment to 'phase down' rather than 'phase out' coal, after a late serious intervention by both China and India.

On a more positive note, senior leaders from South Africa, the UK, the USA, France, Germany and the EU have announced a ground-breaking partnership to support South Africa. South Africa is currently the world's most carbon-intensive electricity producer. The countries agreed to provide US$8.5 billion of climate financing over the next three to five years to help South Africa to make a just clean energy transition away from coal and transform into a new low-carbon economy with lower emissions.

Financial organisations controlling US$130 trillion of assets have also agreed to support net zero and clean technology developments. Many investment banks and lenders have issued new investment guidelines which include stopping lending or financing to coal companies and new coal projects. These should contribute to reducing new coal investments and developments.

COP26 Private Climate Finance Initiatives

At COP26, leading international financial institutions and investment banks have announced new moves to realign trillions of dollars of their future investments and financing towards supporting green investments which will help countries to better achieve their carbon neutrality and net zero-emission targets. A good example is GFANZ: GFANZ has over 450 financial firms which are controlling over US$130 trillion in financial assets globally. They are requiring all their members to set robust, science-based near-term net zero climate targets and develop clear net zero pathways to achieving these.

These international financial organisations and investment banks also agreed to provide new financing and lending to support clean technology developments and renewable energy investments. They also pledged to direct their future financing away from fossil fuel-burning industries, including coal. Many international financial institutes and investments banks have also announced that they will stop future financing and investment support to new coal projects and coal companies. These should help to reduce coal investments and coal growth in future.

COP26 Water & Food Initiatives

At COP26, the water and ocean sectors achieved new major breakthroughs in their climate ambitions. Leading international companies responsible for 20% of global water supplies have agreed to jointly work together to halve their emissions by 2030. They have also agreed to be part of the UN-backed Race to Zero campaign.

The International Water Association, Aguas Andinas and CDP joined together to launch a new water sector initiative. The 50 largest water utility companies globally agreed, as part of the new initiative, that they would accelerate work to build resilient water supplies and wastewater services for more than 1.2 billion people by 2030.

A series of new international water programmes will also be bringing water, climate, economic development, human health, ecosystem restoration and poverty reduction under the same roof. A good international water programme example is the Resilient Water Accelerator which aims to boost water security for 30 climate hotspots by 2030. The Urban Water Resilience Initiative also aims to help to develop new water action plans in 25 African cities.

The Forest Agriculture Commodity Trade (FACT) Dialogue, which is jointly chaired by the UK and Indonesia, has unveiled a new climate roadmap at COP26. It identified four areas of work: international food trade and market development, small holder support, traceability and transparency, plus research and development and innovation. The international dialogue will bring together 28 of the largest consumer and producer countries of beef, soy, cocoa, palm oil, etc.

Nearly 100 leading corporations announced their commitments to halting and reversing the decline of nature. They agreed that they would work together to get nature positive by 2030, as part of a growing movement of companies joining the Science-Based Target for Nature. A good international company example is Burberry, which is a luxury fashion brand and Race to Zero member. They announced their new climate strategy which will help to protect, restore and regenerate nature. They are also expanding their support for farming communities.

The Good Food Finance Network released a list of 14 tools, strategies and policies to promote investments in developing innovations for healthy, sustainable food systems. These included new ways of measuring finance values and assessing land values. These will be followed by finance mobilisation in early 2022.

The Regen10 Coalition, launched at COP26, aims to boost regenerative and resilient food systems. They are aspiring to achieve by 2030 that half the global food production will be made in a way which will benefit people and the planet, with farmers at the heart of the transition.

The UK COP26 presidency also launched at COP26 an action agenda for the transition to sustainable agriculture for healthy diets and resilient livelihoods. The agenda will focus on supporting new research and innovations which will help to cut CO2, reverse nature loss and build resilience in agriculture and food systems. A new US$150 million green investment in agricultural regeneration was announced by the EverGreening Alliance at COP26. This should help to build up the climate resilience of rural communities in Africa.

COP26 US-China Climate Agreement Highlights

At the end of COP26, USA and China announced that they have agreed on a new US-China Climate Agreement. USA and China are currently the world's two largest GHG-emitting countries. Together, they are accounting for about 40% of the world's annual carbon emissions.

The US-China Joint Glasgow Declaration on Enhancing Climate Action in the 2020s was jointly announced on 10 November 2021 by both countries together at COP26. They agreed to increase their various international climate cooperations on reducing each of their emissions so as to better address the global climate crisis (China USA, Joint US-China Glasgow Declaration on Enhancing Climate Action in the 2020s, UK 10 November 2021).

At a time when China and the USA are at odds over other international issues, this new US-China Climate Agreement has declared an important intent to take joint concrete actions on emissions reductions and climate improvements. The two countries agreed to share future new climate policy and clean technology developments. They will discuss and announce new national climate targets for 2035 by 2025. Both the USA and China will also revive a multilateral working group on climate change to improve climate cooperation.

Amongst other key elements in the bilateral declaration, both the USA and China have agreed to develop additional measures to enhance methane emission controls, at both the national and subnational levels. This is the first time the Chinese government has pledged to address the methane issue. The USA has also announced new rules to reduce their methane emissions. The new goal that has been set for 30% reduction of methane by 2030 is significant. This is equivalent to reducing all the emissions from all the cars in the world, all of the trucks in the world, all of the airplanes in the world plus all of the ships in the world, down to zero.

The USA and China also welcomed the important Glasgow Leaders' Declaration on Forests and Land Use. The USA and China highlighted their respective commitments towards the elimination of support for future unabated international thermal coal power generation.

It is generally recognised that the new US-China Agreement in itself is not enough to meet the aspired 1.5°C goal of the Paris Agreement. However, it is the first time that China and the USA have stood up, as two of the biggest emitters in the world, and jointly announced that they are going to work together to accelerate the reduction in emissions. This has sent a powerful message to all the countries. It has also set a powerful international example for other countries to follow. This should help to promote international climate cooperation and climate improvement efforts.

Post-COP26 Glasgow Climate Pact Follow-ups

The COP26 meeting has reaffirmed again how important and essential collective global actions are to addressing and mitigating the global climate change crisis. This is especially important in current times which have been marked by various international uncertainties, geopolitical conflicts and escalating climate impacts. Experts have advised that the world is still not yet on the right track to solve the global climate crisis. However, the progress that had been made over the last year and at the COP26 climate summit have offered some bright spots and a strong foundation to build upon. The good progress also demonstrated that the Paris Agreement mechanisms to strengthen climate ambitions and finances are working, albeit imperfectly and not yet at the pace required globally (COP26 High Level Climate Champions, Nigel Topping, "Time to Bridge the Gap between Awareness and Action" UK February 2022).

The Glasgow Climate Pact that was agreed at COP26 has outlined the key steps for the world and various countries to undertake jointly in their international efforts to tackle the global climate crisis. These joint international actions are essential for the world to have a reasonable shot at reaching the aspired 1.5°C temperature rise goal. These are also essential for building a more sustainable and just future for all countries.

It was generally agreed that the Glasgow Climate Pact that was agreed at COP26 did not do enough to set the world on course to limit global warming to the aspired 1.5°C target. However, it does help to keep that important prospect within reach.

It is encouraging to see at COP26 a new convergence of views by businesses, investors, cities, regions and countries globally. They are sharing more the common understanding and the urgent needs to halve the global emissions, build resilience and end biodiversity loss within the 2020s decade. These key stakeholders are also increasingly confident in their joint ability to collectively drive exponential rates of change globally. Good international examples of that convergence on display at the COP26 meeting in Glasgow included the new international initiatives agreed on limiting deforestation, promoting green finance, reducing methane emissions, etc.

In the push to end deforestation, 141 countries covering 91% of forests have agreed to halt and reverse forest loss and land degradation by 2030. This is backed by nearly £14 billion (US$20 billion) in public and private green finances. New international tools and initiatives were also announced in parallel. Thirty-three financial institutions, with US$8.7 trillion in financial assets under management, have also committed to tackle deforestation which has been driven by agricultural commodities by 2025.

There was also good convergence on green finance and nature-based carbon solutions. A new online investment platform will provide a first-of-its-kind guidance system to help international institutional investors to allocate green capital towards nature-based carbon solutions.

The Regen10 initiative will work with 500 million farmers globally to ensure that by 2030, over half the world's food is produced sustainably. This new food initiative is supported with green finances worth US$60 billion per year.

The new GFANZ comprised financial institutions which collectively covered US$130 trillion in assets under management. They have all committed to support climate finances and green investments to support various countries to reach their carbon neutrality and net zero emissions targets by 2050.

Additional new international initiatives will direct green investments towards climate resilience as well as emission reductions. The new Global Resilience Index will help to measure the climate resilience of countries, companies and supply chains in developing and emerging economies. The International Sustainability Standards Board (ISSB) will create a baseline for high-quality sustainability disclosure standards in the public interest.

On loss and damages involving developing countries, the Scottish government's £2 million (US$2.6 million) contribution to addressing loss and damages was quickly backed with an additional US$3 million contribution from other international philanthropies.

There was also a host of international commitments to accelerate green transport and renewable energy developments. Good international examples include e-bus deployment in Latin America, renewable energy investment in the Caribbean and land restoration in Africa. Experts have forecasted that these green investments are likely to be the beginning of a wave of climate capital and green investments that are being deployed in emerging and developing economies.

Looking ahead, the major emitters will need to ramp up their 2030 emissions reduction targets so as to better align with the aspired 1.5°C target. In addition, more robust international processes will be required to monitor and hold all the different countries and actors accountable for the many commitments that they have made at COP26 at Glasgow. Much more attention is also needed on how to meet the urgent needs of climate-vulnerable developing countries. These are urgently required to help them to deal with climate impacts and in their transition to net zero economies.

It will be a major future challenge to figuring out how to create the right conditions for the trillions of dollars of green investment and climate financing that will be required to drive a resilient zero-carbon transition in markets. These will be essential for the successful implementation of the much-needed climate mitigation plans and green recovery plans in different countries. Potential financial solutions may include long-term or even perpetual green bonds which are similar to those that have been issued previously in wartimes. Other potential green financial instruments may include debt-for-nature swaps and catastrophe clauses in multilateral loans to create more fiscal space for vulnerable economies. Deeper and wider application of different green insurance products may also be considered.

Making the COP26 Agreement credible is the immediate challenge for the year and years ahead. Experts have advised that the current emission trajectories of the existing climate policies are still unacceptable as these are projected to result in a global temperature rise of some 2.7°C. If all the new COP26 targets are in place, then these could lead to a lower 1.8°C temperature rise. Crucially, this optimistic scenario will rely on various targets being fulfilled on time, and ratcheted up to ensure that we do not go beyond 1.5°C. To do that, joint global commitments from businesses, investors, countries, cities and regions are urgently required. These have to be robust, credible and based on science. In addition, international progress should be consistently reported and reviewed.

The new international climate expert panel announced by the UN during COP26 will help to provide a welcome layer of scrutiny over the various corporate and country commitments to achieving their carbon neutrality and net zero-emission targets. These should enhance the integrity of the various commitments made. It should also help to establish key metrics to measure climate progress under the UN-backed Race to Zero and Race to Resilience campaigns.

Enhancing credibility is one of the key elements outlined in the improved Marrakech Partnership for Global Climate Action to enhance climate ambitions globally. This was welcomed by all the parties at COP 26 who agreed to the Glasgow Climate Pact.

At COP 26, various countries also encouraged the High-Level Climate Champions to support the effective participation of non-party stakeholders in the global stocktake. Supporting the stocktake will be a main priority of the Climate Champions. In particular, they will be helping the key stakeholders in various developing countries and at the regional levels to contribute impactfully to the climate mitigation and adaption efforts. They will also provide suitable updates and actual evidence for the various enhanced and credible climate actions that will be implemented.

4
Sustainable Net Zero Strategies of Key Countries

逆境出人才

Nì jìng chū rén cá

Difficult situations force people to rise to the challenges.
Crisis breed wisdom

Global Sustainable Climate Net Zero Policy Overviews

Many governments and countries globally are actively developing their new sustainability strategies plus carbon neutrality policies and net zero plans in follow-up to their commitments to the Paris Agreement and the Glasgow Climate Pact. These countries have all realised the importance of working together with other countries internationally so they can better jointly manage climate change and to better control global warming. There are still many hurdles and challenges to developing suitable new national and international climate and energy policies plus achieving effective joint climate change management globally.

The historic global climate treaty, the Paris Agreement, was signed by many countries in 2016 after reaching agreements in late 2015 in Paris. After the signing of the Paris Agreement, many countries have been developing their new climate policies and sustainability strategies plus new net zero plans in line with their Paris Agreement commitments (Wang, Climate Change & Clean Energy Management, Routledge UK 2019).

Positive developments, post the Paris Agreement, have included new clean energy renewables targets being adopted in different countries globally. A good international example is that at COP22, the leaders of 48 developing nations committed to work towards achieving 100% renewable energy in their respective nations. Another good international country example is that following the signing of the Paris Agreement, 117 countries have submitted their

DOI: 10.4324/9781003142348-4

first nationally determined contributions (NDCs) as required under the Paris Agreement. It is good to note that 55 of these countries have featured new emission reduction targets and clean energy goals.

However, in some other countries, new climate policies developments have been stalling or regressing due to political pressures or changes in governments. A good international country example is the USA when former US President Trump decided to withdraw the USA from the Paris Agreement plus reduced their commitments on the global fight against climate change and global warming. On a positive note, the new US President Biden has expressed strong support for climate change. The USA has now rejoined the Paris Agreement. The USA has also played an active part at COP26 and signed the Glasgow Climate Pact at COP26.

On another positive note, some leading developing countries, including India and China, have emerged as new international leaders in tackling climate change and global warming. During the same periods, many countries globally have also experienced various serious climate-induced extreme weather events which have led to heavy damages with high human and community costs. These have included record heatwaves in Europe and America, hurricanes in Americas, droughts in Africa plus flooding in Asia etc. (Climate Central, John Upton, China, India Becoming Climate Leaders as West Falters, April 2017).

The UN Climate Change Conference of Parties COP 26, in Glasgow UK, has brought together 120 world leaders from 200 countries globally. The final outcomes of COP26, the Glasgow Climate Pact, was agreed after intensive negotiations amongst the 200 countries over the two weeks. Highlights and details of COP26 have been discussed in the previous chapter of this book with international examples (UN Climate Action, COP26 Summary, UN US 2021).

In the Glasgow Climate Pact agreed at COP26, the 200 international countries have agreed to promote accelerate emissions reductions toward the climate goals set in the 2015 Paris Agreement. That new climate accord will hold governments worldwide responsible for emissions cuts which should help to keep the global temperature rises well below 2°C (3.6 degrees Fahrenheit) relative to pre-industrial times, with an aspired target of 1.5°C (2.7 degrees Fahrenheit).

The Glasgow Climate Pact agreed at COP26 also aims to reduce the worst impacts of climate change globally. However, some key stakeholders and climate campaigners have said that it did not go far enough. The Glasgow Climate Pact is also not legally binding on the 200 countries that have signed it. However, it should help to set the global agenda on climate change going forward. It should also help the various countries to develop better new climate sustainability policies, carbon neutrality goals plus net zero plans.

At COP26, in addition to the Glasgow Climate Pact, some leading countries have also made important climate announcements and new climate side deals. Good international examples included the new bold collective commitments to curb methane emissions, to halt and reverse forest loss, to align the finance sector with new net zero targets by 2050, to accelerate the phasing out of the internal combustion engine, to accelerate the phase-out of coal, to end international financing for fossil fuel investments etc.

The details of the COP26 Glasgow Climate Pact plus the new important announcements and new side deals by the different countries have been discussed in more detail in Chapter 3 with international examples.

Post-COP26, many leading countries globally have been developing their new sustainability strategies plus carbon neutrality goals and net zero plans in line with their Paris Agreement and Glasgow Climate Pact commitments. These will be studied and analysed more below in this book with international examples and case studies. These should provide good references and role models for other countries globally. Five key international country case studies will be discussed. These will include China, Demark, UK, Brazil and Spain. We shall be discussing on their new sustainability policies plus carbon neutrality goals and net zero plans. Their details will be summarised below in the following sections in this book with relevant international examples and evidence:

China Sustainability Net Zero Policy & Plans Case Study

China's pledges to achieve carbon neutrality with net zero emissions by 2060 have been important turning points for China and the world. These will have a major impact on the global clean energy transitions plus the global fight against climate change. It will also have major impacts on the leading Chinese private and national companies plus China's energy mix and its fossil fuel markets. The scale of the task is huge, and the detailed roadmap is still being developed. However, international experts have expressed confidence that China will be able to achieve their goals of carbon neutrality with net zero emissions by 2060. These will contribute positively to the global clean energy transitions plus the global fight against climate change (Wang, UK WEG China Oil Company Roundtable Speech UK March 2021).

At a virtual meeting of the UN General Assembly in September 2020, Chinese President Xi Jinping said the country planned "to have CO2 emissions peak before 2030 and achieve carbon neutrality before 2060". This is Beijing's first formal announcement of a long-term plan to lower carbon emissions within a fixed timeline. The strong China commitments to the clean energy transition plus achieving carbon neutrality and emission reductions were further demonstrated in the COP26 meeting in Glasgow in November 2021. The new US-China Climate Agreement was a very important and positive announcement at COP26 with major international impacts.

China is actively developing a new phased carbon and energy transition strategy in line with their commitments to the Paris Agreement and the Glasgow Climate Pact. China's 14th Five-Year Plan (FYP), which started in 2021, has been the main national policy instrument that the Chinese Central Government has been using to pursue its new national climate net zero and energy transition goals. The famous Tsinghua University in Beijing has forecasted that China will have to follow a two-pronged strategy to achieve sufficient emissions reductions in their new sustainability net zero pathways. These will contribute positively to the joint global actions to limit global warming to 1.5 or 2°C.

China will likely include a first-phase plan to achieve their stated lower carbon emissions targets by 2030. This will then be followed by a more well-defined plan to achieve carbon neutrality and net zero emissions nationally by 2060. China is also expected to set peak carbon emission targets for their various major cities, especially in the highly populated and industrialised coastal regions in the coming years. These should be the logical next step after setting the overall country-level climate targets and carbon neutrality goals.

China Clean Energy Transition & Fossil Fuels Reductions Impacts

For the fossil fuel markets in China and globally, the domino effect of the new Chinese energy policy will be significant. China is currently the largest energy consumer in the world. Coal accounted for about 58% of China's total primary energy consumption in 2019. Fossil petroleum fuels were the second largest energy sector which accounted for 20%. These were followed by hydroelectric (8%), natural gas (8%), nuclear power (2%) and other renewables (nearly 5%), according to US Energy Information Administration (EIA) data.

To achieve the aspired 1.5°C scenario, China's total energy consumption will have to peak in 2030. This will be followed by a gradual decline by 2060. This means that over 85% of the total energy consumption and over 90% of the power generation will then have to come from non-fossil fuels, with less than 5–10% of power still coming from coal and fossil fuels sources.

Tsinghua University in Beijing has predicted that the various energy end-use sectors in China will see the increased use of clean electricity to replace the direct combustion of fossil fuels, especially coal and petroleum fuels. The share of primary clean energy and fuels for electricity generation in China has been forecasted to increase from the current 45% to about 85% by 2050. The share of clean electricity in end-use energy consumption in China is forecasted to increase from the current 25% to about 68%.

Looking ahead, the future China energy transition megatrends and scenarios are likely to include four distinct major trends and phases. Coal has almost peaked in China and will likely plateau for about a decade before it will begin to drop sharply. Oil will likely follow a similar trajectory to coal, but with some scope for small additional incremental demand growths in the next decade. Natural gas uses in China has yet to hit its peak by 2030 before it will begin to decline. However, natural gas has an important role as a transition fuel as its emissions are lower than other fossil fuels. National gas is likely to take a greater role than oil in the China national energy mix by 2050. Finally, there will be a steady but undisputable growth trajectory in China for clean non-fossil fuels. These will include clean energy, renewables and nuclear energy sources etc.

Looking ahead, China demands for coal and oil will likely contract the most under China's new emissions plan. These will be worrying developments for the global coal and oil producers, especially Middle East and Australia. China is currently accounting for more than half of the global coal consumption and is the world's largest coal-consuming country. Looking ahead, China's demand for coal and oil fuels is likely to reduce as part of its clean energy transition plans.

China COP Climate & Energy Highlights

At COP26 in Glasgow, China actively demonstrated their commitments to climate change and to achieve carbon neutrality by 2060. China's President Xi Jinping has announced that China will aim for its national emissions to reach their highest point before 2030 and for carbon neutrality to be achieved by 2060. In December 2021, Chinese President Xi also announced the new China 2030 climate targets to the International Climate Ambition Summit with global leaders. These have included new tougher goals on carbon intensity, non-fossil energy share in the primary energy mix and increasing reforestation in China. President Xi also announced that China will be accelerating new clean renewable energy implementations. A good China example is that China's new national wind and solar capacities are planned to reach 1,200 GW by 2030 (Wang, Contribution to UK Windsor Energy Group WEG COP26 Paper led by Lord Howell, UK Oct 2021).

China became the world's largest emitter of carbon dioxide (CO2) in 2006 and is now responsible for more than a quarter of the world's overall greenhouse gas (GHG) emissions. It is important to note that China's per-person emissions are only about half of those of the USA. However, the huge 1.4 billion population in China and its fast economic growth have pushed up its total overall carbon and GHG emissions.

Many international experts have forecasted that reducing China's emissions should be achievable but will require radical clean energy transition shifts. Coal has been China's main source of energy for decades. President Xi has announced that China will "phase down" coal uses from 2026 and will stop building new overseas coal plants. Researchers at Tsinghua University in Beijing have said that China will need to stop using coal for electricity generations by 2050. Coal will be replaced by nuclear and clean renewable energies in different phases.

China is accelerating its clean energy transition from fossil fuels to clean renewable energies quickly. A good international example is that China is now generating more solar power than any other country globally. China's wind power installations are currently more than triple those of other countries globally. China has also announced that the proportion of its energy generated from non-fossil fuel sources will reach 25% by 2030. Many international experts have forecasted that China will be able to reach its national clean energy targets earlier than planned, based on current progress.

China's leads in various green renewable technologies, such as solar panels and large-scale batteries, are supporting their clean energy transitions. These are also helping to reduce China's emissions and air pollution. These are also generating million of new green jobs nationally plus helping to reduce China's dependences on foreign oil and gas imports.

On electric vehicles (EVs), China is now seventh in the world for its percentage of car sales that are new EVs. China is currently making and selling more electric cars than any other country globally by a considerable margin. A good EV example is that about one in 20 new cars bought in China is currently electric-powered. These are important national trends as the transport sector is currently responsible for around a quarter of carbon emissions from fossil fuel combustion. Road vehicles are also the largest GHG emitters globally.

On batteries, experts have forecasted that China will be producing electric batteries with double the capacity of those produced by the rest of the world by 2025. International experts have forecasted that this will enable the storage and release of clean energy generated from renewable sources on a massive scale in China. These will then help to provide a reliable supply of green electricity to consumers across China.

Another important clean energy policy development is that China has included hydrogen as a strategic future clean energy source in their new National Energy Law. This signifies the strong strategic importance of hydrogen in China's clean energy transition plans. Hydrogen is traditionally produced from fossil sources, including gas or coal gasification. The brown hydrogen produced from fossil sources will normally be associated with significant carbon and GHG emissions.

China is currently accelerating the innovative developments of new green hydrogen production technologies using green electricity together with water electrolysis. These are being actively developed by various research institutes in China, with significant future cost reductions being forecasted. Experts are forecasting new green hydrogen production cost reductions of some 80%, which may be achieved by 2030 in China.

It is important to note that getting to net zero GHG emissions and carbon neutrality by 2060 does not mean that China will be stopping carbon emissions completely. It does mean that China will be cutting emissions as much as possible. They will then be absorbing what's left, through a combination of different innovative carbon solutions and approaches. These will likely include CCS, CCU, carbon offsets and international carbon trading.

One important green natural carbon approach is to increase the area of land covered in vegetation and forests, as plants and trees will help to absorb CO_2. China is currently getting greener at a faster rate than many other countries globally. One key improvement area is its national forestry programmes which are designed to reduce soil erosion and pollution. In addition, the replanting of fields to produce more than one harvest per year will help to keep land covered in vegetation for longer. A good forest example is that China is increasing its forest cover nationally with their Green Great Wall Project. They are planting 350,000 km^2 of new forests across China. These forests are stretching some 5,000 km across China.

At the COP26 in Glasgow, China demonstrated their commitment to climate change and shared their five key climate focuses as summarised below:

1. International commitment on sustainable energy transition with substantial carbon reductions. Uphold the UN-centred international system, comply with the objectives and principles laid out in the United Nations Framework Convention on Climate Change (UNFCCC) and the Paris Agreement.
2. International commitments to improving harmony between man and Nature. This includes protecting Nature, preserving the environment and

endeavouring to foster a new relationship where man and Nature can both prosper and live in harmony.

3. International commitments to green development and to seize the enormous opportunities in green transition plus green finance growths.
4. International commitments to improved systemic governance and to follow the innate laws of the ecosystem so as to achieve better ecological balances.
5. International commitments to improved people-centred approaches. Climate and environmental improvements globally will help to improve the well-being of people in all countries across the world.

Looking ahead, China plans to work closely with different countries globally to reach their Paris Agreement targets and to reach carbon neutrality by 2060. Good international cooperations and exchanges in these important areas are very important as the world and China all need to succeed jointly in their decarbonisation and energy transition plans. This will contribute positively to enabling all the countries in the world to achieving the common goal of working together to control climate change globally. A good international example is the new US-China Climate Agreement that was agreed and announced at COP26 by the USA and China. More details on the new US-China agreement have been discussed in Chapter 3.

China Sustainability Net Zero Policies and Pathways

China is currently the world's largest GHG emitter. Hence, China's climate actions will be critical to the world achieving the global carbon neutrality goals and net zero targets in future. The international pledge that was made by President Xi in September 2020 to the UN General Assembly was very important. His two pledges of having CO_2 emissions peak in China before 2030 and for China to achieve carbon neutrality before 2060 represented two very important commitments that have been made by the top leadership in China. The challenge now, however, is how to turn these ambitious goals into reality through new domestic policies and detailed action plans in China (UNFCC, China net zero future goals & policy, UN, US Mar 2021).

China's 14th FYP, covering the period of 2021–2025, has helped to set out China's national economic and social development plans and the long-range objectives toward 2035. The 14th FYP is also the national masterplan for reducing China's emissions in the next ten years toward the 2030 emission peaking goal. The 14th FYP has set out an important target to reduce carbon emissions per unit of gross domestic product (GDP) by 18% in China within the next five years. It has also called for the implementation of supplementary regional absolute carbon caps. It is also locking-in national efforts to achieve carbon neutrality in China by 2060.

China's 14th FYP masterplan has called for the adoption of new national policies and local measures with higher climate impacts. A good example is that China is planning to accelerate its clean energy transition by raising its non-fossil clean renewable fuel share of the primary energy mix in China to 20% by 2025 and to 25% by 2030. China also plans to increase the total installed capacity of solar and wind renewable power plants in China to 1,200 GW by 2030.

Experts have advised that it is likely that the 14th FYP will help to ensure that China's CO2 emissions will peak before 2030. Many experts have forecasted that the emissions from China will most likely plateau earlier by 2025–2030 with the new enhanced national climate policies. The 14th FYP national-level targets are very important. However, the sectoral and local government actions that will be triggered by the national policies and plans will also be very important to help China to achieve its ambitious emission reduction targets.

In early 2021, China's State Council issued the new 'Guideline to Accelerate the Development of a Green and Low-Carbon Circular Economic Development System'. This China Central Government policy document has described important actions in six key areas to reduce emissions. These include industrial production, logistics, infrastructure, consumption, innovation and enabling policies. The national guideline stated the important goal that by 2035, the energy and resource utilisation efficiency in key industries and products in China should reach internationally-advanced levels. China's industrial sectors have accounted for over 65% of the total carbon emissions from China in 2019. So more aggressive decarbonisation of the industrial sectors in China should help to reduce a large portion of China's carbon emissions.

A good China example is that in the transport sector, the Ministry of Industry and Information Technology has issued in October 2021 its New-Energy Vehicles (NEV) Development Roadmap 2021–2035. It aims to improve the new energy and electric vehicles shares of all vehicles sold in China to around 50% by 2035, with the other 50% being eco-friendly vehicles.

On clean energy, China has committed itself to raising its non-fossil fuel share of the primary energy mix to 20% by 2025 and to 25% by 2030. China is also planning to increase the total installed capacity of solar and wind renewable power in China to 1,200 GW by 2030. China is already now the leading renewable energy technology producer and exporter globally. It also has the largest installed fleet of wind and solar plants globally. The total installed capacity of wind and solar power in China has reached over 530 GW by the end of 2020.

To improve clean energy penetrations further, the China National Energy Administration (NEA) has proposed to increase provincial grids' minimum purchase of non-fossil fuel power to 40% by 2030 from 28.2% in 2020. Experts forecasted that this should help China to achieve its 2030 renewable energy development goals ahead of schedule, probably by three to five years.

Renewable innovations in recent years have transformed the economics of clean energy and other clean technologies in China. The plummeting renewable generation costs, with various innovations and cost reduction measures, have meant that it is now cheaper to decarbonise the electricity grid than to use fossil fuels. However, successful decarbonisation will hinge on effective policies being developed and implemented. These should include well-designed prices on clean power, appropriate carbon pricing, good clean energy standards, sufficient climate finance to support green investments, etc.

China's provincial governments are in the process of developing their local regional FYPs, in line with the national FYP. As required by the Ministry of Environment and Ecology (MEE), the provincial governments in China will also be developing their local action plans to ensure that they can peak their CO2 emissions by 2030, in line with national China targets. Currently, a third of provinces in China are planning to set earlier quantitative CO2 peaking commitments. In addition, almost half of China's provinces have commissioned new policy research to help them to develop their new carbon neutrality policies and net zero action plans.

Since 2010, China's central government has undertaken 87 low-carbon pilots in various cities and provinces. These have comprised 81 cities and six provinces across China. Over 60 of these pilots have committed to peak their carbon emissions before 2025. Good China regional examples include Shanghai committed to peaking by 2025. Beijing has also stated that it will maintain a steady carbon emissions decline after peaking in the 2021–2025 time period. More local governments are likely to be putting forward more ambitious targets for their absolute carbon caps and early peaking dates in their new FYPs. So, China is likely to, as a whole, have a far better chance of achieving an early carbon emissions peak than planned.

The People's Bank of China (PBOC), China's financial policy regulator, has also made carbon neutrality a priority in 2021. The PBOC plan has included new financial measures to improve the green finance standards plus for removing fossil fuel-related projects from the green bonds catalogue and adding support for climate-friendly projects in China. It also included mandatory environmental information disclosures and integrating climate change into the risk management system for private and national companies in China. At the local level, PBOC has designated six provinces and nine cities as green finance pilot hubs in China. A good region is Shenzhen in Guangdong. It is one of the key pilot hubs and its municipal government has requested mandatory environmental risk disclosures from all the financial institutions in Shenzhen.

In the international arena, China has continued to show green finance initiative and leadership. A good international example is that EU and China have co-chaired the international task force on sustainable finance, which aimed to harmonise the various sustainable finance taxonomies. Recently, the USA and China have also agreed to resume and rebranded the G20 sustainable finance study group that they have been co-chairing.

Many of China's State Owned Enterprises (SOEs) are also energy giants in China and globally. A good example is China National Energy (CNE), which is the largest coal producer and coal-fired power generator in the world. BAOWU Iron and Steel has become the top producer after reaching 100 M tonnes of product in 2020. The top power companies in China, the so-called Big Five, have accounted for half of China's total installed power capacity.

These SOEs have also started some promising new climate actions in line with the national China plans. Three out of the Big Five power companies have committed to achieve peak emissions before 2025 or to reduce coal consumption. BAOWU Iron and Steel has committed to peak its carbon emissions in 2023. China State Grid released its Action Plan Towards Carbon Neutrality in March 2021, which was the first of its kind among SOEs. Several other big coal and oil SOEs, including CNE, CNOOC (China National Offshore Oil Corporation) and Sinopec, have all kicked off research work to actively develop their new carbon neutrality strategy and net zero action plans. However, short-term improvements are still needed from these energy giants in China to significantly reduce their coal and fossil uses so as to reduce emissions plus to achieve their long-term net zero goals.

Looking ahead, China is expected to roll out more sustainability policies and net zero goals plus enhanced targets and actions from both the Central and Local Governments plus their industrial regulators. These new policies and operational plans taken together should ultimately help China to reduce its long-term GHG emissions trajectory and to meet its carbon neutrality goal and net zero pledge by 2060.

Denmark Sustainability Net Zero Policy Case Study

Denmark has been ranked globally as the country with the highest achievement in climate protection, by the Climate Change Performance Index in 2022. This is based on the facts that Demark has developed strong climate policies and set key climate sustainability carbon neutrality goals and net zero targets. They are planning to achieve 70% emissions reductions by 2030 and climate neutrality by 2050. Under their climate plans, Denmark has committed to reduce GHGs emission by 70% by 2030. This is generally considered to be one of the most ambitious climate emission reduction goals in the world.

A good international achievement example is that Denmark has already submitted its official account of GHG emission reductions as required under the Kyoto Protocol. These official accounts have shown that Denmark has already successfully met its climate obligations under the Kyoto Protocol (Denmark, Climate Agreement for Energy and Industry 2020, Denmark 2020).

The Danish Energy Agency has been publishing two reports each year which evaluate the Danish process towards fulfilling their EU climate obligations. These official publications include the annual Danish Energy Statistics and the Danish Climate and Energy Outlooks. The Danish Energy Statistics have shown the Danish reductions of GHG emissions in a historical perspective. It has also included an assessment of the yearly emissions of CO_2 and other GHGs from Demark. The Danish Climate and Energy Outlook has been showing the expected reductions in future GHG emissions (Denmark Energy Agency, Climate and Energy Outlook Report, Denmark 2021).

Denmark has also enacted the new Danish Climate Law. In 2014, the Danish Parliament passed the new Danish Climate Law. This law is supposed to ensure a stable direction and provide a legal framework around the new Danish climate sustainability net zero policies. The Danish Climate Law has stated that its goal is to transform the Danish economy into a low-emission society by 2050. According to the law, this should result in a resource-efficient society where energy supply is based on clean renewable energy resources. The GHG emissions will be significantly lower together with rooms for sustainable economic growth and developments (Denmark, Integrated National Energy and Climate Plan, Denmark 2019).

Denmark has been making good progress so far on reducing their emissions plus developing suitable new carbon neutrality goals and net zero targets. The net GHG emissions in Denmark in 2018 have amounted to 57.9 million tonnes of CO_2e, which constitutes about 1.6% of the total net emissions of the EU. Since 2005, the country has accomplished a 23% reduction in net emissions, which exceeded the EU's achievement of 16.2%. According to the Danish government, this has been achieved mainly due to good clean energy transitions with significant clean energy sector developments. A good energy example and achievement is that Denmark has successfully decreased the carbon intensity of their primary energy mix nationally.

The Danish land use, land use change and forestry (LULUCF) sector has been a net source of emissions during most of the period. In contrast, the EU overall, land use and forestry LULUCF sector has actually acted as a net carbon sink for EU. According to the Danish Energy Agency, Danish forests have helped to absorb around 170 million tonnes of CO2 annually. However, carbon removals by forests were offset by GHG emissions from soils used in croplands and grasslands plus other agricultural and human activities in Denmark.

In its NECP, Denmark has committed to ensuring that from 2021 their land use and forestry LULUCF emissions will not exceed removals. They are planning to finance afforestation and restoration of carbon-rich farmlands. In addition to enhancing natural carbon sinks, the Danish government has also decided to invest significantly in carbon capture and storage CCS as a critical carbon technology pathway for their transformation towards achieving their climate neutrality goals and net zero targets.

Denmark Sustainability Net Zero Policy &Emissions Intensity Sectorial Analysis

The carbon intensity of the Danish economy is 43% below the EU average. This has made the Danish carbon intensity one of the lowest of all the EU Member States. A decreasing carbon intensity trend has characterised the period from 2005 to 2019. Denmark has halved its emissions per euro of GDP with a 53.3% reduction. This is higher than the EU figure, which has only declined by 44.8%. During the same period, the Danish economy has been growing whilst its emissions have fallen. The Danish government regarded this decoupling between their emissions and economy as an important precondition for meeting their overall emission targets. Looking ahead, they are expecting these positive trends to continue in the coming years. This is also an important international example of a developed country successfully decoupling its emissions and economy. Denmark has demonstrated that the Danish economy has been growing whilst its emissions have fallen over the same period. This will be a very important role model for many countries globally as they try to reduce their emissions significantly in order to achieve their carbon neutrality goals.

In 2019, the transport sector in Denmark accounted for the largest share of the Danish GHG emissions. Since 2005, these transport emissions have decreased by only 0.2%. This has brought the Danish transport sector's share of total emissions from 20% to 28%.

Agriculture is another large emission source in Denmark. It has been responsible for 23% of Denmark's total emissions. Between 2005 and 2019, this sector's emissions fell by only 2% and its share of Denmark's emissions rose by 7 percentage points (p.p.).

The Danish energy industrial sector is also responsible for a large share of its emissions, about some 18%. However, this sector's emissions have more than halved since 2005 by various measures, and they include clean energy transitions. The energy industry emission reductions have contributed considerably to the total emissions reductions in Denmark. Specifically, they have accounted for 21 p.p. out of the 31.3% total reduction.

The manufacturing and construction sector contributed 2 p.p. to the total reductions, by cutting its emissions by 28.9%. The Danish government is planning, with their new energy, industrial and waste strategies, to further reduce emissions by 3.4 million tonnes of CO_2e by 2030. These new policies will include making new funding available to lessen the tax burden on EVs, extend the charging point network, accelerate transition to green buses and ferries, and promote cycling. In addition, the government is providing various incentives to boost solar and wind energy productions plus promote investments in carbon capture, energy storage, large-scale Power to X plants, more subsidies for electrification, more energy efficiency improvements in industry and buildings, lower taxes on green electricity for heating and surplus heat, and a green tax reform proposal. The new waste strategy also aims to achieve a climate-neutral waste sector by 2030 in Denmark.

On agriculture, they are planning to reduce nitrogen losses and banning fertilisers. These measures should result in an annual reduction of 90,000 tonnes of CO_2e by 2030. Further reductions might be made possible by ongoing research covering the use of biochar and feed additives, etc.

Under the Effort-Sharing Decision (ESD), Denmark has adopted a binding target to reduce non-ETS emissions by 20% by 2020 as compared with 2005. To achieve these targets, annual emissions allocations have been determined. The results have shown that Denmark's emissions have remained below their allocation levels every year. An 18.9% reduction was reached in 2019. For the 2021–2030 period, Denmark has committed to a 39% emission reduction, as compared with 2005. The European Commission (EC) has voiced concerns that the Danish NECP lacks a clear strategy to achieve this target. They have estimated that under the policies adopted by 2019, the 2030 target may be missed by 13 p.p.

The Danish sectorial strategies for the transport, energy, agriculture and waste sectors were adopted in 2020. These are expected to help Denmark to increase the feasibility of meeting their 2030 targets. Furthermore, if necessary, Denmark could apply the flexibility mechanism to use LULUCF or ETS credits to comply with the established targets.

GHG emissions from passenger cars are responsible for 60% of the transport sector emissions in Denmark. The emissions from new passenger cars in Denmark were close to the EU average in 2007. There were sharp reductions between 2007 and 2018, which helped to position Denmark below the EU average. In 2018, Denmark was able to achieve, amongst all the EU Member States, the lowest emissions from new passenger cars. The EU-wide target of 130 g/km set for 2015 was met five years in advance. To meet the new target of 95 g/km from 2021, a reduction of 13% from 2018 levels is needed. Relevant measures for further improvements have included the government decision to stop selling cars running exclusively on fossils fuel by 2030, plus the upcoming new tax reforms to incentivise sale of low-emission and electric vehicles.

On clean energy transitions, the renewable energy share (RES) in Denmark was 37.2% in 2019. This was more than 7 p.p. above Denmark's 2020 target. Between 2005 and 2019, Denmark's RES has expanded more than that of any other EU country, by a total of 21 p.p. The main contributing factors were growths in wind and derived clean heat energy sources. According to the NECP, the renewables 2030 target is set at 55%, which is an ambitious target.

Amongst the new renewable initiatives proposed in Denmark were the construction of two new energy islands for offshore wind production and the expansion of the capacity of an existing windfarm. Together, these two initiatives are expected to increase Denmark's current wind capacity by a factor of more than three times.

Denmark is also introducing new renewable policy measures, including new incentives for market-driven expansion of solar and onshore wind power, more subsidies for biogas and other green gasses plus exemption of self-consumption from electricity tax and economic incentives for biomass utilisation.

Denmark is also improving its energy efficiency. In 2019, the Danish primary energy consumption was 2.1% below the 2020 efficiency target of 17.5 M tonnes. The final energy consumption was 0.8% below the target of 15.2 M tonnes.

Looking ahead, Denmark is continuing with their stringent new climate policy developments. The Climate Act was approved by the Danish Parliament in June 2020. It has set legally binding targets of a 70% reduction in GHG emissions by 2030 as compared with 1990 and to achieve climate neutrality by 2050 at the latest. In addition, the Danish government has committed to set new sub-targets every five years. For 2025, experts have recommended a reduction target of between 50% and 54%. A new climate action plan, consisting of separate sectoral strategies, is currently under development. Most of the climate strategies have already been agreed. These will include new green strategies for energy and industry, waste, road transport, green public procurement, sustainable construction and green research. A comprehensive new green tax reform has been proposed. Further new policies and plans are expected, including the new sector strategy for agriculture and forestry in Denmark (EU, European Commission Assessment of the final national energy and climate plan of Denmark, SWD (2020) 903, EU 2020).

UK Sustainability Net Zero Policy & Strategy Case Study

The UK has enacted and implemented various new climate change, clean energy and sustainability policies plus carbon neutrality goals and net zero targets. These have resulted in significant progress in clean energy transformation in the UK. These significant clean energy transitions are accompanied by major shifts away from fossil fuel uses to adopting more clean renewable energy sources, over the last ten years.

A good UK example is the significant reduction in coal power and electricity generation in UK in the last ten years. A decade ago, various coal-fired power plants generated almost a third of the UK's electricity. Under the various new UK government energy policies, there have been big reductions in electricity generation by coal in the UK. In 2019, coal-fired power stations only provided 3% of the UK's electricity requirements. Looking ahead, experts have predicted that the UK will be left with only five remaining coal-fired power plants. These major reductions in coal-fired power plants are in line with the UK government policy and plans to phase out all coal-fired power generation by 2025 (Wang, Renewable Energy Management, Routledge UK 2020).

In the same period, clean renewable energy uses have increased significantly. A good UK example is that renewable energy has grown significantly from supplying only 2% of the UK's power to a fifth, about 25%, of all the electricity produced in the UK. This has represented a significant growth of about ten times, for renewable energy applications. The UK National Grid is also spending around £1.3 billion a year (US$1.63 billion/year) to adapt the UK national electricity grid network to accept variable new renewable energy electricity supplies from various renewable power generators across the UK.

Energy experts in the UK have predicted that clean energy and zero-carbon energy applications will be overtaking fossil fuels as the UK's largest electricity source soon. These have mainly resulted from a dramatic decline in coal-fired power generation, together with rising renewable and low-carbon energy applications.

Looking ahead, UK homes and businesses will be consuming more clean electricity generated by wind farms, solar panels, hydro power and nuclear power reactors in future. These increasing clean energy consumptions will be important real achievements by the UK government new clean energy policies and clean energy transition plans. These should support the UK in achieving its target of carbon neutrality goals and becoming a net zero carbon economy by 2050.

The UK has enacted the new UK Climate Change Act. This has committed the UK government by law to reduce GHG emissions by at least 100% of 1990 levels, plus to reach carbon neutrality and net zero emissions by 2050. This will include reducing emissions from the UK devolved administrations, including Scotland, Wales and Northern Ireland, which are currently accounting for about 20% of the UK's emissions (UK, UK Path to Net Zero Landmark Strategy, UK Oct 2021).

The UK's new Net Zero Strategy has set out how the UK government plans to deliver its emissions targets of Net Zero in 2050 and to achieve a 78% emission reduction by 2035, from its 1990 levels. It has put forward an achievable and affordable vision that should bring net benefits to the UK. It has also outlined new policies and measures for the UK to transition to a green and sustainable future. These have included measures to help businesses and consumers to move to clean power plus supporting the creation of new green jobs, etc. It has also included various green finance initiatives to leverage up to £90 billion of private green investments by 2030. The UK will also reduce its reliance on imported fossil fuels by boosting clean renewable energy applications. These should also help to reduce the risk of high and volatile energy prices in future, plus strengthening the UK energy security.

These green commitments should also help to unlock up to £90 billion of private investment by 2030. In addition, these should help to create 440,000 new green jobs in various green industries across the UK by 2030. These will support UK businesses in gaining a competitive edge in the latest low-carbon technologies. These will also help to develop various new green industries in various UK industrial heartlands.

New green investments in the UK have been announced as part of the new UK strategy. These have included a £1 billion commitment to support the electrification of UK vehicles and their supply chains. There will also be another £620 million support for targeted EV grants and infrastructure, particularly for local on-street residential charge points developments. The UK zero-emission vehicle mandates are aiming to increase the number of zero-emission cars and vans on UK roads in future.

The UK is also working to kick-start the commercialisation of sustainable aviation fuel (SAF) developments. These clean aviation fuels will be made from sustainable materials such as everyday household wastes, flue gasses from industry, carbon captured from the atmosphere, excess electricity, etc. These new clean aviation fuels should produce over 70% fewer carbon emissions than traditional jet fuel on a lifecycle basis. The UK is aspiring to enable the delivery of 10% SAF by 2030 together with £180 million in funding to support the development of new UK SAF plants.

The UK is also setting up a £140 million Industrial and Hydrogen Revenue Support scheme to accelerate industrial carbon capture and hydrogen generation. This should help to bridge the gap between industrial energy costs from gas and hydrogen, plus helping green hydrogen projects to get off the ground. New carbon capture clusters, including the Hynet Cluster in North West England and North Wales plus the East Coast Cluster in Teesside and the Humber, should help to put the UK industrial heartlands at the forefront of this new technology in the 2020s.

The UK government is planning to provide an extra £500 million of green funding to support innovation projects to develop new green technologies. This will bring the total UK funding for net zero research and innovation to at least £1.5 billion. This will support the development of new pioneering ideas and green technologies to decarbonise homes, industries, land and power in the UK and globally.

UK government is also planning to provide £3.9 billion of new funding for decarbonising heating systems and buildings. This will include the new £450 million three-year Boiler Upgrade Scheme.

The UK is also planning to provide a £124 million funding boost to the Nature for Climate Fund. This should help to restore approximately 280,000 hectares of peat in England by 2050. It will also help to treble woodland creation in England. These should help to meet the UK commitments to create at least 30,000 hectares of woodland per year across the UK.

The UK is also planning to provide £120 million of funding towards the development of nuclear projects through the Future Nuclear Enabling Fund. This should support the new UK net zero path to decarbonising the UK's electricity system by some 15 years, earlier from 2050 to 2035.

The new UK policies and spendings brought forward in the UK Net Zero Strategy will mean that, since the former UK PM's Ten Point Plan, UK has mobilised £26 billion of government capital investment for the green industrial revolution in UK. More than £5.8 billion of foreign investment in green projects has also been secured since the launch of the UK Ten Point Plan, along with creating at least 56,000 green jobs in the UK's clean industries.

The UK is also the first major developed country globally to commit in law its climate policies plus its plans to achieve carbon neutrality and net zero targets by 2050. The new UK Net Zero Strategy has also set out new clear policies and proposals for meeting the UK fourth and fifth carbon budgets. The UK NDC has set out the vision and plans to help UK to achieve carbon neutrality and become a decarbonised economy by 2050. These should help the UK to meet its Paris Agreement commitments and to achieve its carbon neutrality goals and net zero emission targets by 2050.

Brazil Sustainability Net Zero Policy & Plans Case Study

Brazil has been actively developing its sustainability policies plus net zero goals and clean energy transition strategies. As part of their updated NDC submission in December 2020, Brazil has set an indicative goal of reaching carbon neutrality and net zero by 2060, conditional on the receipt of financial support from the developed countries. In April 2021, Brazil updated its NDC. It has removed deforestation and has set new sector-specific goals, including emissions reduction goals for 2025 and 2030. At COP26 in Glasgow, the Brazilian delegation has made strong new climate commitments. These included pledges to cut Brazil's carbon emissions in half by 2030 with a new aspired goal of achieving carbon neutrality and net zero by 2050.

Brazil's climate and clean energy policies have helped its growth into one of the world's largest clean biofuel markets. These policies have used the Integrated National Green Regimes (INGR) to promote renewable and clean fuel developments, with key agricultural production systems being operated as part of the national or regional green agendas.

A good country example is the successful growth of clean biofuel productions in Brazil. Brazil has become the world's largest clean biofuel market. Brazilian ethanol from sugarcane are clean fuels which have been proven to be cost-competitive against fossil fuels for transport applications in Brazil. Ethanol production is also more economical in Brazil than in the USA due to several important factors. These included the superiority of sugarcane to corn as an ethanol feedstock. Brazil's large unskilled labour force has also strongly supported the labour-intensive sugarcane production requirements. Whilst the USA and Brazil have produced about the same volume of ethanol, the USA has used almost twice as much land to cultivate its corn for ethanol as Brazil has done to cultivate sugarcane (Wang, Routledge book "Renewable Energy Management in Emerging Economies" UK 2020).

The Brazil Government launched its National Alcohol Program, Pró-Álcool, in 1975, with relevant government policies, as a nation-wide programme. It was financed by the government with the objective to phase out automobile fuels derived from fossil fuels in favour of bioethanol which is produced from sugarcane.

Brazil's 30-year-old ethanol fuel programme is also based on the most efficient agricultural technology for sugarcane cultivation in the world. It uses modern equipment and cheap sugarcane as feedstocks. The residual cane-waste, bagasse, is recycled and used to generate heat and power. These have resulted in very competitive production costs with efficient energy balances. There are currently no longer any light motor vehicles in Brazil running on pure petroleum gasoline. Since 1976, the Brazilian Government has made it mandatory to blend anhydrous ethanol with gasoline, at blending ratios up to 22%.

In Brazil, both sugarcane and ethanol are being produced on an integrated basis to maximise their economy of production. The option to produce more or less of each product is controlled by relative pricing and market demands.

Many experts have suggested that the successful Brazilian biofuel ethanol model and policies have led to good sustainable growth in Brazil, together with strong government policy supports. These successes have resulted from a unique combination of cheap labour, advanced agri-industrial technology and an enormous amount of arable land available in Brazil. Brazil's ethanol infrastructure model has also required huge taxpayer subsidies and government policy support over the decades, before it became commercially viable.

Biopower and green electricity have also grown strongly in Brazil with strong government policy support. In Latin America, Brazil has been the largest overall consumer of biopower and green electricity in the region. Brazil's bioenergy power capacities have been growing steadily in recent years. Over 80% of the biomass-based electricity generation in Brazil has been fuelled by bagasse. These are being produced in large quantities in sugarcane production. Their uses in biopower production have helped to minimise biological waste and promoted circular economy developments in Brazil.

On clean hydropower, Brazil Government energy policies have also promoted clean hydropower plant growth. Substantial clean hydropower capacities have been commissioned in Brazil. In Latin America, Brazil has continued to be the largest hydropower producer. Brazil has also been ranked second globally for new hydropower installations. A good hydropower example is the construction of the new 11.2 GW Belo Monte hydropower project. However, there are also growing public concerns on the potential environmental impacts of new hydropower projects.

On solar renewable power, Brazil Government policies have promoted solar growth. Brazil has continued to rank third for new solar installations and has remained the largest solar thermal market in South America. The decrease in Brazil's solar thermal market was relatively small considering the country's ongoing economic problems. A good Brazil Government policy example is the Brazil social housing programme which has mandated solar water heaters installation in new urban buildings that are being built for very poor families in various cities in Brazil.

On wind renewable power, Brazil has introduced good supporting policies. Brazil has continued to lead the Latin America region in wind power and has also been ranked amongst the global top ten countries, in terms of wind renewable capacity. Wind power has been supplying near to 6% of the overall electricity demands in Brazil. To boost wind energy outputs, many wind companies have been adopting the general move towards building larger wind turbine machines. These have included longer blades, higher hub heights and, in particular, larger rotor sizes. These improvements have driven the wind capacity factors significantly higher within given wind resource regimes in Brazil. These have helped to create further attractive opportunities in the established wind markets as well as new ones. A good wind example is that the average capacity factors for all operational wind farms in Brazil have increased by 2% from some 38% in 2015 to over 40% in 2016, as new wind projects with better technology were brought online.

On biomass renewable power, Brazil policies have promoted the use of biomass from agricultural and wood residues to produce bio-heat for the food, tobacco, and pulp and paper industries. Bioenergy from bagasse has also been used in the sugar and alcohol industries.

On biopower, Brazil has been the largest overall consumer of biopower and green electricity in the Latin America region. Brazil's energy policies have promoted the growth of clean biopower nationally. Bioenergy power capacities have been growing steadily in recent years. Over 80% of the biomass-based electricity power generation in Brazil has been fuelled by bagasse. These have been produced in large quantities in sugarcane production. Their uses in biopower production have helped to minimise biological waste and have promoted circular economy developments in Brazil.

On smart city and climate big data developments, Brazil Government policies have promoted their developments together with high-tech digital IT developments. An exciting smart city big data development example is that in Rio de Janeiro in Brazil, IBM has built an advanced city operation centre. This has been described as the new digital "nerve centre" of the city. It was built initially to help to deal with the floods that had regularly threatened the city. Further developments have enabled the centre to effectively coordinate some 30 different government agencies in the city. The centre has also generated special mobile apps for the citizens in the city. These will help to keep them updated on potential accidents, traffic black-spots and other essential city updates.

Another good climate IT example is Brazil 's AdaptaClima digital Platform. The AdaptaClima IT platform was launched in December 2017 in Brazil to support the dissemination of information and data on climate change to various decision makers. It is an interactive and collaborative virtual digital space for sharing tools plus climate studies and methodologies. The development of the digital platform was coordinated by the Brazilian Ministry of Environment.

All these green policies and new sustainability developments should help Brazil to meet its Paris Agreement commitments plus its COP26 pledges to cut the country's carbon emissions in half by 2030 with an aspired goal of achieving net zero by 2050.

Spain Basque Government Climate Sustainability Net Zero Policy Case Study

The Orkestra-Basque Institute of Competitiveness (OBIC) had invited the author to prepare a new climate policy letter for the Spain Basque Government. The policy letter is titled "Climate Change, Energy Transition and Carbon Neutrality Recommendations". It was submitted and published in the OBIC Ekonomiaz globally (Ekonomiaz OBIC, Wang, Policy Letter for Basque Spain on Climate Change, Energy Transition and Carbon Neutrality Recommendations, Spain December 2020).

This policy letter has focussed on how new climate change, clean energy, sustainability plus carbon neutrality and net zero policies may be conducive to promoting sustainable economic growth in an important industrial economy such as the Spain Basque region. These policy recommendations are based on relevant international developments, especially the latest policy recommendations to the G20 Global Leaders and B20 International CEOs. These have been adapted to offer some relevant key policy recommendations for the Spain Basque Government. These should support them in developing relevant new policies on meeting their Paris Agreement commitments plus their international commitment to achieve carbon neutrality and net zero emissions by 2050 or earlier.

Global Climate Change Impacts on Spain Basque Government Policies

Climate change, clean energy transition, carbon neutrality, climate-resilient infrastructure and water are amongst some of the most pressing global issues with serious drastic international implications. Climate studies and scientific data have indicated that serious climate risks will continuously increase globally in the foreseeable future. Their impacts will grow in a non-linear manner with disastrous impacts globally. Coping with climate risks and achieving carbon neutrality will require all the countries globally to commit to new climate mitigating actions plus providing predictable and effective policy frameworks.

New carbon neutrality goals and net zero targets should be developed so that these can be achieved by countries globally in the second half of the century and preferably by 2050. These should be in line with the Paris Agreement goal of holding the increase in the global average temperature to well below 2°C above pre-industrial levels and pursuing additional efforts to limit the temperature increase to an aspired target of 1.5°C above pre-industrial levels. These should help to significantly reduce the serious risks and damaging implications of climate change globally.

To mitigate further climate change and global warming consequences, governments worldwide should formulate new policies to advance, scale and deploy low-carbon technologies and energy-efficient processes. They should promote innovations, especially on clean energies and carbon recycling. These should help to facilitate their sustainable transformations into new low-emission and carbon neutral economies.

Carbon neutrality, net zero emissions and sustained economic growth can only be accomplished if many multiple policy levers are activated jointly by governments and societies worldwide. In addition to promoting green technologies and innovations, governments globally must also make use of new effective enabling policy frameworks. These can include carbon pricing or taxes plus the elimination of inefficient fossil fuel subsidies, etc. Countries should also strive for a just climate transition which will combine environmental sustainability with creating more equal and inclusive economic growth for its population.

Infrastructures globally are critical for economic growth and human activities. They are also extremely vulnerable to the impacts of climate change. Major climate events in recent years have destroyed critical infrastructure such as roads, bridges, power networks and human dwellings globally. In a time of rapid climate change and intensifying natural hazards, infrastructure systems globally are under pressure to deliver resilient and reliable services. Therefore, there are important urgent needs for various governments and business communities to improve the climate resilience of infrastructures globally via better building design standards, risk assessments and green financing instruments. These are key enablers for improving climate change mitigation, sustainable economic development and improving the quality of life for people globally.

Water is at the source of life plus is key for human and economic activities. The protection of freshwater systems and oceans globally is very important so as to ensure human well-being, economic growth and biodiversity. Globally, growing water demands and climate change have seriously affected various water supplies. These have resulted in water scarcity and droughts in many regions globally. Similarly, the ocean is at great risk due to rising temperatures, increasing amounts of marine litter and pollution, overfishing, plus unsustainable urban development of coastal regions. All countries should put in place new policies that safeguard their freshwater systems and their oceans via good national and international regulations and governance mechanisms.

The global COVID-19 pandemic has served as a serious wake-up call plus a strong reminder of the urgency and importance of the need for new climate and carbon neutrality policies and actions by countries globally. In the post-COVID-19 economy, promoting alternative low-carbon technologies and carbon neutrality would be important to promote sustainable economic growth. These should also boost the creation of more new green jobs by the growing green energy and green finance sectors whilst reducing carbon emissions and climate change impacts. In essence, we must strive to leverage COVID-19 recovery to build back better, improve climate resilience plus promote the green agenda and improve global sustainability.

Spain Basque Economy, Climate & Carbon Outlooks

The Basque region is Spain's fifth largest regional economy. It has a GDP accounting for around 7% of the total national GDP of Spain. The region's exports are more or less evenly balanced between the rest of Spain and markets beyond the Spanish borders. It also has the lowest unemployment rates in Spain.

The Basque region is one of the most important industrial regions in Spain. The Basque Country's economy has been strongly manufacturing-based since the beginning of the 20th century. Manufacturing is accounting for over 25% of the total GDP of the region. The range of industrial productions in the region has been diverse. Industrial activities derived from metal, including the production of steel and machine-tools, are very important for the local economy. However, other sectors such as the chemical and petrochemical sectors and refineries are also noteworthy. These account for a very significant part of the region's GDP. The strongest industrial sectors of the Basque economy are machinery, aeronautic and energy. New technologies plus research and development (R&D) initiatives are also becoming very important. A good example is the growth of technology parks in the region. Basque companies are manufacturing a wide variety of capital goods, durable goods and other intermediate products, for both domestic consumption and exports.

The Spain Basque Government has declared their strong commitments to climate change plus to reduce their carbon emissions and developing various new net zero carbon pathways. They have joined the global Climate Ambition Alliance. This is an international network which is bringing together different regions, cities and companies from around the world that are committed to fighting climate change globally. The Alliance is bringing together different countries, regions and cities that are working toward achieving net zero CO_2 emissions by 2050 or earlier, in line with the Paris Agreement. The Spain Basque Government has joined the global network of over 65 countries, 10 regions, 102 cities, 93 companies and 12 investors which have already joined the global Climate Ambition Alliance.

The Spain Basque Government has also taken part in the meeting of the Steering Committee of the Under2 Coalition. The Spain Basque Government has been a member since the coalition was founded. The Under2 Coalition is a global community of state and regional governments which are committed to ambitious climate actions in line with the Paris Agreement. It is bringing together more than 220 governments representing over 1.3 billion people and 43% of the global economy. Its members are committed to keeping the global temperature rises to under 2°C and are increasing their efforts to reach the aspired target of 1.5°C. They are also committed to achieving carbon neutrality and net zero greenhouse emissions by 2050.

The Spain Basque Government has also declared publicly their commitment to tackling the climate crisis. They have announced that they are establishing a legislative framework to set new carbon neutrality targets for 2050 or earlier. Basque Government has been working on its own climate change strategy, called KLIMA2050 since 2015. Furthermore, external auditors of the UN's Intergovernmental Panel on Climate Change (UNIPCC) panel of experts had visited the Basque region to assess the Basque GHG emissions inventory. This is an audit that the Basque Country has undertaken voluntarily.

Spain Basque Sustainability Net Zero Policy Recommendations

Looking ahead, the Basque Government and companies will have to develop their new climate change policies so they can meet their carbon neutrality goals and net zero target by 2050 or earlier. Global experience has shown that these new climate change, clean energy and carbon neutrality policies will also promote sustainable social and economic growth in an industrial economy such as the Spain Basque region. Relevant policy recommendations will be given based on the latest global research and developments. In particular, they will include recent international work with the G20/B20 Global Taskforce, plus latest policy recommendations to the G20 Global Leaders and the B20 International CEOs. Relevant conclusions from the author's recent Routledge books titled *Climate Change and Clean Energy Management: Challenges and Growth Strategies* and *Renewable Energy Management in Emerging Economies* will also be incorporated. We have adapted these to offer relevant new policy recommendations for the Spain Basque Government plus key actors in the Basque industrial sector and Basque innovation ecosystem. We hope that these will support high-level government policy formulation and developments. The various key policy recommendations are summarised below:

Energy transition and clean energy growth will be critical to ensure the success of the new clean energy and climate policies. It is important for the Basque Government to commit to developing new policies and actions on accelerating the Basque region clean energy transition away from fossil fuels to clean renewable energy as part of their move towards achieving carbon neutrality goals and net zero targets. The government should provide predictable, effective policy frameworks to achieve carbon neutrality by 2050. Sustainability is key and it is most apparent in promoting the sustainable use of energy, local resources, environment, freshwater systems and the ocean. Climate, and the anthropogenic changes to it, calls for strong mitigation actions but it will also require strengthening of various climate-resilient infrastructures and services in the region.

The Spain Basque Government and companies should all now commit to achieving carbon neutrality by 2050 or preferably earlier, as they have announced previously. They have to accelerate new policy formulation and implementation to support the region meeting these important goals. This is in line with the Paris Climate Agreement goal of holding the increase in the global average temperature to well below 2°C above pre-industrial levels and pursuing efforts to limit the temperature increase to the aspired 1.5°C target above pre-industrial levels. These actions should help to significantly reduce the climate risks and the global warming impacts to the region. If no actions are taken, then global temperatures could rise by 4°C by 2100, which could then result in 30–40% destruction of the local and global GDPs. These will have disastrous consequences and very high economic costs.

New policies on promoting the new circular carbon economy (CCE) for the Basque region will be important. These should revolve around optimising various closed-loop regional systems and will be vital to achieving the Paris Agreement goals. CCE policies will encourage efforts to reduce carbon accumulation in the atmosphere through the "4Rs". These will include: Reduce the amount of carbon entering the economy; Reuse carbon without chemical conversion; Recycle carbon with chemical conversion; and Remove excess carbon from the atmosphere. Likewise, various carbon mitigating technologies and energy-efficient processes will be important to achieving the balance between anthropogenic emissions by sources and removals by various GHG sinks.

The Spain Basque Government and companies should promote and deploy suitable low-carbon technologies and energy-efficient processes. They should promote more innovations, especially on carbon recycling and green technologies, so as to transform its economy into a new sustainable low-emission carbon neutral economy quickly. New government policies should be introduced to create an enabling environment for the deployment of relevant low-carbon technologies. New low-carbon technologies should be advanced via effective public policy support. These should include suitable government support for research and development plus promoting international collaborations.

Global experiences have shown that new policies to promote various natural-based solutions and circular economy concepts should generate additional environmental, economic and social benefits. It is recognised that the Spain Basque region and its companies may have different local requirements and timelines to achieving carbon neutrality based on their national or local circumstances. Hence, it is recommended that the Spain Basque Government should, in line with international developments in other leading countries globally, develop new plans and policies to actively support innovative carbon technologies and carbon pricing developments. These should include Carbon Capture Storage and Utilisation (CCSU) and other energy-efficient processes together with a Carbon Emission Trading System (CETS) in line with international standards. The various new low-carbon technologies together with a modern CETS should be central pillars of the Spain Basque environmental masterplan and carbon neutrality policies and roadmaps. It is appreciated that different regions and companies will have to take into account their different local and individual requirements, maturity levels and sector relevance on developing their own specific local policies and action plans. Hence, it is very important that the Spain Basque Government should coordinate and drive all these new policies and actions so as to enable the Spain Basque region to attain their international commitment to achieve carbon neutrality and net zero emissions by 2050 or earlier.

5
Corporate Strategy Developments by Sector

入乡随俗

rù xiāng suí sú

When you enter a village, then you should follow its customs
When in Rome, do as the Romans do

Corporate Sustainable Business Transformation and Net Zero Climate Risks

The World Bank has estimated that the combined revenues of international companies are likely to rise to more than US$190 trillion within a decade. Leading companies, in both the emerging economies and developed countries, have come to recognise the urgent need to consider the rising climate change impacts and climate risks on their future business performances. The potential climate impacts on various business at stake could be enormous. It is very important for both public and private companies to develop appropriate sustainable business strategies with new carbon neutrality and net zero action plans (Mckinsey, Competing in a world of sectors without borders, 2016).

Companies must ensure that they will be able to compile with the growing new climate regulations plus the environmental and clean renewable energy regulations in the countries they are operating in. These new policies are being developed and implemented by various governments and countries globally in line with their different climate commitments, including the Paris Agreement and the Glasgow Climate Pact.

Companies must also take into consideration the growing strong market and consumers' demands for climate and sustainability improvements. CEOs and top management will have to actively reduce their GHG emissions and improve the environmental performance of their companies and production

DOI: 10.4324/9781003142348-5

sites. They will also have to improve their corporate strategies to take account of the rising climate change risks and net zero-emission requirements. Companies have to recognise and anticipate climate-related risks plus many important drivers. These will include changing government policies, clean energy regulatory requirements, product-preference shifts, price volatility etc. (Wang, Climate Change and Clean Energy Management, Routledge UK 2019).

Experts have shown that there are, in broad terms, six different kinds of key climate risks that are likely to affect all leading companies. These risks will include value-chain risks, product risks, governmental risks, consumer risks, stakeholder risks etc. These will be discussed in more detail below with international business examples (Mckinsey, How companies can adapt to climate change, 2015).

Value-chain physical risks are normally related to the damage that could be inflicted by extreme climate incidents, on company infrastructure and other corporate assets, such as factories and supply chain operations. Climate change has led to increased frequency and intensity of extreme weather incidents, such as wildfires, floods, hurricanes or typhoons. The frequency and severity of these climate-induced extreme weather disasters have increased markedly since the 1970s. These have negatively affected many company performances and caused serious damages to various corporate assets and value chains (Wang, Renewable Energy Management in Emerging Economies, Routledge UK 2020).

A good international business climate damage example is Cargill, which is one of the world's largest food and agricultural companies. In 2012, Cargill posted its worst quarterly earnings in two decades. This was caused largely by the serious US droughts, which were induced by climate change. These extreme droughts have led to food crop failures and poor agricultural yields. These have then led to serious reduction in the corporate revenues for Cargill. These, in turn, resulted in Cargill having to post its worst quarterly earnings results even.

Another interesting business example is Western Digital Technologies, which is a major supplier of hard disk drives. In 2011, it posted a sharp decline in corporate revenues, after serious climate-induced flooding in Thailand. This flooding has severely affected most of its manufacturing plants in Thailand. These, in turn, affected their international production and global supply chains. The loss of production also meant a global slump in hard disk supply worldwide. These had severe reverberations for the company plus many other computer manufacturers. It is good to note that Thailand, after experiencing these serious floods, has been implementing the new low-carbon sponge city designs in many of its major cities. These should help to better protect them from the rising flooding risks induced by climate change.

Companies have to undertake urgent actions to prepare for the various extreme climate-induced events which will be occurring more frequently in future. Companies must consider a range of possible climate scenarios plus develop suitable mitigation actions and backup plans. These are required to ensure sustainable business operations and growths.

Digital tools for climate forecasting can help to forecast high-level climate risk probabilities by region, such as for flood, drought, sea-level rises etc. These can also help to predict long-term changes in key climate parameters such as temperature, humidity, or rainfall patterns. Advances in digital technologies and big data systems have helped to improve the accuracy of climate forecasting and weather modelling together with more advanced super computers.

Climate change can also bring serious price risks that can negatively affect companies. These serious price risks could include increased price volatility of raw materials, feedstock supplies to companies etc. A good example is that climate change has resulted in many widespread droughts in many countries, especially in Africa. These could then lead to unexpected high price rises of water supplies to many companies in countries worldwide.

New energy policies and climate-related regulations can also drive up the costs of energy and fuel supplies for companies. Many countries are promoting the clean energy transition from fossil fuels to renewable clean energy. So, companies will have to accelerate their own clean energy transitions accordingly. High-tech and renewable energy industries could also face unexpected price risks in their competition for resources and supplies. A good international business example is the rising competition for rare earth materials. These are critical for the production of advanced battery systems, computer hard drives, televisions, wind turbines, solar photovoltaic systems and electric vehicles. China is currently the world leader in rare earth material production and supply. Other countries are also actively developing their own resources so as to improve their supply chain security and integrity in view of greater global competition.

Rising global warming has also resulted in various extreme weather incidents which have forced companies to cope with the increased risks of production, energy, transport and supply chain disruptions. Many leading companies have been taking proactive steps to manage these serious risks so as to minimise business disruptions and interruptions to their supply chains.

A good business example is IKEA, which has been actively undertaking their clean energy transition away from fossil fuels to clean renewables energy supplies at many of their stores. Looking ahead, IKEA is planning to become largely energy self-sufficient. Their electricity power supply will be based on clean renewable power generation integrated with advanced digital distributed power management systems. These will give IKEA better control of what prices it would have to pay for power and energy supplies, together with improved power security. These will also enable IKEA to better insulate itself against global and regional energy price spikes, plus protect against unplanned power disruptions. In addition, IKEA has also established a new partnership with NESTE. They are exploring new commercial production of bio-naphtha and bioplastic from waste oil recovery in Europe. IKEA is planning to apply these new bioplastics in their packaging and furniture products globally so as to reduce their consumption of plastic chemical materials (Wang, Renewable Management in Emerging Economies, Routledge UK 2020).

Another good international business example is the Germany car manufacturer Volkswagen (VW), which is actively undertaking clean energy transition away from fossil fuel to clean renewable energy for their car manufacturing operations. VW has implemented various hedging strategies against the possibility of rising fossil-fuel prices and has invested €1 billion euros in new renewable energy projects. VW has plans to power their various car manufacturing sites globally through their on-site renewable power production systems which are integrated with advanced distributed power control systems.

Looking ahead, it is expected that more and more leading manufacturing companies will be accelerating their clean energy transition plus go "off grid" and become self-sufficient in their power generation, for both strategic and economic reasons. Like VW and IKEA, it is expected that more and more leading companies will be accelerating their corporate clean energy transition process. They will be reducing their fossil-fuel consumptions and increasing clean renewable energy applications for their manufacturing operations. To generate their own clean renewable power reliably, they will need to employ advance distributed power digital technologies and power storage systems, together with their new renewable power generation systems, which may include solar, wind or biomass. They will also need to ensure that they have good cyber security systems and protection for their new digital power systems so that these will have high reliability and protection against hackers which could cause severe business disruptions.

Climate changes can also induce serious product risks which could seriously affect various company performances and sales revenues. These product risks could result in some core products becoming unpopular or even unsellable due to various reasons. These could cause companies to lose market shares or in severe cases to go under entirely. A good international example is the global ban of CFC due to its damage on the ozone layer. This promoted the development of alternative cooling technologies with new environmentally friendly refrigerants. These changes have had major impacts on conventional air-conditioning systems with chemical refrigerants, which have high global warming impacts. Air-conditioning companies and chemical companies all have to adopt quickly to these mandatory changes or risk serious company failures and prosecutions.

On the positive side, companies are actively developing new greener services and products. Two good business examples are that the construction and infrastructure sectors have been developing new products and services that will cater to the new low-carbon smart cities developments in various leading countries. These have included new energy-efficient buildings, electric-vehicle (EV) charging infrastructure, renewables integration, smart meters, smart grids, congestion-fee systems, plus high-performance green building materials and technologies etc. These have created new green business opportunities for the construction companies which have been willing to undertake relevant corporate transformation to meet the new green challenges.

A good international business example is Saint-Gobain, the international construction and packaging giant. The company has recognised the important implications that climate change will have on its international construction and packaging businesses. It has taken these climate risks into consideration in developing their new sustainable corporate strategies. It has incorporated the development of new sustainable housing technologies at the core of its new green product development strategy. These have helped the company to achieve better sustainable growth and business developments.

Climate changes and global warming can also lead to higher operational risks and uncertainties. A good international business example is that many ski resorts in Europe and USA had suffered significantly lower snow falls, with the abnormally high winter temperatures induced by global warming. Many of these ski resort operators had to apply artificial snow generation so as to ensure that their ski runs have sufficient snow cover for the skiers to enjoy. A good international example is that in the recent Winter Olympics held in 2022 in China, they have to apply artificial snow generation to ensure that their various ski runs have sufficient snow cover for the Olympic skiers to compete on.

Many countries have introduced carbon taxes or tariffs so as to accelerate their clean energy transition in some countries. At COP26, many countries have also committed to phasing-out their coal use and coal power generation. These changes will have major impacts on the coal mining industries, coal mining-equipment manufacturers and related coal supply industries.

Many international utilities and power generation companies have also been changing their traditional power supply business models in many markets globally. They are accelerating their clean energy transition and shifting from fossil fuel to clean renewable energy. A good international example is that the advances in digital distributed power technologies with renewable power generations have resulted in more reliable decentralised clean power generation for different markets. As a result, new clean renewable power systems integrated together with advanced distributed power management systems and energy storage systems are being applied in many countries. These should help to provide reliable clean renewable power. These should also help to provide electricity power access to the 1 billion people in more remote communities, which previously had no access to electricity or power. However, these new systems must also have good cyber security protection built into their digital management systems. These are required to ensure good power supply reliability plus guard against attacks by hackers or terrorists, which can cause severe power supply disruptions.

In the important Business-to-Consumer (B2C) sector, fast-changing consumer preferences are making inroads as consumers have become more willing to pay for greener products globally. Good international business examples include the fast-growing organic food and green groceries sectors which have seen double-digit growths for the past decade in many countries. Consumers are now able to find plentiful supply of organic food in many supermarkets and shops globally to meet their rising demands.

Companies will need to be actively monitoring these emerging megatrends so as to improve their corporate and product strategies accordingly. Companies should adopt a "design to sustainability" approach, in which new products are designed to minimise waste. They should also optimise waste management, including new designs for waste reuses or recycling. Companies have also to redefine their new corporate strategy so as to better align their business interests with climate change mitigation and adaptation. A good international business example is that Siemens has developed a new dedicated environmental portfolio of new carbon-efficient products as part of their new corporate climate change and sustainable product strategies.

Climate change has also raised external-stakeholder risks for companies globally. Whilst these stakeholder risks may vary widely between industries and regions, companies with carbon-intensive activities should proactively manage these potential risks. A good international example is that more than 4,000 corporates have proactively decided to report their carbon exposure on a transparent basis as part of the Carbon Disclosure Project (CDP). Many leading oil and gas majors have also been applying new internal carbon pricings on their evaluation of new fossil projects. These should help to better guide some of their strategic investment decisions.

Around the world, many governments have been introducing new climate change and clean energy policies which could affect the business prospects of many leading corporates. A good international example is that China has launched their new national carbon emission trading programme. This is in follow-up to their successful trial of carbon emission trading pilot programmes in seven major regions in China. The new China national carbon emission trading system will initially cover the electricity power generation sector in China. It is expected that many power companies in China will have to improve their operations and accelerate their fossil to renewable transitions, so as to reduce their GHG and carbon dioxide (CO_2) emissions.

Another good clean energy example is that most US states have introduced new Renewable Portfolio Standards (RPS). These will require a certain proportion of the state's electricity to be produced from clean renewable energy sources.

A good country example is that in Africa, Ethiopia has also developed a new climate masterplan to actively develop its low-carbon economy. This should help Ethiopia to become a middle-income emerging economy country, through low-carbon economic growths with its new climate-resilient green economy strategy.

It is important to recognise the potential political uncertainty of new climate change policies, on both the national and international levels. In particular, changes in government elections and administrations can have significant impacts on climate change and net zero goals in different countries. A good international example is the significant changes in the approaches of the USA to Climate Change and the Paris Agreement, between the Trump and Biden administrations. Former US President Trump had taken the USA out of the Paris Agreement. USA has re-entered the Paris Agreement under President Biden.

Companies have to actively monitor and manage these potential political and regulation changes together with its associated risks. They should be active in understanding the changing political and policy landscapes in the countries that they are operating in. In some cases, leading corporates have to undertake active government lobbying, so that they can help to shape future climate regulations and policy developments. Companies must also develop new climate change strategies so as to put their company in a better position to react quickly and effectively to possible new regulations and policy changes by governments in various countries. Companies should also work with key external stakeholders, such as regulators and various industry groups, to proactively share their perspectives and to provide inputs into future policy formulations.

Climate change has also increased the reputational risks for companies and governments globally. These could be either direct or indirect risks. Direct reputation risks could stem from company-specific actions which could influence the corporate reputation directly. Indirect reputation risk could come in the form of public perception of the whole industrial sector, which could then affect companies indirectly. In the climate change context, negative reputation risks could result in declines in business performance and profitability. A poor corporate reputation in climate change can damage the company sales plus acceptance by consumers and stakeholders. In the worse scenarios, it could lead to consumer boycotts or various protests against the company. It could also damage investor relationships and corporate image. In some worse cases, it has led to ethnical impact investors and shareholders launching various actions against the company board and top management. A good international example is the recent serious shareholder challenges to the Commonwealth Bank of Australia on their perceived poor climate risk management of their housing investments in Australia.

There are also growing global ethnical investor concerns on climate change together with demands for companies to undertake appropriate climate actions. A good international example is that governments plus investors and stakeholders are demanding companies to prepare better disclosures in their environmental, social and governance (ESG) report, which should include new carbon emissions reduction plans plus new carbon neutrality goals and net zero targets.

An actual international example of investors challenging a major business is the recent serious challenges by ethnical investors and shareholders to the top management of ExxonMobil, which is one of the major oil and gas companies. They have severely challenged the company management on their climate and net zero strategies as they do not believe the management has developed adequate climate risk management approaches. These challenges have led to declines in the ExxonMobil share prices plus serious negative impacts to the company reputation both locally and globally.

Investors have also started to lodge serious concerns about potential "stranded" assets. These might include fossil-fuel and coal assets, which are becoming unattractive and unprofitable due to new climate policy and clean energy transition requirements. A good international example of stranded physical assets are the old coal-fired power stations which will have to be phased-out in future so as to reduce environmental pollution and minimise GHG emissions.

Globally, there are growing numbers of customers who believe strongly that sustainability and environmental friendliness should be essential elements of the companies that they would buy their products and supplies from. Good international business examples include the new sustainable startups which are specialising in making clothing from recycled materials. There are rising demands from consumers on these environmental-friendly clothing. These environmental-friendly developments should also help to reduce the emissions and environmental impacts of the international fashion business sector, which is one of the major emitters globally.

Non-governmental organisations (NGOs) are also getting more influential. They are actively monitoring the emissions and environmental performances of different companies. NGOs have also been comparing corporate performance in the climate change area and publishing their results both locally and globally. In addition, university graduates and youth talents are also getting more hesitant to apply to companies with poor climate change and net zero performance records. Responsible company management have to take into consideration these important factors and improve their environmental performances urgently.

In response to these serious climate change impacts and requirements, the management of many responsible companies have taken active steps to improve their climate change strategies and establish new net zero goals. A good international business example is Unilever, the Anglo Dutch conglomerate which is one of the largest good and consumer companies. Unilever has led the FTSE CDP Carbon Strategy risk and performance index. It has improved its carbon efficiency by 40% since 1995. It has announced that its stated corporate environmental improvement goals are to reduce the carbon and water footprints of its various products to half of their 2010 levels by 2020s. Another good international retail business example is Kohl, which has won many international recognitions for its efforts to improve the environmental impacts of its operations and to reduce GHG emissions significantly.

In the digital IT sector, IBM has also won positive recognitions for its good actions pertaining to climate change. These have included setting up new rigorous GHG emission standards for their computer suppliers and IT value chains. IBM won a 2013 Climate Leadership Award from the US Environmental Protection Agency for its supply chain leadership. It was also recognised in 2014 for its good GHG management.

It is encouraging to see many good leading companies understand the importance of climate change and the net zero requirements. They have been actively developing new sustainability strategies and net zero targets. They have also been improving their environmental performances and reducing their GHG emissions. Looking ahead, many companies have still to do more to improve their climate change performances and to develop their new net zero plans. Otherwise, they would be exposed to serious climate risks and suffer serious negative business impacts, including serious product, operational, pricing and reputational damage.

New Corporate Sustainability Net Zero Plan & Strategy Developments

Many leading companies have realised that it is now a real necessity for businesses to develop suitable new sustainability strategies with new net zero goals. At COP26 in Glasgow, over 1,000 international business leaders and CEO have publicly committed to develop new sustainability strategy and net zero plans for their companies to achieve carbon neutrality with net zero emission by 2050. These are in response to the call by UN Framework Convention on Climate Change (UNFCC) that the world's net emissions should fall to zero by 2050 in order to limit the aspired rise in global temperatures to no more than 1.5°C versus pre-industrial levels.

Global business surveys have shown that the majority of top business executives now believe that managing climate risks plus developing good sustainability strategy and net zero goals will be important factors in keeping their jobs. They also believe that other CEOs and executives running businesses which have failed to anticipate and prepare for significant climate risks will be putting their own jobs and those of others in serious jeopardy. In addition, business executives and governments are discovering that there are also large new green business opportunities for companies which are actively progressing on their route to achieving their net zero and carbon neutrality targets. Good international examples include EV, battery, solar, wind and renewable energy manufacturers etc.

Global investments in sustainability and clean renewable energy by international companies have risen strongly in recent years. These investments have taken place via different investment models and various investment channels for different companies. A good international clean investment example is that it has been estimated that the global investments in clean renewable energy facilities have exceed US$ 1 trillion in the last decade. The annual investments in clean renewable energy have also exceeded US$200 billion per year for the past seven years. A good international example is that in 2016, the total new global investment in renewable power and clean fuels was over US$ 260 billion in both the emerging economies and developed countries, as shown in the "International Renewable Energy Association" report (IRENA, 2018).

Looking ahead, experts have predicted that the global clean renewable energy investments are expected to continue their strong upward trends. A good international example is that the Chinese government has announced new major renewables investment plans, as part of their National Five-Year National Plan. They are planning to spend US$ 360 billion on new clean renewable energy projects from 2020 to 2025. These clean energy investments should reinforce

China's position as the world leader in clean renewable energy investments (UNEP, Renewable Investment Global Trends Report, 2019).

Globally, most of the clean energy and renewable electricity investments have continued to be dominated by electricity power generation companies which are owned by big international utility companies or state-owned utility companies. The scale of the various clean energy power plants, including solar photovoltaic (PV), wind power and CSP, has continued to grow with new renewable technical innovations and cost-reduction measures. Some of the key clean renewable power generation equipment have also continued to grow with technological advances and material innovations. A good international renewable example is wind turbines which have continued to increase in size with new material advances and new technological innovations. These have contributed to large and more efficient wind power generation globally (REN, Renewables Global Status Report, 2018).

The leading utility companies in China, Denmark, Germany, India, Sweden and the USA have continued to invest in large-scale renewable energy projects, especially in solar PV and wind power. Interestingly, these leading utility companies are diversifying their businesses as part of their new corporate growth strategy. A good international example is that some leading utility companies have made new investments directly into renewable energy technology companies or have acquired these companies. These strategic investments are in line with their sustainable corporate strategy to improve their innovation supply chain and as part of their drives for new technology innovations.

International analysis has highlighted that many leading oil and gas companies are also undertaking active clean energy transition. These fossil companies have traditionally been working in the fossil-fuel sectors, including oil, gas and coal. Many oil and gas companies have developed new corporate strategies to diversify into new energy companies. They have started to move aggressively into the clean energy and renewable energy sectors. Many leading oil and gas energy companies have developed new clean renewable energy investment strategies and made major announcements. A good example is Shell, which has announced their new clean renewable energy investment strategies, especially in the fast-growing areas of new EV charging and offshore wind developments.

Globally, many major international corporations and institutions have also been making large commitments to purchase clean renewable electricity from different sources, including those from emerging economies. Many leading businesses around the world have also joined the RE100 alliance. This is a global initiative of businesses which have committed to achieving a target of 100% renewable electricity in future. New RE100 corporate members have included major companies in China and India, as well as international heavy industrial corporates (RE100, Report and Briefings, 2019).

Many major companies have been making major purchases of clean renewable energy supplies as part of their new energy and power supply strategies. The bulk of these clean power purchases have been in renewables, such as wind energy and solar PV. Most of the international corporates have been procuring their renewable electricity through renewable energy certificates (RECs). Many major corporates have also entered into new Power Purchase Agreements (PPAs) or applied new direct clean power ownership models.

An increasing number of large international businesses have negotiated and committed to new PPAs for their clean renewable power supplies. Many of these PPAs have contracts undertaken directly with renewable energy generator companies rather than with traditional utility companies. A good international example is that the overall volume of PPAs in 2016 rose to 4.3 GW, which was the second highest amount on record.

There have also been some interesting clean renewable energy community project investments in recent years. These have involved investments by a growing number of local communities in various new renewable projects in many countries. A good international country example is that Canada has seen its first community windfarm starting operation recently. Another good Latin America example is that Chile has been implementing a new dedicated policy for clean community energy projects since late 2015. Chile has now registered 12 new communities to receive investment funds for new community clean renewable energy projects.

A case study on how some of the largest EU companies are developing their new sustainability net zero plans and their new strategies for emission reductions is summarised below with international examples:

EU Company Sustainability Net Zero Emission Reductions Plans Case Study

Leading EU companies have been active in developing their new sustainability net zero plans and their new emission reduction strategies. Experts have forecasted that the EU companies will need to more than double their current level of spendings on new low-carbon capital investments so as to meet the European Commission's new 2050 net zero target (Energy World, Europe's top companies 'must double low carbon investment for net zero' USA, March 2020).

The new energy report has analysed the various low-carbon investments of 882 EU companies to assess whether their investment patterns are consistent with the EU net zero targets. These EU companies have collectively made up over 70% of total European market capitalisation. The analysis has shown that these EU companies allocated some €59 billion to low-carbon capital investment in 2019. Looking ahead, in order to meet the European Commission's new targets, their investments will have to more than double to around €122 billion per year. In terms of overall capital expenditures, low-carbon investments will need to increase from 12% to 25%.

Key sectors for new green investment plus research and development (R&D) include the carbon-intensive transport, energy and materials sectors. These accounted for 50%, 38% and 5% of the total respectively. A good example is the capital investments of €45 billion in the EU clean electric utility sector. These included investments in renewables, infrastructure and enabling technologies, such as demand side response programmes and digitalisation.

Meanwhile, green R&D investments are forecasted to increase to above €65 billion. The bulk of the investment of €43 billion will be in the clean transport sector. These are primarily green investments in developing new electrification and autonomous vehicle technologies.

The green investments by EU companies in 2019 are forecasted to deliver at least 2.4 gigatonnes of CO_2 equivalent in terms of lifetime emissions savings. These are more than the annual CO_2 outputs of the UK, Germany, France, Italy and Poland combined. It is also important to realise that the potential values of new low-carbon business opportunities for EU companies can reach €1.2 trillion. This is over six times the costs of the investments which are needed to realise these green opportunities.

So, there are strong clear business justifications, across many investment sectors for EU businesses to transform into low-carbon businesses. The potential new green business opportunities are high. However, overall current investment levels are still falling short of putting European firms on track to achieve their EU net zero targets. Looking ahead, EU companies will have to accelerate their green investments plus develop their sustainability strategies and net zero plans.

International Company New Sustainability Net Zero Strategy Developments

Leading international companies, in both emerging economies and developed countries around the world, have been actively working on developing their new corporate sustainability strategies and net zero goals together with clean energy transition and sustainable growth plans. These should help them to meet their public commitment to achieve carbon neutrality and net zero emissions by 2050 and to meet their Paris Agreement commitments.

A good international business example is that at COP26 in Glasgow, over 1,000 international business CEOs have committed publicly to actively develop their new sustainability strategies and net zero goals so that they can achieve carbon neutrality with net zero emissions by 2050. These are in response to the call by UNFCC that the world's net emissions should fall to zero by 2050 so as to limit the rise in global temperatures to no more than 1.5°C versus pre-industrial levels.

Looking ahead, it is expected that a rising number of leading international companies globally will be accelerating their development of new sustainability net zero plans together with faster energy transformation from fossil fuel into clean renewable power supplies. Good international business examples include IKEA, VW etc.

IKEA has said publicly that their longer-term corporate direction is for all IKEA Group buildings to become carbon neutral and be supplied with 100% renewable energy. In addition, IKEA is also aiming to improve the IKEA Group's overall energy efficiency performance globally by 25%, as compared with their 2005 performances. Amongst other energy-saving initiatives, IKEA will be using energy-saving light bulbs in all their stores. They will also only have the lights on when warehouses are open. IKEA has also pledged to install extra insulations in their buildings so as to further save on energy for heating and cooling in their stores and warehouses. IKEA has also said that they are going to make sure that all IKEA Group stores, warehouses, distribution centres, factories and offices will be heated and cooled using renewable energy, including wind, water, solar power, biofuels and geothermal energy in future (IKEA, Going Renewables, Sweden 2019).

Volkswagen (VW), the international auto manufacturer, had its corporate reputation severely damaged in 2015 by its roles in enabling its diesel models to cheat laboratory emissions tests in the USA and EU. It has actively developed their new corporate improvement strategies and is now aiming to become a leading provider of sustainable mobility globally. VW has founded a new subsidiary called Elli Group GmbH, based in Berlin Germany. The new unit will develop green auto products and services, especially relating to clean renewable energy and EV charging for its new EV products. VW has said that, they as one of the world's largest automakers, they are going to force the pace to transform the global transportation sector into emission-neutral e-mobility. The new VW business unit is expected to develop a new renewables-based smart charging solution for electric cars. VW believed that they will be entering a strategically relevant and exciting business sector which will offer considerable new green business opportunities. VW believed that these should also help them to strengthen ties with existing customers as well as access entirely new customer groups in the emerging economies and developed countries globally (PV Magazine, Volkswagen green energy supplier, 2019).

Looking ahead, it is expected that more and more international companies will be developing their new sustainability strategies and net zero plans. These should help them to accelerate their clean energy transition away from fossil fuels into renewable energy. These are being driven by new government energy policy plus international requirements to reduce GHG emissions and to improve their environmental performances. Many companies are applying new renewable power generation integrated with advance distributed power storage and digital distributed power management technologies. They are applying advanced digital systems to manage their new renewable power supplies efficiently and reliably. At the same time, they must also improve their cyber security to guard against attacks by hackers or terrorists to these systems, which could result in severe supply disruptions.

International Food Company McDonald Sustainability Net Zero Plan Case Study

McDonald has announced their new sustainability strategy and net zero plans so as to enable it to reach net zero in all its restaurants across the globe by 2050. They have stressed that the new plans for change are also their overall top green business priority.

McDonald announced that it will open its first net zero restaurant in the UK in 2022 as part of its ambitious plans to cut its GHG emissions by 2040. The new restaurant will be stocked with vegan plant-based food. Customer packaging will be compostable and made from renewable, recycled or certified sources. From 2023, all new furniture in McDonald's sites will be made with recycled or certified materials. These furniture will be designed to be recycled or reused when no longer needed. By 2040, it is hoped to cut carbon emissions in the UK as part of its Plan for Change programme.

McDonald is currently one of the largest beef purchasers in the world. Roughly 80% of its total emissions are coming from its international supply chain, in particular its use of beef, chicken, dairy and other proteins. Under their new carbon neutrality net zero-emission plans, McDonald has said that it will develop new guidelines to focus on cutting their emissions in their international supply chains, especially in the agriculture, land use and forestry sectors.

International Oil & Gas Energy Companies Sustainability Net Zero Strategies Overviews

Many of the leading international oil and gas companies have recognised the importance of climate change. They also have to comply with the new clean energy and emission policies that have been introduced by various governments globally, as part of their efforts to meet their Paris Climate Agreements commitments. Many international oil and gas companies are urgently developing their new sustainability strategies and net zero plans plus increasing their clean energy investments. A good international business example is that many leading oil and gas companies have already established new clean energy renewable energy divisions. They are also starting to make significant investments in the clean energy and renewables sectors.

In addition, there are strong drives globally on reducing pollution and plastic wastes. A good international example is that 175 countries have agreed to end plastic pollution in the United Nations Environment Assembly (UNEA) meeting in 2022. Leaders of 175 nations have also agreed to forge a treaty to tackle plastic pollution at the UNEA in Kenya. A negotiating committee will be spending the next two years to hammering out the final international deal. Crucially, the treaty will be legally binding and will address the full life cycle of plastics. The UN Environment Programme has called the new agreement as the most significant multilateral environmental deal since the Paris Climate accord in 2015. This new agreement will have major impacts on oil, gas and chemical companies (UNEA, United Nations Environment Assembly (UNEA) on Plastic Pollution. Kenya March 2022).

The international Oil and Gas Climate Initiative (OGCI) has also been established. It is a CEO-led consortium that aims to accelerate the industrial wide response to climate change. OGCI member companies explicitly support the Paris Agreement and its goals. OGCI members include BP, Chevron, CNPC, Eni, Equinor, ExxonMobil, Occidental, Petrobras, Repsol, Saudi Aramco, Shell, Total etc. They are accounting for over 30% of internationally operated oil and gas productions globally. They are aiming to play active roles in shaping the global pathways to carbon neutrality and net zero emissions by leveraging the collective strengths of OGCI and its member companies. They are aiming to continually improve and build on good international corporate practices to reduce GHG emissions and accelerate transitions to a low-carbon future. Their members have collectively invested over US$7 billion each year in low-carbon solutions. OGCI Climate Investments, a US$1 billion plus investment fund, has invested in new green solutions to decarbonise sectors like oil and gas, industrials and commercial transportation etc.

OGCI announced that they have set their first collective carbon intensity targets. These will aim to reduce the collective average carbon intensity of member companies' upstream oil and gas operations to between 20 kg and 21 kg CO_2e/boe by 2025, from a 23 kg baseline in 2017. These are consistent with the reductions that will be needed to support the goals of the Paris Agreement. This will represent a reduction of between 36 and 52 million tonnes of CO_2e emissions per year by 2025. This will be equivalent to the total CO_2 emissions resulting from energy uses from 4 to 6 million homes.

The new emission targets will cover both CO_2 and methane emissions from OGCI member companies' operated upstream oil and gas exploration plus production activities, as well as emissions from associated imports of electricity and steam. OGCI will also be working on specific actions on emissions reductions from liquefied natural gas (LNG) and gas-to-liquids (GTL) plants.

To contribute to the reduction of their collective average carbon intensity, OGCI member companies are implementing a range of measures in their own operations. These include improving energy efficiency, reducing methane emissions, minimising flaring, electrifying operations using renewable electricity where possible, co-generating electricity and useful heat and deploying carbon capture, utilisation and storage.

Many multinational oil and gas companies have already created new clean renewable energy business divisions. These are tasked to promote their investments in clean energy, renewables plus to promote their clean renewable energy transformations. The oil and gas industry has already seen some of the sector's largest companies, including Shell, Total and BP, announcing that they will be making big investments in renewables and clean energy projects. Recent analysis has shown that Big Oil's cumulative investments in renewable acquisitions over the past five years have reached over US$3 billion. Most of these green investments and acquisitions have been in the solar and wind renewable sectors (CBC Business, Big Oil, 2018).

The rising renewable investments by oil and gas companies have been driven by a number of key factors. These have included climate change, fossil to renewable transformation, GHG emission reductions and technology innovations. In addition, the renewable power generation costs have reduced significantly with technological innovations and cost reductions in recent years. Good international examples include the solar and wind renewable power generation costs being reduced by 50–70% in recent years with various new technological innovations and cost-reduction measures (IRENA, 2018).

Looking ahead, experts are predicting that there will be cleaner renewable growth with rising investments. These are driven by renewable power generation becoming cost-competitive against fossil power generation options. No new government subsidies will be required for future renewable power generation projects. A good industrial example is that renewables generation costs have come down so much recently that the power generation prices for an investment in solar or wind power generation could be cheaper than a natural gas co-generation plant in both emerging economies and developed countries globally.

Looking ahead, energy experts have predicted that natural gas will continue to be an important transitionary fossil fuel for some times in future globally. Many emerging economies and developed countries have promoted natural gas power generation and domestic consumptions as part of their new energy policies to reduce coal and fossil-fuel consumptions plus to improve environmental pollution.

It is important to realise that there are also important complementary roles for natural gas with renewable applications in power generation globally. A good international example is that most wind and solar renewable power generation systems are currently not yet able to supply power reliably and continuously around the clock 24/7. The integration of natural gas with solar or wind renewable power generation may be a win-win partnership in terms of providing reliable power supplies on a continuous basis.

A lot of new investment capital has been coming into the renewable sector from different sources. These included investments from energy companies, pension funds and life insurance companies plus sovereign wealth funds. A good international example is Norway's US$1 trillion government-owned sovereign investment fund. Norway's sovereign wealth fund has announced their new strategic objectives to combat climate change whilst creating value and being good stewards of the national funds. The Norway investment fund managers said, in early 2019, that it would be divesting off their investments in 134 companies which have fossil oil and gas businesses. These included oil and gas companies such as UK-based Tullow Oil, Premier Oil, Soco International, Ophir Energy and Nostrum Oil & Gas. The Norway fund managers have said that they will be retaining their investment positions in Royal Dutch Shell and BP because these two companies have both adopted new clean energy strategies and established new renewable energy business divisions. The Norway fund managers have also announced that they will be redirecting the funds, which they have earned from their oil and gas investments, and investing these in clean energy projects instead (Forbes Energy, Big Oil Dipping into Green Energy, 2019).

At present, most oil and gas companies are continuing with their investments into their tradition oil and gas pillars business, whilst also making new investments into renewables and clean energy businesses. In 2018, experts have estimated that oil and gas companies globally have spent about 1–1.5% of their investment budgets on renewable energy sectors. These have included wind and solar plus power battery storage and carbon capture projects.

CDP, formerly known as the Carbon Disclosure Project, has reported that Europe's Equinor, Total, Shell and Eni have ranked highest for leading the low-carbon transition, whilst China's CNOOC, Russia's Rosneft and USA's Marathon Oil have lagged further behind. CDP has also reported that since 2016, over 145 deals have been made in alternative energy and carbon capture. A total of US$ 22 billion has been invested in renewables and alternative energies since 2010 (CDP, 2017).

A good oil and gas business example is Equinor. They have developed new corporate strategies which is aiming to rebrand the oil and gas company into a broad energy company. As part of their new clean energy strategic shifts, they are planning to invest 15–20% of their future capital expenditures in renewables and new energy solutions by 2030.

Many major multinational oil and gas companies have also come under intensive scrutiny from ethnical investors, climate activists and stakeholders. These stakeholders have been asking the management of various oil and gas companies to become more transparent about how they manage their climate risks and reduce their CO_2 emissions. These have driven many of the oil and gas company management to actively develop new climate and renewable investment strategies. In addition, these have driven some international oil and gas companies, including Chevron, ExxonMobil Corp. and Occidental Petroleum, to join the OGCI which is developing new clean energy and carbon capture solutions. Some other leading oil and gas companies, including BP, Shell, Statoil and Total, have also been reviewing the international carbon emission trading system and carbon tax applications plus discussing these with relevant governments.

We shall examine further below two case studies of leading oil and gas companies on their new renewable corporate strategies and renewable investments together with international business examples.

Shell Sustainability Net Zero Renewables Strategies Case Study

Shell is one of the largest oil and gas energy companies. Its management has been actively developing its sustainability net zero policy plus promoting energy transition. In 2021, Shell announced their ambition to become a net zero-emissions energy business by 2050 or sooner. To achieve this ambition,

Shell highlighted three major corporate changes and transformations. Firstly, Shell will be changing its international operations so as to achieve net zero in all their operations. Secondly, Shell will be significantly reducing the carbon intensity of the products that they are selling. This will mean selling more clean energy products, including hydrogen, biofuels and renewable electricity. The third part is to help their customers who are still dependent on carbon-based energy products to address their emission reductions. These will include the commercial sectors such as aviation, heavy freight and shipping. Potential carbon solutions will include the use of new carbon capture and storage technology or by offsetting emissions through carbon offsets or nature carbon solutions (Shell, CEO Interview on Net Zero by 2050, UK Jan 2021).

Shell is actively developing the details of their new sustainability strategy and net zero plans for each of their business sectors. The latest Shell global energy scenarios have predicted strong future growth in the renewable, clean energy, green transportation and smart cities sectors. It showed that there will be good international business growth opportunities in renewables, clean power, wind, biofuel, EV charging and e-mobility, in both emerging economies and developed countries. Their analysis has shown that the share of electricity in global energy consumption is currently around 22%. Looking ahead to 2070, they have predicted that global electricity consumption will more than double, to over 50% of global energy consumption. These will include growth in many end-user energy consumption areas, as electrification expands more into transportation, home heating and cooking, and industrial sectors. These green growths will be driven by the global decarbonisation efforts to address climate change and to achieve carbon neutrality with net zero emissions (Shell, Sky Scenario, 2018).

As part of Shell's new corporate strategy, a new integrated gas and new energies division has been established. One of its key business objectives is to develop Shell's renewable business and undertake new clean energy investments so as to transform Shell to become one of the largest clean power companies in the world by the early 2030s. Shell is planning to create a new global clean energy business that's more holistic than other companies. They are planning to offer their customers the opportunity to buy all their energy requirements from one integrated energy company which will cover both fossil fuels and renewable energies. They believe that this will be a unique competitive edge for Shell as other power provider and energy competitors cannot make these cross-linkages and integrated customer propositions (Shell, Shell New Energies Scenarios, UK 2019).

A good clean power business example is that Shell has renamed its UK-based energy supplier First Utility as Shell Energy Retail, under the broader Shell

Energy brand. They have started serving all their UK residential customers with 100% clean renewable electricity. Shell's renewable energy offerings are being certified by the Renewable Energy Guarantees of Origin. They will certify that for every unit of electricity that Shell Energy supplies to its customers, a unit of renewable electricity will be supplied into the grid by renewable power generators in the UK. Shell Energy Retail will also be rolling out a range of smart home technology offers to their customers throughout the year. A good example is that they will start with the free Nest smart thermostats for UK customers who sign up for a three-year, fixed-price contract and discounts on home EV charging. Shell is also enhancing customer loyalty by connecting the Shell Energy electricity customers to their existing loyalty system for its fuels network. These will enable their renewable customers to get a discount when they fill up their cars with fossil-fuel products at any Shell fuel retail stations in UK (Shell International, Shell New Energies Units, UK 2019).

Shell also plans to become a major regional clean electric power player in the USA in future. Shell is planning to invest in various deregulated US states where it will be possible for international power companies to compete. A good US example is that Shell has invested in 2018 in the USA retail power supplier 'Inspire Energy', which is already offering clean energy plans in deregulated US states. In 2018, Shell also purchased Texas-based MP2, which has been expanding its power offerings to corporate and industrial customers. Shell New Energies has also purchased a major stake in the US solar developer, Silicon Ranch.

Shell is currently investing US$1–2 billion per year on renewables and new energy solutions. This is still quite small out of a total company capital investment programme of more than US$25 billion. Looking ahead, these clean energy investments are expected to grow further. Good international business examples of recent clean energy investments included the acquisition of the German home energy storage firm Sonnen and the purchase of the Dutch EV charging provider NewMotion. Shell has also invested in two Singapore-based solar firms, Sunseap Group and Cleantech Solar. These two solar companies have been building solar farms for corporate customers across South and Southeast Asia.

In line with global ethnical impact investor development trends, a rising number of international investors and shareholders in Shell have been asking the Shell top management to demonstrate that their investments are a force for good in the world. In response, Shell management has been trying to show these investors that their corporate investments can do good, whilst also delivering good returns.

A good new energy business example is Sonnen, the new Shell Germany clean energy subsidiary. Sonnen has been selling new home-based clean energy optimisation solutions built around a battery system, together with advanced digital software systems connecting and optimising various aspects of energy application in the home. As their customers are purchasing the new clean energy products for their home applications, Sonnen's balance sheet is effectively zero, whilst maintaining a growing and profitable business on a sustainable basis.

Shell's experience in the fossil-fuel industry can actually be an asset in the clean energy sector. Shell's business records have shown that the company has historically been able to find ways to be successful in establishing new difficult and competitive businesses. A good international business example is the successful growth of their international LNG business. In addition, Shell's extensive offshore oil and gas platform experience will also be useful as they expand into building new offshore wind platforms.

In addition, many of Shell's current technical and commercial competences and expertise in the oil and gas sector should also be applied in the new renewable and clean energy sectors. A good example is that Shell's extensive oil fuel retail network experience can be applied in their new EV charging retail venture. The new EV venture is aiming to establish new EV charging stations and retail networks in USA, Europe and Asia.

In other renewable energy sectors, Shell is also actively developing onshore and offshore wind projects in North America, Europe and Asia. On biofuel, Shell has established, together with Cosan, a US$ 12 billion joint venture called Raizen, which is focussing primarily on Brazilian sugarcane and first-generation ethanol.

British Petroleum Sustainability Net Zero Renewable Strategies Case Study

British Petroleum (BP) has announced they have launched a new corporate vision to become a net zero company by 2050 or sooner. BP has also set some new ambitious corporate targets for emission reductions by 2025. BP is planning to bring down their international operational emissions globally by 50%, when compared with their 2019 baseline.

BP's future global energy scenario forecasts have shown that clean renewable energy will be the fastest growing energy segment in the global energy industry. BP is forecasting global renewables growth of over 7.5% growth each year between 2011 and 2030. BP has announced that they are planning to make new investments into the clean renewable energy sector in future. BP's new alternative energy division has strategised to focus its renewable energy portfolio on various clean energy sources, especially biofuels and wind energy. This is in line with the BP corporate forecasts which have predicted that by 2030, various renewable energy supply sources are likely to meet around 6% of total global future energy demands (BP, Global Energy Scenarios, 2018).

On biofuels, BP has invested in various new sugarcane ethanol mills for bioethanol manufacturing. A good international business example is that BP has invested in new sugarcane ethanol mills in Brazil. BP has also been producing biofuel from its biofuels joint venture, Vivergo Fuels, in the UK.

On wind renewables, BP has been developing onshore and offshore wind farms in various locations. A good international wind example is that BP has been developing windfarms in different US states, including Kansas, Pennsylvania and Hawaii.

International IT Digital Company Sustainability Net Zero Strategy Developments

Many international IT digital companies have been actively developing their new sustainability strategies and net zero plans. They are accelerating their clean energy transitions by shifting away from fossil fuel to clean energy globally. Four interesting international IT digital company business case examples, covering Google and Telefónica plus Apple and TSMC, will be discussed in more detail below with international examples. They have all been accelerating their clean energy transition in line with their new corporate sustainability strategy plus net zero plans so as to support the sustainable development of their key global businesses.

Google Sustainability Net Zero Case Study

Google has been active in pursuing its new corporate pledge of achieving carbon neutrality and transforming all of its power supplies to 100% renewable energy supplies. Google claimed that they have become one of the first major companies globally to achieve carbon neutrality. Google also aims to become one of the first major international companies to achieve 100% renewable energy usage. Google has pledged that they are aiming to be the first major international company to operate carbon free by 2030.

Google's key corporate target is for all of its operations to run on carbon-free energy by 2030. This is one of its ambitious moon-shot targets to achieve carbon neutrality and net zero emissions. Currently, Google's international data centres are running at the 67% carbon-free levels. This is a good improvement from the 61% carbon-free level achieved in 2019.

Google has been actively ramping up its acquisition of green renewable power supplies from both emerging economies and developed countries. Google has said that its clean renewables energy transformations are currently on course to enable all its data centres to be powered by renewable energy sources by 2030. They have pledged to purchase enough wind and solar renewable power to support all their global operations. Google has said that reaching its 100% renewable energy goal will take tough multi-year corporate actions and efforts.

Google will also be improving their data-centre energy efficiencies as part of their clean energy transition. The Google engineers have undertaken digital and technical improvements on its data centres in many countries across the world. A good international example is that Google engineers have been able to make the Google data centres 50% more energy efficient than the industrial average. Google has also applied advanced digital technologies, including the use of machine learning and artificial intelligence, in their data centres. These have helped Google to improve their energy robustness and energy efficiency plus meet the rising climate challenges (Computer Weekly, Google datacentres, US 2016).

Google has been active in ensuring that they will have sufficient supplies of renewable energy power supplies for their offices as well as their fleet of data centres. A good business example is that Google has been buying directly from various renewable generators additional wind and solar-generated renewable electricity for their operations. Google has been buying clean renewable power from projects that have been funded by Google company purchases globally. Electricity costs have been one of the largest components in Google's operating expenses. Hence, having a long-term stable supply of renewable electricity power at pre-agreed costs will help Google to achieve better power security and it will also protect Google against future energy disruptions and price swings.

To date, Google's renewable purchasing commitments have resulted in infrastructure investments of more than US$3.5 billion globally, with around two-thirds of the investments in the USA. Google has estimated that these new renewable projects will generate tens of millions of dollars per year in revenues to various local renewable plant owners. In addition, these should also generate tens of millions more to local and national governments in tax revenues.

Telefónica Sustainability Net Zero Case Study

Telecom companies have also been accelerating their renewable digital transformations in light of the serious climate change pressures. A good international example is Telefónica, the international telecom company. Telefónica is the operator behind UK's O2 mobile network. Telefónica has announced their new sustainability net zero corporate target of achieving net zero emissions by 2025 in their main operations and by 2040 at the latest in all their operations globally. To achieve this, they have announced their corporate commitment to reducing emissions in line with the UNFCC 1.5°C scenario. They will also be neutralising their remaining carbon emissions through the purchase of international CO2 absorption and carbon credits, preferably through nature-based solutions.

Telefónica has announced some details of their new sustainability plans and net zero actions. These will include reducing their Scope 1+2 emissions by 90% by 2025 in their main markets, and by 70% globally. They will also act to achieve net zero emissions by 2025 in their main markets. They will be taking into account their Scopes 1+2 emissions plus neutralising residual emissions. They will also reduce the CO2 emissions in their value chains by 39% by 2025. They will also reduce energy consumption per traffic unit (MWh/PB) by 90% in 2025, as compared to 2015 levels.

They have been actively pushing their clean energy transitions by shifting away from fossil energy to renewable energy supplies as part of their new sustainability net zero strategy. Telefónica has said that they are planning to speed up their commitments in fighting climate change and to achieve their Paris Agreement commitments. They are striving to source 100% of their electricity from renewable energy sources by 2030. As of June 2017, 44% of their electricity consumptions have come from renewable energy sources. This is equivalent to the total average power consumption by over 203,000 homes (Computer Weekly, Telefónica Renewable uses, 2017).

Telefónica had also claimed that they are already using 100% renewable power supplies in Germany and the UK, plus 79% in Spain. At its Madrid headquarters (HQ), solar panels have already been generating more than 3 GWh of solar power per year. Telefónica has also now joined the RE100 alliance, which is a worldwide collaborative alliance for businesses which have committed to achieving the 100% clean renewable energy goal in future.

Telefónica believed that its new corporate sustainability strategy and net zero plans have helped them to improve their competitiveness plus reduced operational costs and to make sustainable business growths which are compatible with their corporate sustainability strategy. Their new corporate goal is to have not only the best international digital network with excellent connectivity in technological terms, but also one that is the most efficient and clean in the sector in terms of energy and carbon.

Their Renewable Energy Plan has four key action areas which will differ slightly depending on the local market regulations where it operates. These included the acquisition of renewable energy with a guarantee of origin; long-term PPAs; shorter bilateral agreements and self-production.

In Latin America, Telefónica will be relying heavily on PPAs for clean renewable energy supplies to its operations in the various Latin American emerging economies. A good Latin American business example is that in Mexico, it has already set up a renewable PPA which will be buying solar power to supply its in-country electricity consumptions. They are hoping to sign similar PPA deals in Argentina, Chile and Colombia. Meanwhile, in Brazil, it is acquiring renewable energy through new PPA agreements. In Uruguay, it is installing 16 small solar plants in rural areas to generate 600 MWh of solar energy each year. In Colombia, it recently invested US$1.4 million in new solar photovoltaic generation to replace older power generation equipment which had previously relied on diesel fuels. They have estimated that their fossil to clean renewable energy shifts have helped to eliminate CO_2 GHG emissions of over 470 tonnes per annum.

Apple Sustainability Net Zero Carbon Neutral Strategy Case Study

Apple has announced their new sustainability net zero target to become carbon neutral across its entire international business, manufacturing supply chains and product life cycles by 2030. Apple has announced that the company is already carbon neutral today for its global corporate operations. Their new carbon neutrality and net zero corporate commitments have meant that by 2030 every Apple device that will be sold globally will have net zero climate impacts.

Apple announced that it is already carbon neutral today for all its corporate emissions worldwide. Apple is planning to bring its entire carbon footprint to net zero 20 years earlier than the UNIPCC targets. A good international example is that their Montague windfarm in Oregon, USA is already one of Apple's largest renewable projects, with its 200 MW wind capacity. Apple will use its green wind electricity to power Apple's Prineville data centre in the USA (Apple, Apple commits to being 100% carbon neutral for its supply chain and products by 2030, USA July 2020).

Apple has said that their environmental innovations are not only good for the world but these should also help to make all Apple products more energy efficient. Apple is also planning to bring new sources of clean energy supplies online around the world. Apple is planning to provide more details on its approach to carbon neutrality together with a detailed roadmap, as competitors are actively reducing their climate change impacts. In the Apple 2020 Environmental Progress Report, Apple gave details on its corporate sustainability plans to reduce emissions by 75% by 2030 whilst developing innovative carbon removal solutions for the remaining 25% of its carbon footprints.

Over 80% of the renewable energy that Apple has sourced has come from various renewable projects that Apple has created. To support these efforts and beyond, Apple is establishing an Impact Accelerator Program that will focus on investing in minority-owned businesses that will drive positive outcomes in its supply chains and in communities that are disproportionately affected by environmental hazards. This new accelerator programme is part of Apple's recently announced US$100 million Racial Equity and Justice Initiative, which is focussing on education, economic equality and criminal justice reforms.

Apple's ten-year roadmap aims to lower their international emissions with a series of innovative actions, which will include new low-carbon product designs. Apple will continue to increase the use of low-carbon and recycled materials in its products, innovate in product recycling, and design products to be as energy efficient as possible.

Apple is also promoting recycling innovations. A good business example is that they have developed a new robot called "Dave" which will disassemble the Taptic Engine from their iPhones. This should help to better recover various key materials such as rare earth magnets and tungsten whilst also enabling recovery of steel. This is a new technical innovation in follow-up to its line of "Daisy" iPhone dis-assembly robots.

Apple's Material Recovery Lab in Austin, Texas, is focussing on researching new innovative electronics recycling technologies. Apple is now partnering with Carnegie Mellon University in USA to further develop various new recycling engineering solutions.

Apple has announced that all the iPhone, iPad, Mac and Apple Watch devices which were released in the recent years have been made with new recycled materials and contents. These include 100% recycled rare earth elements in the iPhone Taptic Engine, which is a first for Apple and for any smartphones globally.

Apple announced that it had decreased its carbon footprint by 4.3 million metric tonnes in 2019 through better designs and higher recycled content innovations in its various products. Over the past 11 years, Apple has reduced the average energy needed for its product use by 73%.

Apple is also improving their energy efficiency. They are identifying various new ways to lower energy use at their corporate facilities. They are also helping their various international supply chains to make the same energy improvements. Through a new partnership with Apple, the US-China Green Fund will invest US$100 million in accelerating various energy efficiency projects for Apple's suppliers. The number of facilities participating in Apple's Supplier Energy Efficiency Program grew to 92 in 2019. Together, they have avoided over 779,000 annualised metric tonnes of supply chain carbon emissions. Apple has also invested in energy efficiency upgrades to over 6.4 million square feet of new and existing buildings. These should help to lower their electricity needs by nearly one-fifth and save the company US$27 million in energy costs.

Apple is committed to achieving 100% renewable energy for all its operations globally. A good international business example is that a first-of-its-kind investment fund will help Apple and 10 of its suppliers in China to invest nearly US$300 million to develop renewable projects which should help to generate 1 GW of renewable energy. Apple also has commitments from over 70 of its international suppliers to use 100% renewable energy for Apple production. This is equivalent to nearly 8 GW in commitments to power the manufacturing of its products. Once completed, these commitments will help to avoid over 14.3 million metric tonnes of CO_2e emissions annually. This is equivalent to taking more than 3 million cars off the road each year.

New and completed renewable projects in USA, including Arizona, Oregon and Illinois, have helped to bring Apple's renewable capacity for its corporate operations to over 1 GW. This is equivalent to powering over 150,000 homes a year. Over 80% of the renewable energy that Apple has sourced for its various facilities are now from Apple created projects. These will also help to benefit local communities and other businesses.

Globally, Apple is launching one of the largest new solar arrays in Scandinavia. In addition, they are launching two new renewable projects which will also provide clean power to underserved communities in the Philippines and Thailand. Since 2014, all of Apple's data centres have been powered by 100% renewable energy.

Apple is also actively developing new process and material innovations so as to reduce their emissions further through technological improvements. A good innovation example is that Apple is supporting the development of the first-ever direct carbon-free aluminium smelting process through investments and collaboration with two of its aluminium suppliers. Apple has announced that the new low-carbon aluminium is currently being used in the production of its 16-inch MacBook Pro. Through partnerships with its suppliers, Apple has also reduced emissions from fluorinated gasses by more than 242,000 metric tonnes in 2019. Fluorinated gasses are used in the manufacturing of some consumer electronics components and have contributed significantly to global warming.

Apple is also active in carbon removal. These have included investments in forests and other nature-based solutions around the world. A good nature example is that Apple, in partnership with Conservation International, will invest in new nature projects, including a vital mangrove ecosystem in Colombia. Mangroves will not only protect the coasts but also help to support the livelihood of those communities where they grow. Scientists have shown that mangroves can store up to ten times more carbon than forests on land. Apple, through its partnership work with The Conservation Fund, the World Wildlife Fund and Conservation International, has helped to protect and improve the management of over 1 million acres of forests and natural climate solutions in China, the USA, Colombia and Kenya. A good conservation example is that Apple, in its partnership with Conservation International, is helping to restore degraded savannas in the Chyulu Hills region of Kenya. Apple is also partnering with Conservation International to protect and restore a 27,000-acre mangrove forest in Colombia.

International Chipmaker TSCMC Sustainability Net Zero Case Study

Taiwan Semiconductor Manufacturing Co Ltd (TSMC) is the world's largest contract chipmaker. TSMC has announced that they are aiming to achieve carbon neutrality with net zero emissions by 2050. TSMC has also said that they are deeply aware of the serious global climate change impacts. TSMC announced their commitment to shoulder their corporate responsibility to face the challenges of climate change.

In 2018, TSMC published its Climate Change Statement which stated that it will address climate change through the two key measures of climate impact mitigation and climate risk adaption. At the same time, TSMC adopted the Financial Stability Board's Task Force on Climate-related Financial Disclosures (TCFD) framework to identify and report on potential climate risks and opportunities, as well as to set measurement benchmarks and to manage targets. TSMC has been able to manage and lower the potential financial impacts of climate risks on its operations globally. They have disclosed these results in the TSMC Corporate Social Responsibility Report.

To further address stakeholders' concerns on climate change, TSMC has followed the TCFD framework and published their TCFD report in 2021. They have systematically disclosed their climate management strategy and net zero targets together with appropriate climate control measures. They have also provided a comprehensive description of TSMC's ongoing work and progress in responding to climate change.

In 2020, TSMC established its corporate Net Zero Project. In the same year, TSMC reported that their international offices around the world have achieved net zero emissions of GHGs. To meet its corporate goal of achieving carbon neutrality and net zero emissions by 2050, TSMC will set relevant new climate mitigation measures and emission reduction plans. They will also continue to strengthen their wide variety of green innovations, and actively adopt clean energy transition by shifting away from fossil energy and migrate to renewable energy.

TSMC has set their short-term goals of zero-emission growths by 2025, and of reducing emissions to 2020 levels by 2030. TSMC has announced that it will also continue to actively evaluate and invest in all types of opportunities to reduce carbon emissions.

TSMC has also become the world's first semiconductor company to join the RE100 alliance which commits all its member companies to achieving 100% renewable energy. TSMC will actively adopt the use of renewable energy to meet its short-term goal of zero-emissions growth by 2025.

Banks & Finance Companies Sustainability Net Zero Strategies

Leading banks and finance companies are recognising the importance of climate change and the net zero requirements. At COP26, many leading banks and financial institutions have announced that they are joining the new Glasgow Finance Alliance for Net Zero (GFANZ). Many international banks and financial services companies have been actively developing their new sustainability strategies and net zero plans. Two good global examples are HSBC and PWC. Details of their new sustainability net zero plans and strategies are summarised in two case studies below:

HSBC Sustainability Net Zero Carbon Neutrality Plans

HSBC is one of the largest international banks. They have announced their new corporate targets to achieve carbon neutrality plus net zero carbon emissions across their entire banking customer base and all their global banking operations by 2050 at the latest. They will also provide between US$750 billion and US$1 trillion (772 billion pounds) in climate financing and green investments to help the bank and its clients to make the required green transitions. This pledge is the strongest statement by HSBC on climate change to date.

However, some environmental groups have criticised HSBC for not taking more immediate actions to curb its financing to fossil fuels, especially oil and gas companies. HSBC is currently Europe's second-largest international financier of fossil fuels plus oil and gas companies (Reuter, HSBC targets net zero emissions by 2050, UK Oct 2020).

HSBC announced that it is aiming to achieve net zero emissions in its own banking operations by 2030. Other big UK banks, such as NatWest, have also set similar net zero goals. HSBC's aim to achieve net zero emission across its global operations, including its huge Asia-focussed client base, is one of the most significant pledges made by an international bank to date. Investors and NGOs will be closely monitoring HSBC on how quickly it will pursue its new net zero goals. In addition, HSBC has been careful to state their net zero ambitions mainly as aims or aspirations rather than hard legally binding commitments.

HSBC has come under increasing international pressure from responsible investors, activists, shareholders, politicians and NGOs. It is also facing strong scrutiny on its continual financing of some fossil fuel-linked companies and projects, especially in the developing markets. HSBC has said that it is focussing on expanding its capital market focussed carbon transition policies towards becoming broader ones that will encompass all its activities across financing, asset management, and corporate and retail banking.

HSBC has announced to the international markets that its corporate ambition will be to ensure that its total global financing by 2050 will be net zero. HSBC has said that it will apply a climate lens to its financing decisions plus it will also continue to take into account the unique conditions of its clients across developed and developing economies.

HSBC has said that it will, to help stakeholders to track its journey to net zero, use the science-based Paris Agreement Capital Transition Assessment tool (PACTA) and it will also report on its net zero progress regularly. In addition, HSBC has said that it will work with peers, central banks and industrial bodies to help create a globally consistent, future-proofed standard to measure financed emissions and to contribute to a functioning international carbon offset market.

HSBC has also announced that it will be aiming to invest US$100 million in clean technology, and at donating a further US$100 million towards climate innovation ventures and renewable energy sources. These are in addition to its previous commitment of providing funding to a new natural capital venture.

PWC Sustainability Net Zero Strategy and Plans Case Study

PWC is one of the biggest international financial service companies. It has announced that it will make a worldwide science-based commitment to reach net zero GHG emissions by 2030. It has committed to reducing its total GHG emissions by 50% in absolute terms by 2030, across the whole PWC operation networks. This will include a switch to 100% renewable electricity in all territories that they are operating in. They will also implement energy efficiency improvements in all their offices. PWC is planning to half their emissions associated with business travels and accommodation within a decade. In the 2019 financial year, emissions associated with their business flights alone represented around 85% of PWC's total carbon footprint. The COVID-19 pandemic has accelerated the shift to remote and home working. These have helped to demonstrate the feasibility of new client delivery models, as part of a longer-term transformation of their international financial services (PWC, Committing to Net Zero by 2030, PWC UK September 2020).

PWC has also announced that it will be investing in new carbon removal projects, including natural climate solutions. PWC announced that it will commit to a new corporate practice that for every tonne of CO_2 equivalent that they will emit, they will then remove a tonne of CO_2 from the atmosphere so as to achieve net zero climate impacts by 2030.

These new net zero commitments will build on their 2018 global environment commitments to improve energy efficiencies, go 100% renewable, and offset 100% air travel emissions from FY19 and residual energy use by FY22.

PWC is also working with their clients to accelerate net zero transformations across 157 countries. PWC will build on existing client work in sustainability and net zero transformations. They will also be infusing science-led climate analysis into their areas of service. A good international example is that the PWC Advisory practice will integrate climate risks into relevant engagements and client advisory work. They will be providing clients with various insights about climate risks and new green business opportunities as well as helping them to transform their business processes.

Another major focus area for PWC will be integrating climate-related and other ESG-related factors into their mainstream corporate disclosures and reporting plus governance processes. The PWC Assurance practice will support international organisations to develop high-quality climate disclosure frameworks and measurement standards. They will also help clients to embed these into their reporting and governance processes.

The PWC Tax practice will be helping clients to better understand how net zero transformations will impact their corporate tax strategy plus transparency and compliance obligations. They will also highlight relevant incentives and opportunities plus potential revenue impacts for both public and private sector organisations.

PWC is also working with governments and international organisations to help shape and accelerate the global climate and policy agenda. A good international business example is that PWC is supporting global efforts to develop transparent and robust ESG reporting frameworks and standards. These include working with the World Economic Forum International Business Council, the Financial Stability Board's TCFD, the Global Reporting Initiative (GRI), the Sustainability Accounting Standards Board (SASB), the International Integrated Reporting Council (IIRC) etc.

International State-Owned Enterprises Sustainability Net Zero Strategy Management

SOEs in both the emerging economies and developed countries have been growing and expanding rapidly to become world-class international companies in their countries and globally. It is conservatively estimated that SOEs globally have been contributing more than 10% of the combined sales of the world's largest businesses listed in the Forbes Global 2000. The proportion of SOEs, among the Fortune Global 500 companies, has also grown from 10% in 2005 to over 25% now. The combined SOE corporate sales revenues are currently accounting for more than 6% of the global gross domestic product (GDP) and are larger than the GDP of some key developed economies, including Germany or France. SOEs globally are also recognising the serious threats and risks from climate change. Many SOEs are actively developing their new sustainability strategies and net zero plans to cut their emissions to meet their Paris Agreement commitments.

Energy experts have highlighted that SOEs have been major players in both the fossil energy and electricity power sectors. SOEs have major investments in various fossil sectors, including oil, gas and coal. The Organisation for Economic Co-operation and Development (OECD) has reported that the total SOE investments could amount to over US$300 billion in the G20 countries. SOEs are also major players in the fossil-fuel markets. SOEs have been estimated to own roughly 60% of the coal mines and coal power plants. Experts have also reported that SOEs electricity power generation companies are currently owning more fossil fuel-based generation capacity than those owned by privately-owned electricity-generating companies. As a result, SOEs have been major producers of GHGs and are currently accounting for a substantial quantity of GHG emissions. Experts have estimated that the combined GHG emissions of the top 50 energy-related SOEs in the world will rank third in a list of country-level GHG emissions, just after China and the USA (OECD, SOE transition away from coal and coal-fired power, 2018).

At the same time, SOEs have continued to invest heavily in fossil resources and technologies. Experts have estimated that SOEs are currently responsible for two-thirds of the planned power investments globally, of which more than half are using fossil fuel-based technologies. The International Energy Agency (IEA) has found that, between 2012 and 2017, the share of global energy investment driven by SOEs has increased to 42%, with public sector investors found to be more resilient to changes in the markets for oil, gas and thermal power (IEA, 2018).

Many SOEs in emerging economies and developed countries around the world are beginning to appreciate the serious climate change challenges plus the urgent need for clean energy transition from fossil to clean renewable energy. Many SOEs have been developing new corporate sustainability strategies and net zero plans. They have started investing in new renewables and clean energy projects. New research on the SOE activities in fossil to renewable low-carbon transition has shown that SOEs have major influences on renewable investments, especially in emerging economies. State ownership of some power and utility SOEs has helped to drive these SOEs to invest more in new renewables capacity in line with their government's new clean energy policies. It is encouraging to note that recent research has shown that SOEs in OECD and G20 countries have more than doubled the share of clean renewable energy in their electricity capacity portfolios (OECD, Investment in Low Carbon Infrastructure, 2018).

Looking ahead, the International Renewable Energy Agency (IRENA) has estimated that clean renewable electricity technologies, with ongoing technology innovations, should become cost-competitive with, or even undercut, fossil fuels in the near future. This should further promote the clean energy transition of fossil power to clean renewable power generation (IRENA, 2018).

In addition to the rising cost-competitiveness of renewables, the declines in coal will be driven by global climate change improvements and new environmental policies. The IEA has estimated that, to keep the global temperature increase to well below 2°C, all coal-fired power plant emissions will have to be reduced by more than half by 2030 (IEA, 2018).

These global megatrends have driven more SOEs to develop new sustainability plans and net zero strategies. Many SOEs are reducing their GHG emissions and investing more in new renewables projects.

A good international SOE example is Vattenfall of Sweden. Vattenfall is fully owned by the Government of Sweden and it has invested in power generation facilities globally. Vattenfall has power generation assets in Finland, Denmark, Germany, Poland and the Baltic countries, among others. In 2010, Vattenfall's board and top management adopted new corporate sustainability targets and strategies for the SOE. These included reducing their CO2 GHG emissions by more than 30% by the 2020s. As part of the efforts by the SOE to meet these new targets, Vattenfall's management decided in 2014 to divest off all its lignite coal mines and associated coal-fired power plants in Eastern Germany. Vattenfall's investments for 2018 and 2019 were focussing on renewables including wind power and solar renewable energy together with decentralised digital power solutions plus advanced energy storage and e-mobility (Vattenfall, Road to Fossil Freedom, 2019).

The National Oil Companies (NOCs) in China have also been accelerating the development of their new sustainability plans and net zero strategies plus reducing their emissions and increasing their clean energy investments. More details are summarised in the case study below:

China's National Oil Company (NOC) Sustainability Net Zero Case Study

Chinese NOCs have been growing strongly in the last two decades. A good international example is that both CNPC and Sinopec have been ranked in the top ten largest companies globally in the Fortune 500 global ranking, with CNOOC also rising fast. They have established strong domestic positions in upstream oil and gas exploration and production together with midstream pipeline networks plus downstream refining and oil retailing. They have also been importing rising amounts of oil, gas and LNG to meet China's rising oil and gas demands. The leading Chinese NOCs have followed aggressive growth strategies and expanded into the clean energy sector plus petrochemical and chemical business sectors. In addition, they are also venturing overseas with aggressive acquisitions and are becoming leading global energy players (Wang, UK WEG China Oil Company Roundtable Speech, UK 4 March 2021).

China has pledged to achieve net zero emissions and carbon neutrality by 2060. This will be an important turning point and requirement for all the Chinese NOCs. They are already active in their clean energy transitions by shifting from fossil fuel to clean energy sources. The scale of these tasks is huge and details of the net zero roadmap for China are still being developed.

For the fossil-fuel markets in China, the domino effects of the Chinese energy policy will be huge, as China is the largest energy consumer and producer in the world. To achieve a 1.5C scenario, China's total energy consumptions will have to peak in 2030. This will be followed by a gradual decline to 2060. Then, over 85% of the total energy consumption and over 90% of the power generation in China should come from non-fossil-fuel sources.

China's leading NOCs, including PetroChina, Sinopec and CNOOC, have been developing their new sustainability plans plus net zero targets and carbon neutrality strategies. These come as global energy majors like BP & Shell have announced their new investment plans on renewable energy assets in a low-carbon future. CNPC and PetroChina have become the first Asian state-owned firms to set a target for near-zero emissions by 2050. Sinopec, the second-largest energy company in China, has announced its new sustainability strategy and net zero plans to achieve carbon neutrality by 2050, which is a decade ahead of China's 2060 national net zero-emissions target. CNOOC is implementing the goal to have CO_2 emissions peak before 2030 and achieve carbon neutrality before 2060. CNOOC will be implementing its sustainability strategy and net zero plans with various low-carbon developments. These will include clean energy development, energy-saving, emission reduction projects and efficient energy utilisation.

Sinopec has become the world's largest oil refiner. It is aiming to lead China's green hydrogen push. It is planning to build new hydrogen refuelling stations alongside its existing petrol stations on the east coast. These are strategic moves which Sinopec will proceed with cautiously in line with China's 14th Five-Year Plan (FYP).

China's largest offshore oil explorer CNOOC is also actively expanding into renewables. A good renewable example is that CNOOC is starting its first offshore windfarm.

China's demands for natural gas, which emits half the CO_2 of coal, is set to rise to 15% of the total primary energy consumption by 2030. This is spurred by the increased demands from power generation and residential sectors. Chinese NOCs are active in the natural gas sector. PetroChina has currently included gas power generation into its green investments. CNOOC is planning to raise its natural gas share in total outputs from 19% currently to 30% by 2025. Sinopec is also planning to double its shale gas outputs during the same period.

China's rapidly growing solar and wind markets are already crowded with private manufacturers and state-owned power generators. These are leaving limited space for the NOCs to enter these renewable business sectors in China. So CNPC, Sinopec and CNOOC are developing new innovative renewable market entry strategies. A good business example is that Sinopec is concentrating on new biomass and geothermal developments which have good linkages and synergies with its existing oil and exploration businesses. CNOOC is developing offshore wind generation which has good synergies with its offshore oil and gas platform operation expertise.

The Chinese NOCs are also actively improving their energy efficiencies plus energy-saving management. A good energy example is that Sinopec is planning to implement an "energy efficiency improvement" plan that will accelerate industrial structure adjustments plus phase-out their outdated production capacities.

Chinese NOCs are also working on GHG recovery and utilisation, including carbon capture storage and utilisation (CCSU). A good CCSU business example is that Sinopec will be promoting the recovery and utilisation of high-concentration CO_2 tail gas from their various refining and chemical enterprises. They will also be undertaking CO_2 flooding field tests and methane gas release recovery. The carbon trading transaction volume of enterprises participating in the pilot project has reached over 11 million tonnes of carbon reductions.

Looking ahead, Chinese NOCs are committed to actively developing and implementing their new sustainability strategies plus their net zero carbon reduction plans in line with China's 14th FYP and China's pledge to reach net zero carbon neutrality by 2060.

6
Developments in Clean Energy Transition

冰冻三尺, 非一日之寒

Bīng dòng sān chǐ, fēi yī rì zhī hán

It takes more than one cold day for a river to freeze to three feet deep. Rome was not built in one day.

Global Clean Energy Transition and Net Zero Overviews

The COP26 meeting in Glasgow has highlighted that clean energy transition is an important and essential element of the new sustainability strategy and net zero plans of various governments, countries and companies globally. Many governments have developed and enacted new policies and regulations to accelerate clean energy transitions in their countries. These are in-line with their commitments at the Paris Agreement and to reduce greenhouse gas (GHG) emissions globally. The new clean energy transition policies enacted by many countries have started to significantly change their primary energy mix with reductions in fossil-fuel consumptions whilst boosting clean renewable energy applications.

Clean energy transition is an important pathway to transform the global energy sectors toward sustainable clean energy by transitioning from fossil-based energy and fuels to zero-carbon clean energy resources. The objective is to reduce carbon dioxide (CO_2) and GHG emissions to acceptable levels. These will also help to limit the climate change impacts and to reduce global warming in-line with the Paris Agreement targets. Clean energy transitions will involve countries and companies actively shifting their energy production and consumption away from fossil sources which release a lot of GHGs, to clean energy sources that release little to no GHGs. Key clean energy sources include renewables, hydropower, wind, solar, biofuel etc. Other key energy transition improvement

DOI: 10.4324/9781003142348-6

strategies will include reducing the carbon intensity of the energy supply mix, increasing energy efficiency, prioritising environmental protection, improving actions based on science, plus promoting environmental education and awareness. Clean energy transitions should help to reduce GHG emissions and generate broader socio-economic benefits. These benefits should include reduced pollutions, better air qualities, lower human health impacts, reduction of ozone layer damage, depletion of natural resources plus generation of new green jobs and low-carbon start-ups.

Clean renewable energy investments globally have grown by over US$1 trillion over the last decade in different countries across the world. International Renewable Energy Agency (IRENA) has also reported that the global clean renewable energy growths and transformations have already helped to create over 10 million new jobs in the clean energy sector in various countries. Looking ahead, it is expected that clean renewable energy growth should continue with annual investments of over US$200 billion per year for the foreseeable future (IRENA, 2018).

The global energy demands have been growing slowly with low demand growth rates of about 0.9% over the five-year period of 2011–2016. In 2017, the global energy demands increased by over 2%. However, global energy demand in 2020 fell sharply by 4% with the global COVID-19 pandemic. This was the largest global energy decline since World War II and the largest ever absolute decline. Looking ahead, global energy demands are likely to rise again as countries globally recover from the COVID-19 pandemic. This may result in global energy demands surpassing the pre-COVID-19 levels.

An analysis of the energy growths of different countries has shown that more than 40% of the energy growths in recent years have been driven by China and India, which have been the two fastest growing major economies globally. It is also concerning to see that 72% of the increased energy uses have been met by fossil sources or fossil fuels. Only a quarter of the energy rise was met by renewables with the remainder by nuclear energy (IEA, Energy & CO2 Report, 2017).

With clean energy transition, natural gas demands globally have grown faster than oil with annual growth rates of around 3% year on year. These natural gas growths have been driven by many countries and companies which have viewed natural gas as a cleaner transitional fuel in their energy mix. China alone has accounted for almost 30% of the global gas growths in recent years. In the past decade, about half of the global gas demand growths have come from the power and electricity generation sectors, plus the industrial and building sectors (Wang, Renewable Energy Management, Routledge UK 2020).

It is good to see that renewables and clean energy sources have enjoyed the highest growth rates of any energy sources in recent years. Renewables and clean energies are currently helping to meet a quarter of the global energy demand growths. It is interesting to note that China and the USA have led the renewable and clean energy growth globally. Together, they have contributed around 50% of the recent increases in renewables-based electricity generation capacities globally. The EU, India and Japan have also contributed significantly to the renewable transformation globally. Wind power has also accounted for 36% of the growth in renewable-based power outputs.

The global electricity demands have increased by 3.1%, which was significantly higher than the overall increases in energy demands. China and India together accounted for 70% of these electricity growths with their high economic growth. These increases in electricity demands have been mainly met by power generated by gas, coal, renewables and nuclear energies globally.

Looking ahead, the global energy consumption is expected to rise by over 40% from now to 2030–2035. The bulk of the new incremental energy growths, estimated to be over 90%, are expected to be generated by the emerging economies. China and India energy growths are expected to account for more than half of the total incremental energy increases globally with their continued high economic growths. By 2035, the energy consumptions in the non-Organisation for Economic Cooperation and Development (OECD) emerging economies are expected to increase by 65–70% relative to their 2012 levels (IEA, World Energy Outlooks, 2018).

Energy experts have also forecasted that after more than a century of continuous energy growths, global energy demand growths are likely to peak or plateau around 2030–2035. The main strategic drivers include the industrial sector shifting to lower consumption service industries, heavy industry getting more efficient, improved energy efficiencies etc. A good international energy example is that China's total energy consumption for steel production by 2035 should be halved as a result of the steel companies in China using more efficient blast and arc furnaces (McKinsey, Global Energy Perspective, 2019).

Clean renewable energy applications around the world are expected to rise for the foreseeable future. Wind and solar powers currently only constitute a small slice of the overall energy mixes globally. However, they have accounted for more than half of the new energy capacity that has been installed in the recent years. Looking ahead, experts have forecasted that new solar or wind technologies should enable solar and wind power generation to become cost competitive against fossil power generation. As a result, new wind and solar power generation capacities have been forecasted to increase significantly by a factor of 13 and 60, by 2050. Looking ahead to 2035, clean renewable energy sources are expected to make up more than 50% of the total power generation capacities globally.

Looking ahead, energy experts have also predicted that fossil-fuel growths are likely to decline very fast in future. However, fossil-fuel uses are still unlikely to vanish completely by the end of 2100 around the world. Looking ahead, the growths in oil and coal demands globally are expected to slow down further. Experts are forecasting oil peaking in the early 2030s. Gas demands globally are expected to grow until 2035. This is mainly due to its currently perceived role as an interim transitional fuel in many countries globally. Experts have forecasted that natural gas growths are likely to plateau around 2035 and then decline post-2035, largely because of increasing competition from renewables. These are likely to lead to a peaking in global carbon emissions in the period 2025–2035. This will then be followed by a likely decline in carbon emissions globally with an eventual fall of roughly 20% in carbon emissions by 2050 (McKinsey, Global Energy Perspective, 2019).

In comparison to emerging economies, the energy demands of the advanced developed economies of North America and Europe are expected to grow only very slowly in the short and medium terms. Looking ahead to beyond 2030, the energy demands of the advanced developed countries could even fall further if both their clean energy transition policies and energy efficiency improvement plans would work as planned (Wang, Energy Markets in Emerging Economies Growth Strategy & Outlooks, 2016).

Looking ahead to 2035, oil is expected to be the slowest growing of all the major fossil fuels globally. The bulk of the new net oil demand growths are expected to come from the emerging economies outside the OECD. The combined oil demand growths from China, India and the Middle East will likely account for the bulk of the new net oil demand growths globally. The key emerging economies in Asia are also expected to show the largest growths in liquid fossil oil fuels consumption globally, with China accounting for the bulk of the total increases. The non-OECD emerging economies share of the world liquid fuel consumptions is expected to grow substantially over time. These are driven by their higher economic growths and their transport sector growths.

Coal is expected to, after oil, be the slowest growing fossil fuel globally. Most of the net growths, estimated to be above 85%, in the global coal demands to 2035 are expected to come from China, India and emerging economies. Experts expect that these countries would be continuing with their coal power generation applications for the time being. At COP26, many countries have agreed to a phasing-out of coal applications globally but no firm dates have been agreed.

Natural gas is generally expected to be the fastest growing of all the fossil fuels. This is mainly due to its currently perceived role as a cleaner interim transitional fossil fuel in many countries. Non-OECD emerging economies are expected to generate over 75% of the new gas demand growths globally in the next decade. Liquefied natural gas (LNG) exports from the major gas producers to the key gas-consuming emerging economies are expected to grow more than twice as fast as the averaged global gas consumption growths.

Looking ahead, nuclear energy generation is also expected to continue to rise to 2035. China, India and Russia are expected to account together for over 95% of the growth of nuclear power globally. In the developed countries, especially USA and EU, nuclear power outputs are expected to decline with some planned plant closures. Some EU countries are developing new nuclear power strategies and plans to improve their energy security and to reduce their reliance on Russian gas imports.

Many countries are also actively developing hydrogen as a future clean fuel. Hydrogen produces zero emissions at the various points of use. It can be stored and transported at high energy density in liquid or gaseous forms. It can be combusted or used in fuel cells to generate heat and electricity. Natural gas is about 8.5 times as dense as hydrogen. The denser natural gas is easier and more energy efficient to move than hydrogen. However, hydrogen partially makes up for that fact by being more energy dense per unit mass. Hydrogen is about three times more energy dense per unit mass than natural gas. Energy experts have forecasted that the production cost of green hydrogen is likely to reduce significantly in the next ten years with the various international developments and innovations globally. These innovations and cost reductions should help to promote more new green hydrogen clean fuel applications globally.

Looking ahead, experts have forecasted that the clean energy transition and renewable energy growths globally will continue with annual investments of over US$200 billion per year for the foreseeable future. The major growths areas will be mostly in the solar and wind renewables energy sectors. Hydroelectric power is also expected to grow moderately to 2035. Nearly half of the new net hydroelectric power growths are expected to come from China, India and Brazil. There will also be growths in the biofuel and geothermal sectors in various countries globally. There will also be major international developments in green hydrogen developments. These clean renewable energy applications will contribute to emissions reductions globally. These should help countries globally to better meet their Paris Agreement commitments (REN, Global Status Report, 2018).

COP26 Clean Energy Transition & Net Zero Highlights

The important international COP26 meeting, held in Glasgow in November 2021, has highlighted that clean energy transition is an essential and critical element of the new sustainability strategy and net zero plans of various governments and companies globally. Many countries and governments have developed and enacted new policies and regulations to accelerate clean energy transitions as part of their new sustainability strategy and net zero plans. These should help them to better meet their Paris Agreement commitments. Looking ahead, clean energy transition and clean renewable energy growth are expected to accelerate. These are driven by the various new government policies and clean energy targets announced at and around the COP26 meeting. Some of the key announcements and their details will be discussed in more detail below with international examples:

Three big European power companies have raised their 2030 clean energy transition targets. Enel announced that they are aiming to have 154 GW of renewable and battery storage capacity in place by 2030. Enel has also brought its net zero target forward by ten years to 2040, from 2050. SSE has cut its targeted Scope 1 and 2 emissions for 2030 to about half of what it has previously planned. SSE is also planning to treble its renewable energy outputs in the foreseeable future. RWE is planning to add 2.5 GW of renewables capacity per year out to 2030. This is a significant increase from their previously planned target of only 1.5 GW per year (COP26 UN Climate Champions, The Power and Freedom of Net Zero, UK March 14, 2022).

The adoption of the Versailles Declaration at COP26 has meant that the EU Member States have asked the EU Commission to prepare a detailed plan to cut EU gas dependency on Russian gas imports. This should help to improve EU energy security and promote the growth of clean energy applications in EU.

The EuroAfrica Interconnector will be providing 2,000 MW of clean electricity between Egypt, Cyprus, Greece and Europe. This will help to form a "clean electricity highway" connecting the national electricity grids of Egypt, Cyprus and Greece through a 1,396 km subsea HVDC cable.

The Xlinks Morocco-UK Power Project will be a new clean electricity generation facility that is entirely powered by solar and wind energy combined with a battery storage facility. It will be located in Morocco's renewable energy rich region of Guelmim Oued Noun. It will cover an approximate area of 1,500 km^2. It will be connected exclusively to the UK via a new 3,800 km HVDC subsea cable for green electricity exports. The project is also facilitating just transition by creating nearly 10,000 green jobs during construction in the region, whilst simultaneously creating associated jobs in the UK via submarine power connectors.

Coal was a major area of discussions at COP26. After intensive debates, 44 countries and 32 companies and regions have agreed to sign the COP26 President Alok Sharma's statement on clean energy transition from coal to clean power.

The Powering Past Coal Alliance also welcomed seven new subnational governments, three new energy companies and 11 new financial institutions joining the alliance. They and other members of the alliance are committed to ending unabated coal power uses globally.

The Beyond Oil and Gas Alliance was launched on 10 November 2022 at COP26. It is an international coalition of governments and stakeholders working together to facilitate the managed phase-out of oil and gas productions in designated countries globally.

The Africa Green Hydrogen Alliance and LatAm Green Hydrogen Alliance have been launched at COP26. They are made up of countries and industry leaders from different regions globally who support accelerating green hydrogen and zero-carbon industry developments.

The Green Hydrogen Catapult announced at COP26 that their collaborations should help to drive the costs of green hydrogen productions across a key tipping point to below US$2/kg. They have also increased their green hydrogen production target from 25 to 45 GW over the past year. They are promoting an international collaborative approach to scaling up green hydrogen productions in both developing and developed countries globally.

Twelve countries have committed to the largest increase ever in product and energy efficiency. A global goal of doubling the energy efficiency of lighting, cooling, motors and refrigeration by 2030 was supported by the Climate Group's EP100 initiative of 129 international businesses.

The Global Energy Alliance for People & Planet announced that it will be mobilising at least US$10 billion for the rollout of renewable electricity for a billion people by 2030. It has issued a call for transformational country programmes. These should help to unleash a robust pipeline of renewable projects in different countries globally.

The plan of establishing a Global Offshore Wind Alliance in 2022 was announced at COP26. It aims to rally governments and international businesses to join forces to increase their offshore wind ambitions. These should help to implement more offshore wind power generation towards 2030 and beyond.

The new International Sustainability Standards Board (ISSB) has agreed to develop a new global environmental, social and governance (ESG) baseline and framework for high-quality sustainability reporting and ESG disclosure standards. This should be in the public interest, as it will promote better global transparency and standards. It also marks the start of international collaborations between different leading investor-focused sustainability disclosure organisations, with them agreeing to collaborate together in one international board.

The Race to Zero's power producers have announced that they are aiming to reach over 750 GW of renewable energy by 2030. They are also promoting renewable electricity demand growth globally.

Ten international pharmaceutical companies announced that they will be joining forces to cut their indirect emissions by shifting to renewable energy. The pharmaceutical and medical technology sectors have joined the Race to Zero campaign to halve their emissions within the 2020s.

Global Energy Transition and Clean Energy Growths Outlooks

Global investments in clean energy transition plus clean renewable power and clean fuels have been growing strongly in recent years. Global spendings on clean energy transitions to low-carbon energy sources have risen by more than a quarter in 2021. These have been driven mainly by the growth in electric vehicles (EVs) and new renewable power installations globally. Total clean energy transition investments have reached US$755 billion in 2021. This is a significant jump of 27% from a year earlier in 2020. These record-breaking investment figures have shown that there are strong investor appetites for the growth of clean energy applications and development of renewable technologies. These should all contribute to preventing the worst effects of global warming. However, experts have advised that investments have to ramp up significantly in future to achieve the aspired target of net zero carbon emissions by 2050.

Looking ahead, experts have estimated that some US$2.1 trillion of investments will be required in the clean energy transition sector from 2022 to 2025. These investments will amount to nearly three times of the 2021 levels. These investment figures will include spendings on renewable electricity, electrified heat, energy storage and nuclear power. New government sustainability strategy and net zero plans plus new energy transition policies across all regions will likely generate even more green investments globally.

In 2021, the biggest share of green investments and energy transition spendings have gone to new renewable energy projects, such as wind farms and solar parks. The renewable sector has attracted investments of some US$366 billion in 2021. This was a net increase of 6.5% from the 2020 green investments figure. Most of the new renewable investments have concentrated in Asia. In the Americas, Europe, the Middle East and Africa regions, their green investments in new renewable projects in 2021 were almost similar or flat when compared to 2020.

Renewable energy capacities globally will need to grow rapidly to provide sufficient amounts of clean power for countries to reduce their emissions and meet their Paris Agreement commitments. These will include displacing fossil fuels power generation from the world's electric grids and replacing these by clean renewable power generations. In addition, more clean electricity generation will be required to meet new sources of clean electricity demands, especially those for EVs charging.

Investments in the electrified transportation sectors have risen significantly globally. These have included EVs, zero-emission vehicles plus their supporting infrastructure, including EV charging and batteries. Their total green investments have risen by 77% in 2021 to US$273 billion globally. Experts have forecasted that these green investment figures will likely have to rise even further in future and these are likely to surpass the total investments on renewable energy (Bloomberg NEF, Energy Transition Investments 2021, US 2022).

Global investments in clean renewable energies have continued to be focusing primarily on the solar and wind renewable power sectors. Asset financing of green utility projects, such as wind farms and solar parks, has dominated global clean renewable investments in recent years. There have also been significant cost reductions in both the solar and wind renewable power generation sectors in recent years. These significant cost reductions have been achieved with various new technology innovations and new cost reduction measures. Looking ahead, renewable energies are likely to become cost competitive against fossil fuels and fossil power generation in the near future. This should promote more clean renewable power projects and investments (IRENA, 2018).

The global clean renewable power generation sector has continued to attract far more clean investments than for fossil-fuel power generation plants or nuclear power plants. A good international example is that in 2016, it was calculated that nearly US$250 billion of clean investments have been committed to construct new renewable power generation plants globally. These clean renewable investments were about double that of the US$134 billion of committed investments for new fossil and nuclear power plants. These included some US$114 billion of investments in new fossil fuel-fired generating capacity and US$30 billion for new nuclear power capacity. Overall, clean renewable power generation has been accounting for over 60% of the total new power-generating capacity investments globally in recent years (Wang, IOD Climate Finance Green Investment Paper, 2018).

Globally, clean renewables energy investments in the developing countries and emerging economies have overtaken those in the developed countries for the first time in 2015. However, in 2016, clean investments in developed countries retook their lead over the developing countries. These have mainly resulted from the new clean energy transition and the clean energy policies that have been introduced by various governments globally in-line with their Paris Agreement commitments. The green investment trends in the renewable energy sector have been varying widely by regions globally. China has been leading the global renewable energy investments with about 30–35% of the global investments. Europe was second at 25% and the USA was third with 20%, whilst Asia-Oceania was fourth at 10–15%. The Latin America, Middle East and Africa regions have each accounted for about 3–5% of the global renewable investments (Wang, Renewable Management in Emerging Economies, Routledge UK 2020).

The top ten countries globally with the highest clean energy investments have included three emerging countries and seven developed countries. The top five countries included China, the USA, the UK, Japan and Germany. The next five countries included India, Brazil, Australia, Belgium and France.

However, there have also been significant increases in clean energy investments recently in some specific countries across the world. A good country example is Thailand, which has increased its renewable investments by 4–5% to US$1.5–2 billion. These investments have led Thailand to become the Asia's emerging economy with the third highest clean renewable energy investments, after China and India (UNEP, Renewable Investment Global Trends Report, 2019).

In recent years, renewable power generation has been achieving their largest annual capacity increases. These have been driven by the new clean energy transition policies and regulations that have been enacted by most countries in-line with their Paris Agreement commitments. Solar PV has seen record new capacity additions in emerging economies and developed countries globally in recent years. These have accounted for more new capacity additions than other renewables and fossil power-generating technologies. Solar PV has represented about 45–50% of newly installed clean renewable energy power capacity globally. Wind and hydropower have accounted for most of the remaining new renewable power capacity additions globally. Wind power has contributed about 30–40% and hydropower has contributed about 15%.

Experts have calculated that globally more new clean renewable energy power capacities have been added annually, than all the fossil-fuel capacities combined in recent years. These have been driven by both the new clean energy policies enacted by different governments and renewable power generation becoming cost competitive against fossil power generations. Experts have also reported that renewable power generation has grown to supplying about a quarter, near to 25%, of the global electricity demands. Hydropower has been providing the majority of the renewable power at over 16%. The other renewable power sources, including solar, wind, geothermal and biopower, have been supplying the remaining 9% of global renewable power consumption.

The top countries with installed clean renewable electric power generation capacity have continued to be China, the USA, Brazil, Germany and Canada. China has continued to be the global renewable power leader, with more than one-quarter of the world's clean renewable power installed capacity.

The ongoing growth and geographical expansion of renewable energy have also been driven by new energy policies plus continued technology innovations and cost reductions in renewable technologies. Significant cost reductions have been achieved in both solar PV and wind power with new technological innovations and manufacturing cost-cutting initiatives. Solar PV and onshore wind power have already become cost competitive against power generation by fossil fuels and nuclear power generation in an increasing number of countries globally. These have been due, in part, to new renewable innovations plus the declines in component prices and improvements in generation efficiency. A good international example is that the competitive bid prices for new off-shore wind power stations have reduced significantly in Europe in recent years. These have contributed to making wind power more attractive for both onshore and offshore applications.

These clean renewables energy cost reductions are particularly important for developing countries and emerging economies. These have enabled to make new clean renewable energy installations more attractive. In particular, new renewable electrical supply systems have become attractive for clean electricity supplies to remote and difficult-to-access locations. These include islands or isolated rural communities where electricity prices have previously been high and their access to traditional national electricity grid connections has traditionally been difficult and uneconomical in the past.

Many developing countries will be bringing online an increasing amount of new power-generating capacity in order to meet the rapidly rising electricity demands from their growing populations and communities. They have increasingly turned to clean renewable technologies which might be grid-connected or off-grid. They have also been introducing new supporting policies such as competitive tendering or feed-in tariffs (FITs) in order to support their new clean renewables energy growths. A good international example is the growth of new clean renewables electricity generation systems integrated with advanced IT distributed power systems and energy storage systems. These advanced integrated renewable energy systems have become particularly attractive for supplying clean electricity to remote rural communities and villages in developing economies worldwide.

Looking ahead, IEA has forecasted that the pace of clean energy transition and clean energy growth in different countries globally is likely to accelerate further in future. They have forecasted that clean energy renewable capacity growths globally should be on track to accelerate across the globe in the foreseeable future. China and the EU are set to overshoot their current clean energy targets. There will also be significant renewable growths in the USA and India. These significant renewable growths are being driven by improved competitiveness plus ambitious clean energy goals and new clean energy policy supports (IEA, Energy Transition Outlooks, Paris 2022).

The China clean energy transition and net zero case study, with relevant clean energy details and examples, will be given below in this chapter:

China Clean Energy Transition and Net Zero Case Study

The recent economic growths of China have created one of the biggest and fastest growing energy markets globally. The energy markets in China have been undergoing significant clean energy transitions recently. These have been driven by China's new sustainability strategy and carbon neutrality net zero policies which are in-line with China's international pledge to achieve carbon neutrality and net zero emissions by 2060. Experts are optimistic that China should be able to reduce their emissions nationality so as to achieve their carbon neutrality and net zero-emission goals by 2060 plus meet their Paris Agreement commitments.

The clean energy transitions in China have already resulted in significant reductions in China's fossil-fuel consumptions, especially in gasoline and diesel. Looking ahead, China's fossil fuels and oil products consumption will most likely reduce further in the foreseeable future. On the other hand, China's natural gas and clean renewable energy applications have been growing significantly. Looking ahead, clean energy applications should continue growing for the foreseeable future. Details of China's clean energy transition will be discussed in this case study with relevant business examples below (Wang, House of Lords WEG Paper, 2018).

In recent years, China has been leading the global renewable energy investments. China alone has accounted for over 30% of the clean renewable investments of the whole world. Europe was second at 25% and the USA was third with 19%, whilst Asia-Oceania was fourth at 11%. The three regions of Latin Americas, Middle East and Africa have each accounted for 3% of the global renewable investments (REN, Global Status Report, 2018).

On renewable and clean energy investments, the China Government National Energy Agency (NEA) has announced that China is planning to invest some 2.5 trillion yuan or over US$360 billion into new renewable projects in China, in-line with their National Five-Year Plans (FYP). They have also announced that China, which is now the world's largest energy market, will undergo significant clean energy transformations. It is planned that China will shift away from coal power generation towards using natural gas and clean renewable power generation. They have also forecasted that these higher renewables and clean energy investments in China should help to create more than 13 million new green jobs nationally in China. The China NEA has also forecasted that the total installed renewable power generation capacity in China, compromising of wind, hydro, solar and nuclear power together, should be contributing to about half of the new electricity generation capacities in China by 2030 (China NDRC, 13th Five Year Plan, 2016).

The China National Development and Reform Commission (NDRC) has said that solar power will be receiving some 1 trillion yuan or over US$140 billion of new planned green investments. China is planning to increase its solar power capacity by five times. This is estimated to be equivalent to installing about 1,000 major new solar power plants across China. In addition, some 700 billion yuan or US$100 billion of new investments are being planned to go into new windfarms across China. Another 500 billion yuan or over US$70 billion of new green investments are planned to go into new hydropower stations across China. New green investments by China into new tidal and geothermal power generation facilities are also planned in future. In addition, there are major new developments in new green hydrogen productions.

In addition, China has announced its new national 'Ecological Civilization' environmental transformation programme. This national programme is planned to generate new green renewable investments of between US$470 billion and US$630 billion in the period up to 2030.

Leading economists have forecasted that the China Central Government will only be providing some 15% of these new green investments from public funds. The private sector, companies and businesses in China will have to generate sufficient extra new green finance to fund at least 85% of the required future green investments across China. These planned new green investments should also help to promote more economic growths and developments of various Public Private Partnerships (PPP) across China.

In addition, China has been introducing a new China Carbon Emission Trading Scheme (CCETS) nationally in different phases. They have already introduced the CCETS for the power sector in China in the first phase, as it is one of the highest emission sectors. They are planning to expand the CCETS to cover other important industrial sectors in future. The introduction of the new national CCETS scheme is estimated to create new carbon trading and financing values ranging from US$9 to 60 billion in future. In addition, these should create many new green jobs in the growing green finance and carbon trading sectors in China.

The growth of new energy vehicles and EVs has also been encouraged in the China government policies. China is already one of the world's largest EV markets. Experts have forecasted that there should be further significant growth of EVs in China in future.

These planned new green investments and climate financing in China should create excellent opportunities for international cooperations. These should also promote good opportunities for knowledge sharing and cooperation between the leading international banks, finance houses, investment firms plus professional service companies globally with their equivalent companies and counterparts in China.

Global Clean Energy Innovations and Cost Reductions Outlooks

The ongoing developments in clean renewable energy technologies have led to many new innovations and significant cost reductions in various renewable technologies. Large cost reductions have been achieved, particularly for solar PV and wind power generations. Both solar PV and onshore wind power have become cost competitive against new fossil fuels and nuclear power generation in a rising number of locations globally. These have been due, in part, to declines in component prices and improvements in generation efficiency. A good international example is that the competitive bid prices for offshore wind power generation have dropped significantly in Europe recently. These have made wind renewable power plants, both onshore and offshore, more attractive green investment versus traditional fossil power generation plants (Wang, Renewable Energy Management, Routledge UK 2020).

IRENA has reported, in their recent Global Renewable Cost Analysis Report, that the costs of generating power from onshore wind have been reduced by over 20% since 2010 whilst the cost of solar photovoltaic (PV) electricity has also been reduced by over 70% in the same time period. With further renewables power generation cost reductions expected for these and other clean renewable energy options, IRENA has forecasted that key renewable energy technologies should be competitive on price basis against fossil power generation by 2025. Globally, solar PV plus onshore and offshore wind power schemes have reduced in costs significantly, with various innovation and cost reductions. They are now cost competitive against fossil power generation in most countries globally. IRENA has forecasted that offshore wind and Concentrated Solar Power (CSP) power generation costs should be further reduced to a range of US$0.06–US$0.10 per KwH by 2025. These should enable all the key renewable technologies to become cost competitive against traditional fossil power generation options in the near future (IRENA, Global Renewable Cost Analysis Report, 2021).

The latest analysis by Bloomberg New Energy Finance (BNEF) has also shown that the benchmark levelised cost of electricity (LCOE), for offshore wind power generation, has fallen by over 20% in recent years. LCOE aims to measure the all-in costs of producing a megawatt-hour (MWh) of electricity from a new project. LCOE will take into account all the various costs of development, construction and equipment, financing, feedstock, operation and maintenance which are all required to support the electricity power generation facilities. Onshore wind and PV solar power generation have also become cheaper. The improvements in the cost-competitiveness of these low-carbon renewable options have been achieved due to a combination of technology innovations, greater economies of scale, stiffer price competitions and manufacturing improvements. The LCOE per MWh for onshore wind, solar PV and offshore wind power generation has been reduced by some 50%, 85% and 55%, respectively, since 2010. These major cost reductions have resulted from new innovations and cheaper components. The global over-supply of renewable modules has also resulted in sharp price reductions.

Various renewable innovation and cost reductions have enabled solar PV and onshore wind power generation to become the cheapest sources of new bulk renewable power generation in most countries. Offshore wind power generation has often been seen as a relatively expensive power generation option when compared to onshore wind or solar PV. However, various recent changes and improvements are helping to make offshore wind power generation more attractive. A good international example is the sharp reductions in the capital costs of large offshore wind facilities resulting from larger advanced wind turbines together with new lighter stronger wind turbine blade materials.

A major problem for renewable power generation has been that they are dependent on variable sunlight and wind availabilities. These have produced intermittent electricity supplies that are unattractive and impracticable for the power industries and cities electricity supplies. In the past, expensive battery storage systems were required to ensure continuous power supply and grid stability. In recent years, there have been interesting innovative developments of a new generation of dispatchable baseload (24/7) renewable energy systems coupled with advance energy storage technologies. These new integrated systems can potentially help to generate reliable and affordable stable green electricity supplies to industrial and residential consumers. These should help to supply stable green renewable power on a continuous reliable basis, which will be independent of the variable sunlight and wind availabilities.

Clean energy power storage systems have shown significant innovations and cost reductions in recent years. One of the most striking cost reductions has occurred in lithium-ion batteries. Experts have shown that the benchmark LCOE for lithium-ion batteries has fallen significantly. These significant cost reductions have helped to open up many new interesting opportunities for many clean renewable power storage system developments. Battery power storage systems integrated with solar or wind power projects are starting to compete strongly in many markets globally against fossil power generation options. In many cases, clean renewable power generation plants have not required any government subsidies to be cost competitive against coal-fire and gas-fired generation for the provision of dispatchable power. These new clean renewable power generation units integrated with advanced energy storage options should be able to deliver clean power reliably whenever the grid needs the power. This is a significant improvement for renewable power supplies which in the past have only been available when the wind is blowing or the sun is shining.

Electricity demands in cities globally are also fluctuating during the day, with pronounced peaks and lows inter-day. Meeting the peak power demands has previously been dominated by fossil power generation, such as coal power generation, open-cycle gas turbines and gas reciprocating engines. These traditional fossil power generation routes will now face strong competition from the new clean renewable power generation units integrated with advanced power storage systems, together with digital distributed power management systems. Experts have shown that these new integrated renewable power generation systems with advance storage and management systems should be able to provide reliable electricity supplies around the clock to industrial and residential consumers with all the latest developments (BNEF, Battery Power's Latest Plunge in Costs, 2019).

The new clean renewables power systems integrated with battery storage system and distributed power management systems are particularly important and attractive for developing and emerging economies. These should make clean renewable energy installations much more attractive, particularly to provide electricity supplies to remote locations, such as islands or isolated rural communities. Traditionally electricity supplies to these remote communities and village have been limited, as it has been very expensive to connect them to national grid systems. Many developing countries have increasingly turned to clean renewable power supply with advanced power storage and management systems, which might be on-grid or off-grid. They have also been introducing supporting policies such as tendering or FITs to support their new clean renewables energy growths.

A good international example is the increasing use of new clean renewables electricity generation systems integrated with distributed power management and advanced battery storage systems in many developing countries globally. These are becoming especially attractive for supplying electricity to remote rural communities and villages in developing economies worldwide. These new renewable developments should help to supply clean electricity to over 1 billion people worldwide, who currently do not have easy access to electricity globally. These new renewable power developments should help to promote just transition in developing and emerging economies globally.

Global Electricity Power Energy Transition Net Zero Developments

The electricity and power generation sectors are two of the largest contributors of GHG and CO2 emissions globally. B20 expert studies have shown that the emissions generated by the electricity and power sectors globally are the third highest sectorial emissions globally (B20, Energy and Sustainability Position Paper, KSA 2020).

The clean renewables electricity power generation sector has been growing fast globally. There are now noteworthy clean renewable electricity and power developments in most key regional markets of the world. These are in follow-up to the new sustainability strategy and net zero policies introduced by various countries, in-line with their Paris Agreement commitments. The various major clean electricity and power developments in key countries and markets globally are summarised below with international examples (Wang, Renewable Energy Management, Routledge UK 2020).

China has been leading the world in installing new renewable clean power and electricity capacities, particularly in solar PV, wind and hydropower. A good country example is that China has allocated over US$360 billion of investments in their latest national FYP for new clean renewable energy investments. A lot of the new investments will be in new solar PV and wind power facilities which should help to increase China's total renewables capacity significantly. There will also be significant new green investments in other renewable energy systems, including hydro, bioenergy plus green hydrogen and geothermal. These green investments should all help to meet China's ambitious national renewable energy targets. These should also help to reduce China's GHG emissions and to meet its Paris Agreement commitments.

Other countries in Asia have also been investing in clean renewable power too. Most of the renewable electricity and power generation in Asia have traditionally been from hydropower. However, the hydropower share of renewable power supplies has been decreasing in recent years relative to other renewable power supplies, especially solar PV and wind power. A good Asian example is that in India, both new wind power and solar PV capacities have increased substantially. Biopower generation in India has also been growing fast, especially in the remote rural communities. Both Indonesia and Turkey have been investing in new geothermal renewable power installations.

Oceania countries have also been promoting clean renewable energy applications. Australia has been leading the Asia Pacific region in clean renewable electricity installed capacity. The bulk of renewable power generation in Australia has been from hydropower, with close to 60% share. This is followed by wind power at over 30%. In recent years, solar PV capacities have been growing quickly in Australia, which has abundant solar resources as well as fossil reserves.

In Europe, clean energy and renewable energy supplies have been continuing their ongoing growth trends. New clean renewable power plants have accounted for a large majority, over 85%, of all new power installations that are being built in the EU in recent years. Most of the new renewable power installations have been dominated by wind power and solar PV.

The new EU clean energy and renewables directive, the "Clean Energy for All Europeans Package", has been causing some concerns for the renewables sector in the EU. There have been serious concerns from many stakeholders, including manufacturers, project developers, plus investors and financing institutions. Their concerns have been largely about the new proposals to remove priority access and dispatches for renewable energy. Other serious concerns included the removal from the new 2030 EU targets, the renewable energy and energy efficiency targets plus binding national targets. There are also concerns about the planned mandatory replacement of FITs by competitive tendering for new renewable projects in the EU (EU, Clean Energy for all Europeans, 2018).

In the USA, there have been strong growths in new clean energy and renewable installations despite the federal policies introduced by the previous President Trump administration on promoting fossil fuels and coal applications. Clean electricity generation by wind energy and solar PV have actually increased substantially. In 2020, renewable energy sources accounted for about 12.6% of total US energy consumption and about 19.8% of the total electricity generation in the USA. Experts have forecasted that the annual share of US electricity generation from renewable energy sources will rise from about 20% in 2021, to 22% in 2022, and then rise further to 24% in 2023. These increases are resulting from the continued rise in new renewable power generation capacities, including new solar and wind electricity and power plants, in the USA.

In Canada, hydropower has continued to be the dominant source of clean renewables power generation on a national basis. For newly installed clean renewable power plants, new wind power generation plants have been the largest source of new clean power generation that have been installed over the past 11 years in Canada.

Various Latin American countries have also been promoting clean renewables power plants. Some countries have achieved high shares of national electricity generation with variable renewable energy systems. Two good Latin America country examples include Honduras, which has managed to supply near to 10% of its electricity nationally with solar PV, plus Uruguay, which has used wind power to supply over 20% of its national electricity consumption recently. In addition, a number of Caribbean Island states, including Aruba, Curacao, Bonaire and St. Eustatius, have all managed to achieve clean renewable energy shares of over 10% in their total nation power mix.

Many African countries have also been promoting clean renewables energy applications. Two good African country examples are Egypt and Morocco. Egypt, followed by Morocco, has been leading the Middle East North Africa (MENA) region in installing new renewable power generation capacities. Both countries have significant amounts of hydropower capacity installed. South Africa together with Ethiopia have been leading sub-Saharan Africa in their total installed renewable power capacities. Their clean renewable power generation capacities have reached 5% of their total national electricity generating capacity in recent years.

South Africa and several countries in northern Africa, including Algeria, Egypt and particularly Morocco, have also become important markets for CSP. They have also become the new centres of green industrial manufacturing activities for solar PV modules and wind turbine components in Africa. These new clean renewable energy manufacturing capacities have helped to create new green jobs and employment opportunities to support the new low-carbon economy developments in Africa. Several Africa countries, including Ghana, Senegal and Uganda, have commissioned new solar PV plants recently. Kenya is one of the few countries worldwide to have brought additional new geothermal capacity online. Several new large hydropower projects have also been under development in various African countries, but some have caused serious environmental concerns.

Middle East countries have also started actively promoting clean renewable energy applications. Currently, the renewable capacities, including solar PV, wind power and CSP, in the Middle East region are comparatively small. A number of different Middle East countries have been building and considering new wind power and solar PV projects. They have been developing new domestic renewables manufacturing capacities. These have also helped to create new green jobs and employments in the region. Renewables projects are being planned in Jordan, Oman, Saudi Arabia, the State of Palestine and the United Arab Emirates (UAE) (REN, Global Status Report, 2018).

Substantial new green investments will have to be made in various emerging economies and developed countries globally to upgrade their national power electricity grids so that these can better accommodate their variable clean renewable energy supplies. Good country examples include the modification and expansion of the national electricity grids in India, China and Jordan. These should enable the national grids in these countries to better transmit the rising amounts of variable renewable power supplies that are being generated in these countries. These major investments in grid improvements together with reforms in their national power markets are essential for these countries to better utilise their newly installed clean renewable power plants.

The developments of new off-grid clean renewable energy power systems and supplies will be very important for the more than 1 billion people world-wide, who currently do not have easy access to electricity supplies from their national grids. Most of these people are living in remote rural communities in the emerging economies, especially in sub-Saharan Africa and Asia. New clean renewable power generation systems integrated with advanced power storage and digital distributed power off-grid energy management systems should enable them to enjoy easier electricity access from their remote locations. These new advanced integrated renewable power systems should help to offer new cost-competitive power supply options for these people, especially those living in rural areas which are far away from the national grids in their countries. Many countries have been considering these new cost-effective off-grid renewable power options to provide clean electricity access for their remote villages and rural communities as part of their new sustainability strategy plus new net zero goals and just transition plans.

A good international example is that the number of off-grid solar PV power generation systems integrated with power storage and decentralised power distribution systems have been increasing rapidly in many rural communities in developing economies in Asia and Africa. Multilateral and bilateral financing institutions globally have also been providing ethnical impact green investment funds to enable accelerated deployment of these new integrated renewable power projects to supply clean electricity to remote communities (Wang, FT Asia Climate Finance Summit, 2018).

Globally in both emerging economies and developed countries, there have also been expanded applications of new decentralised electricity mini-grids, together with clean renewable power supplies. These have been driven in part by the strong desires to improve the reliability of power supplies in the face of rising numbers of extreme weather events, which have been occurring more frequently due to climate change. These included hurricanes, typhoons and flooding. These extreme weather incidents have caused more frequent power cuts in many countries globally. So many leading international companies, especially those in the IT, digital and data service sectors, have decided to make major new investments in their own secured renewable power generation and storage systems to ensure their power security.

A good international business example is that the leading international IT and data companies in the USA and other developed countries have been investing heavily in their own secured electricity mini-grids together with stand-alone renewable power generation and storage capacities. These have also resulted in a rising number of interconnections of these new local mini-grids with regional or national electricity grids in many developed countries.

In a rising number of developing countries, renewables power mini-grid systems have been applied. These are also helping to meet the important UN goal of providing electricity access for all, especially for remote villages and rural communities. These should also promote just transition globally (UNFCCC, Distributed renewable power generation and integration, 2015).

Looking ahead, there are also some ambitious plans to consider whilst inter-connecting existing national electricity grids across different countries. These super-grids across key regions should help to promote the transmission and sharing of renewable electricity and power across different countries. These plans are still in the very early stages of consideration. There are many tech-nical, commercial, legal, controls and political hurdles to overcome. Good international regional super-grid examples include the potential new future super-grids being discussed for Europe, Africa, Asia and America. Many of these potential new super electricity grids should help to advance the integra-tion and sharing of renewable electricity and power supplies across different countries and continents. These should then help to promote clean renewable power and green electricity growths globally. These will also help to improve international power security across different countries and regions globally.

Global Clean Renewable Energy Supply Chains Risks & Improvements

Global demands for clean renewable energy components, material and tech-nologies have increased significantly. The clean energy markets in different regions are expected to continue to grow exponentially. Experts have fore-casted that they are likely to reach values of some US$23 trillion globally by 2030. These significant growths in the renewable energy markets and appli-cations are driven by countries seeking to diversify their energy systems with more reliable clean energy sources as part of their new clean energy transition policies plus sustainability strategy and net zero plans. However, various serious global incidents, including the COVID-19 pandemic, have highlighted the serious risks and shortcomings in the global renewable supply chains. Many countries and experts are urgently studying these serious supply chain problems. They are also urgently developing different improvements options so as to improve the robustness of the renewable supply chains in different countries. These improvements are essential for different countries to achieve their planned clean energy transitions in-line with their new sustainability strategy and net zero policies plus to meet their Paris Agreement commitments.

A good international country example is the new US renewable supply chain strategy which has just been published by the US government in 2022. The key points are summarised in the international case study below.

US Clean Energy Transition Supply Chain Strategy Case Study

The USA is accelerating its clean energy transitions in-line with its new sustainability strategy and net zero plans plus to meet its Paris Agreement commitments. The US Department of Energy (DOE) studies have shown that without new US domestic raw materials production and manufacturing capacities, the USA will have to continue to rely on clean energy imports in future. They believe that this will then expose the USA to serious supply chain risks and vulnerabilities. In addition, the USA will also lose out on the enormous new green job creation and new employment opportunities that will be generated by the clean energy transitions. In addition and in many cases, the USA has also untapped the potential to support greater domestic renewable energy and component productions.

A new US strategy was developed by the US DOE in response to US President Biden's Executive Order 14017 on America's Supply Chains. The new US DOE "America's Strategy to Secure the Supply Chain for a Robust Clean Energy Transition" is the first comprehensive US plan to build the US Energy Sector Industrial Base (ESIB). This will be required to support the rapidly accelerating transition to clean energy across USA. It is also part of the US Government's approach to revitalise the US economy and domestic manufacturing by securing the most critical supply chains across the USA (US DOE Office of Policy, America's Strategy to Secure the Supply Chain for a Robust Clean Energy Transition, USA FEBRUARY 24, 2022).

The new US clean energy supply chain strategy should lead to the development and buildup of stronger, more resilient and diverse renewable energy supply chains in the USA. These should then help the USA to better meet their climate change goals and net zero targets plus to meet their Paris Agreement commitments. It should help to establish the USA as a leader in clean energy innovation and manufacturing globally. These should also help to create millions of new green jobs in the USA plus contribute to economic growth and just transition across the USA.

The new US clean energy supply chain strategy has also summarised the crucial elements of the new US clean energy supply chain, together with key new technologies and cross-cutting topics. It has also covered various actions that the US government is employing or will be developing to strengthen the US domestic clean energy supply chains. The proposed policy strategies and actions should help in laying out a comprehensive US government approach to create new programmes and build on existing programmes. The DOE report has proposed more than 60 different actions by both the US Federal and State governments plus Congress. These should help the USA to better capture the new economic and employment opportunities that are inherent in the clean energy transition. The US DOE will be working with several other Federal Agencies and Congress to accomplish the proposed improvements to the US energy supply chain strategy.

The US DOE report has built on detailed reviews of the new clean energy supply chains of different critical industrial products. These have included semiconductor manufacturing and advanced packaging, large capacity batteries, critical minerals and materials, cybersecurity etc.

Meeting the US national climate goals of 100% clean electricity by 2035 and achieving a net zero emissions US economy by 2050 will involve a massive buildup of clean energy technologies and accompanying scale-ups in its supply chains, both domestically and globally. The US clean energy transition process should help to create significant opportunities for the USA to establish global leadership in the global clean energy market, especially in several renewable technologies which are currently poised for exponential growths. These will include solar, wind, nuclear, grid improvements, plus battery storage and green hydrogen.

Taking urgent actions now to address the various risks and vulnerabilities and maximise opportunities should enable the USA to reinvest and modernise their various manufacturing bases across the USA. This will help to create millions of new high-quality green jobs across the USA. It should also help to increase access to clean energy sources across the USA. It should help to build up a clean energy economy and improve public health in communities across the USA.

Through various deep assessments, the US DOE has identified various ways to increase the productivity in various key clean energy areas. These include carbon capture materials, electricity grids including transformers and high-voltage direct current, energy storage, fuel cells and electrolysers, hydropower including pumped storage hydropower, neodymium magnets, nuclear energy, platinum group metals and other catalysts, semiconductors, solar photovoltaics, wind, commercialisation, competitiveness, cybersecurity, digital components etc.

To address the various supply chain risks and vulnerabilities plus to maximise strategic opportunities, the USA DOE has proposed seven key action areas. These include: (1) Increasing raw material availability; (2) Expanding domestic manufacturing capabilities; (3) Supporting formation of and investment in diverse, secure and socially responsible foreign supply chains; (4) Increasing the adoption and deployment of clean energy; (5) Improving end-of-life energy-related waste management; (6) Attracting and supporting a skilled workforce for the clean energy transition; and (7) Enhancing supply chain knowledge and decision making.

Looking ahead, the US DOE is planning to implement a full suite of existing and new US government policy tools to address the new US clean energy supply chain challenges and opportunities. These will include expanding US government financial grants to support domestic manufacturing capabilities and job creation, leveraging foreign direct investment in US-based clean energy technology manufacturing, promoting the adoption of traceability standards to improve global supply chain mapping capabilities, plus supporting carbon foot-printing of energy supply chains.

Global Hydrogen Net Zero Innovation and Developments

Many countries and governments globally have been actively developing hydrogen as a new future green clean fuel. Hydrogen produces zero emissions at the various points of uses. It can also be stored and transported at high energy density in both the liquid and gaseous forms. It can also be combusted or used in various fuel cells to generate heat and electricity. Natural gas is about 8.5 times as dense as hydrogen. The denser natural gas is easier and more energy efficient to move than hydrogen. However, hydrogen partially makes up for that fact by being more energy denser per unit mass; in fact, hydrogen is about three times more energy denser per unit mass than natural gas.

Many universities and research institutions are working on different new green hydrogen production processes together with new technology innovations and innovative cost reduction ideas. Experts have forecasted that the production costs of green hydrogen are likely to be reduced significantly in the next ten years with the various potential new developments and innovations globally. A good international country example is China, which is actively working on new hydrogen developments and innovations. The details are summarised more in the international country case study below:

China Hydrogen Net Zero Development Plans Case Study

China has identified hydrogen (H2) as a future strategic clean fuel. They believe that hydrogen can play many important roles in China's clean energy transitions plus its carbon neutrality and net zero plans. Hydrogen can help to reduce carbon emissions and improve the decarbonisation of the transport and industrial sectors in China. These should help to contribute significantly to achieving the Chinese national goal of achieving carbon neutrality and net zero emissions by 2060, as President Xi (XJP) has announced in his UN speech.

An important policy signal is that China has included hydrogen as a specific clean energy source in the new national energy law of China. This helps to signify the future strategic importance of hydrogen in China. China's Fourteenth National FYP has also included hydrogen in its various development plans.

Hydrogen has traditionally been produced from various fossil sources, including gas or coal gasification. These fossil processes all involve significant carbon emissions. Looking ahead, China is developing potential new innovative green hydrogen (H2) production processes using renewables and water electrolysis. These are being actively developed by various research institutes and universities in China. They are making good progress and with potential future large cost reductions being forecasted. The research in China is aiming to develop new innovative processes to produce green hydrogen by integrating water electrolysis with renewable energy power supplies. These should be cleaner and cheaper than other hydrogen production processes. Experts are forecasting that production cost reductions of some 80% may be possible by 2030.

China is also preparing important new promotional policies for hydrogen H2 plus fuel cell vehicles (FCV). These could lead to future China's FCV growth overtaking that of EVs. FCV could potentially have faster refuelling, carry heavier loads and cover longer distance capacities, in comparison to EV. The new China's FCV Notice has stipulated that the current purchase subsidies for FCVs will be replaced by pilot demonstrations in selected cities for an initial phase of four years. Key focus will be on the research, innovation and application of key new FCV components. The key supports from China Central Government will be in the form of financial awards and grants to the selected cities rather than purchase subsidies for consumers. These should help to accelerate the development of new China urban hydrogen (H2) hubs.

The new hydrogen FCV policies in China have been developed based on the successful 'China EV Ten Cities, Thousand Vehicles program' but with some important modifications. Starting with only a few hundred EVs in 2009, China has now become the largest EV market in the world and currently has a stock of over 3 million EVs. The future targets for FCVs in China are very ambitious. From a 2019 stock of about 6,000, there is a goal to get to 50,000 FCVs in 2025, and then 1 million FCVs in 2030 across China.

The 2022 Winter Olympics in Beijing and Zhangjiakou was a key opportunity for FCV demonstration and developments. This was just like the 2008 Summer Olympics in Beijing for EVs and plug-in electric vehicles (PEVs). The Zhangjiakou municipal government operated 16 new hydrogen refuelling stations and 2,000 FCVs during the Winter Olympic Games in 2022. Daily hydrogen production of some 34 tonnes/day were achieved for the refuelling of the 2000 FCVs being operated during the Winter Olympics.

The new special hydrogen financial awards to approved pilot cities in China should also help to promote the developments of hydrogen across China. These will include improved hydrogen production and transportation, key technology innovations, improving components of the fuel cell, improved hydrogen refuelling infrastructure, and vehicle marketing. These should bring in many more stakeholders to the frontstage than just vehicle manufacturers. These should include additional key stakeholders in energy generation, fuel cell components and materials plus special equipment. These should be good on the national level, because various major cities in China can focus on their comparative advantages to grow into future hydrogen (H2) hubs and smart cities in China.

In summary, China has identified hydrogen as a strategic future clean fuel. They are actively developing their future green hydrogen (H2) plans and policies. Many details have to be developed plus many strenuous research and development tasks have to be accomplished. However, experts have forecasted that the outlooks for technology innovation and cost reductions are looking bright. These new green hydrogen developments in China should contribute strongly to China achieving their important goal of achieving carbon neutrality and net zero emissions by 2060, as President Xi (XJP) has announced in his UN speech.

7
Developments in Sustainable Transport

英雄所见略同

Yīng xióng suǒ jiàn lüè tóng

The views of different heroes are generally similar.
Great minds think alike.

Global Sustainable Transport Net Zero Developments

Global energy demands in the transport sector have been rising continuously by some 2% annually on average since 2005. The transportation sector has been accounting for over a quarter, some 28–30%, of the overall energy consumption globally. More seriously, the transportation sector globally has been generating over one-fifth, about 23–25%, of the energy-related GHG emissions of the world. This is largely due to the fact that fossil oil fuels, especially gasoline and diesel, have been the dominant transport fuels being used in various countries globally. Fossil oil fuels have been accounting for over 90% of the final energy consumption in the transport sector globally (REN Global Status Report 2018).

In follow-up to the historic Paris Climate Agreement in December 2015, the international community has been focussing increased attention on the decarbonisation of the transport sector. Many countries have submitted nationally determined contributions (NDCs) that have referred specifically to promoting clean renewable energy applications in their transport sector. A good country example is that New Zealand has linked EVs to renewable energy developments in their NDCs.

Various governments globally are developing new medium- to long-term strategies to decarbonise their transport sector. These new country transport policies and strategies will often involve long-term structural changes which closely link

DOI: 10.4324/9781003142348-7

the transport sector with clean energy transition and meet new carbon neutrality goals. A good international country example is Germany's climate and transport action plans. These are aiming to significantly reduce the GHG emissions from the transport sector in Germany by some 40–42% by 2030 (Wang, Climate Change and Clean Energy Management, Routledge UK 2019).

There are various potential options to decarbonise the transport sector globally. These include gas vehicles, EVs, hydrogen vehicles, biofuel, public transport, bike sharing, etc. The main focus of recent international climate and decarbonisation discussions has been on the electrification of road transport and EV developments. A good international example is the rising focus on implementing new reliable EV charging networks in developed and developing countries. These new charging systems can be integrated with clean renewable electricity supplies. These developments should help to reduce emissions plus support further EV sales in different countries globally.

There are good opportunities for renewable energy and clean fuel applications in the transport supply chains. These will include the use of liquid biofuels, biofuels blended with conventional fuels, natural gas vehicles, renewable electricity for EV charging, etc. In addition, there should be good green investment opportunities in establishing new infrastructure and retail station networks. These will be important to support liquid and gaseous biofuel supplies plus the charging of EVs using renewable electricity or hydrogen produced by renewable electricity, etc.

Biofuels, which include ethanol and biodiesel, have represented the majority of clean transport fuel supplies globally. These biofuels have been supplying around 4% of the road transport fuels in selected countries globally. The global ethanol productions have remained relatively stable in recent years. There have been some biofuel decreases across Europe and in Brazil. These have been offset by the increases in the USA, China and India. The global biodiesel productions have been growing faster with substantial increases in the USA and Indonesia. These biodiesel growths have been fuelled by supporting policies in different countries. There have also been strong public concerns and government policy drives against diesel fossil fuels in many countries. These are mainly due to serious concerns about the high GHG and particulate emissions from fossil diesel fuels. These should promote the global shift from fossil diesel fuels to biofuels or clean fuels globally.

The various technologies for producing, purifying and upgrading natural gas and biogas for use in the transport sector have become relatively matured. The gas infrastructure and supply chains for gas vehicles based on natural gas fuels have been growing slowly but steadily internationally. A good international example is the growth of liquefied petroleum gas (LPG) and biogas vehicles in China. These include the growth of taxi fleets, fuelled by LPG or biogas, in Beijing and other leading cities in China. There are several barriers to broader gas and biogas penetrations in the transport sector. These included the lack of regulations regarding access to natural gas grids plus the lack of suitable infrastructure and retail networks for gas and biogas supplies to the transport sector. The decentralised nature of biogas feedstocks and their comparatively high economic costs have also been affecting growth. Most of the biogas production for transport purposes have been concentrated in Europe and the USA.

The electrification of the transport sector has been rising in recent years with the growth of EVs globally. These growths have helped to expand the potential for greater integration of clean renewable energy with EV charging. These include clean electricity supply to trains, light rail, trams, plus two- and four-wheeled EVs.

Looking ahead, further electrification of the transport sector globally should create new markets for clean renewable energy applications. The growth of clean renewables energy in various national power grids should provide more clean electricity supplies for new EVs and electrified transport charging systems globally. Some EV service providers and utility companies have started offering new services provisions to charge EVs with clean renewable electricity supplies. A good international example is the new customer service offerings on EV charging by various electric car sharing and rental companies in the UK and the Netherlands.

On a very limited scale, some car companies in several countries have been developing new EV prototypes that can use solar photovoltaic (PV) directly. Interesting international examples include new passenger car prototypes with solar PV charging features in China and Japan plus solar-powered buses in Uganda. These are still in early stages of development with relatively limited applications globally.

The key barriers to electrification in the road transport sector have continued to include relatively high EV purchase costs plus limited driving ranges and the short battery life of EVs. The lack of national EV charging infrastructures in various countries have also limited EV sales and growth. In most developing countries, there are additional barriers to EV growth with the lack of robust local clean electricity supply infrastructure plus limited availability of EV electricity charging retail stations. However, various improvements are currently being actively developed internationally. A good international business example is that some leading international oil and energy companies are actively developing new EV charging stations which are linked with their existing oil fuel retail station networks in various countries globally.

Looking ahead, some leading countries, including Germany, India, the Netherlands, the UK and Norway, are seriously discussing a gradual phase-out of the internal combustion engines (ICEs) as part of their sustainability strategy and net zero plans. A good international example is that some countries are seriously considering the possible phasing-out of diesel engine cars by 2025–2030 and then petrol engine cars by 2030–2040. These plans will need extensive consultation and careful development to ensure public acceptance in various countries globally.

The international aviation transport sector has accounted for just over one-tenth, around 10–15%, of the total energy used in the transport sector globally. In 2017, the International Civil Aviation Organization (ICAO) announced a landmark agreement by 66 nations, which accounted for 86% of the global aviation activity. These countries have agreed to jointly mitigate GHG emissions in the aviation sector as part of their new carbon neutrality and net zero plans. The new international agreement will support the production and use of sustainable aviation fuels. These new clean aviation fuels should include clean aviation fuels produced from biomass or different types of wastes.

The use of biofuels in aviation has already moved from a theoretical concept to a business reality for a few airlines in recent years, such as 2016. A number of significant agreements for the provision of aviation biofuels have been signed internationally. In addition, there has also been various ongoing development work on new electric airplane prototypes and new solar-powered planes (IRENA, Biofuels for Aviation, 2017).

The marine shipping transport sector globally has been consuming less than one-tenth, around 7–10%, of the total energy used in the transport sector globally. The International Maritime Organization (IMO) has agreed to a new 0.5% sulphur cap in marine fuels globally. This new cap will limit the future burning of heavy fuel oils in ships. This will have big impacts on various oil refineries globally. The sulphur cap should contribute to GHG emission reductions from ships which are in line with global climate change concerns. These caps should promote cleaner shipping fuel applications, including liquefied natural gas (LNG) and renewable fuels applications in ships.

The integration of various renewable energy application into ships is also being investigated. In theory, clean renewable energy sources, including wind and solar energy, could be incorporated into shipping designs and operations. A good international example is that there has been some research into developing new wind energy-assisted propulsion technologies for ships but more developments are required.

For ship propulsion, the use of biofuels or other renewable-based fuels, including hydrogen, can also be considered. There are also some new development activities associated with the use of clean gaseous fuels for ships. A good international example is the deployment of LNG-fuelled ships in Australia. These may also offer new green opportunities for biogas incorporation (Seatrade Maritime News, IMO 2020 Sulphur Regulation, 2018).

The railway transport sector has accounted for around 2% of the total energy used in the transport sector globally. The bulk of railway trains globally, around 50–60%, have been fuelled by fossil oil products and fuels. Over one-third, about 35–40%, of railway trains have been powered by electricity. The share of clean renewable electricity in the total energy mix of the world's railways has increased by three times. A good international example is that renewable electricity supplies to railways have risen from 3.4% in 1990 to nearly one-tenth, around 9–10%, globally.

Some other countries have even reached much higher penetrations of clean renewable electricity usage in their railways. A good international country example is that all the electric trains in the Netherlands have been converted to clean wind energy generated electricity. A few other railways have also implemented new projects to generate their own electricity from renewables. These included new wind turbines on railway land and solar panels on railway stations. Good international example of these renewable power railway applications can be found in India and Morocco. Chile has also announced the construction of new solar PV and windfarms to help to produce renewable electricity to power their Santiago subway trains. The testing of new smart on-board dynamic energy management systems in both intercity and urban trains has also been taking place to improve railway energy efficiency plus to help manage and store variable renewable electricity supply for use on trains.

COP26 Sustainable Transport & Clean Fuel Highlights

In the international COP26 meeting, held in Glasgow in November 2021, sustainable transportation and clean fuels were major areas of discussion. There were important new sustainable transport declarations and announcements made at COP26. These are summarised below with international examples:

Over 100 national governments, cities, states and major businesses have signed the Glasgow Declaration on Zero-Emission Cars and Vans. They have committed to end the sale of internal combustion engines by 2035 in leading markets and 2040 worldwide. At least 13 countries have also signed a similar memorandum of understanding (MOU) to end the sale of all fossil fuel-powered heavy-duty vehicles and trucks by 2040.

Many leading companies, countries, regions and cities have committed to accelerating the roll-out of new EV charging infrastructures. They agreed that these will be important to promote further EV sales and growth globally.

Some leading Latin American cities, including Bogotá, Cuenca and Salvador, have announced that they will be turning their public transport fleets to zero-emission fleets by 2035. These should help to decarbonise their transport sector, which is one of the region's biggest GHG emitters.

Over 200 businesses from across the international shipping value chains have committed to scale up and commercialise new zero-emission shipping vessels and clean shipping fuels by 2030. They have called on governments globally to develop and enact appropriate regulations and infrastructure to enable a just transition by 2050 in the global shipping sector.

Nine leading international companies and big-name brands globally, including Amazon, IKEA, Michelin, Unilever and Patagonia, have jointly announced that they will be shifting 100% of their ocean freight to ships that are powered by zero-carbon fuels by 2040. This should promote shipping companies to accelerate shifting their ships to use zero-carbon fuels globally.

Nineteen countries have signed the Clydebank Declaration, to support the establishment of zero-emission shipping routes. These countries have agreed their collective aims to create at least six zero-emissions maritime corridors by 2025 whilst aspiring to see many more corridors in operation by 2030.

Twenty-eight leading shipping and wind energy companies have launched Operation Zero. They have committed to work together to accelerate the decarbonisation of shipping operations and maintenance vessels working in the North Sea offshore wind sector. They have agreed to aim to deploy zero-emission operations and maintenance vessels in the region by 2025.

The international shift to sustainable aviation fuels is approaching an important breakthrough. Over 80 aviation industry businesses and large corporate customers are aiming to boost the supply of clean aviation fuels to meet 10% of the global jet fuel demands by 2030. This will be a 1,000-fold increase from current situations. These should help to save 60 million tonnes of carbon dioxide (CO_2) emissions per year plus help to create 300,000 new green jobs.

Three-quarters of the corporate sector commitments that have been submitted to the Science-based Targets Initiative so far this year have been aligned with the aspired target of limiting global warming to 1.5°C. The corporate memberships of the International Business Ambition for 1.5°C's campaign have also grown strongly from 28 companies to 1,000 companies in two years. They are representing a total amount of US$23 trillion in market capitalisation globally.

Regional Sustainable Transport Net Zero Developments

International surveys have shown that the road transportation sectors in different countries have accounted for about 75% of the total transport sector energy consumptions globally. Different regions globally have their unique mix of vehicle types plus fuelling requirements and infrastructure. The major mega-trends in sustainable road transport developments plus clean transport fuel developments for different regions across the world will be discussed in more detail below with international examples.

In Asia, fossil oil fuels are still the dominate transport fuels in different countries in the region. However, there has been continuous growth in ethanol and biofuel productions for clean transport fuel applications in various Asian countries. A good Asian example is that China, India and Thailand have been leading the Asia region in biofuel productions. The production of biodiesel has also continued to rise in other countries in Asia, especially in Indonesia.

On biogas, both China and India have established new biogas infrastructure, into which biogas could be fed in for transport uses. A good country example is that India's first biomethane-fuelled bus has started operations recently. India is also planning more biogas stations, biogas buses and routes across the country.

In China, EV sales have risen significantly with the government's New Energy Cars program. China has become the largest EV market for passenger EVs globally. China has also become the world leader in electric two-wheel motorbike sales globally. China has overtaken both USA and Europe in the cumulative sales of EVs. China has also become the largest global electric bus market, with many plug-in electric buses operating on its roads. Experts have forecasted that China is likely to account for more than 50% of the global electric bus market by 2025. These rising EV numbers in China should help to reduce GHG emissions from China plus help China to achieve its carbon neutrality and net zero-emission goals by 2060.

In Japan, EV sales have been declining recently, but they still accounted for about 8% of the global market for passenger EVs. Japan has also been accelerating hydrogen applications for transportation developments. A good international example is that Japan has deployed many new hydrogen buses at the international Olympics games that were held in Japan in summer 2021.

In Europe, the rising interest in electric mobility and EVs has contributed to the recent declines in clean biofuel productions. The total production of both ethanol and biodiesel has been declining across the EU region. However, there were also some increases in ethanol production in some countries, including Hungary, Poland, UK and Sweden. In the EU, biogas and biomethane production has grown to gain more market shares in the transport fuel market. A good international example is Sweden, which provided record shares of biomethane, over 70%, in its supply of compressed natural gas (CNG) for its transport sector. Four of the world's five largest producers of biogas for vehicle fuel are now based in four 4 EU countries, including Germany, Sweden, Switzerland and the UK.

The EU regional sales of EVs have also been increasing in recent years. These have accounted for nearly one-third of the global passenger EV sales. Norway has been leading the EU region in total EV sales. Netherlands is second with UK third and France in the fourth position. Netherlands has also built and commissioned a first-in-the-world, solar-controlled, bi-directional clean electricity charging station for EVs.

In Africa, the production of biofuel and ethanol has risen in recent years. There have been some EV sales in South Africa and Morocco. Some biogas and biomethane road transport pilot projects have also been launched in South Africa in recent years.

In North America, USA has continued to be the largest producer of biofuels. The US government has been supporting biofuel developments with supportive agricultural policy together with US federal renewable fuel standards. The production of both ethanol and biodiesel has increased recently, which reversed recent declines. USA is also one of the five largest producers of biogas for vehicle fuel uses worldwide. Renewable biogas has accounted for about 20–35% of the gas fuels used in the transport sector. EV sales have also increased in the USA with rising consumer demands. The US EV sales have accounted for about one-third of the passenger EV sales globally.

In Canada, the ethanol biofuel production has decreased whilst biodiesel production has increased. EV sales have also increased significantly with rising consumer demands in Canada.

In Latin America, Brazil has become the second largest producer of biofuels globally after the USA. However, there has been recent declines in both ethanol and biodiesel production in Brazil. There have also been decreases in both ethanol and biodiesel production in Colombia and Peru. On the other hand, the production of biofuels has increased in both Argentina and Mexico. Argentina, Brazil and Colombia have also developed natural gas infrastructure into which biogas could be incorporated and transmitted. The EV markets in Latin America are still in their early development stages. Looking ahead, there may be good future growth opportunities as various countries in Latin America push ahead with their carbon neutrality and net zero plans.

Global Electric Vehicle Growths and Developments

The transport sector and motor vehicles globally have been major contributors to GHG emissions and climate change impacts around the world. Climate change concerns and the green transport drives globally have promoted the growth of EVs in different countries globally. Transport experts have forecasted that the number of EVs globally could rise to over 100 million by 2035. Looking further ahead, the number of EVs globally could further rise to over 200 million EVs globally by 2040.

EVs encompass any road transport vehicles that will use electric drives. The electric charging of various EVs is normally provided by external electrical sources such as from city grids or home charging points. Some EV technologies have been hybridised with fossil-fuel engines. A good international example is the plug-in hybrid electric vehicles (PHEVs) that are available from some leading international car manufacturers.

Looking ahead, a new third variant of EV or zero-emission vehicles will be the use of fuel cells to convert hydrogen directly into electricity. Smart EV charging systems are also using growing quantities of variable renewable energy supplies from different renewable generators for EV charging (REN, Renewables Global Status Report 2017).

The electrification of both the road and rail transport sectors globally has been expanding. These expansions have enabled the greater integration of clean renewable energy with the transport sectors. Good international examples include the use of green electricity to power trains, light rail, trams as well as for charging of two- and four-wheeled EVs.

Political interest from different countries and government in electric mobility has increased following the Paris Agreement plus the Glasgow Climate Pact that was agreed at the COP26 meeting. These have sparked off broader debates and commitments by different countries on accelerating the electrification of their transport sectors which are in line with their Paris Agreement commitments (REN, Renewables Global Status Report 2018).

Global deployment of EVs for road transport, and particularly passenger vehicles, has grown rapidly in recent years. The EV passenger car market (including PHEVs) is currently only accounting for a small portion of the global passenger car sales but these are rising fast. The top five countries for passenger EV deployments include China, the USA, Japan, Norway and the Netherlands. Together, they have accounted for over 60–70% of the global EV sales. China and the USA have been the market leaders in EV unit sales. Norway is the market leader in terms of EV country market penetration.

China's EV market has seen dramatic growth in recent years. EV sales nationally have increased significantly with strong government support and rising consumer interests. China has now surpassed the United States to become the country with the largest number of passenger EVs on its roads.

In most countries, even those with strong incentives, EVs have continued to represent a small share of their total passenger vehicle sales. Norway is the only market globally where the EV market shares have reached a high mass market penetration level. Norway currently has the highest EV market penetration rates globally. These high market penetrations have been driven by a set of strong government incentives. These included EV exemption from sales and registration taxes, as well as the construction of extensive national EV charging infrastructure. EVs sales have represented about a third of all new passenger vehicle registrations in Norway.

Although electrically driven passenger cars have experienced the most rapid market growth in recent years, electrical drives have also been applied in other transport modes, including trains, trams, buses plus two- and three-wheeled vehicles. A good international example is that in Europe, over 5,500 electric buses have been operating on the road. Around 90% of these electric buses were connected via overhead electric wire networks which are linked to the city grids.

EV manufacturers and electric utilities have been developing and experimenting with new "smart" charging and vehicle-to-grid technologies. These new innovations should enable EVs to be charged by variable clean renewable electricity supplies from the city grids together with advanced renewable energy storage systems. A good international example is Netherlands, which has become an international leader in the use of variable renewable electricity supplies for EV charging via advanced smart charging systems.

There are currently some significant challenges for EV scale-ups to meet market expectations. Some of the most important challenges include limited EV drive ranges, limited availability of EV charging infrastructure and a lack of uniform charging standards. There are currently also three different plug types for the rapid charging of EVs: firstly, the CHAdeMO network, which works only with Asian-made vehicles; secondly, the SAE Combo plug, which fits in with German and some US-made vehicles; thirdly, Tesla's Supercharger network, which only fits Tesla electric vehicles. These three EV plug standards are currently all competing in the EV marketplace globally. Looking ahead, these should be harmonised by different countries and manufacturers globally, if possible, so as to further promote EV sales and growth globally.

Global Auto Company Electric Vehicles Transformations

Global EV growth has led to the emergence of many new EV manufacturers in different countries globally. Good international examples of different market leaders of passenger EVs include Tesla, Renault, Nissan and BYD.

BYD has been selling over 100,000 vehicles annually in China and overseas markets. BYD has achieved an impressive 13% market share in China and globally. BYD was started as a battery manufacturer in 1995 and has been a relative newcomer in the automotive industry. Renault-Nissan (France-Japan) has become the global market leader in terms of cumulative sales of EVs across different countries. The other leading global EV players include Tesla from USA and BMW from Germany (REN, Renewables Global Status Report 2018).

Several long-established traditional ICE vehicle manufacturers have also been realigning their corporate strategies and future plans so as to increase the share of EVs in their future sales. A good international example is the Volkswagen (VW) Group from Germany. It has announced ambitious plans to bring more than 30 pure-electric EV models to the car market in the next few years. VW has also set new sales targets of selling 2–3 million EVs annually by 2025 which will be equivalent to 20–25% of its total projected global sales of all vehicles. As part of their new product strategy, covering ICE, EV and ZEVs, VW has also announced new research and development (R&D) plans to research and develop new battery technology as a new core competency. VW has also expressed interest in building their own new battery factories to supply batteries for their growing EV productions globally.

Another good international car manufacturer example is Daimler AG in Germany, which announced in 2016 that it would be investing US$10.5 billion or EUR 10 billion in EV manufacturing. Daimler is planning to design and manufacture over ten new different EV models by 2025.

The rapid emergence and growth of electric drives, as a serious alternative to the traditional ICEs, have opened many new opportunities for new market entrants to the global automotive market. Good international examples include Tesla and BYD, both of whom have quickly become global market leaders in EV manufacturing in different regions. Tesla was founded as a new EV company in 2003 in USA, whilst BYD was started as a battery manufacturer in China.

Some successful international high-tech companies have also been showing interests in becoming involved in the growing EVs business, including Apple and Google. A good example is that Apple in USA has started to make major investments in EVs. Apple has been spending more on R&D in recent years and on EV vehicles and related services than it has done on several other Apple products combined. Google has also been interested in EV applications, especially in autonomous electric vehicles (AEVs). Google has set up a special business unit which is actively researching and developing AEV driving applications.

In addition, several other international consumer electronic and real estate companies have also announced their interest to enter the global EV market. A good international example is that in China some 200 mostly small medium enterprises (SMEs) in China have been reported to be developing and marketing their new EVs. They are aspiring to follow the successful footsteps of BYD in China. The PRC Government has recently announced new plans in March 2022 that they will be regulating more in the EV sector in China so as to ensure that it will compromise only top-quality companies.

Serious development hurdles for EV and ZEVs have included their limited driving ranges plus their battery capacity and life expectancies. Many manufacturers have been working on advancing various battery technologies so as to increase the EV driving ranges. Two good international examples include two new mid-priced EV models from Renault-Nissan and General Motors from USA, which have claimed to have longer driving ranges of more than 300 km each.

Many international EV manufacturers have also announced plans for developing new EV models with a driving range of up to 500–600 km. A good international example is Daimler AG, which has announced that its new EQ battery EV will have an aspired driving range of up to 500 km. VW Group has introduced a new concept e-Golf model with an aspired driving range of up to 600 km. VW has also announced that their new EVs will be sold at similar costs to their diesel-based equivalent.

On EV charging systems, various EV manufacturers plus oil and energy industries have been actively developing new EV charging stations in different countries. These developments should help to address the current shortage of EV charging stations in various developed countries. A good international example is that in Europe, they have been working together to expand the EV charging infrastructure and networks to include over 100,000 charging stations which will also include 10,000 fast EV charging stations.

In Europe, several leading auto manufacturers, including the BMW Group from Germany, Daimler AG, Ford Motor Company from USA and the VW Group, have announced that they will be jointly forming an important new joint venture on EV charging systems. They will be working together to build up a new network of high-powered 350 kW EV charging stations in Europe. These should enable longer EV travel ranges plus faster charging for EVs across different EU countries. These rapid charging stations should be able to allow

EVs with a range of 400 km to reach a full charge in some 12 min only. These much faster charging times should be attractive to new EV owners and should help to promote more customer acceptance of EVs in different countries. Some companies have even advertised that EV owners should be able to enjoy a cup of coffee at the cafes of their new EV rapid charging stations, whilst their EVs are being rapidly charged at the same time.

In the USA, Nissan and BMW have also announced plans to install new EV fast charging stations across USA. These will be equipped to work with both the CHAdeMO and SAE Combo connectors. Major US electric utilities have also joined efforts to expand EV charging infrastructures in various US states.

Reducing battery costs and improving recycling are the key strategic drivers for future EV battery market development and growth. For EV competitiveness in general, the mega global trends towards longer battery lifetimes and higher energy storage densities plus green recycling are the critical future R&D goals globally.

In the aviation sector, there has been various research into electric airplanes. A good example is the solar-powered aircraft, called the Solar Impulse 2, which has successfully completed an around-the-world flight after a 16-month voyage. There are also various R&D developments for new electric power passenger planes in different countries.

The research on exploring different methods to integrate renewable energy supplies into the charging stations for EVs has also been growing. A good international example is the installation of what is reportedly the world's first solar-controlled, bi-directional charging station for EVs in Utrecht, the Netherlands. This project has been undertaken as part of the Netherlands National Living Lab Program.

There have also been other innovative offerings in EV service provisions emerging globally. A good international example is that some EV service providers, including car sharing companies in the UK and the Netherlands, have begun offering new service provisions for their customers to buy renewable electricity to charge their EVs.

In addition, an increasing number of EV companies have been working to integrate renewable energy technologies directly into their EVs. A good international EV example is the Hanergy Holding Group from China. It has introduced four concept EVs which will use solar power directly to extend their driving ranges. Hanergy announced that they have plans to produce these solar EV vehicles commercially within three years.

Details of the new major EV investment plans by Toyota are summarised in the international business case study below:

Toyota EV Net Zero Transformation Case Study

Toyota, the world's largest car maker, has announced that they are planning to make a major investment of US$35 billion into their strategic shift towards producing more EVs globally. This is an important strategic move as the world's biggest carmaker has made the strategic business decision to set itself up for direct competition with Tesla and to join other leading international car manufacturing groups in their push towards achieving net zero carbon neutrality.

Toyota's new strategic business plan marks a major increase in its EV targets as it now aims to sell over 3.5 million EVs annually by 2030. Toyota also plans to launch 30 new EV models by 2030 in a new EV product line-up which will also include sports cars and commercial vehicles as well as passenger EVs.

Toyota's new EV investment plan is an important corporate decision and signals a major strategic business shift. Toyota has in the past argued that a longer-term fix for global warming should be a mix of hybrids, EVs and hydrogen-powered vehicles instead of a single bet on battery-powered cars. Although Toyota's investment plans are still trailing behind the VW €52 billion pledge on EV, it will dwarf the US$17.7 billion investments that were announced by its rival Nissan.

Toyota is planning to split its US$35 billion investment equally between EV car development and continuing investment in new battery improvements. Toyota has also said that their high-end Lexus brand will be at the forefront of their aggressive EV push.

Toyota's latest ambition for net zero emissions follows its major announcement that it would be ready, from 2035, to only sell zero-emission vehicles in western Europe. This was based on the assumptions that sufficient renewable energy supply capacity plus electric charging and hydrogen refuelling infrastructures will be put in place by then in Europe. Europe is currently accounting for about 10% of Toyota's global sales.

Global Battery Developments and Innovations

A critical success factor for both future EV and renewable market growth will be in the important areas of new battery improvements and battery cost reductions globally. These new future improvements in longer battery lifetimes and higher energy storage densities will be very important for improving the driving ranges and lifetimes of future new EVs. In addition, the development of suitable new battery systems which are suitable for green recycling will be important to meet the new environmental and recycling requirements that are being introduced by different countries globally in line with their Paris Agreement commitments.

Li-Ion batteries are nowadays representing the most commonly used battery technology in EVs. This is due to both their high energy density and increased power per mass battery unit. These have allowed the development of some types of batteries with reduced weight and dimensions at competitive prices.

Globally, CATL remains the largest battery manufacturer by capacity. CATL takes the top spot, with its batteries being installed in 32.6% of all EVs manufactured in 2021. In 2021 alone, CATL's installed power battery capacity was 96.7 GWh. This was a significant increase of some 160% over the 36.2 GWh achieved the previous year.

Looking ahead, the global growth of EVs will require a dramatic scale-up in the lithium-ion battery supply chain and lithium-ion battery manufacturing capacities in different countries. In 2020, there was about 630 GWh of global battery production capacity, with nearly 75% of that in China. Leading battery companies have announced ambitious plans to boost global battery production capacities significantly. Experts predicted that battery capacity could rise by over 3.65 times of the 2020 levels, to about 2,300 GWh by 2025. Looking ahead, industry experts have forecasted that lithium-ion battery production capacity could rise further, by over 5.4 times of the 2020 levels, to about 3,400 GWh by 2030 with the expected global EV growth.

EV battery improvements will be critical for promoting future EV sales and growth. The price of lithium-ion battery packs, which was US$1,000 per kWh in 2010, has already been reduced significantly by over threefold to below US$300. Experts have forecasted that battery pack prices could be further reduced by another threefold to less than US$100 by 2026. These lower battery prices should then further promote EV sales and growth globally (BNEF, EV Battery Pack Cost Forecasts, 2018).

Battery capacity boosting technology innovations will also be important for improving EV battery capacity and life. Technical advances in cathodes, anodes and electrolytes should increase the capacity of batteries by 80–110% by 2025. These technological improvements should generate over 40% of future battery cost reductions. A good technical example is that new battery cathodes will incorporate new layered–layered structures. These should help to eliminate dead zones in batteries. These should then help to improve future battery cell capacity by some 40%.

Battery manufacturers have also been developing high-capacity silicon anodes. These new silicon anodes should increase battery cell capacity by over 30% over the traditional graphite anodes that are currently being used today. Researchers are also developing new cathode–electrolyte pairs which should increase cell voltage to 4.2 V by 2025. These are significant increases from the 3.6 V to date. These should help to further increase battery cell capacities by some 15–20%, over current-day norms.

EV automakers will have to carefully balance their projections of the pace and trajectory of declining battery and energy storage prices against how other power train technologies and fossil-fuel prices will develop. A good international example is that future scenarios which would project a relatively quick decline in battery prices plus flat or slowly rising petroleum prices would favour more battery-electric-vehicle (BEV) development. On the other hand, other scenarios anticipating a slower decline in battery prices, as well as increases in petroleum prices, would favour more PHEV developments.

EV manufacturers will also have to develop suitable enterprise risk management systems and risk mitigation strategies to manage these potential product development risks. These should then allow them to hedge their future development strategies and risks in light of the long product development cycles. These should also allow them to better choose the right investment and development strategies amidst a range of potential technological options and uncertainties.

It is interesting to note that many innovations that will enable battery improvements and price reductions for automotive lithium-ion batteries are most likely to be realised first or faster in other faster moving high-tech consumer sectors, including consumer electronics and smartphones. The global demands for cheaper and better performing batteries in these important consumer sectors have been intense. Their development cycles are normally more compressed as these are critical for their continual growth and success.

Other important industrial sectors globally could also face big disruptions, from future battery and energy storage improvements. The emergence of cheaper improved battery and energy storage systems could seriously undermine the future profitability of the traditional capital-intensive fossil-fuels-based assets in the electricity generation and petroleum sectors globally. A good international business example is that power companies globally could face new challenges if low-cost battery storage would enable the wider use of renewable energy power generation integrated with battery storage and advanced distributed power management systems. Another good disruptive example is that the wider adoption of EV charging could alter the patterns of electricity demands in many key markets. In addition, the race between EVs and advanced ICE technologies could accelerate the international reductions in demand for fossil oil transport fuels globally, including gasoline and diesel. These should help to contribute to international GHG emission reductions and reduced pollution globally. These, in turn, should allow countries globally to better achieve their carbon neutrality and net zero goals plus to meet their Paris Agreement targets.

Looking ahead, international companies will also have to start to develop innovative means of recycling cobalt, lithium and other key materials from used EV batteries. These should promote the development of new cost-competitive recycling processes to extract these high-grade metals from various used EV batteries. These materials are used in cathodes of lithium-ion batteries, which are the most common type of battery in EVs globally.

A good new international recycling example is Sumitomo Metal's recent new battery recycling technology breakthroughs. These should help to bolster Japan's recycling of these valuable materials from used EV batteries. These, in turn, should benefit Japan's EV battery makers and EV car manufacturers.

Using its expertise in copper refining, Sumitomo Metal has developed an innovative process to cheaply extract copper, nickel, cobalt and lithium from used EV batteries. Their new recycling process will involve first crushing and then heating the resulting powder to specific temperatures, whilst adjusting the oxygen levels. Sumitomo Metal is planning to construct and bring their new EV battery recycling facility online in Japan by 2023. It will have the capacity to process 7,000 tonnes of crushed EV batteries a year. The new recycling plant should help to extract 200 tonnes of cobalt a year. These should be sufficient for making 20,000 EV batteries using nickel-manganese-cobalt cathodes (Sumitomo, Achieving Battery to Battery Recycling, Japan Mar 2022).

Other international companies, like JX Nippon Mining & Metals and Umicore, are also working on innovative ways to recycle valuable materials from used EV batteries. However, they have been struggling to keep their recycling process costs down, as their processes will require expensive chemicals. In contrast, Sumitomo Metal said that they can extract materials from used EV batteries at a relatively low cost and at commercial volumes with their new process. Sumitomo has claimed that its recycling process will remain competitive even if mined lithium values will fall to around US$5 or US$6 per kg, or if nickel and cobalt prices return to past lows.

Rising EV battery demands globally have sent the international prices for these valuable materials surging fast globally. Sourcing sufficient materials for EV battery production has become increasingly challenging for various businesses worldwide. Lithium prices have more than doubled over a year to nearly US$30 per kg. Cobalt prices have also risen about 80% to around US$60,000 per tonne. In addition, many of these materials carry serious international supply chain and compliance risks.

A good international example is that about 70% of the world's cobalt is mined in the Democratic Republic of Congo in Africa. Some leading international automakers have been trying to minimise their supply risks. A good business example is that Tesla has already made the strategic business decision to secure their own mining rights to lithium in Nevada in USA so as to guarantee their own future lithium supplies.

International pressure is also growing to use more recycled materials in EV batteries. Looking ahead, new EU regulations are being developed by the EU. These are looking set to require future EV batteries to contain a minimum of 12% recycled cobalt and 4% recycled lithium and nickel by 2030.

So, leading EU auto and EV companies are accelerating their various EV battery recycling developments. A good EU business example is that the VW Group has begun testing new ways to extract these valuable materials from disposed EV batteries. These developments should promote the recycling of these valuable materials. These will also help to reduce wastes and promote the growth of circular economy in EU and globally.

Sustainable Public Transport Net Zero Developments

Many countries and communities globally are recognising the importance of their urban public transport and public transit systems. These are very important for the efficient functioning of major cities globally. Public transport is also more energy efficient than private vehicle uses and will emit less GHGs than private vehicles. These should contribute to reducing GHG emissions from different cities and countries. These will have important bearings on the carbon neutrality and net zero plans of various countries plus their ability to meet their Paris Agreement commitments.

In COP26, various countries and cities globally have committed to further reduce the emissions from their public transport sector as part of their new carbon neutrality and net zero plans. A good international example is that some leading Latin American cities, including Bogotá, Cuenca and Salvador, have committed to turn their public transport fleets to becoming zero-emission fleets by 2035. These should help to decarbonise their transport sector, which is one of the region's biggest GHG emitters.

Many leading car companies have also, in addition to passenger EVs, been working on new electric buses and public vehicle developments for the public transit, railway and freight transportation sectors. A good international example is that Siemens from Germany has announced that they have made significant advances with their long-distance pure-electric trucks which could transform the European freight transport sector. In addition, different innovative EV companies in California, Singapore and Switzerland have announced that they have been actively researching and exploring the potential of autonomous electric buses.

Clean renewable energy supplies have also been increasingly used in different countries globally to providing electric charging for public transit vehicles and systems. A good international example is that Chile has announced that Santiago's subway system, which is the second largest in Latin America after Mexico City, will be powered mostly by clean electricity generated by solar PV and wind energy. This is part of Chile's national renewable energy drives and clean energy transition plans.

In Africa, Uganda has launched Africa's first solar-powered bus. These buses will use electric batteries charged with solar power which will help to extend the driving ranges of the buses. An Australian company has also announced plans to launch a solar-powered jeepney for use in the Philippines. In Bangladesh, new inexpensive solar-powered three-wheeled ambulances will be used to provide emergency services to the rural areas of Bangladesh.

The global COVID-19 pandemic has also shown that effective public transport systems are vital to keeping cities running globally. These will help to serve essential workers in health care, emergency services, food services and urban residents. The COVID-19 pandemic lockdowns have also put incredible strain on public transit systems worldwide. A good international example is that the US San Francisco BART system has lost some US$ 55 million a month at the peak of the COVID-19 pandemic. This was caused by decreased ridership and less sales tax revenues, during the most serious periods of the COVID-19 pandemic (WRI, Safer, More Sustainable Transport in a Post-COVID-19 World, USA April 2020).

In COP26, many leading cities and mayors have made new carbon neutrality and net zero commitments. These have created good opportunities for the scaling-up of the electrification of their public bus fleets. Experts have shown that the total lifecycle costs of electric buses are now nearing the costs of traditional fossil diesel fuel buses. However, electric buses have higher upfront costs, which are creating some entry barriers for many cities. A good country example is China Shenzhen. To help Shenzhen become the first city in the world to convert its entire public bus fleet to electric buses, China's national government has provided a subsidy of US$150,000 per bus. Chile also has strong national policies to promote electric buses transition and investments. Other countries and cities globally can consider similar incentives and provide new stimulus packages to help other cities globally to get over the initial electric bus procurement humps. These should then help cities globally to better achieve the significant air quality improvements and reduced GHG emissions benefits of wider electric buses applications.

In some other countries, support may be more helpful to be directed at the supply side. A good international example is that in the USA, e-bus supply from manufacturers currently cannot keep up with the rising demands from different cities in USA. So, ramping up electric bus manufacturing in USA should help to meet the rising demands and also create more new green jobs.

In other countries, more incremental upgrades may be the best green investment approach. A good international example is that in some African cities hundreds of independent minibus operators are the dominant mode of public transport. These minibuses are mostly running on fossil fuels and are major sources of GHG emissions from these African cities. A good African city example is that Kigali in Rwanda has been introducing larger capacity public transit buses featuring "tap-and-go" cashless payments. They are providing free Wi-Fi, which is a high-demand item in many African cities. They have also been installing covered bus stops for the passengers to use. These should all help to attract more urban residents to use more public transportation.

Sustainable Shipping Net Zero Developments

International surveys have highlighted that the international marine shipping sector has been accounting for about 3% of the GHG emissions globally. The GHG emissions from international shipping operations are also rising. These have already risen by 4.9% in 2021 from 2020, surpassing the pre-pandemic levels. Experts have predicted that these shipping emissions, if left unchecked, could grow further by 50% from 2008 levels by 2050. This will then make the global target of achieving carbon neutrality with net zero emissions by 2050 all but unattainable globally.

In the international COP26 meeting, there has been significant progress in zero-emission shipping commitments with many new initiatives announced. These included new initiatives to establish new zero-emission shipping routes, accelerate the shipping sector's decarbonisation plus to ensure just and people-centred transitions. Some of the key shipping announcements and deals are summarised below with international examples.

The Climate Vulnerable Forum of 55 countries called at COP26 for a mandatory levy on international shipping emissions which will be in line with limiting global warming to 1.5°C. They also called for the revenues to be used for urgent international climate mitigation actions.

Various countries and the private sector are already moving in the green shipping direction. A good international example is that the ports of Los Angeles and Shanghai, along with C40 Cities, have agreed to create the world's first green shipping corridor, between the USA and China.

One of the largest international shipping companies, AP Moller-Maersk has announced that it will move forward its carbon neutrality and net zero targets up to 2040, from 2050. This is in response to growing international customer demands for green shipping transport and clean technological advances. It is aiming to reduce its absolute international shipping emissions by 35–50% between 2020 and 2030.

In COP26, over 200 leading international businesses from across the international shipping value chains have all committed to accelerating the scale-up and commercialisation of their zero-emission shipping vessels and fuels by 2030. They have called on governments globally to enact the right regulations and put in place appropriate infrastructure to enable a just shipping transition by 2050 globally.

Nine leading international companies and big-name brands globally, including Amazon, IKEA, Michelin, Unilever and Patagonia, have announced that they will be shifting 100% of their ocean freights to green shipping vessels which will be powered by zero-carbon fuel by 2040.

Nineteen countries have signed the Clydebank Declaration to support the establishment of new green zero-emission shipping routes. These countries have agreed their collective aims to create at least six zero-emission maritime corridors by 2025 whilst aspiring to see many more in operation by 2030.

Twenty-eight international shipping and wind energy companies have launched Operation Zero. They have committed to work together to accelerate the decarbonisation of shipping operations and maintenance vessels working in the North Sea offshore wind sector. They are aiming to deploy zero-emission operations and maintenance shipping vessels in the region by 2025.

In addition to cutting emissions, the shipping industry's race to zero emissions must also support a just and equitable transition for its workers and services globally. The International Chamber of Shipping, the International Transport Workers' Federation and the UN Global Compact have joined forces to promote the just transition of the international shipping sector and its workers so as to achieve a zero-emission shipping industry globally. These will include training and educations as well as major new green investments in emission reductions from ships globally.

It is also important to build up the climate resilience of coastal and port communities globally. It is also critical to improve their infrastructures which have already suffered from various extreme climate impacts, including severe storms, flooding and rising sea levels. Experts have forecasted that various coastal urban areas could face more than US$1 trillion per year in various damages and costs by 2050. These will be due to the damaging impacts of various extreme climate incidents, including rising sea levels, flooding and extreme storms.

Green investments in the climate resilience and new green business opportunities of ports and coastal communities will be important for many countries globally. A good international example is that major ports and coastal communities could become future hubs for clean offshore power systems, such as wind and tidal power renewable systems. The green electricity generated can be exported to national grids with connections to domestic power grid systems. These should help to further decarbonise cities and create new green jobs. Work to restore and protect the shipping ports and coastal communities can also help to buffer coastal zones against economic declines plus the rising sea levels and extreme storms.

Turning the COP26 Clydebank Declaration for Green Shipping Corridors into reality will be especially important to the shipping sector's global race to zero-emission reduction efforts. In it, 22 countries have committed to establish at least six green zero-emission shipping routes by 2025. They have agreed to catalyse and accelerate the maritime sector's decarbonisation efforts. These should help to unlock new green business opportunities plus generate new green jobs and socio-economic benefits.

The UN held its international One Ocean Summit in France in February 2022. It is a good opportunity for governments, multilateral institutions, business leaders and civil society to work together to accelerate the roll-out of green shipping corridors, showcase zero-emission ships plus improve the climate resilience of ports and coastal communities.

There are also important international developments on clean shipping fuel transitions. Shipping experts have shown that there are currently around 50,000 merchant vessels out at sea or docked at a quay somewhere. These ships criss-crossing multiple trade routes around the world are generating a staggering 3% of the world's CO_2 emissions. This is equivalent to the same GHG emission volumes from Germany (BBC, The shipping giant banking on a greener fuel, London March 2022).

There are various international moves to promote the clean transition of shipping fuels from fossil fuels to cleaner sustainable fuels. The EU is working hard to cut shipping fuel CO_2 emissions. They are developing several EU schemes designed to make the use of fossil shipping fuels more expensive. However, a major problem for shipping firms is that the alternative cleaner shipping fuels are currently still only produced in tiny quantities compared with the traditional marine fossil fuels.

Some leading shipping companies are actively developing new clean shipping fuel alternatives. A good international example is that Maersk has made the important commercial decision to order 12 green ocean-going ships which will run on methanol. Each new green ship will cost US$ 175 million (£130 m) and is capable of carrying 16,000 containers. Maersk has estimated that these new smaller ships could save 1.5 million tonnes of CO2 per year, or 4.5% of its international shipping fleet's GHG emissions. These new green ships will hopefully help to kick-start the global market for clean shipping powered by methanol, which is potentially a clean shipping fuel for the international shipping industry.

However, experts have warned that it will be challenging to source enough green methanol to keep these ships running globally. There are only 30,000 tonnes of green methanol fuel being produced now in the world every year. Experts have forecasted that it is likely that the green methanol production capacities globally will have to be increased by at least 15 times to fuel all Maersk's new ships.

Methanol is part of the alcohol family of chemicals that are being used in paints, plastics, clothing fabrics and pharmaceuticals, and as a vehicle fuel. Unlike hydrogen, which is also promoted as a green fuel, methanol does not need to be stored under pressure, or extreme cold. Many ports also already have the appropriate infrastructure to handle methanol. It is also relatively easy to handle on ships, and the methanol ship fuel technology is well known.

Most methanol is currently produced from natural gas. Green methanol does not rely on fossil fuels and can be made in a couple of ways. Biomethanol is produced from biomass, such as agricultural wastes. Heat, steam and oxygen are used to convert the biomass into useful biofuels, including methanol. There's also e-methanol which is produced by using renewable electricity to split water into oxygen and hydrogen, which is combined with CO2. Methanol is also a hydrocarbon fuel and will generate GHG emissions. In its favour, green methanol has a much lower carbon footprint when compared to other traditional marine fossil fuels.

The Danish firm, European Energy, is amongst the very few green methanol producers globally. It is planning to supply 10,000 tonnes of e-methanol for Maersk's first new shipping vessel. The construction of a commercial-scale green methanol plant near Aabenraa in southern Denmark will start in 2022. Operations hopefully will begin in 2023. Once fully commissioned and ramped up, it is hoped that the plant will produce at least 30,000 tonnes of green methanol a year. The plant will harness solar power and CO2 from biogas production. Manure collected from nearby farms will be the main raw material source for biogas production.

Scaling-up is one of the biggest challenges for green methanol production globally. Compared to conventional marine fuel, green methanol is currently twice as costly. In addition, the new shipping vessels are 10–15% more expensive to build.

Looking ahead, ammonia or hydrogen may be a better long-term clean fuel solution for clean zero-emission shipping fuels. However, their technologies and commercial production processes are also still being actively developed globally. Greater international cooperation should be encouraged so as to accelerate these important developments.

8
Developments in Sustainable Smart Cities

美名胜过美貌

měi míng shèng guò měi mào

A respected brand name is always better than just beautiful packaging
Good reputation last forever

Climate Impacts & Challenges on Global Cities

Climate changes and global warming have serious implications for all the major cities around the world. Some of the most serious negative impacts and damages on leading cities around the world have been caused by the various extreme weather events induced by climate change and global warming. These include strong hurricanes, typhoons, extreme heat summers, freezing cold winters, extreme heavy downpours, flooding, droughts, etc. These extreme weather incidents have caused serious damage to various cities and communities across the world with heavy financial costs and damage.

UN's Intergovernmental Panel on Climate Change (UNIPCC) and scientists globally have studied the serious climate impacts and risks that are affecting cities and urban populations globally. The rising concentration and interconnection of people, infrastructure and assets within and across cities and into the rural areas have created serious challenges and risks to many cities globally. International surveys have shown that urban populations have grown by more than 397 million people between 2015 and 2020 globally. More than 90% of these population growths have been occurring in Less Developed Countries (LDC). The most rapid growth in urban vulnerability has taken place in unplanned and informal settlements, plus in smaller to medium urban centres in low- and middle-income nations. These have led to serious consequences, as their adaptive capacities are often limited (UNIPCC, AR6 Assessment Report, UN USA Feb 2021).

DOI: 10.4324/9781003142348-8

Cities and urban populations around the world are suffering various major climate impacts and risks. These include serious exposures to extreme climate incidents and their impacts. These include heatwaves, urban heat islands, extreme precipitation and storms. In combination with rapid urbanisation and the lack of climate sensitive planning, these are exposing marginalised urban populations and key infrastructures to the serious risks and impacts of climate-induced extreme weather incidents. A good international example is the serious wildfires which have occurred in many countries, including the USA, Australia, etc.

The COVID-19 pandemic has also generated serious urban impacts and has affected many vulnerable populations. The impacts on the health, livelihoods and well-being of residents are felt disproportionately by economically and socially marginalised people globally. Urban areas and their infrastructures globally are very susceptible to both compounding and cascading risks. In particular, these include risks arising from interactions between extreme weather events and increasing urbanisation. Losses and damage can become systemic when affecting entire urban systems. These can also jump from one system to another. A good international example is the serious droughts that have affected rural food productions in various regions globally, especially in Africa. These have contributed to serious urban food insecurity and shortages in various countries across the world.

The UNIPCC and scientists globally have also highlighted that many coastal cities and their communities are disproportionately affected by climate change and extreme weather incidents, such as flooding, storms, etc. These are, in part, due to the exposure of multiple assets, economic activities and large coastal populations which are often concentrated along narrow coastal zones. Scientists have detected and measured the early impacts of accelerating global sea level rises induced by global warming. The damages include subsiding coastlines, flooding at high tides, water-table salinisation, ecosystem and agricultural transitions, increased erosion and coastal flood damage globally.

Coastal and island settlements with high inequality are particularly prone to climate impacts. A good international example is that coast cities with a high proportion of informal settlements, as well as deltaic cities are very prone to land subsidence. Small Pacific Island States are also highly vulnerable to climate impacts, especially the global sea level rises and extreme storms induced by climate change.

Experts have predicted that the climate risks to coastal cities and communities will likely increase by at least one order of magnitude by 2100, if there are no significant joint climate adaptation and mitigation actions globally. Coastal populations exposed to serious climate risks in coastal cities, for instance, to a

100-year coastal flood, are expected to increase by some 120+% if the global mean sea level would rise by 0.15 m relative to current levels. The flooding risks will double if the sea levels rise by another 0.75 m globally. The flooding risks will triple if the sea level rises reach 1.4 m globally. These global flooding forecasts have been made by international scientists based on current assumptions with present-day populations and sea protection heights.

Scientists have measured that the average sea levels around the world have risen by about 8 in. or 20 cm in the past 100 years. Looking ahead, scientists are predicting that sea levels could rise further in the next 100 years. These are driven by climate change and global warming which are causing the accelerated melting of the polar ice caps and sea warming globally. Ocean scientists have conservatively estimated that sea levels globally could potentially rise by a further 1–4 ft., or 30–100 cm, by the end of 2100. These high sea level rises would be large enough to cause serious flooding of many coastal cities, including New York, Hong Kong etc., plus various Small Pacific Island states, such as Vanatu. Good international examples of the serious flooding risks include various famous beach resorts, such as Hilton Head, and leading coastal cities, such as Bangkok, Boston and Hong Kong. These have all been forecasted to be experiencing much more frequent and serious flooding risks by 2100.

Looking ahead to 2050 and 2100, many coastal and low-lying cities around the world are all expected to be seriously affected by more flooding risks and incidents. These cities will have to invest heavily in various new flood defences. These should include seawall protection plus sponge city designs and catchment ponds. These should help these cities to better survive and control these potential serious flooding risks.

Major cities around the world are going green and actively developing their new sustainability strategy plus net zero plans. Many cities are actively transforming their energy mix and promoting clean energy transition as part of their commitments to the Paris Agreement. They are actively transforming their energy mixes away from fossil fuels to use more clean renewable energies, such as solar, wind, hydro, bioenergy and geothermal. These clean renewable energy applications will help these cities to reduce their greenhouse gas (GHG) emissions. These cities should then be able to better meet the rising future energy requirements by their growing populations and economic developments. In addition, it will also help to reduce pollution and lower GHG emissions plus minimise their climate change and global warming impacts. Good international examples of leading green cities in the world include Copenhagen, Amsterdam in Netherlands, Stockholm in Sweden, Vancouver in Canada, Curitiba in Brazil, Reykjavik in Iceland, London in the UK and San Francisco in the USA. Looking ahead, experts have forecasted that over 100 cities across the world, from

Addis Ababa to Auckland, will be using more than 70% renewables in their primary energy mix as a result of their clean energy transition (Asian Development Bank, Green Cities, 2012).

A good international city example is that in the USA, some 58 leading cities and towns, including Atlanta and San Diego, have committed to move to 100% clean energy in future as part of their clean energy transition drives. Meanwhile, Burlington in Vermont has claimed to be the first US city to get all its energy from entirely clean renewable sources. Another good international example is in Latin America, where almost half of Brazil's greenest cities have been powered entirely by hydropower and clean renewable power supplies.

There are large variations in how different cities are undertaking their clean energy transitions and transforming their energy mixes away from fossil fuels to clean renewable energy. A good international example is that most of the 100 leading cities in North America are reporting their energy mix are or aspiring to achieve some 70% of clean renewable energy in their city's energy mix. On the other hand, a majority of Latin American cities that are reporting their energy mixes have already passed that important threshold and are using more than 70% renewable energy in their urban energy mixes.

Energy experts analysing the various city clean energy transformations have found that many leading cities in the developing world are actively supporting the clean energy transformations. They are capitalising on their local natural resources and renewable energy availability. The pioneering clean energy transformation activities in these developing cities have been largely driven by local economic needs plus the political commitments of their local and national governments. These should help them to generate new green economic growth plus reduce their GHG emissions and better achieve their Paris Agreement commitments.

Climate change and global warming are also imposing serious challenges to the availability of clean renewable energies to different key cities of the world. A good international example is that in Latin America, the production of green electricity from hydropower has been changing drastically between different years due to extreme droughts induced by climate change in some key Latin American regions. Looking ahead, some cities in the developing world, especially in Latin America, will have to further diversify their energy mixes into different clean renewable energy sources, including solar, wind, hydro, geothermal, bioenergy, etc. This would then help them to provide more sustainable clean power generations together with good energy security for their local population whilst protecting their local environment (CDP, Global City Report, 2016).

Looking ahead, scientists have predicted that the global population is likely to grow further and reach around 9.7 billion by 2050. Urbanisation is also expected to accelerate across the world. These could lead to more than 50 mega-cities, which are cities with more than 10 million inhabitants, being formed worldwide. It is important that the relevant municipal authorities should ensure that these mega-cities will function properly plus at the same time be attractive places for their inhabitants to live and work in. One solution is for major cities to adopt the new sustainable smart city design concepts, which are being adopted by many leading cities globally. Good international examples include Singapore, Dubai, London, Shanghai, New York, etc. These cities are also aiming to use big data, interconnectivity, and smart algorithms to help them to rise to the mega-city challenges.

The UNIPCC and scientists globally have also been studying the various potential climate adaptation plans, opportunities and gaps for major cities globally. They have found that many major cities in various countries are developing their climate adaptation plans. However, a few of these have not been implemented to date. As a result, there are significant urban adaptation gaps which are existing in many global regions and for all hazard types. Current climate adaptations in many cities are also considered inadequate to cope with the current serious risks posed by climate change and the associated climate hazards.

Looking ahead, experts have forecasted that the continual rapid growths in urban populations in major cities globally are likely to continue. However, these urban population have many un-met needs for a healthy environment, affordable housing and sustainable infrastructures. These should create new international opportunities to integrate inclusive adaptation strategies into sustainable smart city developments globally. These may include retrofitting older buildings, upgrading existing infrastructure, new urban designs, etc. Municipal governments and urban communities should work together to develop better nature-based solutions with safeguards and to develop better inclusive processes of climate adaptation and mitigation into everyday urban planning and development.

International experience has suggested that key new smart city climate adaptation options should include a mix of infrastructure, nature-based, institutional and socio-cultural measures and interventions. Potential mitigation and improvement options should include a range of vulnerability-reducing measures. Potential avoidance measures could include disincentivising developments in high-risk areas plus addressing existing social vulnerabilities. Potential accommodation measures could include elevating future housing developments away from the rising sea levels or flooding risks. Potential advanced measures could include building up and out to sea. Potential staged and managed retreat measures could include landward movement of people and developments. Potential hard and soft protection measures could include building new coastal flooding defences, such as new sea walls or coastal wetlands.

Disaster risk management, climate services and risk sharing should also help to expand the solution space and option ranges. These should help to increase the feasibility and effectiveness of developing other new options. There is high confidence in the economic and ecological feasibility of green infrastructure and ecosystem services, as well as sustainable urban water management. However, experts have warned that various institutional barriers, such as those in the form of limited social and political acceptability, may have to be overcome.

There are many good co-benefits and synergies for smart city climate adaptation and mitigation actions. Urban climate adaptation measures can enhance social capital plus improve livelihoods and ecological health as well as contribute to low-carbon smart city future developments. Urban planning, social policy and nature-based solutions with safeguards can bring greater flexibility as well as additional co-benefits for sustainable development of smart cities. Participatory inclusive planning for smart city infrastructure provision and risk management in informal, precarious and under-serviced neighbourhoods should be encouraged. The inclusion of indigenous local knowledge will be vital. There should also be good communication and efforts to promote local leadership, especially amongst women and youth, so as to promote just transition and inclusive approaches together with better equity and inclusivity co-benefits.

Green finance and good governance are essential for smart city improvements. Key innovations in adaptation in social policy and nature-based solutions with safeguards have not yet been matched by similar innovations in adaptation finance. Governance capacity, financial support and the legacy of past urban infrastructure investment have constrained how smart cities and settlements can adapt to key climate risks. Limits to smart city climate adaptation are often most pronounced in rapidly growing urban areas and smaller settlements. Climate financing has also been successfully applied to large-scale city engineering and infrastructure projects, rather than city maintenance or social innovations.

Access to green finance is often difficult for city, local and non-state stakeholders, especially in conditions where governance is fragile. Climate governance will be most effective when it has meaningful and ongoing involvement of all societal stakeholders from the local to global levels. Key stakeholders to be involved should include city residents and households, communities, municipal governments at all levels, private sector businesses, non-governmental organisations, etc. Indigenous peoples, religious groups and social movements should also be actively involved in the various adaptation and mitigation actions for smart city developments globally.

COP26 Sustainable Net Zero City Highlights

Many leading cities and their municipal governments globally have recognised the serious threats of climate change and global warming. They are developing their individual sustainability strategies and net zero plans to reduce emissions and to meet their Paris Agreement commitments. Many leading cities have also agreed in the various international climate meetings and COP meetings to work together to jointly achieve their carbon neutrality and net zero goals. Details of these good international cooperations are summarised below with international examples.

In the COP24 meeting, many cities and mayors have agreed to work together to try to limit global warming to below 2°C and then work together to further achieve the 1.5°C aspired target, as proposed in the IPCC 1.5°C report. In line with these new global consensus and agreements, many city leaders and municipal governments have been improving their environmental management and net zero plans. These have included enacting new firmer emissions reductions requirements and clean energy transition targets together with appropriate new municipal policies.

In the COP26 meeting held in Glasgow in November 2022, the impacts of climate change on major cities together with potential improvements were discussed extensively. There were many important international announcements covering new global climate alliances between major cities and new climate deals between major cities. The key COP26 city announcements and highlights of major city deals are summarised below:

New agreements to improve climate resilience in cities globally were reached in the COP26 meeting. The UN-backed Race to Resilience campaign launched a new metrics framework that will, for the first time, allow cities, regions, businesses and investors to measure the progress of their work in building resilience to climate change. Experts have estimated that these could affect 4 billion urban residents who are the most at risk by 2030. Over 2.3 billion people and 100 natural systems in over 100 countries are so far being covered by the work being carried out by the Race to Resilience's partner initiatives.

The urban green built sectors in various cities globally have achieved some major breakthroughs in their climate ambitions in COP26. A good international example is that over US$1.2 trillion of real estate assets under management have now joined 'The Race to Zero'. Over 100 small medium enterprise (SME) construction companies in ten countries, plus 20% of international architects and engineers, have also joined the climate campaign. The percentage of construction companies who are members has also doubled in the last two months.

On city climate resilience improvements, 33 leading cities globally have joined the 'Cities Race to Resilience' campaign. A good city example is Edinburgh city in Scotland UK joining the climate campaign.

London Mayor Sadiq Khan has become the new chair of the 'C40 Global City Alliance' (C40). This is the coalition of over 97 international cities, representing over 700 million people and a quarter of the global gross domestic product (GDP). The C40 City Mayors Migration Council Task Force will champion new international green ethnical investments. These will be used to boost climate adaptation and reduce displacements in migrant communities plus facilitate dignified movements as part of their new C40 climate agenda.

In the COP26 meeting, new international land use agreements were also agreed. These will improve future city land uses and conservation globally.

After the first week of COP26, new government commitments on international emission reductions were announced. These should help to close the emissions gap to better limit global warming to the aspired 1.5°C target, by around 9 gigatonnes per year (if fulfilled). This will leave around an extra 13 Gt of further emission reductions to go, according to the new analysis by the Energy Transition Commission. The global leaders' declaration at COP26 to protect forests and on transition to sustainable land use should account for the biggest chunk of that reduction at 3.5 Gt.

On green city buildings, 42 international businesses announced that they have signed the World Green Building Council's (GBC's) updated commitment to drive operational emissions from buildings globally to net zero by 2030. It will address embodied emissions, covering initial construction as well. US$1.2 trillion in real estate assets under management has now committed to halving emissions by 2030. Internationally, 20% of architects and engineers have also agreed to join the climate campaign. These should help The Race to Zero on its path to achieving net zero before 2050.

Major cities globally have committed to further reduce their emissions at COP26. A good international example is that San Francisco has joined Los Angeles, Mexico City, Oslo and Budapest in committing to at least halving the GHG emissions from the initial construction of buildings by 2030, with a 30% reduction by 2025. These are key parts of the C40s Clean Construction Declaration.

On city infrastructures, a new international guide 'The Infrastructure Pathways' should help practitioners and city planners globally to build new green city infrastructures. These should be developed in a way that will adapt to the changing climate and can also withstand climate change-related disruptions.

A Global Resilience Index was launched and went live globally at COP26. This should help to improve the way that insurers, financiers and investors globally better measure the climate resilience of different cities, countries, companies and supply chains.

The Soros Economic Development Fund (Or Open Society Foundations) has announced at COP26 that it will provide extra climate financial supports. They are channelling these to achieve equitable, community-driven climate resilience and green energy transformations in cities and countries globally which are most vulnerable to climate change, including small islands and developing states. The fund is now considering specific new green investments in these areas globally.

The Windows on Resilience programme has brought over 6,000 people through the Resilience Hub at COP26. These should help to elevate the voices of people on the frontlines of climate actions. It should also help to facilitate more international discussions on shared climate challenges and solutions.

Mission Innovation, which is a coalition of 23 governments, is launching four new missions for international collaborations. They are aiming especially to advance technologies for industry, cities, carbon dioxide (CO_2) removals and bioeconomy.

On green transport, over 100 national governments, cities, states and major businesses have signed the Glasgow Declaration on Zero-Emission Cars and Vans. They have committed to end the sale of internal combustion engine cars by 2035 in leading markets and then in all markets worldwide by 2040. At least 13 countries have also signed a similar memorandum of understanding (MOU) to end the sale of fossil fuel-powered heavy-duty vehicles and trucks by 2040.

Many leading cities and municipal governments have committed to accelerate the roll-out of more electric vehicle (EV) charging infrastructures in their cities. This should promote the growth of EVs and create extra green jobs. They have also called on other cities to recognise its importance and to follow suit.

Many cities globally have announced their commitments to accelerate the green transformation of their public transport fleets. A good international example is that some major Latin American cities, including Bogotá, Cuenca and Salvador, have announced that they will be turning their public transport fleets into zero-emission fleets by 2035. These should help to improve the green transformation of the Latin American transport sector, which is one of the region's biggest emitters.

The £27.5 million Urban Climate Action Programme was launched at COP26 to provide technical assistance to at least 15 mayors of mega-cities in developing countries. The programme should help them to deliver on their new goals to reach net zero emissions and build better resilience to climate change.

The UN-backed Race to Zero announced they have now reached 1,049 cities and local governments, representing 722 million people globally. These have the potential to reduce global emissions by at least 1.4 gigatonnes per year by 2030. Amongst those, 593 cities globally have committed to shift towards more resilient and sustainable energy systems; 501 cities are also working to build zero-carbon buildings; 415 cities have agreed to improve their waste recycling and aim to shift to zero waste; and 222 cities have committed to divest away from fossil fuels and to promote clean energy transition. In addition, 68 states, regional and city governments have signed up to a range of ambitious sectoral actions to accelerate climate progress by 2030. These will include new green projects on clean transportation, the built environment, clean energy, nature-based solutions, waste recycling, green agriculture, environmental justice, plus better intergovernmental cooperations and planning. Meanwhile, 33 cities and more than 76 regional governments have now committed to help build climate resilience within the decade as members of the UN-backed Race to Resilience campaign. A good international member state example is Maharashtra, which is India's largest state by GDP with a population of over 124 million.

On coastal cities, the Great Blue Wall initiative was launched at COP26. This will champion an Africa-led 2030 roadmap to conserve and restore marine and coastal biodiversity, while building up the climate resilience of coastal cities and communities. These should help to unlock the development of a regenerative blue economy that should benefit at least 70 million people plus contribute to just transition and net zero developments globally.

Smart Cities Sustainable Net Zero Developments

There has been rising urbanisation globally and almost half of the world's population are now living in urban cities around the world. Looking ahead to 2050, experts have projected that the international urban city populations are likely to rise further to 75% of the world's population. Cities and municipal governments globally have been developing their sustainability strategies plus their new carbon neutrality and net zero goals in line with their Paris Agreement commitments. City planners globally have also been advocating that it will be important to improve low-carbon city designs globally. These should support more cities transforming into smart low-carbon net zero cities in future. These cities should have the appropriate improved green environment to better sustainably support their rising city population. It will also be important to retrofit and improve older cities globally so that they can also become smart low-carbon net zero cities in future. The potential key challenges and improvements that are required for smart low-carbon net zero cities globally will be discussed more below with appropriate international examples (BBC, How will our future cities look, Feb 2013).

City planners globally have been working together via various international city research alliances. A good leading international university example is the Imperial College London Digital City Exchange. Their research on leading cities globally has shown that many large international cities may be reaching their breaking points. These have been brought about by various worsening city problems. These serious city problems include rising traffic jams, longer queues, delays on public transport, power outages, worsening pollution, rising congestion, poor air and water quality, etc.

In addition, the air quality and environmental pollution in many major cities globally are getting worse to very poor levels, which may be hazardous for their urban populations. Hence, there are urgent needs for the major cities in the world to prioritise their efforts on their clean energy transitions. These will help them to achieve major reductions in GHG emissions plus to meet their Paris Agreement commitments (Imperial College's Digital Economy Lab, Digital City Exchange, UK 2019).

There has been widespread recognition internationally that the commitments made by national governments and cities under the Paris Climate Agreement will be very difficult to achieve without concerted action by major cities globally. Many city mayors around the world have shown strong commitment to tackling climate change together with a willingness to collaborate internationally to achieve these strict climate goals jointly.

A good international city example is the C40 Cities Network. This is a global network of the mayors of some of the world's leading mega-cities. They have agreed to work together to address the key climate change challenges to major cities globally and to meet their Paris Agreement commitments. The C40 City group is actively developing new sustainability strategies plus new net zero plans and pathways for cities globally. These include potential new emissions-reduction options that cities will have to adopt in order to keep the global average temperature rise within the aspired target of below 1.5°C as advocated in the IPCC 1.5C Report (C40 City & Arup, Deadline-2020 City Report, 2018).

Experts have advised that it is generally recognised that the challenges to cities to limit their temperature increase to 1.5°C will be immense. Many major cities globally are already stretched to meeting multiple and competing priorities. International city leaders must develop their new sustainability strategies and new net zero plans plus determine the critical actions to reduce their current emissions trajectory further. They have to work proactively with all city stakeholders to build and invest in the appropriate new smart city low-carbon net zero infrastructures. City leaders have also to enact suitable policies and incentives that will be required to make significant progress toward achieving these green net zero targets. City leaders will also need to prioritise appropriate climate actions around key city initiatives that will catalyse systemic changes in their cities. The key priority climate actions should include urban greenification, decarbonisation, green buildings, improved energy efficiencies, better waste management and recycling improvements. These key action areas for international cities will be described in more detail in the sections below with various international examples (Mckinsey report, Focused acceleration: A strategic approach to climate action in cities to 2030, 2018).

Urban greenification will be very important for future smart low-carbon net zero city designs and developments. Sustainability experts have advised that future cities will have to become green carbon-neutral smart cities. These future green carbon-neutral smart cities will need to undertake significant clean energy transformation by replacing their fossil fuel with clean renewable energy supplies. Low-carbon public and private transportation systems will also have to become essential parts of these low-carbon net zero cities. These may include EVs, green public transport fleets and bike-sharing schemes. These future net zero smart cities should also include new green zero-emission buildings and green skyscrapers. These could include new living and office spaces which will vie with floating greenhouses plus high-rise vegetable patches and green roofs. These city greenification improvements should help to reduce GHG emissions and lower pollution in various cities. These should also help to improve the city air quality significantly whilst raising the living standards for the urban residents.

Decarbonising the electricity grid and power supplies for cities around the world will be an important requirement for cities globally to achieve the 1.5°C IPCC target. These will include a massive expansion of large-scale clean renewable power generation plus the phasing-out of fossil-fuel power generation systems. These should help to decarbonise the city electricity grid and power supplies globally. Major cities and their residents are normally the major customers for their urban electric utility suppliers and generators. These should give them significant leverage to shape the emissions profile of the electricity supplies that are being consumed within their metropolitan areas. Capturing this opportunity will not be easy and cities have to work together with key stakeholders to achieve these goals. Utility companies and regulators will have to play central roles in ensuring that the overall mix of green renewable electricity supplies would be appropriately balanced at a city system level. In addition, critical new power components such as advanced energy storage systems and smart grids should be put in place with appropriate infrastructures so as to ensure overall electricity supply reliability to the major cities globally.

City leaders and municipal governments will also have essential roles to set clear new decarbonisation goals and targets. These will be key for aggregating clean energy demands for clean renewable power supplies plus promoting energy efficiency. In addition, municipal governments should promote shifting more urban energy consumption to green electricity, especially in the transportation plus heating and cooling sectors in their cities. Through focussed acceleration, and close collaboration between utility companies and regulators, city experts have forecasted that major cities globally should be able to achieve a grid energy mix of 50–70% clean renewable energy in future. The clean renewable energy sources should include solar and wind, together with other zero-emission clean energy generation sources such as hydro or hydrogen. These clean energy transformations in cities globally could help to capture 35–45% of the total emission reductions needed by 2030 globally. In addition, the significant cost reductions in renewable power generation, especially solar and wind, should help to maintain future city electricity costs to the same level as now or even lower than current fossil power generation prices.

A major area of improvement in smart cities will be to optimise and improve the energy efficiency of buildings in the cities. In buildings around the world, heating and cooling have accounted for 35–60% of their total energy demands. These heating and cooling energy requirements have also produced nearly 40% of the GHG emissions from buildings.

Looking ahead, reducing energy uses and emissions from buildings in cities globally will be very important. However, these may not be easy and there may be many challenges. These will require significantly more focussed efforts and commitments than most cities have currently undertaken. These will include raising building standards for new construction, retrofitting building envelopes, upgrading HVAC and water-heating technology, and implementing lighting, appliance, and automation improvements. To realise good progress in these areas will require city leaders and municipal governments to work closely with building owners, both residential and commercial, plus real estate developers and building occupants. Combined actions by all parties should help to reduce energy costs and reduce emissions from buildings. In addition, these should also provide more resilient, comfortable spaces to live, work and play for future smart city residents through to 2050 and beyond.

The UNIPCC has, in its latest 2022 climate report, suggested that cities globally should incentivise green building developments. Since the UNIPCC's 5th Assessment Report in 2014, an increasing number of new zero-carbon buildings have been constructed in various leading cities in different regions globally. Improving green building electric heating, more efficient appliances and better lighting, plus the circular use of materials have been the key green building improvement areas. However, progress must also be accelerated in different cities globally to retrofit the older buildings. City leaders and building owners should work together to ensure that these older buildings are retrofitted with the latest green technologies so as to improve their energy efficiency and accelerate their clean energy transition. Municipal governments should also accelerate their developments of new green building guidelines for construction and use, as well as building energy codes. These will be essential to drive further progress in green building developments globally (UNIPCC, Global Climate Report, US Apr 2022).

The UNIPCC has also proposed that cities globally should redesign their transport systems to focus on shifting city transport systems to zero- and low-carbon transport systems. Experts have predicted that if cities do not change their current transport emission trajectories, then CO_2 emissions from the city transport sectors are set to increase by up to 50% by 2050. Cities will need to implement a suite of actions to avert these rising emission trends. The UNIPCC has found that cities can reduce their transport-related fuel consumption by about a quarter through a combination of more compact land use and the provision of car-free infrastructure, like pedestrian lanes and bike pathways. These shifts by cities toward better low-carbon, highly accessible urban designs should also improve the well-being of urban residents by reducing congestion and air pollution. Simultaneously, electro-mobility options like battery EVs, which is currently the fastest-growing segment of the auto industry, and electric railways charged by clean power have already helped to reduce transport-related GHG emissions in many cities globally and must continue to accelerate.

For the hard-to-decarbonise transport systems, such as the shipping and aviation sectors, various innovations in advanced clean fuels, including biofuels, hydrogen, ammonia and synthetic fuels, are emerging as potential future viable options. However, these will need more international developments and innovation together with more green financing and government policy supports (UNIPCC, Global Climate Assessment Reports, US Apr 2022).

City leaders and municipal governments globally have also been considering a wide range of various potential green mobility and transport options. These will include optimising the various public and private transportation mixes, including bike-sharing schemes plus future hybrid and electric vehicles mixes. A good international city planning example is that various leading municipal governments use green mobility and land-use planning to transform the transport systems around their cities. Many leading cities, including London, Amsterdam and Hague, have implemented dedicated cycle lanes in their urban designs.

The key to reducing emissions through various city transportation modes will be to ensure that all city residents will have access to a variety of attractive, affordable low-carbon green mobility options. Public transit-oriented transport developments can help to promote smart densification through better land-use planning. These will also lay the foundation for more multi-modal transportation systems which should help to reduce carbon emissions in cities in the longer term. Various initiatives in cities to encourage walking and cycling can also help to improve city lifestyles and improve urban resident health. Targeted enhancement of mass transit systems, such as the introduction of bus rapid transit (BRT) on main transport arteries, can also help to reduce traffic jams plus lower GHG emissions in cities. In addition, cities can accelerate emissions reductions by promoting the sales and uptake of the next-generation clean vehicles, including EVs, zero-emission cars and new energy cars. A good international example is that many municipal governments have accelerated zero-emission car growths in their cities by undertaking various car licencing and registration incentives. New autonomous vehicle digital technologies can also be used to optimise freight transport and delivery in cities. Experts have forecasted that focussed acceleration in these various green transport action areas can potentially contribute to emissions reductions of 20–45% of the 2030 targets, depending on the urban income levels and population density. These green improvements can also help to promote sustainable net zero city economic developments, raise the GDP of cities, reduce congestion and improve city efficiency. In addition, these should help to improve the quality of life for city residents by alleviating local air pollution and improving equitable access to green mobility options in major cities globally.

Future smart sustainable net zero cities will also need to tackle waste recycling and reduce emissions in a resource-effective way. Experts have advised that smart cities should adopt a prioritised approach involving the "highest and best use" approach. These would involve first reducing waste generation and repurposing as much useful finished products as possible. There should be increased recycling, composting and recovering of various waste materials for useful purposes. Cities will also need to manage waste disposal to minimise emissions of any remaining organic matter. A good international example is that methane emissions from various city waste landfill sites globally have been shown to have major impacts on emissions from cities and are major contributors to global warming. Reducing wastes should help to reduce GHG emissions and improve energy efficiency. Innovative models for waste management can help cities to rethink their needs for traditional waste collection and disposal infrastructures.

Some forward-looking cities are already going further and planning their transition to achieve a full "circular economy" with better waste recycling. These will involve shifting resource consumption from linear flows to continuous reuses and recycling. Waste experts have estimated that waste-management improvements in cities globally could help cities to achieve up to 10% of the emissions reductions that will be needed by 2030. These improvements will also provide additional benefits, including improved local resource resilience, waste reduction and improved energy efficiency.

Sustainable Net Zero City Transformation Benefits Case Study

Many major cities globally are developing their sustainability strategies and new net zero plans in line with their Paris Agreement and COP26 commitments. Various stakeholders have questioned what are the major economic and social benefits to these cities and their residents by their push to become new smart low-carbon net zero green cities. Analysis of the green transformations undertaken by some of the leading cities around the world has identified various major benefits. These included lower pollution, improved air quality, reduced GHG emissions, greener buildings, better living environments, etc. A good international green net zero smart city case example is Copenhagen in Denmark. Details of its sustainability strategy and net zero developments plus the associated economic and social benefits are summarised in the international case study below.

Copenhagen Sustainable Net Zero City Transformation Case Study

The impetus for Copenhagen's climate net zero plans and the drives for carbon neutrality started when Copenhagen hosted the COP15 global climate conference in 2009. City leaders believed strongly that they had to walk the talk plus set an international example for other cities globally. There have been lots of challenges plus setbacks during their transformation journey. However, Copenhagen is now well on its way to achieving their goal of becoming a carbon-neutral net zero green smart city by 2025.

Copenhagen has been undertaking rapid transformations and clean energy transitions which have helped to create new jobs, new economic activities and setting up of new businesses. The city government of Copenhagen has been moving actively toward meeting the goals of its 2025 Climate Plan to become the world's first carbon-neutral city by 2025.

A good green example is that Copenhagen has been working hard to reduce and offset their carbon and GHG emissions with clean energy transformations.

Copenhagen city officials have reported that their new climate policies and net zero plans have helped to improve the city environment as well as improve the Denmark capital city's sustainable economic developments and global competitiveness. By focussing on reducing carbon emissions and becoming more sustainable, the city is helping to enhance their citizens' health, well-being and comforts. These have also helped to improve their standards of living and employment opportunities (John Berger, Copenhagen, Striving to Be Carbon Neutral: The Economic Payoffs, July 2017).

Economists have forecasted that each time Copenhagen spends US$1 on its climate net zero planned improvements, it will also help to generate US$85 in private green investments elsewhere in the city. Economic studies have shown that the Copenhagen climate plans and actions should be generating an economic surplus of almost US$1 billion over its lifetime, which is a very significant economic benefit. In addition, there are additional benefits, including improving living standards, reduced pollution, better environment and improved air quality.

In line with the Copenhagen 2025 Climate Plan, the city government is aiming to reduce Copenhagen's carbon emissions by 37% with new clean energy transition policies and targets. The city is also planning to purchase international carbon offsets via the Carbon Emission Trading Schemes (CETS). These combined strategic moves should enable Copenhagen to achieve a total of 63% carbon reductions that would be required to become a carbon-neutral city. It is recognised that although the purchased carbon offsets will, in principle, help to result in net zero carbon emissions, the local effects of residual carbon emissions will still be felt.

Copenhagen has succeeded in reducing its carbon emissions by more than 40% since 1990. These have been achieved despite its population having grown by over 50% in the same period. The city is now home to nearly 600,000 people, with greater Copenhagen comprising an additional 2 million people. As the city's population increased between 2005 and 2014, its economy also grew by 18% in the same period. By contrast, its per capita CO_2 production has fallen by 31%, which is very good. These impressive reductions have been achieved mainly due to the city's clean energy transition plans and massive climate protection efforts. The city has managed to hold onto the various climate gains.

An impressive result is that the residents of Copenhagen have become the Danes who are producing proportionately less carbon than other Danes living elsewhere in Denmark. With 40% of Denmark's population living in greater Copenhagen, the city is only emitting 30%, or a per capita emission of 2.5 tonnes per person, of the whole nation's averaged per capita carbon emissions.

These notable accomplishments in carbon emission reductions have been achieved by much hard work. A good example is that Copenhagen has been transforming its private and public transport systems. It has also been encouraging its residents to use various low-carbon transportations. These have led to about 45% of all road trips now being made by bicycles. Over 75% of the cyclists have also been riding year-round despite the cold winters. The city has put in place a good bike-sharing system with dedicated bike lanes plus routes where cyclists can travel safely at designated speeds.

The city government has also increased the proportion of its cars running on clean fuels, including electricity, biofuels or hydrogen, by up to 64%. The city has established the ambitious goal of having all the city vehicles converted to run on clean fuels by 2025. They have also been implementing carbon-neutral public bus services. A good example is that the city will be converting their existing bus fleets, which are running on diesel, to run on clean fuels in future.

Copenhagen has also been improving its energy efficiency with major new green investments. A good example is that energy-efficient district heating systems are being used to heat approximately 98% of the city. All the heating in the city is planned to be done by energy-efficient district heating by 2025. There will be no chimneys on the roofs of individual houses as there would be no individual heating in the houses or flats in Copenhagen in future.

The improvements in energy efficiency in Copenhagen have resulted in significant savings to consumers and businesses in the city. The adoption of various innovative energy-efficient technologies has helped to bring new green products and technologies to the city. These energy-efficient improvements have also helped to lower production costs, which have made the city's economy more competitive.

Copenhagen city government has also developed specific new green investment strategy for their low-carbon transformations. A good example is that the city has been actively reducing the emissions from its district heating systems. Copenhagen has been producing heat from municipal wastes. They are building a biomass-fuelled power plant named BIO4 at Amagerværket to replace a 600-MW coal power plant. The new waste to power electricity generation plant has been designed to reduce CO_2 emissions by a massive 1.2 million tonnes per year.

Copenhagen's clean energy transformations and smart city transitions have demonstrated that these can help major cities globally to reduce their GHG emissions whilst generating significant economic and social benefits. Copenhagen city leaders have said that it has not been expensive for Copenhagen to go green. In addition, it also helped to improve the environment of the city and has created more green employment for the city residents. City officials have reported that going green has been very good for the local economy and has helped to create more new local green jobs for the residents. It has also helped to create a more vibrant city which is more liveable for its residents. These are important achievements for a world-class competitive smart carbon-neutral city. These can also be a very good international role model for other major cities to follow globally.

International Smart City Carbon Neutrality Sustainable Developments

Leading cities globally are developing their sustainability strategies and new net zero plans so as to achieve their carbon neutrality targets and to meet their Paris Agreement commitments. Many cities are accelerating their clean energy transitions by reducing the use of fossil fuels and promoting clean energy transition. They are promoting various clean renewable energy applications, including solar, wind, hydro, bioenergy and geothermal. These clean energy transformations should help the cities to better meet their rising energy requirements as well as lower GHG emissions and reduce pollution. Some leading cities have also committed to move to 100% clean energy in future as part of their Climate Action Plans. A good international city example is Copenhagen in Denmark, which is aiming to become carbon neutral by 2025 as part of their ambitious climate plans.

Decarbonising the electricity power generation and electricity supply grid of major cities around the world is an important requirement for these cities to achieve their clean energy transformation and to meet the 1.5°C UNIPCC aspired target. Power generator, utility suppliers and grid companies have to work together to ensure that the overall mix of clean energy sources would be appropriately balanced together with reliable supply security to all the customers in each of the cities. In addition, critical components, such as energy storage and smart grids, should be in place to ensure grid reliability and efficiency.

A good international example is that in UK, the electricity and energy systems in the major cities in UK have been changing to maximise supply reliability and economic benefits for businesses and households. Over a quarter of UK's electricity is now being generated by renewable sources, including wind, solar and waste. New advanced energy storage technologies are being applied and the costs for future energy storage systems have started to decline significantly. The UK Government Ministry BEIS and Ofgem have put forward new plans to upgrade the UK smart grid and smart energy systems so that consumers in the major UK cities will have more control over their energy uses. They are also applying innovative new technologies, such as smart electricity metering etc. (UK BEIS, Smart City & Grid Developments Report, July 2017).

There has also been good international cooperation on new smart materials plus clean battery research and innovations. A good international example is that UK and China have been cooperating on new battery and new material research, particularly on graphene. Graphene is seen by many researchers as one of the world's thinnest, strongest and most conductive materials. Scientists have been forecasting that graphene could revolutionise aircraft and car designs plus create new battery and new material applications. Graphene was first isolated from the graphite mineral at the University of Manchester by Andre Geim and Kostya Novoselov in 2004. They were both awarded the Nobel Prize for Physics in 2010 for their discovery.

China has now included graphene as one of the strategically important new materials in its National Five-Year Plans (FYPs). A new five-year UK-China research programme between China's Beijing Institute of Aeronautical Materials (BIAM) and the National Graphene Institute (NGI) at The University of Manchester, UK has been established. The key objectives of the joint research are to develop new graphene-based polymers which can be used in new batteries, new aircrafts plus high-speed trains and zero-emission vehicles. These new graphene polymers should make them both lighter in weight and more robust in performance. Specifically, the researchers will be focussing on developing new graphene-based composites with enhanced mechanical and conducting properties, together with improved electrical and thermal conductivity. These new materials should be very important for new applications in new smart grids, new EV charging stations, new battery and new energy storage system designs.

Two international sustainable city clean energy transition case studies, covering China and Sydney, are summarised below with international examples:

China Smart City Sustainable Clean Energy Transition Case Study

China is shifting its future city developments so that these will be in line with its global pledge to achieve carbon neutrality with net zero emissions by 2060. These future smart green city development strategies will include key themes on climate change, net zero designs and green developments. The Chinese Government has started implementing their new concept of "ecological civilization" nationally. These are in line with a famous motto by President Xi Jinping, who has said that: "The Green Mountains and Green Rivers are as valuable as Mountains of Gold and Rivers of Silk". In China, it is common to describe environmentally healthy rivers and water in shades of green.

There are important smart city transformation plans and developments being undertaken in various major cities and key economic regions in China. China has some of the largest cities in the world. Two good mega-city examples are Beijing and Shanghai. The urban population of Beijing is 25 million and that of Shanghai is 34 million. These have made them two of the largest mega-cities in China and amongst some of the largest mega-cities globally. The urban population in China is currently representing 57% of the 1.38 billion total population. Looking ahead, it is expected that with the rising urban migration across China, these could further raise the urban population in China to about 60% by 2025. Experts have estimated that around 250 million Chinese farmers and peasants would be moving from rural regions to urban cities, to become seasonal migrant workers in the big cities.

Putting this rural-urban migration in China into the global perspective, the Global Commission on the Economy and Climate has forecasted in their recent report that more than 2 billion extra people are expected to be moving into different cities globally in the coming decades (Global Commission on the Economy and Climate Report, 2018).

China is also in a period of transition with new urban cities being planned. A good city example is Xiongan, which is a new state-level special economic area in the Baoding area of Hebei in China. It is situated about 100 km southwest of Beijing and active urban developments are ongoing. Xiongan is part of the new green low-carbon smart city development masterplan for the Greater Beijing region in China. Xiongan represents a fundamental change in China's national strategy and its long-term city planning strategy. It will share some functions with the capital in Beijing but it can also take over some tasks from Beijing. A lot of the non-core central and municipal government functions and administrations that are currently in Beijing will be moved out to Xiongan. A good example is that Peking University has planned to invest and move some of their research functions from Beijing to Xiongan. The main functions of Xiongan will be to serve as the new development hub for the Beijing Tianjin Hebei economic triangle.

The implementation of this new smart city project will include significant green investments and sustainable developments. A good example is that the Central Government has forbidden some polluting industries from entering the new city area. In addition, some real estate development projects have been stopped until their detailed environmental planning and reviews are finalised by relevant government agencies. Xiongan will also include various new smart city designs with advanced modern technologies. These will include smart highways, subways, green buildings and green transportation systems (Xinhua, China to create Xiongan New Area in Hebei, Beijing 2017).

There are good international exchanges and cooperations ongoing between the key Chinese city mayors and other international city mayors plus urban designers. A good international example is that the British Town and Country Planning Association (TCPA) experts have been discussing with China city mayors and urban designers about various new low-carbon smart city designs. They have been exchanging views and learnings on various new potential city and urban designs with low-carbon buildings and green public transport systems. These international exchanges and cooperations should help China's major cities in their smart city transformations plus promote international cooperations and exchanges. The clean energy transformations in the key Chinese cities should also help to reduce their GHG emissions and lower pollution. These should improve their environment and the living conditions for their residents (Wang, Sino-British Summit Paper, China NDRC Renewables and Smart City Plans, 2017).

The PR China Government has been actively supporting EVs and new energy car deployment in their cities across China. The Chinese Government's support for new EVs has helped to create a new world-class new energy and electric car industry in China. These have helped to create many new green jobs plus promoted green economic developments and exports. A good international example is that the Chinese new energy car company, BYD Auto, has overtaken both Mitsubishi Motors and Tesla Motors to become the world's second largest plug-in electric passenger car manufacturer, after Renault-Nissan. In addition, the new electric car growth in China should also help to reduce China's oil consumption and improve its energy security. It will also help to reduce air pollution and carbon emissions in China.

Currently, China already has the world's largest fleet of light-duty plug-in EVs. China has overtaken both USA and Europe in the cumulative sales of EVs. China has also become the world's largest electric bus market globally. Looking ahead, China is expected to account for more than 50% of the global electric bus market by 2025. The rising number of EVs in China should also reduce GHG emissions from the cities and help to achieve China's Paris Agreement commitments.

Sydney Smart City Sustainable Clean Energy Transition Case Study

The City of Sydney in Australia is one of Sydney's central boroughs. It includes the central business district (CBD) and many inner-city residential areas too. The City of Sydney is home to around 250,000 residents. The City of Sydney in

Australia has been undertaking active clean energy transitions. It is shifting its energy mix away from fossil fuels so that it will be running on 100% renewable energy sources.

A good clean energy transition example is that Sydney is using locally sourced clean energy supplies from wind and solar farms in New South Wales. This should help to lower its CO_2 emissions by around 20,000 tonnes each year. The clean energy shift should also provide an estimated savings of AUD$500,000 (€308,000) per annum over the next decade (Euronews Living, City of Sydney now runs on 100% renewable energy, EU July 2020).

The residents in the City of Sydney will benefit from green renewable energy supplies and improved air quality. All the City's operations, including streetlights, swimming pools, council buildings and even the historic Sydney Town Hall, will be running off entirely renewable energy sources. This is the biggest green energy deal in Australia's history. It is estimated to have a total green investment value of over AUD$60 million (USD 40 M or €37 M) overall.

The City of Sydney Lord Mayor has said that the new AUD$60 million renewable electricity deal will also help to create more new green jobs locally in the new wind and solar farms in Glen Innes, Wagga Wagga and the Shoalhaven areas.

The City of Sydney has been carbon neutral since 2007, a feat which was certified in 2011. This has made the district the first city government in Australia to reach this important carbon neutrality milestone. The next target is to further reduce its GHG emissions by 70% by 2030. Roughly three-quarters of the City's power is wind-generated, and the rest will come from solar power. Renewable energy supplies will come from three different renewable sources in New South Wales. These will include the Bomen Solar Farm, Sapphire Wind Farm and Shoalhaven Solar Farm.

The Shoalhaven Solar Farm is particularly interesting as it is being developed alongside a not-for-profit (NGO) community enterprise, called the Repower Shoalhaven. The farm will also be used to power houses in the region. This should help to lower the energy bills for local residents. Once completed, Shoalhaven will generate enough green renewable electricity to power some 1,500 homes in the region.

9
Developments in Sustainable Finance and Green Investment

国以民为本

Guó yǐ mín wéi běn

The foundation of a country is made up by its people
People are a country's roots

Climate Sustainable Net Zero Green Finance Developments

Climate change and global warming have led to a rising number of extreme weather incidents in various countries globally. These include hurricanes, typhoons, heavy rainfall, flooding and droughts. These climate-induced extreme weather incidents have caused serious economic and social damage globally. These damages can run into millions and in some cases billions. A good international example is the serious wildfires that have occurred in the USA and Australia.

Many countries and businesses globally have recognised these serious climate risks. They are developing their sustainability strategies and new net zero plans together with suitable remedial actions. Globally, climate finance and green investments are growing fast in different countries. These are required to fund the many new green investment projects that are being implemented in various countries and companies. These are also required to reduce their emissions and to meet their Paris Agreement commitments.

The COP26 meeting in Glasgow in November 2021 has highlighted the huge climate finance and green investment requirements globally. Economists have forecasted that in order to reach the proposed net zero targets globally by 2050, around US$9.2 trillion per year of green capital spending on new physical assets for clean energy and land uses would be required, starting from 2021. These new green investment projects can also lead to the creation of some 15 million new green jobs globally (McKinsey, Net Zero Transition report, US 2021).

DOI: 10.4324/9781003142348-9

Economists have also calculated the potential climate finance and green investment required in different regions globally. In Asia Pacific, economists predicted that climate finance and green investments could add US$47 trillion to the region's economies by 2070. On the other hand, inactions or failures to act jointly could also wipe out US$96 trillion from the region's economies by 2070. In Europe, reaching net zero emissions by 2050 could add €730 billion (US$ 825 billion) to the European economies by 2070. On the other hand, inactions or failures to act could lead to damage amounting to €6 trillion (US$6.7 trillion). In the USA, climate actions and green investments could lead to a US$3 trillion gain in the US economy by 2070. However, inactions or failures to act could led to a US$14.5 trillion loss in the US economy.

Global green investments in clean energy transitions have reached a record high of US$755 billion in 2021. This is a significant growth as it is up by 27% relative to 2020. These are encouraging growths but more are required in future. Looking ahead, in order to achieve carbon neutrality and net zero on a global scale, the world will require US$125 trillion in climate investment by 2050 in various countries globally. Research commissioned by the United Nations Framework Convention on Climate Change (UNFCCC) has shown that these massive climate finance and green investments will be required to meet the aspired global carbon neutrality goals and net zero targets.

These various important strategic drivers and requirements have led to significant growth in climate finance and green investments globally. However, there are many challenges and issues for sustainable climate finance and green investment growths in future. Details of the climate finance and green investments growths and challenges, with relevant international examples, will be discussed in more detail in the following sections below.

Global Climate Finance and Green Net Zero Investments Growth Challenges

Globally, the climate finance and green investment financial sectors have been growing fast in recent years. Many economists have expressed their views that these are probably still not growing fast enough to meet the global climate challenges. A good international example is that the global investments in the clean energy transition and renewable power growths have been growing strongly in recent years. These have exceeded US$200 billion per year for the past seven years globally. Despite these rising investments, the total global investments in clean energy sectors are still much lower, say at about one-third, when compared to the total ongoing investments in the fossil energy and fuel sectors globally.

The current large financing and investments gaps between clean energies and fossil investments have posed major challenges internationally. Looking ahead, these big investment gaps will need to be reduced quickly. Countries and companies globally will have to accelerate their implementation of new green projects so as to reduce their emissions in-line with their Paris Agreement commitments.

Looking ahead, leading climate agencies globally have forecasted that over US$90 trillion of new green investments would be required between now and 2030 to achieve the aspired carbon neutrality goals and net zero targets globally. These new green investments and climate finances will have to come from both the public and private sectors. Economists have forecasted that leading governments globally will likely only provide a small amount of public green funding to seed green investment growths in their countries. The bulk of the new climate finance and green investment fundings will have to come from private and corporate sources globally.

A good international example is that in the UK, the Committee on Climate Change (CCC) has estimated that the total investment required to meet the UK's new climate plans and carbon budgets will amount to some £22 billion (US$24 billion) per year, which would represent about 1% of the UK gross domestic product (GDP). These will likely involve a public seed investment of only £2.2 billion, which is about 0.1% of UK GDP annually. The remaining green investment and climate finance funds will have to be generated by the UK private and corporate sectors (CCC, The 2014 New Climate Economy Report, UK).

Many developing economies, particularly China and India, have been growing fast. The developing countries and emerging economies also have high demands for climate finance and new green investments. These will generate additional new requirements for climate finance expertise and new international green investment opportunities.

A good international example is that China has announced that their new national 'ecological civilisation' green transformation programme will require new green investments of between US$470 billion and US$630 billion in the period from now to 2030. It is expected that the PRC Central Government would provide some 15% of green seed public funding. The private and corporate sectors in China will then have to generate at least 85% of the required future green investments and climate financing funds.

Many countries, stock markets and regulators are also introducing stricter ESG reporting requirements for their public listed companies. There is also growing pressure from many ethnical investors and responsible investor groups on many multinational companies, especially on the leading international oil and gas companies.

Globally, ESG reporting and investments are growing fast. Financial experts have estimated that some US$26 trillion of ESG investments globally are currently being invested in-line with the international ESG criteria. A good international ESG example is that in the USA alone, about US$6–7 trillion of investments are being invested and managed in-line with the ESG principles and criteria.

The Climate Action 100+ group has also reported that multinational companies focussing on the triple ESG bottom lines, including economics, environment and social, have been outperforming other broader market indices globally. Investment experts have also reported that well-managed clean renewable infrastructure investments have been bringing steady and stable returns in recent years. These are enabling them to be more attractive investments for international investors and mutual funds globally.

COP26 Climate Finance & Green Investment Highlights

In the COP26 meeting in Glasgow in 2021, sustainable climate finance and green investments were some of the major areas of discussion amongst the country leaders and delegates. The key discussion points plus the new global alliances and deals announced at COP26 are summarised below:

The Glasgow Finance Alliance for Net Zero (GFANZ) was established at COP26 by leading financial institutions and international banks globally. The companies which have joined the GFANZ have over US$130 trillion of private capital assets globally. These GFANZ companies have all committed to transforming their companies and the global economy to achieve the new global carbon neutrality goals and net zero targets. GFANZ has grown to compromise 450 international companies from over 45 countries. These GFANZ company commitments should help to deliver the estimated US$100 trillion of climate finance and green investment funds that will be required to achieve the carbon neutrality goals and net zero targets over the next three decades. These should amount to about 70% of the total green investments required globally, according to a new analysis commissioned by the UN High-Level Climate Action Champions.

The Bank of America has announced the creation of a new climate finance funding vehicle. It will provide green investment funds for new clean energy projects. These will include approximately 8 gigawatts in shovel-ready wind and solar renewable projects plus electric vehicle (EV) charging infrastructure projects in the Caribbean.

Leading international financial institutions, with around US$8.7 trillion in total assets globally, have committed to tackle and reduce deforestation globally. They will support deforestation by focussing on better management of the various agricultural commodities in their investment portfolios by 2025. They will, in particular, focus on palm oil, soy, beef, and pulp and paper.

The Global Energy Alliance for People and Planet has announced that they will launch a new green energy transition fund of some US$10 billion. The new fund will focus on accelerating and scaling up equitable energy transitions for a billion people in the developing and emerging economies by 2030.

The African Green Finance Coalition announced that they would be helping various African countries to work together to build up their climate finance capacity and credibility. They will also be actively supporting various new green investment opportunities across the African continent. This should enable different African countries to look ahead and tap into the international financial markets for their new climate and green investment projects.

The leading companies in the AFR100 initiative have called on peer companies to raise US$2 billion of green investment capital. They will use these green investments to accelerate Africa's locally led restoration of degraded land, before the COP27 meeting which will be held in Egypt in November 2022. This is in support of the US$400 million green finance capital that has already been mobilised.

Eight Pacific Island States, including Fiji, Kiribati, Papua New Guinea, Samoa, the Solomon Islands, Tonga, Tuvalu and Vanuatu, have announced that they will be the first countries in the region to receive climate finance advisors through the new Climate Finance Access Network. These should help them to build up new climate finance capacity in these Pacific Island States. These should also help to develop the new green investment project pipelines across the various islands in the region.

Bloomberg Philanthropies announced at COP26 that it would launch a new international campaign to phase out coal globally. The campaign is aiming to close a quarter of the world's 2,445 remaining coal plants and all 519 proposed coal plants by 2025. It will also be expanding its efforts to an additional 25 developing countries where coal power is projected to rapidly grow. It is already working in seven countries and the EU to phase out coal facilities.

Over 100 private and public organisations have partnered together for the launch of the Climate Resilience Hub at COP26. These international organisations announced that they would be supporting a global climate resilience campaign as part of the UN-backed Race to Resilience campaign.

The UN-backed Race to Zero campaign's international membership has grown to 5,235 businesses, 67 regions, 441 financial institutions, 1,039 educational institutions and 52 healthcare institutions. They have all committed to actively reduce each of their greenhouse gas (GHG) emissions by half between 2020 and 2030.

The international Cities Race to Zero also announced at COP26 that their international membership has now grown to include 1,049 cities globally.

A new Global Resilience Index was launched at COP26 to improve the ways that international insurers, financiers and investors will measure the climate resilience of countries, companies and supply chains globally. A number of new climate grants and green investments have also been set up. These will go towards building climate resilience in at-risk countries. This will include US$100 million from the Green Climate Fund to support new climate technology developments.

The UN's Net Zero Asset Owner Alliance, which is responsible for US$10 trillion in assets, announced at COP26 that it would commit to phase out most of their thermal coal assets by 2030 in various industrialised countries and then worldwide by 2040. Thirty-three GFANZ members are now part of the Powering Past Coal Alliance, with 11 new firms also joining them at COP26.

At COP26 in November 2021, the then UK Chancellor Rishi Sunak announced new UK requirements for firms in the UK to publish their plans for new net zero and decarbonising actions through to 2050.

The International Financial Reporting Standards Foundation (IFRSF) also announced that the new International Sustainability Standards Board (ISSB) will be developing a new globally consistent climate and sustainability ESG disclosure standard for the financial markets globally.

At COP26, the International Network for Greening the Financial System and Carbon Disclosure Project (CDP) have agreed to jointly explore how financial transparency can help to shift the global financial markets and systems towards achieving a more secure, climate resilient world. They are studying new international financial disclosure systems and mechanisms which can help to promote and catalyse these global shifts.

On blue bonds, Latin America and the Caribbean will be receiving their first blue bonds. IDB Invest will be issuing an AUD$50 million, ten-year fixed rate blue bond. The proceeds will support various sustainable water projects which will help to promote clean water and sanitation developments for people and communities in the region.

At COP26, the international financial sector has stepped up to protect forests globally. Thirty-three major financial institutions with US$8.7 trillion in assets under management have committed to phase out deforestation by better management of agricultural commodities in their commodity portfolios by 2025.

Two dozen countries and foundations, which have recognised their central stewardship over forests and nature, announced at COP26 that they would provide US$1.7 billion of green financing to support climate resilience improvements for indigenous peoples and local communities from 2021 to 2025. Their key focus will be to advance forest tenure rights and promote recognition of their key roles as the guardians of forests and nature globally.

On green investments advice, a newly launched nature-based solutions online investment platform pilot was launched by Capital for Climate at COP26. It should provide a comprehensive green finance and investment guidance system. It should help various international institutional investors to better understand why and how to improve allocation of their green investment capital towards nature-based solutions for climate change. This is likely to be of particular interest to green investors who have committed to reach net zero emissions before 2050. These should include the 400 plus financial institutions, which have over US$130 trillion in assets under management, that are members of the GFANZ, as announced at COP26.

On sustainable aviation, the global shift to sustainable aviation fuels has approached an important breakthrough after COP26. Over 80 aviation industry businesses and large corporate customers have announced that they are all aiming to boost the use of green aviation fuel to some 10% of global jet fuel demands by 2030. This will represent a huge 1,000-fold increase from today. These shifts from fossil aviation fuels to clean sustainable aviation fuels should help to reduce 60 million tonnes of carbon dioxide (CO_2) emissions per year. In addition, economists estimated that these green investments should help to create 300,000 new green jobs. The new sustainable aviation fuel transition projects and new green job creations will require significant climate financing and green investments globally. These should help to reduce GHG emissions significantly globally and contribute to the global carbon neutrality goals and net zero targets.

Global Sustainable Green Finance Country Developments

Leading countries globally are increasingly recognising the serious threats of climate change and global warming. These were demonstrated by the 200 countries attending the COP26 meeting held in Glasgow in November 2021.

Governments and countries also expressed serious concerns about the negative impacts of the rising number of extreme climate-induced incidents on their cities, communities, banks and companies. In particular, many governments and countries expressed concerns about how prepared and robust their banks and companies are in preparing themselves to handle these serious climate risks and extreme weather incidents.

A good international example is that an Aviva-sponsored Economist Intelligence Unit report has forecasted that up to US$43 trillion of assets could be lost by 2100 as a result of the various future extreme weather events induced by climate change and global warming (The Economist Intelligence Unit, The Cost of Inaction: recognising the value at risk from climate change, 2015).

Many countries globally have been actively promoting their climate finance and green investment developments. They have recognised that these would be required to fund the various new green investment projects that will be required to reduce their GHG emissions in-line with their net zero plans plus to meet their Paris Agreement and Glasgow Climate Pact commitments.

A good international country example is that the UK Government *Department of Business, Energy and Industrial Strategy* (BEIS) has launched the *UK Green Finance Taskforce Initiative* (GFI) to encourage the growth of the climate finance and green investment sector in the UK. These green finance developments should then better support UK's net zero transition and to achieve their target to achieve carbon neutrality by 2050. Economists have generally agreed that in order to accelerate the various new green investments, via debt or equity financial channels, the leading banks, corporates and lenders will all need to understand the associated climate risks and impacts better (UK GFI Green Finance Initiative Report 2017).

The European Commission has also published new legislative proposals on sustainable green finance. These new measures will have major impacts on asset managers, banks and companies in the EU. They will have to integrate various ESG factors and risks into their corporate management systems. There will also be new formal obligations for EU companies and banks to better disclose how sustainability and climate risks will be integrated into their organisational management and corporate services provided to clients. EU companies will have to pursue lower carbon emission objectives plus comply with new EU "low carbon" or "positive carbon impact" benchmarks.

Another good international country example is China. Green finances and green bonds have been growing steadily in China. The concepts of ESG and green financing are being increasingly accepted and supported by the PRC Government and regulators plus banks, financial institutions and listed companies in China. In particular, there is strong support for improving the ESG standards and governance systems for State Owned Enterprises (SOEs) and banks in China to comply with. More details on China's latest climate finance and green investments developments are summarised in the case study below with relevant business examples.

China Climate Finance and Green Investments Case Study

Climate finance and green investments, especially green bonds, have been growing steadily in China. The important concepts of ESG plus climate finance and green investments are also being increasingly accepted and supported by the various PRC Government ministries and regulators plus leading financial institutions and listed companies. The key developments and outlooks in these areas will be discussed in more detail below:

Leading PRC commercial banks have been very active in promoting climate finance and green investments in China, especially through their green credit business. Data released by the People's Bank of China (PBOC) have shown that by the end of September 2021, the green credit balance of 21 major banking institutions in China had reached over 14 trillion yuan or more than US$2.2 trillion. This has represented a significant growth of more than 21% in nine months, as compared to the beginning of the year 2021.

Furthermore, there are also important ongoing policy discussions on whether the risk weighting of green assets can be or should be reduced in China. These are being closely watched by commercial banks as any breakthroughs and new policy changes in this area will provide stronger incentives for green credit business growths in China.

The Green Bond Market in China has been growing well. It is expected that green bond issuances in China should exceed US$100 billion in 2022. However, China's Green Bond Market currently still remains a small share of the overall China bond market and there is large potential for future growth. Looking ahead, it is expected that an increasing number of green asset-backed securities and infrastructure green bonds will be issued in future.

Looking ahead, it is also expected that there will be further regulations of the Green Bond Markets in China. A good regulatory example is that the China Green Bond Standards Committee is working on the harmonisation of green bond standards and market access of green bond verifiers. These potential new future regulations of China's Green Bond Market should improve its transparency and raise market confidence (Guo Peiyuan, SynTao, The concept of responsible investment is increasingly recognized and accepted by Chinese financial institutions, March 2019).

Climate finance and green investments have also been growing fast at the local government and provincial levels in China. Local governments and provincial administrative regions have been releasing various new local green finance policies. These new local policies have covered green bonds, green credit, green equities, green insurance, green development funds, environmental finance and other local green finance areas. Looking ahead, it is expected that more local governments across China will be promoting green finance and more new local green finance policies will be released in future. It is anticipated that various local governments in China will continue to issue more local policies to support the development of green finance locally. These are expected to include policy signals and facilitation measures, substantive financial incentives, regulate standards and quantify assessments, etc. These should help to deepen local green finance policy developments, especially for the new green finance pilot zones in various leading provinces in China.

Climate finance and green investments have also been important elements of the China Belt and Road Initiative (BRI), which includes considerable amounts of green investments. Since the launch of the BRI, the international community has been closely following the environmental and social impacts of the various BRI projects and investments. There have also been good international cooperations by China with various countries.

A good international example is that in November 2018, the Green Finance Committee (GFC) of the China Society for Finance and Banking and the UK City of London jointly released the Green Investment Principles for the BRI. It advocated the incorporation of international sustainability principles in various BRI asset classes, financial products, project implementation, management of participating agencies and other management processes. These Principles have been endorsed by many large financial institutions and enterprises in China and globally. It is anticipated that these green investment principles will play important roles in greening the various BRI projects and investments. Chinese and international financial institutions will be closely following these Principles. These should encourage better management of the environmental and sustainability risks of the BRI investments in China and globally.

On international green finance cooperations, China has been continuously enhancing potential international cooperations on climate finances and green investments with leading financial regulators and institutions globally. A good international example is that China has undertaken various bilateral and multilateral green finance cooperations and pilot green finance programmes with the

UK, France, Germany, Luxembourg and other countries. These have covered green finance fields such as financial regulations, green bonds and information disclosure. A good international example is the UK-China joint pilot on the G20 Taskforce on Climate Finance Disclosures (TCFD). Looking ahead, these growing trends of international cooperation are expected to continue with greater participations by leading financial institutions in China with overseas financial institutions.

On FinTech, there are rising fintech applications in green investment and climate financing. There are also interesting developments of new innovative green inclusive finance. Good examples of potential new fintech applications include providing more abundant, accurate and effective data through cheaper and faster means, reducing search costs, improving the pricing of ESG risks and opportunity costs, optimising measurements, recording and verification of sustainability indicators, plus offering sustainable financing in a more creative and inclusive way.

With the strong growth of internet and IT companies in China, there are also strong growths and developments of new fintech technologies in China. Looking ahead, it is anticipated that fintech companies will be increasingly applying new fintech technologies to support the growth of inclusive climate financing and responsible green investments. These will cover important climate just transition areas, especially in how to combine climate improvements with poverty reductions in China.

Chinese regulators are also working actively to enhance the environmental and climate disclosure requirements in China. This will include new regulations requiring listed companies in China to disclose environmental administrative penalties and carbon policies. A good example is the new policy encouraging carbon emissions disclosures that were issued by the China Securities Regulatory Commission in July 2021.

China has also enacted the "Plan for the Reform of the Legal Disclosure System of Environmental Information". It was issued by China's Ministry of Ecology and Environment (MEE) in May 2021. The MEE has issued these new disclosure regulations which will require domestic entities in China to disclose a range of environmental information on an annual basis, effective from 8 February 2022. The new rules will apply to all listed companies and bond issuers which have been subjected to certain environmental penalties in the previous year and other entities identified by the MEE, including those that discharge high levels of pollutants. These covered entities in China must disclose relevant information on the various environmental topics. These would include environmental management, pollutant generation, carbon emissions, contingency planning for environmental emergencies, etc. Listed companies and bond issuers must also disclose climate change, ecological and environmental protection information related to investment and financing transactions, etc.

Global Green Finance and Clean Renewable Energy Investments Growths

Globally, climate finance and green investments in clean renewable power and clean fuel developments have been growing strongly in recent years. One good international financial example is that experts have calculated that these green investments have been exceeding US$200 billion per year for the past seven years. Another good international investment example is that it is worth noting that for the fifth consecutive year, the total investments in new renewable power generation capacities globally have roughly doubled those of the investments in fossil-fuel power-generating capacity internationally. These green investments should contribute to various countries and companies globally on achieving their new net zero targets and carbon neutrality goals plus their Paris Agreement commitments (REN, Renewables Global Status Report, 2017).

Global investments in clean renewable energy projects in recent years have been focussing on solar power, followed closely by wind power. Asset finance of utility projects, such as wind farms and solar parks, has dominated the global clean energy investments. IRENA has shown that there have been significant reductions in clean renewable power generation costs with new technological innovations in recent years, especially in solar and wind renewable power generation. Internationally, the clean renewable power generation sector has continued to attract far more clean investments than investments for fossil power- or nuclear power-generating plants. Overall, clean renewable power generation has been accounting for over 60–70% of the total new power-generating capacity investments globally.

Globally, clean renewables energy investments in both developing and emerging economies have been growing fast. These are mainly due to the clean energy transition and new net zero carbon neutrality policies introduced by various countries, as part of their Paris Agreement commitments. The green investment trends in clean renewable energy have been varying widely by regions globally. Clean renewable investments have particularly been growing strong in China, India, the USA, Europe, Australia, Middle East, Africa, Asia-Oceania and Latin America.

International surveys have shown that China has been leading the global clean renewable energy investments with 32% of the global investments. Europe was second at 25% and the USA was third with 19%, whilst Asia-Oceania was fourth at 11%. The Americas, Brazil and the Middle East and African region each accounted for 3% of the global clean renewable energy investments.

Globally, the top ten countries in clean investments have included three emerging countries and seven developed countries. The top five countries included China, the USA, the UK, Japan and Germany. The next five countries included India, Brazil, Australia, Belgium and France.

Global Climate Finance and Green Investment Financial Institutions

The international growths of climate financing and green investment funds have been supported by a variety of international green financial institutions plus central banks and commercial banks. Different green finance instruments are currently being used internationally. These include debt financing, green bonds, blue bonds and ESG investments.

Globally, debt financing has been making up the majority of the green investment funds that are going into new clean energy investments and new utility-scale renewable energy projects. These have included non-recourse loans, green bonds or leasing for different renewables projects. At the corporate level, there have been various debt borrowings by different utility or project developers. A good international example is that various international commercial banks have been active in providing project-level debt financing for clean renewable energy projects in different countries globally.

In addition to international commercial banks and bond issuers, the other major sources of debt financing for new clean renewable power assets have been borrowings directly from the different national and multilateral development banks globally. Development banks have also been providing major financing to green renewable projects globally. A good international example is that Germany's KfW has provided US$39 billion for climate finance and green investment projects. These have included US$8 billion for renewable energy projects and US$20–25 billion for new energy efficiency projects.

Another good Asian example is that the Asian Development Bank (ADB) has also provided US$3–4 billion of climate finance and green investments to support new clean renewable project investments in developing member countries in Asia (REN, Renewables Global Status Report 2017).

Green bonds have also been an important asset class for clean energy investors around the world. These have included various qualifying debt securities issued by development banks, central and local governments, commercial banks, public sector agencies and corporations plus asset-backed securities and green mortgage-backed securities and project bonds. Green bonds issuances have been growing strongly globally. A good international example is that G7 countries, including France, the USA, the UK, China, Germany, etc., are all active in issuing green bonds to fund their various climate and clean energy projects.

A good international country green bond example is that the UK has become a world leader in the structuring, underwriting and listing of international green bonds. The green bond market in the City of London, UK has grown significantly in recent years. Looking ahead, it is expected to grow even further with various new future green bond issuances planned. However, there is also more to do in terms of domestic pound sterling green bond issuances.

Institutional investors, such as insurance companies and pension funds, have tended to be more risk-averse. They have been more interested in the more predictable cash flows of renewable projects that have already been built and are in operation. In Europe, direct investments by institutional investors in clean renewable energy projects have been growing and are expected to grow further in future.

Leading electric utility companies have continued to be an important source of on-balance-sheet financing and project-level equity financing. A good international utilities example is that some of the largest European electricity utility companies have been actively investing in new clean renewable energy projects, as part of their clean energy transition and carbon neutrality drives.

Central banks around the world have also agreed that climate change is a serious financial risk to their countries and the world. The leading central banks of various countries globally have been developing different new climate finance and green investment policies. IEEFA has found that currently most central banks, beyond risk discovery, have limited use of active monetary policy measures to mitigate climate risks. The bulk of various central bank actions toward climate change to date have been focussing on the fundamental needs for improved disclosure and risk discovery for the various financial institutions in their country. IEEFA has also highlighted that the Central Bank of China, the PBOC, has been active in promoting green finance in China. Details of PBOC green finance policies and actions will be summarised in the international case study below with relevant financial examples (IEEFA, China Central Banking and Climate Action Steers Credit to Decarbonize, US Apr 2022).

China Central Bank Green Finance & Investment Growth Case Study

China has announced internationally its pledge to achieve carbon neutrality and net zero emissions by 2060. The PBOC has been active in greening China's financial systems. Climate risks have been seen as a serious threat to China's financial market stability.

Chinese President Xi Jinping has announced an international pledge that China will reach their CO_2 emission peak by 2030, plus achieve carbon neutrality with net zero GHG emissions by 2060. After the President's announcement, efforts in China to foster more climate-friendly lending have intensified. IEEFA have reported that they have found that the PBOC's actions to steer credit into decarbonisation efforts are bold and novel, when compared to other central banks globally (IEEFA, China Central Banking and Climate Action Steers Credit to Decarbonize, US Apr 2022).

The PBOC has introduced the important concept of the "five pillars" of green finance that it will be building to support the climate finance and green investment efforts in China going forward. These five key pillars will include green finance standardisation, green financial information disclosure and supervision, green finance incentive mechanisms, green financial products and markets, and international green finance cooperation. The PBOC has ratcheted its climate actions higher with conventional, unconventional and experimental measures plus new services. These should help to fortify the development of those five new pillars of green finance within China's unique economic, political and financial environment.

The PBOC has introduced different new green finance measures. A good example is that PBOC has extended new green loans which can cut 0.8% of the country's annual CO_2 emissions from coal power plants in China. Another key measure is the introduction of a new green finance facility that will provide discounted central bank credits to various state and commercial banks in China that are lending to enterprises which are actively engaged in carbon emission reductions projects.

The PBOC has launched the Carbon Emissions Reduction Facility (CERF) in China just after the Conference of the Parties (COP26) Finance meetings held in Glasgow in 2021. The new CERF will have substantial impacts on financing China's carbon reduction efforts. The CERF will offer attractively priced green funding to banks in China. These will be conditional on green loans extended to borrowers who should be able to produce proven, audited and consistent decarbonisation results. The CERF will also provide banks in China with the option to refinance 60% of the qualified loan principal at 1.75% from the PBOC. This should be an attractive source of one-year green credit at the moment. It is just 25 bps above deposit funding at 1.5% and at least 75 bps below China's interbank and bond market funding above 2.5%.

A positive result is that by the end of 2021, within its first month of operation, the PBOC has refinanced green loans to 2,817 borrowers in China. Together, they have promised to cut a total 28.76 million tonnes of carbon emissions annually. These amounted to some 0.8% of China's annual CO_2 emissions from the coal power sector. This is a strong positive start. However, the CERF's real test will come as actual emission reduction results come through plus when third-party audits are conducted and the PBOC assesses both for rollovers.

Climate Finance and Green Investment Challenges

The growth of climate finance and new green investments internationally has varied greatly between different countries globally. Despite the recent strong growths of the green investments and climate finance sectors globally and the increasing deployment of clean low-carbon technologies, the equity and debt financing for new clean green investment projects are still facing various challenges and issues globally.

The key reason for these challenges and disparities was that there have been some financiers and funders who have not been willing to take the significant early-stage financial risks in cleantech and climate startups. This has meant that many pioneering low-carbon technology startups have been struggling to attract the green investment capital that is required for them to grow and scale up to the commercialisation stage.

There are also several serious financial concerns weighing on the sector and holding back its ability to grow. One major international challenge has been that there is a low appetite for investment banks and funds to invest in green startups which have long lead times to commercial development. In many instances, these long lead times have been unavoidable due to the long research and development (R&D) periods. In general, cleantech startups have required longer investment timescales. In many cases, they have also required more upfront investment capital, to scale up to the commercialisation stage when compared to other digital technology companies. A good international example is that the first investment to exit journey time for a renewables hardware startup could take more than ten years. These longer timescales have meant that their early equity investment rounds have been typically unattractive and unsuitable for many closed-end financially motivated investment funds. These international investment funds typically have a ten-year duration, which are common in the UK and other key international financial hubs.

By contrast, the growths in international green venture capital (VC) funds have been stronger. The growth of this new green VC has been primarily driven by the longer-term strategic motivations of their financial backers and ethnical investors. They have also been facing some serious issues and challenges. One critical issue has been that some knowledge spill-over market failures have reduced their commercial competitiveness. New low-carbon startups have to struggle hard to acquire the necessary new skills, knowledge and technologies that are required to help them to deliver the returns necessary to justify venture equity investments. There has also been serious competition from other fast followers who have benefited from spill-over knowledge generated by the innovators and pioneers.

A good international example of green VC growth is that a lot of green finance and climate investments in Europe and EU have been generated by different corporate venture capital (CVC) funds. These have often been set up by various ethnical investors or impact investment funds (EU European Commission, Framework for State aid for research and development and innovation. 2014).

The longer time-frames that are required for cleantech developments have caused serious financial concerns and challenges for investors globally. The vulnerability to knowledge spill-overs has also been high. These have led to increased risk and have reduced the appetite for green investments. The start-stop nature of some government grant fundings for early-stage R&D has also increased the risks of the technology incubation stage and lengthened the prototype development process.

As some of the cleantech companies mature, the absence of a liquid secondary market has dis-incentivised VCs looking to move their capital onto the next opportunity. Private equity or institutional investors have also significantly different time horizons to venture capitalists. These differences have made it more difficult for VCs to exit and monetise their green investments. The situation has also been further compounded by the need for patient capital in new physical technology investments. These have then, in turn, lengthened and complicated potential buy-outs and their due diligence processes.

These various green finance challenges are likely to seriously affect the growth of some countries into low-carbon economies and cleantech hubs. Hence, different governments should seriously consider these challenges and develop suitable policy support and financial incentives to support their green finance growths to better support cleantech developments at different stages of their value chains.

One good potential policy support option is for governments to consider setting up a Green Investment Accelerator (GIA) for early-stage green climate technology grant funding. There have been similar accelerators which have worked well for the health, life sciences and infrastructure system sectors. Governments should consider new incubators with comparable mechanisms to focus on supporting early-stage cleantech and climate technology developments. These GIAs should include multi-year, multi-call schemes to provide fast track grants for early-stage cleantech startups. These should encourage new VC funding growths from suitable pre-qualified institutions with a good green VC track record. These would then provide suitable financial support to green startups at different stages of their development. These should then help to develop a thriving green ecosystem, with coordinated government and investor supports. These schemes would also need multi-year commitments, with regular calls for applications announced well in advance. These green fundings should also be complemented by funding from public funding bodies such as research councils or research institutes, which have clean growths and clean renewables energy developments as key objectives in their core programmes.

An international good example is that UK has already set up a successful Innovate UK Investment Accelerator pilot in health, life sciences and infrastructure systems. UK has been considering setting up a comparable mechanism to support early-stage cleantech and climate technology startups. This could be complemented by funding from the Research Councils UK which has clean energy growths as a key strategic objective in their core programmes.

Another interesting green finance support option is that governments should consider establishing a dedicated public-private green VC fund. Governments should consider setting up a new green VC fund to leverage their public seed grant fundings and to raise further capital from the private sector. The new green VC fund should focus on backing early-stage cleantech companies and small and medium enterprises (SMEs) in their initial growths and developments. These should also encourage more green capital to enter into the early-stage green investment market. This should support the growth of more and larger climate finance and green investment deals.

Annually, government agencies globally have also been spending tens of billions of pounds on the procurement of private sector goods and services. These could present significant opportunities to support selected innovative private sector cleantech companies to scale up through supplying specialist cleantech services to the public sector. The public sector should also take a strategic approach to public sector clean energy purchasing by considering the new opportunities presented by new cleantech companies. These should help to demonstrate lower-cost, clean energy services which could be scaled up to provide services to the wider economy.

Many international finance companies are recognising the importance of climate change and green finance. A good international example is that at COP26, the Glasgow Financial Alliance for Net Zero (GFANZ) was established by various major international financial institutions. GFANZ is comprised of leading financial companies which have over US$130 trillion of private capital assets globally. These financial companies have all committed to transforming the economy and industries globally so as to achieve the UNFCC net zero targets. GFANZ has grown to 450 firms from 45 countries. These GFANZ commitments can help to deliver an estimated US$100 trillion of green climate finance that will be required for new net zero investments over the next three decades. These should amount to 70% of the total green investments that will be needed globally to achieve the net zero targets.

Two international finance case studies, covering the green climate finance initiatives by two leading international finance institutions, Blackrock and Gate Foundation, are summarised below:

Blackrock Green Finance Case Study

BlackRock is currently the world's largest financial asset manager. It has US$10 trillion in assets under management as of January 2022. Blackrock has announced that they believe that addressing the climate change challenges can help to provide various good opportunities for their climate finance and green investments businesses.

A good international investment example is that they believe that the next 1,000 global investment unicorns will mostly be in the green business sector. Unicorns are company startups that have grown to have a market valuation of over a billion dollars. These could include new green companies that are developing clean energy technologies, green hydrogen, green agriculture, green steel and green cement (Blackrock CEO, Green Investments, USA CNBC October 2021).

Experts have forecasted that to achieve the global carbon neutrality goal and net zero carbon emissions target by 2050 is going to require massive improvements in various industrial and manufacturing processes plus clean technology developments. These will require large amounts of green investments together with a large amount of ingenuity and innovations plus international cooperations.

Blackrock has said that they are seeing rising demands from investors internationally to put their money into new green investment projects and climate technology developments. Blackrock, as one of the leading asset managers globally, is at the nexus between owners of capital and assets that they are investing in on behalf of investors globally. They are seeing that investors and asset owners globally are actively looking for suitable future green investment opportunities. These include new green opportunities coming from the clean energy transition and new net zero pathway developments.

At present, some environmental and climate-friendly technologies are still more expensive than their carbon-emitting counterparts. These price differences are sometimes described as a green premium. A good international green premium example is that sustainable aviation fuels are currently costing at least 140% more than kerosene, which is the traditional fossil aviation fuel.

In addition to private finance institutions, leading international financial organisations, such as the International Monetary Fund (IMF), the World Bank and central banks of different countries globally, must also play leading roles in climate finance and green investments. They should help to ensure that suitable capital and financing globally will be encouraged to be invested in new green investments and new climate technology developments globally. A good international central bank example is that the green initiatives from the PBOC on promoting climate financing and green investments in companies in China are actively reducing their emissions.

Bill Gate Foundation Green Finance Case Study

Bill Gate Foundation's climate investment fund is moving forward with their ambitious green finance plans. They are planning to funnel billions of dollars into new emerging green clean climate technology developments globally.

A good international example is that their fund, Breakthrough Energy, has put out a Request for Proposals (RFP) for green projects in Europe through Breakthrough Energy's Catalyst programme. This has come after the Catalyst programme released its first RFP for similar projects in the USA recently (Bill Gate Foundation, Green Finance Climate Fund, US 2021).

The Catalyst programme was launched with the aim of enabling a zero-carbon economy through public-private partnerships (PPP). It has already fundraised US$1.5 billion towards its US$3 billion target. It is planning to use the money raised to boost four different kinds of new green technologies developments. These include green hydrogen fuels, sustainable aviation fuels, energy storage and new technologies that will help to capture CO_2 in the air.

The Catalyst programme also plans to work on new PPP with the US Department of Energy (DOE). It plans to funnel US$1.5 billion over three years into joint projects with the US DOE after the US Congress passed the bipartisan infrastructure bill. US President Biden signed that bill into law in November 2021. It should help in unlocking US$1.2 trillion in new green investments. These should include tens of billions of dollars to promote various green technology developments. These will include EVs, updating airports, makeover the power grid, building new "hubs" for clean hydrogen and directing air capture and pipelines for captured carbon. It is estimated that these PPP could help to trigger up to US$15 billion of additional climate financing and new green investments in the USA.

Green Finance Companies ESG Developments and Improvements

Many governments and regulators from different countries globally have introduced new ESG policies and measures. These are aiming to improve the governance and oversight of green finance institutions and companies globally. Many countries and leading stock markets globally have implemented the new ESG regulations and reporting requirements for all their publicly listed companies and banks to comply with. A good international example is the Hong Kong Stock Exchange (HKEX), which has introduced strict ESG regulations and reporting requirements for all the listed companies in Hong Kong to comply with.

The ESG standards are an assessment framework (non-financial) for business performance and the work environment of companies and banks globally. Their ESG reports will be used to evaluate the performance of companies, banks and organisations in the three key areas of Environment, Social and Governance. The ESG has gained so much importance recently as it has been incorporated by many countries and stock markets in their new regulations for international banking and financing evaluations and reporting.

Globally, many governments, regulators and stock exchanges have included mandatory ESG requirements in their new regulations and requirements. Good international examples include both the UK and US stock markets. The ESG reporting is now an integral part of global corporate, banking and financing reporting and evaluations. Leading public listed companies globally will have to comply with the ESG regulations. They will have to prepare and publish their ESG reports annually together with their financial reporting. These ESG reports will be reviewed by the regulators, investors and various financial institutions. The reports will have important impacts on the performance evaluations and credit ratings of various companies by various financial institutions and credit rating agencies. These will then have big impacts on the future financing and invest-ability of companies and organisations globally.

However, many key stakeholders globally have also voiced serious ESG concerns. In particular, experts have commented that that the current accounting and reporting standards for ESG are not adequate and will need improvements.

A good international example is that the G20 Finance Ministers, in their international G20 Finance Minister meeting, have also voiced similar concerns on the international ESG framework and reporting standards. The G20 Finance Ministers have agreed to commission and establish the international TCFD. The taskforce is tasked by the G20 Finance Ministers to develop the new international TCFD framework to improve ESG reporting by companies and banks globally.

These various international developments are helping to build momentum towards the development of new global ESG methodologies and solutions under the newly created ISSB. These developments should help to improve the global standardisation of ESG and TCFD data, reporting and ratings across different companies and countries globally. There should also be room for various future approaches with continuous improvements. In addition, these new key developments should allow governments, regulators, stakeholders and investors globally to be able to better evaluate and compare various companies and portfolios across a core set of ESG metrics, on a more transparent and fair basis globally.

The IFRSF has announced, in early 2022, the release of the first exposure drafts of proposed standards for company sustainability and climate-related disclosures that have been developed by its ISSB. These new ESG international standards are aiming to address the demands by global capital markets for more comprehensive and consistent sustainability information from companies together with a more comprehensive global baseline of sustainability disclosures. The new proposals have envisioned sustainability-related financial information being reported alongside company financial statements. These new international requirements will require companies globally to disclose how sustainability-related financial information will be related to key information in their financial statements (IFRS, New Sustainability and Climate Disclosure ESG Standards, US Mar 2022).

The ISSB has stated that it is working closely with international organisations and jurisdictions to support the inclusion of the new ESG standards into various jurisdictional requirements in different countries globally. The new proposals have built upon the recommendations of the G20 TCFD, which was commissioned by the G20 Finance Ministers. It has also incorporated industry-based reporting requirements from SASB, which was recently integrated into the IFRS. The ISSB is planning to build on the SASB standards. They will be embedding the various industry-based standards development approaches into their own new standards development process.

Two important new ISSB draft publications in 2022 included the "Exposure Draft IFRS S1 General Requirements for Disclosure of Sustainability-related Financial Information" and "Exposure Draft IFRS S2 Climate-related Disclosures" (ISSB, Draft International ESG Standards, US 2022).

IFRS S1 has set out the new sustainability-related financial information reporting requirements for companies. These new proposals will require a company to disclose material information about its exposure to all significant sustainability-related risks and opportunities. It should include detailed information about the impacts and dependencies on people, the planet and the economy, if these are material to the assessment of the company's enterprise value. Disclosures required under the new standard will include relevant information to enable investors to understand the company's governance processes that will be used to monitor and manage sustainability risks and opportunities. It will include the integration of these risks into the company's overall risk management process. It will address the company's strategy for addressing significant sustainability-related risks and opportunities. It will also cover how the company measures, monitors and manages these risks and opportunities. These will include the various metrics and targets used plus the company's assessment of its performance towards its targets. The proposed new ESG standards will also require disclosure of sustainability-related information across a company's various value chains. These should include activities, resources and relationships along its supply, marketing and distribution channels.

IFRS S2 will require companies to disclose material information enabling investors to assess the effects of significant climate-related risks and opportunities on the enterprise value chains. The proposal takes a similar 'Governance, Strategy, Risk Management, and Metrics and Targets' approach as IFRS S1. Required information under the new standard will include the governance processes, controls and procedures which are being used to monitor and manage climate-related risks and opportunities. It should include relevant information about how climate change may affect the company's business models and processes. It should also include strategy and cash flows, and the identification of physical climate change risks and transition risks related to the shift to a low-carbon economy. Companies would also be required to report on their corporate plans to address climate-related transition risks and opportunities. These should include how they are planning to achieve the required climate-related targets, or how they aim to adapt to climate-related value chain risks.

Additionally, these climate-related standards would require companies to disclose their absolute Scope 1, 2 and 3 emission information, which should be calculated using the GHG protocol. These requirements will go beyond the USA SEC's recently proposed climate disclosure rules, which would require Scope 3 information only if they are material, or if the company has a stated emissions reduction goal that includes Scope 3. The ISSB has stated that "The requirement to disclose Scope 3 emissions reflects the importance of providing information related to a company's value chain".

The ISSB has initiated a 120-day consultation period in 2022 to collect relevant international feedback on their new draft ESG proposals. They are planning to issue the new improved international ESG standards by the end of 2022.

10

Carbon Reductions and Net Zero Carbon Solutions

种瓜得瓜

Zhòng guā dé guā

If you plant a melon seed, then you should get a melon when it is grown. You reap what you sow.

Climate Change Carbon Impacts and Carbon Solutions Developments

Climate change and global warming have been described as two of the biggest challenges that are confronting the whole world. CO_2 has been shown to be one of the key GHG emissions that has been causing global warming globally. Scientists have shown that the concentrations of CO_2 in the earth's atmosphere had been rising exponentially. International measurements have shown that CO_2 concentrations have been rising at rates of about 0.17% per year, since the industrial revolution. These rises have been mainly caused by the combustion of fossil fuels, especially coal and fossil oil fuels. In addition, large-scale deforestation activities in various countries have also helped to reduce the earth's natural capacity to reabsorb CO_2 via photosynthesis. In 2015, global CO_2 concentrations had risen passed 400 ppm. This was more than 40% higher than the pre-industrialisation CO_2 concentration of 280 ppm. In 2020, despite the global COVID-19 pandemic, the global average amounts of CO_2 hit a new record high of 412.5 parts per million.

The IEA has, in their Global Energy and CO_2 Status Report, reported that the international emissions from different fossil-fuel applications have increased globally. Higher electricity demands in various countries have been responsible for over half of the growth globally. The global power generation sector has accounted for nearly two-thirds of the GHG emission growths. Coal used

DOI: 10.4324/9781003142348-10

in power generation alone has generated over 10 gigatonnes CO2 emissions. These coal-related emissions have been generated mostly in Asia, China, India, and the USA. These have contributed significantly to some 85% of the net increase in GHG emissions. It should also be noted that in the same period coal-related emissions have declined for Germany, Japan, Mexico, France and the UK. These have resulted from the various coal abatement measures that have been introduced by these countries (IEA, Global Energy and CO2 Status Report of 2018, 2019).

These rising CO2 and GHG emission levels have contributed to worsening global warming and climate change impacts globally. Experts have warned that climate change and global warming could potentially cause massive damage and economic losses of US$1–4 trillion by 2035 globally. Economists have forecasted that the resulting "carbon bubble" could potentially cause global financial losses and damages larger than the 2008 financial crisis. Many countries across the world have already been suffering major climate-induced economic losses. Looking ahead, the negative impacts of various extreme climate-induced incidents are likely to worsen more in future. These will include typhoons, hurricanes, flooding, droughts and wildfires (BBC Environment, Carbon 'bubble' could cost global economy trillions, June 2018).

Many countries and governments globally have been developing and enacting new climate policies and clean energy transition requirements. These should help to reduce their GHG emissions as part of their Paris Agreement commitments. These include improved energy efficiency, reduced fossil-fuel consumption, increasing renewable and clean energy applications, etc. The application of various carbon solutions and new carbon technologies will also be very important to reduce emissions and to minimise global warming. These would include international carbon emission trading, applying new low-carbon technologies with advanced carbon capture technologies, including CCS, CCSU and BECCSU. These will be discussed in more detail in this chapter with international examples and case studies.

Some scientists and energy companies have forecasted that fossil fuels, including oil, gas and coal, will continue to play significant roles in the global energy mix, if new carbon technologies, such as CCS, can be developed and deployed successfully. There is a lot of work still required to develop these new carbon capture technologies, including CCS plus CCU and BECCS. More technology innovations are required to enable these carbon processes to become both cost-competitive and technically reliable so that they can become viable future robust carbon solutions.

An important driver for international carbon improvements will be the international carbon pricing. Global warming and climate change have incurred huge financial losses and high social costs to different countries around the world. The various carbon and social costs can vary significantly from country to country depending on their specific social and economic conditions. The US Environmental Protection Agency (EPA) has estimated that the global averaged social cost of carbon would typically be about US$41/tonne (272 yuan). Good international examples of various carbon social costs include that India's social costs are about US$86 per tonne, the US costs are close to US$48, Saudi Arabia costs are some US$47, plus China, Brazil and the UAE costs are about US$24.

Carbon pricings have had marked impacts on emission reductions in countries where there has been good policy support for carbon emission trading systems (CETS) with a level of price certainty provided. To encourage decarbonisation, a carbon price floor should be considered. Most international carbon markets have yet to yield significant emissions reductions to date. Key reasons include low-carbon prices plus over-allocation of carbon credits and poor carbon management (Nature Climate Change, Country Level Social Cost of Carbon, Sept 2018).

To mitigate the rising carbon issue globally, various new innovative carbon solutions are being developed. These include international carbon offsets and CETS plus potential new carbon capture technologies, such as CCS, CCU and BECCS. These various potential carbon technologies and solutions will be discussed in more detail below with international examples and case studies.

COP26 Carbon Market Agreements and Announcements

One important and surprisingly good outcome from the international COP26 meeting held in Glasgow in November 2021 was an agreement between world leaders on a new set of rules for regulating the international carbon markets. This will allow countries globally to trade their carbon credit rights, which should help to reduce GHG emissions globally. This will essentially support the transfer of emission reductions between countries whilst also incentivising the private sector to invest in climate-friendly carbon solutions (The Conversation, COP26 agreed rules on trading carbon emissions, USA Dec 2021).

These are important developments of Article 6 of the Paris Agreement, which aims at promoting integrated, holistic and balanced approaches that will assist governments in implementing their nationally determined contributions (NDCs) through voluntary international cooperation. These international carbon cooperation mechanisms, if properly designed, should make it easier to achieve the carbon reduction targets plus raise ambitions via various international market mechanisms and non-market approaches as stipulated in Article 6.

COP26 has confirmed the role of the Voluntary Carbon Market Mechanism (VCM), to channel international finance, technology and capacities from various countries to different climate mitigation activities, particularly in the developing countries. These will support the transfer of various carbon mitigation outcomes and emissions reductions globally. These should also help different countries to better meet their NDC and to achieve their Paris Agreement commitments.

The United Nations Framework Convention on Climate Change (UNFCC) summaries have shown that at COP26, the various countries reached new agreements for international carbon market mechanisms. These will essentially support the transfer of emission reductions between countries whilst also incentivising the private sector and companies to invest in climate-friendly solutions (UNFCC, COP26 Outcomes: Market mechanisms and non-market approaches (Article 6), US 2022).

Simultaneously, the various countries and parties at COP26 have also reached agreements on the various international non-market approaches which should enable stronger cooperations between countries on mitigation and adaptation globally. Countries have agreed to the implementation of new rules for three key instruments that should help the various parties to cooperate more to meet their intended emission reductions and adaptation aims as captured in their national climate action plans under the Paris Agreement (Nationally Determined Contributions, or NDCs).

The first two of these instruments involve international cooperations which will help to result in the smoother transfer of emission mitigation outcomes between different countries. It will support the transfers from the country that have achieved their emission reductions to another country that will acquire these reductions. The instruments have been designed to enable and incentivise private sector involvements. Under the non-market approaches, countries are enabled to work together to achieve mitigation and adaptation, as well as sustainable development and poverty reduction.

Decisions on implementation rules were adopted for all three instruments. Firstly, guidance was adopted for cooperative approaches where parties in bilateral arrangements can recognise the transfer of emission reductions between them. These should enable mitigation programmes, such as international emission trading systems in different countries to link with each other.

Secondly, rules, modalities and procedures were adopted for the new UNFCCC mechanism, which provide credits for different emission-reducing activities. These should enable a company in one country to reduce emissions in that country and then have these reductions credited so that it can then sell these credits to another company in another country. Then that second company may use these credits for complying with its own emission reduction obligations or to help it meet its new net zero targets.

Thirdly, the various countries have adopted a work programme to support non-market approaches that are being implemented between the different parties. The work programme should help different countries plus their institutions and stakeholders to develop better cooperations in a number of important areas, such as the development of clean energy sources.

These new COP26 carbon market agreements will help the world to move closer towards the Paris Agreement goal of holding the global average temperature rise to as close as possible to 1.5°C. Strengthened international cooperations should enable the different parties to be more ambitious in their actions to curb GHG emissions and to build resilience to climate change. These should make it more cost-efficient for different countries to meet their NDCs. These should also enable them to consider going further in their mitigation than their NDCs had intended, or to adopt extra adaptation actions resulting from deeper emission reduction efforts.

These new COP26 carbon market agreements should also encourage more private sector involvements. Both the cooperative approaches and the UNFCCC mechanisms should incentivise the private sector to implement more mitigation activities across the world. These can cover a range of sectors and technologies, such as energy efficiency, transport and reforestation. These new carbon mitigation activities will also allow for the development of international carbon credits. These can then be transferred internationally and used in other countries towards meeting the aims of NDCs or other compliance uses. These instruments should deliver important investment signals to the private sector, which should help to support different countries to achieve a bigger scale in their climate mitigation actions. These, in turn, should help to contribute to stronger international climate adaptation actions.

The new COP26 carbon market agreement will have big implications for different governments at various levels and for the private sector globally. For the private sector, the adoption of these rules should enable new mitigation activities to start. In particular, these will include implementing mitigation projects under the new UNFCCC mechanism. In addition, many activities that are already operating under the clean development mechanism (CDM) of the Kyoto Protocol will now be able to move over to the new UNFCCC mechanism. They can use the new rules that have been adopted which support these transitions.

After the new COP26 carbon market agreements, international parties will have to work together on the next steps to deliver real benefits globally. For cooperative approaches, countries that are cooperating already to deliver their NDCs with cooperative approaches will now start to provide the details of those approaches through their reports. The purposes of these reports are to allow for accurate accounting of international transfers and to provide transparency as to the way in which countries are cooperating globally.

For the project mechanisms, the bodies that supervise the CDM and the new UNFCCC mechanism have agreed to meet each other further in 2022. They will work together to start to deliver the rules for new projects and the processes for transitioning existing projects over to the new system under the Paris Agreement.

In relation to cooperations that do not involve carbon credits, a committee will start to meet in mid-2022 to implement the programme of work that the Parties at COP26 have agreed in Glasgow. Further aspects will be worked on by the various parties in the SBSTA meetings in 2022–2023 so as to add and develop some more details for implementation.

Carbon Solutions Global Developments and Outlooks

To mitigate the serious carbon emission issue globally, various new innovative carbon solutions and new carbon removal technologies are being developed by different countries and companies globally. These should help them to reduce their carbon emissions plus meet their Paris Agreement targets and commitments.

After the COP26 new carbon agreements, carbon offsets and CETS developments will become increasingly important carbon solutions for countries and companies to consider.

New carbon capture technologies are also being actively developed by various countries and companies. These include Direct Air Capture (DAC), CCS, CCU and BECCS. There are also innovative technologies for DAC being developed globally.

These various potential carbon solutions will be discussed in more detail in the various relevant sections below together with relevant international examples and case studies.

Carbon Offsets and Emission Trading Developments

With the new carbon market agreements that have been reached at COP26, carbon offsets and international carbon trading will become increasingly important carbon solution measures to help countries and companies globally to meet their carbon neutrality goals and net zero targets.

Carbon offsets will enable countries, cities and businesses to better control and offset their residual carbon emissions after implementing all their carbon emission reduction measures. In addition, it will also provide a critical source of green finance for new renewable energy developments plus emission reduction projects around the world. A good international example is that the global voluntary carbon offset market was only valued at around US$ 1 billion in 2021. Looking ahead, carbon experts have forecasted that the global Voluntary Carbon Offsets market size is projected to grow strongly and more than double by 2027 with a CAGR growth rate of more than 12% per year over the period.

Tackling rising carbon levels using carbon offsetting was first adopted at the Kyoto Treaty conference in Japan in 1997. Over the past 20 years, the design, operation and administration of various carbon offset schemes have been developing and improving. Today, carbon credits generated by voluntary offset schemes are subjected to rigorous industry standards. These should provide a comprehensive methodology framework plus an independent verification process and an international registry to ensure that these emissions reductions are real, permanent and unique. The UN has also endorsed carbon offsets as a valid way to reduce carbon emissions quickly and cost-effectively. These should help countries, cities and companies globally to speed up and scale up their green transformations to achieve their carbon neutrality goals and net zero targets (Wang, Climate Change and Clean Energy Management, Routledge UK 2019).

Various companies around the world have already collectively invested nearly US$4.5 billion over the past decade to purchase nearly 1 billion of carbon offsets from green projects globally which have reduced or sequestered GHGs. Overall, international carbon offset buyers have purchased about one-quarter as many offsets as the carbon emissions they have reduced directly. Experts have estimated that carbon offsets have helped to increase these companies' collective carbon mitigation impacts by some 25%.

A study by Imperial College London (ICL) on 59 carbon offsetting projects has shown that the purchasing of carbon credits by various companies has created a host of additional benefits. These include creating more green jobs and incomes, conserving local ecologies, improving access to clean water and health care, enhancing skills acquisition and promoting gender equality. The ICL research has estimated that when a business would offset one tonne of its CO_2 footprint then it should generate an additional £530 (US$664) in benefits to the communities where the carbon reduction projects are based. The costs of purchasing a tonne of carbon offset have typically been below €45 (USD 45) to date. These values would obviously vary globally depending on the projects participating in the research study. The results still demonstrated that the wider economic, environmental and social impacts of using offsets would be considerable. The ICL study has also found that businesses investing in carbon offsets have also reported additional benefits such as enhanced brand images plus more engaged employees and better market differentiation for their products or services (Imperial College London & ICROA, Unlocking the hidden value of carbon offsetting, 2014).

Carbon offsetting, as part of an overall corporate carbon management strategy, should enable companies to cost-effectively reach their goals of carbon emissions reductions, which may normally be beyond their business's economic or technical competence. These have provided good opportunities to accelerate businesses to respond to the urgent needs to reduce GHGs in line with their Paris Agreement commitments. International experience has also shown that carbon offsets should also bring a host of wider environmental, economic and social benefits to communities in other parts of the world. Carbon offsets can also help to enhance the brand images and reputations for a participating company's products and services plus make these more attractive for their customers (BP, Carbon Neutral Management Plans, London 2017).

International companies have rallied around a few reputable third-party carbon offset certificators. These should ensure that their carbon offsets are properly certified. A good example is the Gold Standard, which has worked since 2003, to ensure the efficacy of carbon offset programmes. To date, they've helped over 80 non-governmental organisations (NGOs) and 1,400 projects globally to make a genuine difference in their carbon offsets and carbon emission reductions. Other well-documented carbon offset programmes include Verra's Verified Carbon Standard Program, Climate Action Reserve. A good international example of successful carbon offsets global applications is summarised in the international case study below:

Carbon Offsetting Company Atmosfair Case Study

Atmosfair is based in Germany and has been involved with carbon offset projects globally. To date, their efforts have helped to keep almost 4 million tonnes of carbon away from the atmosphere. The bulk of their projects, over 90%, are actively reducing carbon in the air. The other 10% are working to provide developing countries with appropriate resources that they will need to reduce their own carbon emissions. Their carbon offset projects have included funding new renewable energy and clean energy transition projects worldwide. A good international example is the provision of clean efficient cooking stoves in developing countries like Nigeria, Rwanda and India. All the Atmosfair carbon offset projects have either been already certified by the Gold Standard or been submitted to them for approval.

Forest Natural Carbon Solution Developments

Many governments and countries globally have been putting in place appropriate new policies and measures to meet their Paris Agreement commitments. Experts have predicted that there are likely to be big gaps between the commitments that countries have made under the Paris Climate Agreement and the emissions reductions that would be required to avoid the worst consequences of global warming.

A good international example is that according to the UN Environment's Emissions Gap Report 2017, current pledges from governments would represent only about half of the emission reduction that would be required to avoid a 2°C temperature rise, and just one-third of what would be required to limit warming to 1.5°C (UN Environment, Emissions Gap Report, UN US 2017).

Whilst these climate emissions gaps are significant, the UN Environment has suggested that these gaps could still be closed by various cost-effective means. One of the major contributors to closing the carbon emission gap naturally will be by forests globally. A good international example is that experts from the UNFCCC have reported that some 6.3 gigatonnes (billion tonnes) of CO2 emission reductions by forests globally have already been achieved over the past six years. These have included forests in Brazil, Ecuador, Malaysia and Colombia. To put this into perspective, this is equivalent to more than all the annual emissions from the USA being absorbed naturally by forests.

These showed that forests should be a central part of the international carbon solutions for climate change and emission reductions globally. The UN International Panel on Climate Change (UNIPCC) has suggested that if deforestation would end today and degraded forests were allowed to recover, then all the tropical forests on earth could help to reduce the current annual global carbon emissions by some 24–30%. Hence, the world's tropical forests should potentially have the capacity to contribute to about one-quarter to one-third of the near-term carbon solutions that will be required to control global warming and climate change (Center for Global Development book, Why Forests? Why Now?, 2016).

In addition, saving forests globally will not only help fight climate change but also help to protect the 1.6 million people globally who are currently dependent on forests for their livelihoods. In addition, enormous amounts of CO2 and pollutants were released into the atmosphere when forests were cleared and burnt by human activities in various countries. Other human activities such as selective logging and drainage of carbon-rich peat swamps have also generated significant emissions. The burning of forests after logging in different countries has generated large amounts of carbon emissions and air pollution in various countries. A serious international example is the heavy air pollutions that have occurred in South East Asia which have been caused by the burning of forests after logging in Indonesia and South East Asia annually. In extreme cases, these serious air pollutions have affected surrounding countries as far as Singapore and Malaysia.

A good international forest carbon offset case study is given in the international case study below.

Norway Gabon Forests Carbon Offset Case Study

Norway is generally recognised as one of the most sustainable countries globally. Norway is currently undertaking a bold innovative natural carbon offsetting project with forests in Gabon.

Norway has decided that for a ten-year period, from 2016 to 2025, it will pay US$10 for each tonne of carbon that the forests in Gabon will absorb. Gabon is one of the few remaining countries in the world with almost pristine forests.

This is a highly effective plan on reducing deforestation plus reducing emissions naturally and improving air quality. It is also a tangible method of helping the development of the local economies in Gabon and supporting international just transition.

Carbon Dioxide Direct Air Capture DAC Developments

Experts have advised that DAC is expected to play an increasingly important and growing role in various net zero pathways globally. Capturing CO_2 directly from the air and then permanently storing it will help to remove CO_2 from the atmosphere. This can provide a way to balance emissions that are difficult to avoid. These will include emissions from the long-distance transportation and heavy industrial sectors. DAC can also offer a carbon solution for legacy emissions globally.

DAC is a technological method that uses various chemical reactions to capture CO_2 directly from the atmosphere. When air is moved over these chemicals, they will selectively react with and remove CO_2 from the air whilst allowing the other components of air to pass through.

There are currently 19 DAC plants operating worldwide. They are estimated to be capturing more than 0.01 Mt CO_2/year. The latest DAC plant to come online, in September 2021, is capturing some 4,000 tonnes CO2/year for storage in basalt formations in Iceland. A new 1 million tonne Mt CO2/year DAC capture plant is in advanced developments in the USA.

Looking ahead, IEA has given more information in their IEA DAC Report and their Net Zero Emissions by 2050 Scenario. The IEA has forecasted that DAC technologies could potentially help to capture more than 85 Mt of CO2 in 2030 and then increase significantly to around 980 Mt CO2 in 2050. These future DAC developments will require large and accelerated scale-ups from the current amounts of almost 0.01 Mt CO2 today. More technological innovations and cost reductions will be required to make DAC to become a more competitive carbon solution in future (IEA, Direct Air Capture (DAC) Report, Paris 2022).

Various countries and companies globally have been working actively on developing new innovative DAC developments. The IEA reported that since the start of 2020, various governments globally have committed almost US$4 billion in funding specifically for DAC developments and deployments. These include US$3.5 billion to develop four DAC hubs and a US$115 million DAC prize programme in the USA. More new research and development (R&D) fundings for DAC are also expected to be forthcoming in other countries globally, including Australia, Canada, Japan, the UK, etc.

The USA has also launched a Carbon Negative Shot during COP26. It has identified DAC to be amongst a portfolio of CDR approaches with the potential to remove CO2 and durably store it, at scale, for under US$100/tCO2.

Private and philanthropic investments in DAC are also growing globally. Leading DAC companies have raised around US$125 million in capital since the start of 2020. Leading international companies that have invested in early DAC projects include Microsoft and United Airlines.

DAC is also one of the four technologies that Breakthrough Energy Catalyst is targeting for up to US$1.5 billion in future investments. It is also an eligible technology for the US$100 million Carbon Removal XPRIZE that was announced in 2021.

Carbon Capture and Storage CCS Developments

CCS has become one of the most promising potential future carbon reduction technology solutions globally. The UNIPCC has defined CCS as a process involving the separation of CO2 from industrial and energy-related sources. Then, the CO2 is transported to a suitable storage location which will provide long-term storage and isolation of the CO2 from the atmosphere. Hence, CCS would typically integrate four key elements, including CO_2 capture, compression of the CO_2 from a gas to a liquid or a denser gas, transportation of pressurised CO_2 from the point of capture to the storage location and then isolation from the atmosphere by storage (UNIPCC, Special Report CCS SRCCS, 2005).

Experts have estimated that the contribution of CCS on the global carbon removal could be as high as 20% of the total required international carbon emission reductions to be achieved by the end of 2100. Various international studies have shown that CCS should be included as one of the key carbon emission reduction options and a key future carbon solution for two good reasons. Firstly, the costs of the overall emission reduction actions could be lowered with CCS. Secondly it is very difficult to reduce carbon emissions globally to sufficiently low levels without CCS.

The CCS technology can currently help to capture up to 90% of CO_2 released from the burning of fossil fuels in electricity generation and various heavy industrial processes, such as cement plus iron and steel production. Looking ahead, technological innovations and cost reduction improvements can help to improve the CCS carbon capture efficiency together with lowering the overall CCS costs (Ghent, The Breakthroughs of CCS/CCU, 2017).

CCS technologies will likely play major roles in the clean energy transitions in different countries globally. CCS can contribute to decarbonising existing and new fossil-fuel power plants plus the production of low-carbon fossil-fuel-based blue hydrogen. Blue hydrogen can then be used for hydrogen fuel cell mobility in the transport sector and in heating plus as a clean feedstock in various industrial sectors.

Industrial CO_2 emissions are major sources of emissions globally. These can be captured and stored by CCS using different methods. The main ones include post-combustion, pre-combustion and oxyfuel. Post-combustion technology helps to remove CO_2 from the flue gases that are generated by burning fossil fuels. Once the CO_2 has been captured, it can be compressed into the liquid state and transported by pipelines, ships or road tankers. The compressed CO_2 can then be pumped underground, usually to depths of 1 km or more, to be stored into depleted oil and gas reservoirs, coal-beds or deep saline aquifers, where the geology is suitable for long-term CO_2 storage.

At the moment, there are around 25–30 large-scale CCS projects or pilots being operated in different countries worldwide. Looking ahead, CCS experts have advised that there are likely to be some 135 additional commercial CCS facilities in the project pipeline from a diverse range of industrial sectors globally. These include cement, steel, hydrogen, power generation and direct air capture (Global CCS Institute, CCS Report, 2015).

The potential net reduction of carbon emissions to the atmosphere through CCS will depend on several key factors. These would include the fraction of CO_2 captured, the increased CO_2 production resulting from loss in overall efficiency of power plants or industrial processes due to the additional energy required, transport and storage leakages plus the fraction of CO_2 that can be retained in underground storage over the long term.

A good international CCS example is that a conventional fossil-fuel electricity power generation plant incorporating CCS could potentially help to reduce CO_2 emissions to the atmosphere by more than 90% when compared to a conventional power plant without CCS. The optimal degree of carbon emission reductions will depend on the trade-offs between the amounts of emissions reduced plus the costs of capture and the properties of the underground storage facility in which the CO_2 is stored.

Currently, there are three main CCS technology pathways, which include geological storage, enhanced oil recovery (EOR) and mineral carbonation. Storing CO_2 deep underground is currently the most mature CCS option because it can rely on experience from the oil and gas sector. In addition, it can be implemented by applying known proven technologies. It should be noted that although the individual component technologies required for capture, transport and storage are well-understood and some even technologically matured, the largest challenge for CCS deployment would be the successful integration of each of these component technologies into large-scale integrated demonstration projects, especially for industrial applications of CCS (Cuéllar-Franca & Azapagic, CCSU Technology Review, 2015).

Public perception and concerns have also played very large parts in the overall acceptance process for CCS projects. A good international example is that some key stakeholders have seen CCS as quite risky and one that has potential serious environmental impacts. Potential perceived risks would include CO_2 leakages plus the alteration of groundwater chemistry. The risks associated with geological CO_2 storage have generally been assumed to be similar to those of existing industrial activities, such as oil and gas production, natural gas storage and acid gas injection (Global CCS Institute, 2015).

The EU has included CCS in its EU Climate and Energy Package as an important option to achieve its long-term emissions reduction goals. CCS has also been accepted as one of the few potential options to reduce unavoidable emissions from industrial processes, such as the production of steel, on a sufficiently large scale. A good international example is that a new legal framework, the EU "CCS Directive" has been set up to ensure CCS safety plus to minimise risks and any negative environmental effects (European Commission, CCS Directive, 2012).

The three key CCS technologies will be discussed in more detail below together with relevant international examples and case studies.

CCS Geological Storage Technology Overviews

The CCS geological storage technological process has been applied at different locations globally. It would normally comprise the capturing of CO_2 from point emission sources from power plants or industrial installations. Then, the captured CO_2 will be compressed, transported and injected into suitable geological formations. The CO_2 would be stored as either a compressed gas, a liquid or in a supercritical state in various designated locations, including geological and ocean storage locations globally.

In the geological storage case, the CO_2 would normally be stored at depths of 800–1,000 m in suitable geological formations. These may include depleted oil and gas reservoirs, deep saline aquifers and coal-bed formations. A good international example of CCS geological storage that has been demonstrated successfully is in Norway at the Sleipner gas field which has been operating since 1996.

In the case of ocean storage, captured CO_2 would normally be injected directly into the deep ocean to depths of greater than 1,000 m. In contrast to geological storage, ocean storage still has not been tested on a large scale, even though it has been studied for over 25 years. There have been various serious concerns about unknown biological impacts, high costs, impermanence of ocean storage plus public acceptance concerns. Experts advised that more studies and developments will be required on CO_2 ocean storage before it can be widely applied.

Enhanced Oil and Gas CCS Technology Overviews

EOR is a CCS technology which has been actively applied in the oil and gas sectors globally. These have helped to produce more oil and gas from various discovered oil and gas fields. EOR can be applied after these oil and gas fields have already gone through the primary and secondary production phases. After the primary and secondary production phases, there would normally still be about 50–70% of oil and gas remaining in the reservoirs. The operator could then choose to produce more oil and gas in a tertiary recovery phase by injecting heat, chemicals and/or gases into the fields. These techniques would be part of the EOR package.

Carbon dioxide flooding or CO_2-EOR has been one of the most proven EOR methods applied globally. It would involve injecting almost pure (at least 95%) CO_2 into a depleted reservoir. These will make the oil swell and become lighter. This would then result in the oil detaching away from the rock surfaces. The oil would then flow more freely within the reservoir. Then, the oil could be collected and recovered.

These EOR techniques have led to higher oil recoveries globally. Best practices globally have generally helped to recover an extra 5–15% of the original oil in place (OOIP) using this EOR method. Normally, the injected CO2 and water would be separated from the oil when these reach the surface. Then, they could be recovered and re-injected for further EOR.

Similarly, CO2 could be used to extract more natural gas from coal deposits. These would normally be un-mineable by the enhanced coal-bed methane recovery (ECBM) technology. For difficult gas fields, the enhanced gas recovery (EGR) technology could be applied (Cuéllar-Franca & Azapagic, CCSU Technology reviews 2015).

A good international EOR example is that the use of CO2 flooding for enhanced oil production has been widely used in various locations in USA and Canada. The first large-scale testing of CO2-EOR took place in the 1970s in the huge Permian Base in Texas and New Mexico in USA. The injected CO2 would normally originate from three different sources: firstly, natural hydrocarbon gas reservoirs normally contain CO2 as an impurity; secondly, CO2 produced from natural CO2 reservoirs; and thirdly, CO2 from industrial or anthropogenic sources. In all three cases, the gas would need processing in order to bring the CO2 concentrations to the right levels of 90–98%. The main sources of CO2 used today would be naturally occurring CO2, because of its lower costs and wider availability.

Even though the monetary benefits of CO2-EOR would not occur as quickly as gas or oil drilling and exploration, they are eventually continuous and substantial. CO2-EOR should lead to longer term positive returns. A good international EOR example is the first CO2 flooding projects in the Permian Base in Texas, USA which have been operating since the 1970s. These are still under operation today and have been producing nearly 1 million barrels of oil per year. Forty years after the reservoir was denoted as "depleted", CO-EOR have helped to produce more oil and gas from these fields. These have helped to generate more revenues, taxes and employment plus CO2 storage at the same time. The economic and social benefits of enhanced oil recovery should offset some of the capture and storage costs, making this CCS option more cost-effective.

Mineral Carbonation CCS Technology Overviews

Mineral carbonation is another CCS technology option that has been applied globally. These would normally involve reacting the CO2 with metal oxides, resulting in the formation of carbonates with heat releases. This is a natural process which would permanently fixate CO_2 in a solid mineral phase.

There are differences between in-situ and ex-situ carbonation. The former is similar to geological storage. Normally, CO_2 would be injected into silicate-rich geological formations or alkaline aquifers, resulting in carbonates. The latter would involve carbonate natural minerals or industrial residues. These would include slag from steel production or fly ash, and they would require additional energy inputs.

A good international example is the CarbFix Project in Iceland. In this project, CO_2 from a geothermal power plant was injected into basaltic rocks that were 400 and 800 m deep. After two years, about 95% of the injected CO_2 had disappeared. These had reacted with the volcanic rock to form carbonate minerals. The actual reaction rates were much faster than predicted. The resultant CCS cost was at a relatively low cost level of some 17 US\$/t CO_2. These actual results have demonstrated that carbonation could be a safe long-term storage for anthropogenic CO_2 emissions globally (Cuéllar-Franca & Azapagic, CCSU Technology review, 2015).

Carbon Capture Utilisation CCU Developments

CCU technologies are being actively developed by various countries and companies globally. It can potentially become one of the important future carbon reduction solutions globally with appropriate new technological innovations and cost reduction improvements.

Carbon capture and utilisation (CCU) is different from CCS in their final treatment of the captured CO_2. Instead of transporting the CO_2 captured to a particular location for long-term storage, the CO_2 will be used as a new raw material for transformation into various new value-added products with different new innovative conversion technologies. CCU processes have the potential to reduce both CO_2 emissions whilst creating useful commercial products with new innovative technologies. These could then potentially lead to many new clean business opportunities for various new green product developments.

At present, the overall CO_2 emission reduction potentials would be limited by the available market potential for CO_2-based products. One important scientific fact is that CO_2 is a relatively inert molecule. As a result, most of the current industrial uses of CO_2 are highly energy intensive. Some good international examples of the current commercial industrial applications of CO_2 include the production of urea, inorganic carbonates and pigments, methanol, salicylic acid and propylene carbonate. Looking ahead, these markets are likely to grow significantly as new cost-effective CCU technologies become available.

Experts have estimated that if the currently known CCU processes were to be deployed in the most efficient ways, then they could potentially help to remove or use up about 300 million tonnes of CO_2 per year. These should help indirectly to reduce CO_2 emissions by around one 1 Gt per year. This will be equivalent to about 5% of the total net CO_2 emissions globally.

One of the most important CCU options is the direct utilisation of CO_2. Pure CO_2 is being currently used directly in various applications. A good international CO_2 example is that in the food industry, CO_2 is used to carbonate beverages and in food processing, preservation and packaging. Furthermore, CO_2 can be used to decaffeinate coffee by bathing the steamed coffee beans in compressed CO_2, which would then remove the caffeine without eliminating the flavour. For the various international food and beverages market applications, suitable purification processes will need to be applied to produce the extremely high purity CO_2 levels required.

Some other potential CO_2 direct applications would include the provision of CO_2 to greenhouses to maximise plant growth rates, such as tomatoes. CO_2 has also been used as a refrigerant gas in large industrial air-conditioning and refrigeration systems. CO_2 has also been applied in fire extinguishers and dry fabric cleaning. In the pharmaceutical industry, CO_2 could be used as a respiratory stimulant or as an intermediate in the synthesis of drugs. Most of these industrial applications are restricted to sources which would produce CO_2 streams of very high purity, such as ammonia productions. Moreover, the CO_2 sequestration capabilities of these market applications are currently relatively low.

Another interesting CCU possibility is the conversion of CO_2 into clean fuels. These would normally involve the hydrogenation of CO_2. A good industrial example is CO_2 and hydrogen (H_2) being brought together via new innovative catalytic processes to produce large volumes of chemicals such as methanol, dimethyl ether (DME) and ethanol. These can then be used to produce various clean fuels for use in the transport sector globally. The main constraint for these methods is primarily the availability of hydrogen on a cost-efficient basis. As we have discussed in earlier chapters in this book, there is currently a lot of work in developing new green hydrogen processes in many countries and universities globally. Experts have forecasted that these should help to promote more cost-effective green hydrogen productions globally in the near future.

Hydrogen can be produced through water electrolysis. However, this would require a lot of energy, which would then increase the cost of hydrogen significantly. A good industrial example is that the current averaged manufacturing cost of hydrogen, produced by alkaline water electrolysis and operated with wind power, would correspond to over 6–7 US\$/kg depending on the clean electricity sources. However, there is currently a lot of R&D work on developing green hydrogen production processes globally. Experts have forecasted that the green hydrogen production costs are likely to be reduced significantly, say by 70–80%, in the next five to ten years with new technological innovations and cost reduction measures.

As a clean fuel, ethanol has several advantages over methanol due to its safer handling properties and better compatibility to gasoline. Other hydrocarbon fuels could also be produced using a hydrogenation reaction. However, these would require higher energy and are less favourable process options.

CO_2 could also be utilised as a feedstock to produce various useful chemicals. The conversion of CO_2 to urea has been significant and is being applied commercially in different locations. However, the conversion to other chemicals has been limited to a few commercial applications on a modest scale.

An exciting new CCU chemical development has been the new MTO MTP process for the conversion of CO_2 to chemicals. These would normally involve the catalytic hydrogenation of CO_2 together with synthesis gas reactions. A good process example is CO_2 and hydrogen (H_2) being brought together via new innovative catalytic processes to produce large volumes of valuable chemicals such as ethylene, propylene, methanol, DME, etc. The main constraints would be the availability of suitable large quantities of CO_2 and H_2 for economic commercial operations of these big complex industrial chemical plants.

Photo- and electrochemical/catalytic conversions of CO_2 also have potential interesting new possibilities. Solar energy can be used to directly or indirectly reduce CO_2 via biological routes. The biological photochemical reduction of CO_2 will be based on reproducing nature's photosynthesis process. Sunlight, water and CO_2 together with new innovative catalysts will help to convert CO_2 to CO and then convert it into other interesting organic compounds. A barrier to this methodology is the efficiency of the catalysts that are necessary for the reaction plus the costs of the materials used for synthesis. A lot of advances have been made in new catalysts in recent years. Experts have forecasted that there may be further interesting breakthroughs in future.

There are currently several companies which have successfully operated CCU plants with clean renewable energy to chemically produce green fuels from CO_2. A good international example is the current market leader, which is Carbon Recycling International (CRI). It is an Icelandic company which has been producing methanol based on CO_2 and hydrogen with renewable energy. It has developed an innovative approach to use the abundant geothermal energy available in Iceland to split water into green hydrogen and oxygen. The resultant green methanol has been sold to the international market, where it has been used to blend with gasoline and to produce biodiesel. The CRI plant has been shown to release 90% less CO2, when compared to the production of the same amount of energy from fossil oil fuels. Their annual production of green methanol has amounted to about 5 million litres per year.

The conversion of CO2 into useful materials via mineral carbonation could be another potential interesting CCU option. CO2 can be used in combination with industrial residues and wastes. These could include steel and blast furnace slags, cement kiln dust and waste cement, fly ashes, municipal waste incineration ash, mining wastes and asbestos. These industrial waste left-overs have interesting CO2 fixation potentials and can be turned into valuable commercial products when these are reacted with CO2.

A good international industrial example is the production of cement and building materials out of slags from stainless steel manufacturing. This is currently being done by Carbstone Innovation NV which is a Belgium-based company. The storage capacity of these applications is rather limited and small scale, when compared to the amount of CO2 to be stored globally. These new technologies also still need to further demonstrate their commercial viability on a large industrial scale.

The IEA has also suggested that CCU can be a potential cost-efficient carbon solution strategy to tackle emissions from existing coal- and gas-fired power plants. Around one-third of today's coal and gas power generation plants were built only in the last decade. So, retrofitting them with new CCU facilities should allow them to continue operation with reduced CO2 emissions to the atmosphere. These should help to avoid the expensive costs of early retirement whilst also helping to reduce CO2 emissions globally.

In its recently published report, the IEA has identified four potential important pathways in which CCU can contribute to successful clean energy transitions and reducing CO2 emissions globally. CCU can be retrofitted to existing fossil power and industrial plants that may otherwise still be emitting 8 billion tonnes of CO2 in 2050, which is around one-quarter of today's annual energy-sector emissions. CCU can be used to tackle emissions in sectors with limited other options, such as cement, steel and chemicals manufacturing, plus in the production of synthetic fuels for long-distance transport. CCU can be used in the production of low-carbon hydrogen from fossil fuels, which can become a low-cost option in several regions around the world. CCU can help to remove CO2 from the atmosphere by combining it with bioenergy or direct air capture to balance emissions that are unavoidable or technically difficult to avoid. These various pathways will need further developments but can become potential interesting CCU options globally (IEA, IEA Report on CCU too Expensive? Paris 2021).

Bioenergy Carbon Capture Storage BECCS Developments

BECCS is being developed as a potential new future carbon reduction technology in different countries globally. The challenges associated with BECCS technology are large and complex. Biological carbon mitigations will normally involve CO_2 uptake by living organisms, which can be via photo-synthetic or electro-synthetic processes. Photosynthetic micro-organisms will use solar energy to naturally convert CO_2 into organic carbon and create a significant amount of biomass. Experts have estimated that these organisms have already been converting around 100 Gt per year of carbon into biomass annually globally. They have been doing these via some highly sophisticated natural biological mechanisms for carbon fixation and utilisation. These could potentially become attractive new carbon reduction technologies but would need much more developments plus proofing.

Similarly, micro-algae can be used to convert CO_2 into clean biofuels. There is a lot of research on optimising micro-algae's higher photosynthetic efficiencies so as to convert CO_2 to achieve a high biomass productivity of valuable biofuel and non-fuel co-products. The photosynthetic efficiency of micro-algae would be in the range of 3–8%, which is much higher than that of terrestrial plants and which is normally only about 0.5% on average. Micro-algae can also be used biologically to fix CO_2 from flue gas, without having to separate it via innovative developments. These could make microalgal bio-refineries poten-tially more economic and commercially attractive. These micro-algae could then serve as feedstocks for the fermentation of CO_2 to biofuels, biodiesel, fermentative bioethanol and biobutanol. The cultivation of algae could take place in open-pond systems or in new innovative closed bioreactors. These would require good supplies of water, nutrients and CO_2 plus good continuous mixing. After the photosynthetic biomass production, the biomass would need to be separated and processed into biofuels that are suitable for market appli-cations. These could be potentially interesting BECCS pathways but would require further developments.

CO_2 could also be sequestered by anaerobic bacteria by metabolism under spe-cific conditions. These processes are dependent on and enabled by the catalytic activities of certain specific enzymes which are present in anaerobic CO_2-sequestering organisms, such as Archaea. The end products of these anaerobic fermentation processes could include various useful chemicals, such as alcohols and biogas. These could then be used as clean fuels or as raw materials for con-versions into other products. For these metabolism processes, the operational parameters, such as pressure, temperature, hydraulic retention time, etc., are of extreme importance. These would require further developments and research.

A good international commercial application of these innovative anaerobic BECCS technology has been undertaken by LanzaTech. It is an innovative biotech company that was founded in New Zealand. They have discovered suitable microbes which would treat waste gas from power plants, steel mills, etc. in the LanzaTech Biological Fermenter. The CO_2 would be converted by the microbes in the reactor into clean fuel, such as ethanol, and other by-products. These would then be separated in a downstream hybrid separator into sellable clean fuels and other by-products for sale into the local markets. Currently, it has been successfully operating two plants at steel mills in China, where commercial operation had begun in 2015. Experts have calculated that the ethanol which has been produced this way has helped to cut the equivalent carbon footprint by 60–80% (LanzaTech, Biological conversion of carbon to products through gas fermentation, NZ 2019).

Experts have advised that, in general, various BECCS technologies still need further developments globally. However, these could provide potential interesting future net zero pathways in different countries. There are also considerable uncertainties plus potential impacts on resources, biodiversity and soil health. More developments are urgently required to identify and promote BECCS deployment, where these can be beneficial for carbon reductions. Good governance and financial incentives are also required to stimulate high-quality BECCS developments for future commercial applications globally (Imperial College London, Bioenergy with carbon capture and storage BECCS paper, 2018).

Sustainable Carbon Net Zero Solutions in the Energy and Chemical Sectors

Globally, the oil and gas plus energy and chemicals industrial sectors have accounted for about 60% of the global CO_2 emissions. These high carbon emissions have primarily been generated by fossil-fuel uses, including coal, oil or natural gas. These fossil oil and gas fuels have also been providing over 80% of the global energy supply in recent years.

International studies have shown that coal uses globally have generated the highest amount of GHG emissions. A good coal example is that it is interesting to note that in producing the same amount of energy, coal is almost twice as polluting as natural gas. On the other hand, the GHG emissions from fossil fuels and oil products are somewhat lower than the emissions from coal but higher than those from natural gas. Hence, many countries globally are currently boosting their natural gas consumptions as gas is seen as an interim transition fuel in these countries' clean energy transitions (IEA, 2015).

In contrast with the steel sector, the oil and gas plus energy sectors have a plethora of possibilities to generate clean power, which would help to reduce their emissions of CO_2 and other GHGs. These include the wider applications of clean renewable energies, such as wind, solar, hydro, geothermal and nuclear power. These are all proven renewable technologies which could generate clean energy without the release of GHGs. In addition, there have been major innovations and significant cost reductions in all the clean renewable energy power generation technologies in recent years. IRENA has found that many of the clean renewable power generations are already cost-competitive against fossil power generation in many countries globally.

Most leading oil and gas plus energy and chemical companies globally have been developing their carbon neutrality plans and new net zero targets. Many leading companies have been developing new corporate strategies which will promote clean energy transitions by incorporating more clean renewable energy applications into their business portfolios, in addition to fossil fuels. Most companies have seen these clean energy transition shifts as a necessary evolution as part of their climate change strategy and net zero plans. The pace of their clean energy transformations will be heavily influenced by the international prices of oil, fossil fuels and economic growth in different countries.

Investments in clean renewable energy have been growing swiftly globally. A good international example is that record amounts of green investments of above US$200 billion per year have been provided to new green renewables projects globally in recent years. As the green investments in renewables have gone up, the costs for renewable power generation have also been reducing with various innovations and cost improvements. A good international renewable example is that the capital cost for a typical solar photovoltaic (PV) rooftop system in Europe has decreased by 90% in the last 25 years, as a result of the various innovations and cost improvements.

Leading energy companies have also been looking at the various CCS and CCU technologies from different perspectives. A good international example is that some leading fossil energy companies have predicted that in the long term, their fossil power plants would have to be shut down unless they can integrate them with new CCS or CCU facilities or convert these to renewables.

It is important to note that the situation of the oil and gas plus energy sectors is very different from the steel and cement industrial sectors. For the steel and cement sectors, they will have to apply CCS or CCU in order to continue operation and to reduce their CO_2 emissions significantly. Otherwise, they will face shutdowns or serious penalties.

Most of the CCS and CCU developments in the oil and gas plus energy and chemical sectors have focussed on major power generation plants to date. This is because they are ubiquitous and would provide the largest source of CO2. One of the most interesting future technological developments in CCU would be to convert CO2 into clean fuels or clean chemicals to meet future market demands globally. Experts have forecasted that there would be large markets of considerable sizes for the various synthetic clean fuels and clean chemicals globally. There are still many technical challenges and commercial hurdles on the various CO2-to-fuels/chemicals conversions pathway. These include high costs in both operational expenditures (OPEX) and capital expenditures (CAPEX). The CO2-based synthetic fuels will also have to compete with other fossil-based fuels and biofuels.

The international regulatory frameworks surrounding CCU are also unclear. A good international example is that it has been unclear whether converting CO2 to clean fuels or green products would mean that no carbon allowances would have to be paid in EU-ETS. These uncertainties would need to be resolved so as to promote more clean fuel and chemicals developments.

There are also interesting new green business cooperation opportunities in CCS and CCU for energy and chemicals companies together with cement and steel companies globally. A good international example is that some energy companies have offered new carbon solutions services which include CCS and CCU technologies for their own use as well as a service to their international clients.

A very interesting international development is that a cement company will always have CO2 as a by-product of its cement production. Looking to the future, a potential business option is that the cement company could choose to cooperate with or pay an energy company to take over its huge amount of CO2 so as to avoid paying enormous carbon allowances. The energy company would then convert the CO2 to clean synthetic fuels or chemicals via innovative new technologies. Then, the energy company could sell the clean fuel and chemical products that they have converted from CO2. So, the companies can potentially earn extra revenues from applying new CCU technologies whilst also reducing their GHG emissions.

The chemical industry has been in an interesting position with regard to CCU technologies applications. The chemical industry globally has been responsible for generating close to 20% of industrial CO2 emissions globally. The chemicals sector could also be providing the important necessary chemical technology knowhow on the various new chemical conversion techniques for future CCU applications for both themselves and their clients globally. Hence, the chemical industrial sector can be on both the supply and demand side of new CCU technologies developments and applications globally.

Many chemical companies are also more interested in the supply and conversion of carbon monoxide (CO) instead of CO_2. An important physical-chemical fact is that the utilisation of CO is thermodynamically much more efficient than CO_2. As such, the CO molecule is already being used as an important raw material for multiple chemical manufacturing applications by leading chemical companies globally.

Chemical experts have advised that the costs of producing chemicals via CO conversion processes are currently still much higher than in the conventional oil or gas processes. The chemical products made from CO must currently compete commercially against their fossil-based equivalents in the global chemical markets. Several important drivers could help to offset these economic hurdles. Firstly, an increase in the international oil price could reduce the difference in production costs between fossil-based and CO-based chemicals significantly. A second driver would be to give international official recognition that CO-based products are more environmentally friendly than their fossil-based equivalents. This could be done by specific government policy support or by means of international sustainability labels. This would then help the emergence of a new international market for green chemicals, in which customers would be willing to pay a 'green premium' price for these green chemical products. In addition, these should help green chemical companies to create more competitive advantages over other traditional fossil chemical companies. In addition, green chemical products should also help to improve the international brands and images of chemical companies globally.

There should also be interesting win-win business cooperation opportunities by international chemical companies with steel companies in the treatment and reduction of carbon emissions. A good international example of a win-win cooperation between leading chemical and steel companies is in the steel mill gas sector. Normally, steel mill gases will contain large amounts of CO, aside from CO_2. When this CO reaches the air, it would normally react with oxygen in the atmosphere to form CO_2 in just a matter of seconds. By better utilising the CO from the steel mill flue gases, CO_2 emissions should be indirectly reduced. This is because the CO would not then react to form CO_2. This should help to reduce GHG emissions plus provide useful by-product manufacturing via suitable new CCU technologies. More work would have to be done to further develop these promising new chemical CCU technologies. These innovations should help to reduce CO_2 emissions and minimise global warming.

Some leading chemicals companies have already been successfully applying new CCU technologies and have built new commercial CCU plants in different countries. A good international example is SABIC in Saudi Arabia. More details of its new CCU plant are summarised in the special CCU case study below with international examples.

SABIC Major CCU Project Case Study

CCU has been a key component of the new corporate decarbonisation and net zero strategies of the Saudi Arabic Basic Industry Company (SABIC) in Saudi Arabia. SABIC was founded in 1976, with the clear vision of making use of waste hydrocarbon gases which were then being flared as a by-product of crude oil production in Saudi Arabia. SABIC has been successfully recovering these hydrocarbon gases and then utilised these for manufacturing base chemicals and specialty chemical products for the past few decades.

SABIC has also been developing various sustainable solutions for its chemical manufacturing. A good international example is that SABIC has been applying advanced CCU technologies to help to capture CO_2 emissions from their chemical plants and then converting these into valuable chemical products. More details will be given in the industrial CCU case study below.

SABIC, together with other leading companies globally have all agreed that addressing climate change and reducing the amounts of CO_2 emissions to the atmosphere are some of the greatest global challenges to date. At SABIC, they have responded by reducing CO_2 emissions from their chemical plants in Saudi Arabia and by applying advanced CCU technologies in their integrated chemical manufacturing bases.

A good international CCU example is that SABIC has built a new mega-carbon CCU plant in Saudi Arabia. This new CCU plant started operations in 2015 at United, which is an important SABIC chemicals affiliate in Saudi Arabia. This CCU plant is the largest facility of its kind in the world. It uses proprietary CCU technologies to capture 500,000 MT/y of CO_2 from their production of ethylene glycol (EG). These CO_2 emissions have previously been emitted into the atmosphere. The captured CO_2 is then converted into valuable chemical feedstocks for various industrial processes. SABIC has advised that the amount of CO_2 they have captured is equivalent to planting over 11 million trees. Experts have calculated that these amounts of trees would be required to be planted to capture the equivalent amount of CO_2 emissions (Sabic, Creating the world's largest carbon capture and utilization plant, KSA 2021).

The traditional CCS technology will capture CO_2 from industrial or power-sector sources. Then, CCS will store the capture CO_2 in a suitable geological formation. The newer processes of CCU will capture the CO_2 emissions. Then, CCU will purify the captured gas for conversion into commercially viable products. These could include clean chemicals, fertilisers and clean fuels. So, CCU technologies could allow the captured CO_2 emissions to be used as valuable feedstocks for the production of clean fuels and green chemical products.

SABIC has taken into account some of the serious challenges that CCS has come up against globally in the development of their CCU strategy. These include uncertainties over the potential storage capacity and potential leakages plus public environmental resistance and concerns.

SABIC has developed their new CCU corporate strategy after evaluating all the available alternative and complementary technologies, including CCU and CCS. These detailed evaluations were necessary in order to meet the ambitious climate change and carbon neutrality targets in the most sustainable manner.

SABIC has set an ambitious target to reduce their GHG intensity by 25% and material loss intensity by 50% by 2025, versus their 2010 baseline. CO_2 is normally formed as an inevitable by-product of the EG manufacturing process. SABIC is also uniquely positioned to share the by-products that would otherwise be wasted, given the close proximity that their various chemical manufacturing facilities share with each other in their integrated chemical manufacturing bases in Saudi Arabia.

As part of their new CCU masterplan, SABIC scientists have developed a suitable purification process unit to remove the various impurities from the CO_2 vent streams based on proven technologies. Once the CO_2 is purified, it is then channelled through a network to other SABIC affiliates to produce various valuable chemical products. These included urea, which is a key agri-nutrient that will enable more plentiful harvests and methanol production. The CCU plant is also producing high-grade liquefied CO_2, which is used widely in the food and drink industry.

This ambitious new CCU project is a good international example of both SABIC and the Saudi Arabia Government's drive to turn "Emissions to Value" (E2V) and to develop a "carbon circular economy". These new CCU technological innovations have been recognised by the G20, during the G20 Energy and Ministerial meeting in June 2019 in Osaka, Japan, as a good basis for reducing GHG emissions globally. They have recognised these CCU developments as an integral part of the global effort to mitigate climate change and to reduce GHG emissions globally (Sabic, Creating the world's largest carbon capture and utilization plant, KSA 2021).

Bibliography

1 ABC News, South Australia Biogas Human Waste Pilot Plant, Australia April 2019.

2 ACS America Chemical Society, Selective Electrochemical Reduction of Carbon Dioxide Using Cu Based Metal Organic Framework for CO2 Capture, USA 2018.

3 Africa Dev Forum, Electricity Access in Sub Saharan Africa, World Bank USA 2019.

4 Albright & Calderia, Reversal of ocean acidification enhances net coral reef calcification, February 2016, Nature USA, 2016.

5 Apple, Apple commits to be 100 percent carbon neutral for its supply chain and products by 2030, USA July 2020.

6 Amadeo K, Carbon Tax, Its Purpose, and How It Works, USA June 2019.

7 APEC, Update of 2009 APEC Report on Economic Costs of Marine Debris to APEC Economies, APEC Singapore 21 March 2020.

8 APEC, Life Cycle Assessment of Photovoltaic Systems in the APEC Region Report, Singapore, April 2019.

9 Asia Development Bank, ADB Signs Landmark Project with Icelandic, Chinese Venture to Promote Zero-Emissions Heating, ADB Manila 2018.

10 Asian Development Bank, Green Cities, ADB Manila 2012.

11 Assessment Agency (EU EDGAR), Emission Database for Global Atmospheric Research, EU Belgium 2011.

12 B20 Energy, Sustainability and Climate Taskforce Policy Recommendation Paper to G20 Global Leaders, Riyadh, Saudi Arabia KSA, Nov 2020.

13 Bank of England, Quarterly Bulletin: The Bank of England's Response to Climate Change, UK Q2 2017.

14 BBC, The shipping giant banking on a greener fuel, London UK March 2022.

15 BBC, How will our future cities look? BBC London UK, 17 February 2013.

16 BBC Environment, A new global agreement - the Glasgow Climate Pact - was reached at the COP26 summit, UK Dec 2021.

17 BBC Environment, Climate change: Low-carbon revolution 'cheaper than thought', UK Dec 2020.

18 BBC Environment, Coal power developers 'risk wasting billions', BBC UK, 12 March 2020.

19 BBC Environment, Carbon Bubble could cost global economy trillions, UK June 2018.

20 BBC News, Stephen Hawking's warnings: What he predicted for the future, UK 15 March 2018.

21 BBC News, Climate change impacts women more than men, UK 8 March 2018.

22 BBC Science, European Sentinel satellites to map global CO2 emissions, London July 2020.

23 BBC Science, Greenland and Antarctica ice loss accelerating, BBC UK, 12 March 2020.

24 BBC Science & Environment, What is Climate Change? BBC UK September 2020.

25 Bill Gate Foundation, Green Finance Climate Fund, US 2021.

26 Bill Gate, Bill Gate Notes, Travel without contributing to Climate Change, USA August 2020.

27 Bill Gate, Bill Gate Notes - Covid 19 is Awful but Climate Change is Worse, US July 2020.

28 Blackrock CEO, Green Investments, USA CNBC October 2021.

29 BlackRock, Global ESG Company Study, USA 2020.

30 Bloomberg, Global ESG Investment Study, USA 2021.

31 Bloomberg, Aramco, Exxon Make Move to Join BP, Shell in Carbon Curbs, US June 2020.

32 Bloomberg, Tesla Finishes First Solar Roofs, USA August 2017.

33 Bloomberg, All Forecasts Signal Accelerating Demand for Electric Cars, USA July 2017.

34 Bloomberg, India's Blue Sky Pledge Gives Power to Country's Green Bonds, By Anindya Upadhyay, USA July 24, 2017.

35 Bloomberg, China Boosts Solar Target for 2015 as It Fights Pollution, USA 2015.

36 Bloomberg, Beijing to Shut all Major Power Plants to Cut Pollution, USA 2015.

37 Bloomberg BNEF, Energy Transition Investments Report 2021, US 2022.

38 Bloomberg BNEF, Green Bond Pasted 1 Trillion USD, Bloomberg, USA Oct 2020.

39 Bloomberg BNEF, Colossal Six Months for Offshore Wind Support Renewable Energy Investment in First Half of 2020, USA July 2020.

40 Bloomberg, BNEF, Miners Begin Cleaning Up Their Act with Renewables, USA, 10 March 2020.

41 Bloomberg BNEF, A Decade of Renewable Energy Investment Led by Solar, USA 6 Sept 2019.

42 Bloomberg BNEF, Battery Power's Latest Plunge in Costs Threatens Coal and Gas, USA 26 March 2019.

43 Bloomberg BNEF, Electric Vehicle EV Battery Pack Cost Forecasts, USA 2018.

44 Bloomberg, BNEF Bullard: Tech Investments Are Powering Up Clean Energy, USA Oct 2018.

45 Bloomberg BNEF, The future of China's power sector. From centralised and coal powered to distributed and renewable? USA, 14 October, 2013.

46 BNP Paribas AM, Revised coal investment policy, Paris 2019.

47 BNPP AM, Sustainability roadmap to deliver Paris-aligned investment portfolio by 2025, Paris 2019.

48 Boao Forum for Asia, 2015 Forum speeches & proceedings, BFA Hainan PRC 2015.

49 Boao Forum for Asia, 2014 Forum speeches & proceedings, BFA, Hainan PRC 2014.

50 BP, Carbon Neutral Management Plans, London 2017.

51 BP, Global Energy Scenarios, London 2018.

52 C40 City & Arup, Deadline-2020 City Report, UK 2018.

53 Cambridge Qian Wang et al. 'Molecularly engineered photocatalyst sheet for scalable solar formate production from carbon dioxide and water.' Nature Energy UK 2020.

54 Canada Ecofiscal Commission Report on Carbon Pricing, Canada, April 2018.

55 Canada Global News, Worried about the climate and carbon taxes, Canada 2018.

56 Canada Govt Agriculture and Agri-Food Dept, Holos Climate change agriculture model, Canada 2018.

57 Canada Govt Agriculture and Agri-Food Dept, Climate change and agriculture, Canada 2018.

58 Carbon Brief Food & Farming, Rise in insect pests under climate change to hit crop yields, UK 2018.

59 Carbon Tracker UK, Carbon Majors Report, UK 2017.

60 CBC Business, As renewable energy grows, so does interest from Big Oil, USA 10 May 2018.

61 CDP, The Annual Carbon Majors Report for 2017, UK 2017.

62 CDP, Global City Report, UK 2016.

63 Center for Global Development, Why Forests Why Now Report, USA 2015.

64 CGIAR, Fighting Floods by Sponge Cities, Udon Thani Thailand, Thailand 2018.

65 Chartered Management Institute, 'Winning Ideas – Top 5 Management Articles of the Year' London UK, Feb 2016.

66 Chevron, Chevron produces renewable alternative energy with geothermal energy, USA 2010.

67 China Carbon Forum, China Carbon Pricing Survey, Beijing China 2017.

68 China Dialogue, Expert Roundtable: Is China still on track to reach its Paris targets?, China June 2018.

69 China Dialogue, Five Things to know about the China National Carbon Market, China Dec 2017.

70 China Ministry of Industry and Information Technology, New-Energy Vehicles Development Roadmap 2021–2035, Beijing China October 2021.

71 China National Bureau of Statistics, Statistical Communiqué of the People's Republic of China on the 2014 National Economic and Social Development, China 2015.

72 China's State Council, 14th China Five Year Plan, Beijing China 2021.

73 China State Council, New Guideline to Accelerate The Development of a Green and Low-Carbon Circular Economic Development System in China, Beijing China 2021.

74 China USA COP26, Joint US China Glasgow Declaration on Enhancing Climate Action in the 2020s, Glasgow UK 10 November 2021.

75 China Water Risk, Top 10 Responsible Investment Trends for 2019 In China, China 18 March 2019.

76 Climate Policy Info Hub, The Global Rise of Emissions Trading, EU 2018.

77 Christian Aid, Counting the Costs – A Year of Climate Breakdown, UK Dec 2018.

78 CIFOR Center for International Forestry Research, Forests and Climate Change, Indonesia 2019.

79 City of London Corporation, Total tax contribution of UK Financial Services, UK 2017.

80 CleanTechnica, World's First Advanced Offshore Wind Power Radar System Now Operational, USA 2016.

81 Columbia University, Committee on Global Thought, USA 2019.

82 Construction Enquirer, First net-zero carbon London office project approved, UK July 2020.

83 CSO Energy Acuity, Global Renewables Top Ten Companies, UK 2019.

84 ClientEarth, Review of UK companies' climate disclosures, UK 2016.

85 Climate Central, John Upton, China, India Becoming Climate Leaders as West Falters', Canada April 2017.

86 Climate Action Tracker, China, US and EU post-2020 plans reduce projected warming, USA 2013.

87 Comiso & Hall, Climate Trends in Arctic as observed from Space, WIREs Climate Change, USA 2014.

88 Computer Weekly, Google to hit 100% renewable energy target for datacentres in 2017, USA 2016.

89 Computer Weekly, Telefónica increases use of renewable energy to fight climate change, USA 2017.

90 COP26 High Level Climate Champions, Nigel Topping, Time to Bridge the Gap Between Awareness and Action, UK, February 2022.

91 COP26 Climate Champions, COP26 & Global Clean Energy Climate Updates, UK Nov 2021.

92 COP26 President Alok Sharma, COP26 Climate speech, Chatham House UK 2022.

93 Craig Idso, CO2, Global Warming & Coral Reefs: Prospects for the Future, USA 2009.

94 Cuéllar-Franca & Azapagic, Carbon Capture Storage Utilitisation Technology Review, USA 2015.

95 Daily Mail, WHO, Air pollution big killer than smoking, UK March 2019.

96 Deloitte, Global CxO Sustainability Report, UK 2022.

97 Denmark Government, Integrated National Energy and Climate Plan, Denmark 2019.

98 Denmark Government, Climate Agreement for Energy and Industry 2020, Denmark 2020.

99 Denmark Govt Energy Agency, Climate and Energy Outlook Report, Denmark 2021.

100 Dominic Barton, China half a billion middle class consumers, by Global MD of Mckinsey & Co, in The Diplomat, USA, 30 May 2013.

101 Drax Power Station Announcement, Drax closer to coal-free future with fourth biomass unit conversion, UK August 2018.

102 DuPont, Sustainable Energy for a Growing China, May 2013, USA, 2013.

103 Dutch Marine Energy Centre, FORESEA Funding Ocean Renewable Energy through Strategic.

104 DW, Nile dam project: Talks stall between Egypt and Ethiopia, Germany 2019.

105 European Action project, Netherlands 2019.

106 Economist Intelligence Unit, The Cost of Inaction: Recognising the value at risk from climate change, UK 2015.

107 EEA European Environmental Agency, Agriculture and climate change, EU Brussels 2018.

108 EIA, Explosion of HFC-23 super greenhouse gases is expected, USA 2015.

109 Ekonomiaz OBIC, Henry Wang, Policy Letter for Basque Spain on Climate Change, Energy Transition and Carbon Neutrality Recommendations, Basque Spain, December 2020.

110 Elsner, Kossin & Jagger, The Increasing Intensity of the Strongest Tropical Cyclones, Nature 455, no 7209, USA 2008.

111 Energy Narrative, Is 2¢ a kWh solar power real? By Jed Bailey. USA 15 February 2018.

112 Energy Research Institute, China 2050 high renewable energy penetration scenario and roadmap study, USA 2015.

113 Energy Foundation, Statement on China's Launch of the National Emissions Trading System, USA Dec 2017.

114 Energy World, Europe's top companies 'must double low carbon investment for net zero' USA, March 2020.

115 Environmental Defence Fund, Five reasons to be optimistic about China's new carbon market, USA Dec 2017.

116 Eversheds Sutherland Law Briefing Paper, UK Industrial Decarbonisation Strategy Paving the Way to Net Zero, London UK March 2021.

117 EU ESCO Committee of China Energy Conversation Association. Notice on the Disposal of Hydrofluorocarbon., European Commission, Joint Research Centre (JRC)/Netherlands Environmental, EU Brussels, July 2015.

118 Euronews Living, City of Sydney now runs on 100% renewable energy, EU July 2020.

119 European Commission EU, Assessment of the final national energy and climate plan of Denmark, SWD(2020) 903, EU 2020.

120 European Commission EU, CCS Directive, EU Brussels 2012.

121 EU, European Commission Assessment of the final national energy and climate plan of Denmark, SWD(2020) 903, EU Brussels 2020.

122 EU, Clean Energy for all Europeans, EU Brussels 2018.

123 EU, Directive 2014/95/EU, Brussel 2018.

124 EU, Framework for State aid for research and development and innovation, Brussels 2014.

125 EU Commission, Causes of climate change, EU Brussels 2019.

126 EU, Clean Energy for all Europeans, EU Brussels 2018.

127 EU, An EU Strategy on Heating and Cooling, EU Brussels 2016.

128 EU, New Renewable Energy Directive to 2030, EU Brussels, November 2016.

129 EU Environment Agency EEA, Renewable energy in Europe Report, EU Brussels 2017.

130 Euronews Living, City of Sydney now runs on 100% renewable energy, EU July 2020.

131 Fenby Jonathan, Will China Dominate the 21st Century? London, UK, 2014.

132 Fidelity, Global ESG Investment Survey Study, UK London 2021.

133 Financial Post Canada, Ottawa to return 90% of money it collects from carbon tax to the Canadians who pay it, Canada 2018.

134 Fine and Tchernov, Coral reef impacts by low ocean PH, USA 2006.

135 Fisher R, Ury W, Patton B, *Getting to Yes: Negotiating Agreement Without Giving In.* New York, NY, Penguin Books, USA 1991.

136 Forbes Energy, Big Oil Is Feeling The Heat And Dipping Into Green Energy, USA April 2019.

137 French National Centre for Scientific Research CNRS, Climate-driven range shifts of the king penguin in a fragmented ecosystem, France 2017.

138 G20/B20, Energy, Sustainability & Climate Taskforce White Paper, KSA 2020.

139 G20 Sustainable Finance Study Group, Sustainable Finance Synthesis Report, UK 2018.

140 G20 TCFD, Task Force on Climate-related Financial Disclosures (TCFD) Report, USA July 2017.

141 Ghent University, The Breakthroughs of CCS/CCU, Netherlands 2017.

142 Global Commission on the Economy and Climate. Global Annual Report, USA 2017.

143 Global CCS Institute, Global CCS Report, UK 2015.

144 Global CCS Institute, Yanchang-petroleum-report-1-capturing-co2-coal-chemical-process, UK 2015.

145 GPCA and McKinsey report "Thoughts for a New Age in Middle East Petrochemicals" released at 10th GPCA Forum, Dubai UAE, November 2015.

146 Greg Rogers 'Planning a Successful TCFD Project' Linkedin blog, USA November 2018.

147 Green, F & Stern, N., China's "new normal": Structural change, better growth and peak emissions, LSE Grantham Research Institute on Climate Change and the Environment, London UK 2015.

148 Greenwich Council London UK, New E-Car Club for Low Emission Neighbourhood, UK 2019.

149 Guardian, World Largest Liquid Air Battery Starts Construction in UK, London June 2020.

150 Guardian, Fossil fuels produce less than half of UK electricity for first time, UK June 2019.

151 Guardian, London Energy customers locked into District Heating Systems, UK 2017.

152 Guo Peiyuan, SynTao, The concept of responsible investment is increasingly recognized and accepted by Chinese financial institutions, Beijing PRC March 2019.

153 Harford T, Can Solar Power Shakeup the Energy Market, BBC UK 11 Sept 2019.

154 Harvard Business School, "Should You Make the First Offer?", USA July 2004.

155 Hong Kong Civic Exchange, Pathways to Net Zero Carbon Emissions by 2050, Hong Kong, July 2020.

156 Hong Kong Stock Exchange, Report on the analysis of environmental, social and governance (ESG) practice disclosure, Hong Kong 18 May 2018.

157 Huidian Research, Indepth Research and Forecast of China Ethylene Industry for 2013–2017, Beijing PRC 2013.

158 Hunter, Estimating Sea level extremes under conditions of uncertain sea level rises, Climate Change 99, no 3–4, USA 2010.

159 ICIS, Global Annual Base Oil Conference, London UK Feb 2018.

160 IEA, IEA Direct Air Capture (DAC) Report, Paris France 2022.

161 IEA, Report on if CCUS too Expensive? IEA Paris 2021.

162 IEA IPCC Fatih Birol & Hoesung Lee, Energy is at the heart of the solution to the climate challenge, Paris July 2020.

163 IEA, CFI, Joint Report on Energy Investing: Exploring Risk and Return in the Capital Markets, Paris, 2020.

164 IEA, Outlook for biogas and biomethane: Prospects for organic growth, World Energy Outlook special report Fuel report, IEA Paris March 2020.

165 IEA, Report & Roadmap for energy conservation & GHG emission reductions by catalytic processes, IEA Paris, 2013.

166 IEA, Global Energy & CO2 Report, Paris of 2019, Paris France 2019.

167 IEA, Global Energy and CO2 Status Report of 2018, Paris France March 2019.

168 IEA International Energy Authority World Energy Outlook IEA WEO Report, Paris 2017.

169 IEA, WEO Special Air Pollution Report, Paris 2017.

170 IEA, World Energy Outlook 2015. International Energy Agency, Paris, 2015.

171 IEA, *World CO2 emissions from fuel combustion: Database documentation.* International Energy Agency, Paris, 2015.

172 IEA, Energy Balances. International Energy Agency, Paris, 2014.

173 IEA, Energy Technology Perspectives. International Energy Agency, Paris, 2014.

174 IEA, World Energy Outlook 2014. International Energy Agency, Paris, 2014.

175 IEA, World Oil Market Report 2012, IEA Paris 2012.

176 IEA, Energy Technology Perspectives. International Energy Agency, Paris, 2010.

177 IEEFA, China Central Banking and Climate Action Steers Credit to Decarbonize, US Apr 2022.

178 IEEFA, ExxonMobil Empty Climate Risk Report & Shareholders wants Transparency, USA April 2018.

179 IFRS, New Sustainability and Climate Disclosure ESG Standards, US Mar 2022.

180 IHA, Hydropower Sustainability Assessment Protocol Presentation, India 2015.

181 IHA, SEforALL and IHA to partner on new hydropower preparation facility model, Germany, 17 November 2017.

182 IKEA, IKEA Goes Renewables, Sweden 2019.

183 IMF, "Fiscal Implications of Climate Change" International Monetary Fund, Fiscal Affairs Department, USA March 2008.

184 IMF, World Economic Outlook Database. International Monetary Fund. Washington D.C., USA 2015.

185 Imperial College London, BECCS Deployment Report, London UK 2018.

186 Imperial College London, BECCS, Bioenergy with carbon capture and storage, UK 2018.

187 Imperial College London Business School, Cormacka & Donovan, Estimating Financial Risks from the Energy Transition, UK June 2020.

188 Imperial College London Business School, UK Business Leader Summit and Survey, London April 2020.

189 Imperial College London CCFI, Climate Risk? A Field Guide for Investors, Lenders and Regulators, UK Mar 2022.

190 Imperial College London CCFI, Climate Risks and Investment Impacts, Charles Donovan Director at the Centre for Climate Finance and Investment, Imperial College London Business School, UK 2018.

191 Imperial College London, Climate change and environmental pollutions have serious impacts on heart and lung health, by Maxine Myers, Joy Tennant, Mr Martin Sayers, UK 12 March 2018.

192 Imperial College London Digital Economy Lab, Digital City Exchange, London UK 2019.

193 Imperial College London & ICROA, Unlocking the hidden value of carbon offsetting, UK 2014.

194 International Carbon Action Partnership (ICAP), Lessons learnt from Chinese Pilot ETSs Cap setting and allowance allocation, UK 2014.

195 International Zero Emission Vehicle ZEV Alliance, Zero Emissions Target Announcements, USA 2015.

196 Independent, UK Met Scientists warn CO2 levels expected to rise rapidly in 2019, UK Mar 2019.

197 INSEAD, Artificial Intelligence AI Holistic Approach to the Humans+Machines Loop, France 2019.

198 IOT Agenda, Using technology to save nature, USA 2017.

199 IPCC UN, Special Report CCS SRCCS, UN USA 2005.

200 IRENA, Global Renewable Cost Analysis Report, Abu Dhabi 2021.

201 IRENA, Investments in Renewables Analysis, Abu Dhabi 2018.

202 IRENA, Biofuels for Aviation, Abu Dhabi 2017.

203 ISSB, "Exposure Draft IFRS S1 General Requirements for Disclosure of Sustainability-related Financial Information," US 2022.

204 ISSB "Exposure Draft IFRS S2 Climate-related Disclosures." US 2022.

205 Japan Government, Blueprint towards a possible hydrogen society by 2040, Tokyo 2017.

206 John Berger, Copenhagen Striving To Be Carbon Neutral: The Economic Payoffs?, UK July 2017.

207 King Abdullah Petroleum Studies & Research Centre KAPSARC 2014 Discussion Paper on Lowering Saudi Arabia's Fuel Consumption & Energy System Costs without Increasing End Consumer Prices, KAPSARC Riyadh, Saudi Arabia, March 2014.

208 KPMG, Investment in PR China Report, UK April 2012.

209 LanzaTech, Biological conversion of carbon to products through gas fermentation, New Zealand 2019.

210 LSE Grantham, What should investors know about the current state of corporate climate action? LSE TPI Commentary, UK 24 March, 2020.

211 LSE Grantham Institute, Post COP24 Forum, London Dec 2018.

212 LSE Grantham Institute & Future Earth, Sustainability in the Digital Age Survey, Montreal Canada June 2020.

213 Lord David Howell column in Japan Times, "Oil and money, A combo that faces a cloudy future', Japan Oct 2018.

214 Lord Nicholas Stern, Financing climate ambition in the context of COVID-19, LSE Grantham, London May 2020.

215 Lord Nicholas Stern, Chair, Grantham Research Institute, London School of Economics and Political Science speech, Post COP24 Forum 'Where do we go from here?' LSE London, Dec 2018.

216 Lu SM, A global review of enhanced geothermal system (EGS), Elsevier Netherlands 2018.

217 Marine Energy.biz, Third MaRINET2 Call Provides €1.2M Testing Boost for Renewables, UK 2019.

218 Marine Renewables Canada MRC, State of the Sector Report 2018, Canada 2018.

219 McKinsey, Net Zero Transition report, US 2021.

220 Mckinsey, COP26 made net zero a core principle for business. Here's how leaders can act, USA November 12, 2021.

221 Mckinsey, Climate hazards getting worse and which countries are most vulnerable, USA Jan 2022.

222 Mckinsey, COP26 made net zero a core principle for business, USA Nov 2021.

223 Mckinsey, Road Freight Net Zero, Zero Emission Trucks Report, EU 2021.

224 Mckinsey, The State of Internal Carbon Pricing, US 2021.

225 Mckinsey, The zero-carbon car: Abating material emissions is next on the agenda, USA Sept 2020.

226 Mckinsey, Asia Climate Risks & Responses, Mckinsey Global Institute, USA August 2020.

227 McKinsey, Global Energy Perspective, USA 2019.

228 Mckinsey, The future of Electricity rate design, USA 2019.

229 Mckinsey, Bringing Solar Power to the People, USA June 2018.

230 Mckinsey, Smart City Developments and Improvements. USA Mar 2018.

231 Mckinsey Consulting, Bringing Solar Power to the People, USA June 2018.

232 Mckinsey, Disruptive trends that will transform the auto industry, USA 2017.

233 Mckinsey, How Solar Energy can Finally Create Values, USA October 2016.

234 Mckinsey, Competing in a world of sectors without borders, USA 2016.

235 Mckinsey, How companies can adapt to climate change. USA July 2015.

236 Mckinsey Quarterly, Battery technology charges ahead, By Russell Hensley, John Newman, and Matt Rogers, USA March 2018.

237 Mckinsey Quarterly, Peering into energy's crystal ball, Scott Nyquist, Mckinsey, USA July 2015.

238 Mckinsey Quarterly, The Disruptive Power of Solar Power, by David Frankel, Kenneth Ostrowski, and Dickon Pinner, USA April 2014.

239 Mike Parr, Diverting fossil fuel investments to renewables is not enough, Euractiv, Brussels April 2019.

240 Mining.com, Scandinavian Biopower to invest in a biocoal plant in Mikkeli Finland, UK 2016.

241 MIT, Study reveals chemical link between wildfire smoke & ozone depletion, USA Feb 2022.

242 MIT, Sense-able Cities Lab, USA 2019.

243 MIT, Climate forecasts, USA 2017.

244 MIT USA, MIT Climate Action, USA 2017.

245 Nagoya University, Evaluating the contribution of black carbon to climate change, Japan 2018.

246 NASA, Global Climate Change Sea Level Rise Data, USA 2019.

247 NASA, What is Climate Change, USA May 2014.

248 NASA Jet Propulsion Lab & CIT, Key Indicator Global Climate Change, USA Aug 2014.

249 National Research Council, Ecological Impacts of Climate Change, Washington USA 2008.

250 National Resources Defense Council, The Consequences of Global Warming on Glaciers and Sea Levels, USA Aug 2014.

251 National Geographic, The Big Thaw, USA 2019.

252 Nature, Climate Change, Country Level Social Cost of Carbon, USA Sept 2018.

253 Nature, Albright, Reversal of ocean acidification enhances net coral reef calcification, USA 2016.

254 NCA, USA Fourth National Climate Assessment, USA 2018.

255 Nerem, Proceedings of the National Academy of Sciences on Sea level rises, USA 2018.

256 New York Times, How to play well with China on USA President Obama & PRC President Xi Jingping meetings in June 2013, New York Times, New York, USA, 2013.

257 New York Times, In Cyberattack on Saudi Firm, U.S. Sees Iran Firing Back, USA 2012.

258 NOAA, Climate Change Atmospheric Carbon Dioxide, USA 2018.

259 NRDC, Global Warming, USA March 2016.

260 National Snow & Ice Data Centre NSIDC, Glacier and Climate Change, USA 2019.

261 NSIDC National Snow & Ice Data Centre, 2018 Winter Arctic Ice Report, USA 2018.

262 Ocean Panel The, The Ocean Transition Full Paper, Japan 2020.

263 OECD MENA Task Force on Energy & Infrastructure 2013 Report on Renewable Energies in the Middle East and North Africa MENA: Policies to support private investment, with inputs by Henry Wang and other OECD MENA Task Force team members, OECD, Paris, 2013.

264 OECD, Investment in Low Carbon Infrastructure, OECD Paris 2018.

265 OECD, SOE transition away from coal and coal fired power, OECD Paris 2018.

266 OECD, The greening of agriculture, agricultural innovation and sustainable growth, Paper prepared for the OECD synthesis report on agriculture and green growth, Paris November 2010.

267 OECD, Green Growth Declaration, Paris France 2009.

268 OECD, "Environmentally Related Taxes and Tradable Permit Systems in Practice" OECD, Environment Directorate, Centre for Tax Policy and Administration, Paris, June 2008.

269 OECD, Smith, S. "Environmentally Related Taxes and Tradable Permit Systems in Practice" OECD, Environment Directorate, Centre for Tax Policy and Administration, Paris, June 2008.

270 Offshorewind biz, Shell and CoensHexicon Co. Ltd agreement for a floating offshore wind farm in South Korea, UK June 2019.

271 OPEC, World Oil Outlooks of 2014, Vienna Austria 2014.

272 OPEC World Oil Outlooks of 2013, Vienna Austria 2013.

273 OPEC IEA IEF Energy Conference 23 March 2015, Riyadh Saudi Arabia 2015.

274 Orkestra-Basque Institute of Competitiveness, Ekonomiaz Policy Letters for Basque Spain, Spain Dec 2020.

275 Oxford University, Jennifer Allan, i Charles Donovan, ii Paul Ekins, iii Ajay Gambhir, ii Cameron Hepburn, iv, David Reay, v Nick Robins, vi Emily Shuckburgh, vii Dimitri Zenghelisvii, A net-zero emissions economic recovery from COVID-19, UK May 2020.

276 Oxford University, Smith School of Enterprise and Environment, From the Stockholder to the Stakeholder: How Sustainability Can Drive Financial Outperformance, UK 2016.

277 People's Republic of China, "Technology Roadmap for Energy-Saving Vehicles", Beijing, October 2016.

278 People's Republic of China, National Action Plan on Climate Change (2014–2020), Beijing 2014.

279 People's Republic of China, Energy Development Strategy Action Plan (2014–2020), Beijing 2014.

280 People's Republic of China, Second National Communication on Climate Change of The People's Republic of China, November, Beijing 2012.

281 People's Republic of China, China's 12th Five Year Plan, Twelfth Five-Year Guideline, 2011–2015, Beijing 2011.

282 People's Republic of China, China's 13th Five Year Plan, Thirteenth Five-Year Guideline, 2016–2020, Beijing 2016.

283 People's Republic of China, China's pledge to the Copenhagen Accord. Compilation of information on nationally appropriate mitigation actions to be implemented by Parties not included in Annex I to the Convention, Beijing 2010.

284 PRC Ministry of Civil Affairs, Interim Measures for the Administration of Investment Activities of Charitable Organizations for Value Preservation and Appreciation, Beijing PRC 2018.

285 PRC New FDI Measures: Management Measures for Approval and Filing of Foreign Direct Investment (FDI) 外商投资项目核准和备案管理办法, MOFCOM, Beijing, PRC, May 2014.

286 PRC Government, The Catalogue of Priority Industries for Foreign Investment in Central and Western China中西部地区外商投资优势产业目录, PRC Government, Beijing, PRC 2013.

287 PRC Government, 2013 Catalogue of Investment Projects Approved by Government (2013) 政府核准的投资项目目录 (2013年本), PRC Government, Beijing, PRC, 2013.

288 PRC Supreme People's Procuratorate, Opinions on Enhancing Cooperation and Coordination in the Prosecution of Public-Interest Litigations to Legally Fight against Pollution, Beijing PRC, January 2019.

289 PDO Petroleum Development Oman, Mirrah Solar Project, Oman 2019.

290 Plasteurope, IKEA NESTE Polyolefins from bio-naphtha Commercial-scale pilot plant, Belgium 2018.

291 Politico, 5 Takeaways from COP24, Paris, USA Dec 2018.

292 Power Engineering International, The Three Ds of Modern Power, USA May 2017.

293 Pricewaterhouse Coopers (2013) China M&A 2012 Report, PWC UK, May 2013.

294 Princeton University, Earth's oceans have absorbed 60 percent more heat than previously thought, USA Oct 2018.

295 PV Magazine, Volkswagen is all set to become a green energy supplier, Germany January 2019.

296 PWC, Committing to Net Zero by 2030, PWC UK September 2020.

297 RE100, Report and Briefings, USA 2019.

298 REN21, Renewables 2017 Global Status Report, Paris 2018.

299 REN21 Renewable Energy Policy Networks for 21st Century, The Renewables 2017 Global Status Report, REN21 Secretariat, Paris, 2017.

300 Reuter: HSBC targets net zero emissions by 2050, earmarks £772 billion green financing. UK Oct 2020.

301 Reuter, Exxon asks U.S. regulator to block climate-change resolution: Investors, USA 2019.

302 Rik van dan Berge & Wang Henry, Report on Clean Coal Technology in China – A Strategy for Netherlands, Twente University, Netherlands 2009.

303 Royal Society, Climate Change Global Warming, London UK 2008.

304 Royal Society, Global Responses to Climate Change, London UK, 2014.

305 Sabic, Creating the world's largest carbon capture and utilization plant, KSA 2021.

306 Sabine Christopher, The Oceanic Sink for Anthropogenic CO_2, USA 2004.

307 Satoshi Ikeda, Chief Sustainability Officer, Financial Services Agency, Japan Why Japan is leading the TCFD wave, FSA Japan 24 March, 2020.

308 Saudi Arabia, Vision 2030 National Plan, Riyadh 2016.

309 SCMP, China's national carbon trading rollout expected to have major impact on key industries, Hong Kong April 2017.

310 SCOR, Report of the Ocean Acidification Group, Vienna Austria 2009.

311 Seatrade Maritime News, IMO 2020 Sulphur Regulation, UK 2018.

312 Seymour & Busch, Centre for Global Development, "Why Forests? Why Now?", Washington DC, USA 2016.

313 Slovenia Times, China's path to a green economy, Slovenia July 2017.

314 Stephen Hawking, BBC Environment News, Climate Change Tipping Point, UK 2018.

315 Seatrade Maritime News, IMO 2020 Sulphur Regulation, UK 2018.

316 Shell, CEO Interview, Net Zero by 2050, UK Jan 2021.

317 Shell CEO Interview, Resilience and Change in a Year like no Other, Netherlands, January 2021.

318 Shell International, Shell New Energies Scenarios, London UK 2019.

319 Shell International, Shell International New Energies Units, UK 2019.

320 Shell International, Shell Sky Scenario, London UK 2018.

321 SOAS Corporate note, Key takeaways from the 5th Plenum of the 19th Central Committee China, SOAS, London UK October 2020.

322 SOAS, London University, Chinese City-Clusters: A Regional Development Strategy, London April 2020.

323 Sumitomo, Achieving Battery to Battery Recycling, Japan Mar 2022.

324 Sustainable Energy for All, Progress Toward Sustainable Energy 2015, UK June 2015.

325 Techtarget, How climate change threats can inform cybersecurity strategies, USA 2018.

326 The Global Commission on the Economy and Climate, The 2018 New Climate Economy Report NCE, USA 2018.

327 The Global Commission on the Economy and Climate, "The New Climate Economy Report: Better Growth Better Climate", USA 2014.

328 The National, China largest net importer of crude oil report 6 Mar 2013, USA 2013.

329 The World Meteorological Organisation WMO, State of the Climate report, USA November 2018.

330 TheCityUK, Key facts about the UK as an International Financial Centre, UK 2017.

331 Toyota, Sustainability Environment report 2018, Japan 2018.

332 UCL, Will three billion people really live in temperatures as hot as the Sahara by 2070? UCL, London, May 6, 2020.

333 UCL Efthymiopoulos Ioannis PhD Thesis, Recovery of lipids from spent coffee grounds for use, UCL London UK 2018.

334 UK Climate Change Committee CCC, Finance-Advisory-Group-Report-The-Road-to-Net-Zero-Finance Report, London UK Dec 2020.

335 UK Green Finance Team GFI, Green Finance Initiative Report, London UK 2017.

336 UK Government, UK Path to Net Zero Landmark Strategy, UK London Oct 2021.

337 UK House of Commons Environmental Audit Committee, Green Finance Inquiry Oral Evidence Published Records, London UK, 20 February 2018.

338 UK Parliament, The Energy and Climate Change Committee, UK CCS Competition, UK 2016.

339 UK House of Lords, Electric Car & Battery Storage New Program Review, UK July 2017.

340 UK Met Office, Climate Summaries 2018, London, UK Jan 2019.

341 UK Met Office, Climate Projects 2018, UKCP18, London UK 2018.

342 UK Met Office, Warming: A Guide to Climate Change, UK 2011.

343 UK Government BEIS, Smart City & Grid Developments Report, UK July 2017.

344 UN Environment Program, The Global Trends in Renewable Energy Investment Report, US 2019.

345 UN, COP22 Marrakech Roadmap for Action, Marrakech Morocco, 2016.

346 UN, Greening the Economy with Agriculture Report, USA 2012.

347 UN, United Nations Fact Sheet on Climate Change on Africa, USA 2018.

348 UN Brundtland Commission Report, Our Common Future, WCED UN USA 1987.

349 UN Climate Action, COP26 Summary, UN USA 2021.

350 UN Environment, Emission Gap Report, UN USA 2017.

351 UN Environment, Global Emissions Gap Report, USA 2017.

352 UN Habitat & MIT, Floating City to fight Climate Change, USA 2019.

353 UN Intergovernmental Panel IPCC, Report on Climate Change, USA 2017.

354 UN, Sustainable Development Goals SDG, NYC USA 2015.

355 UNEA, United Nations Environment Assembly (UNEA) on Plastic Pollution. Kenya March 2022.

356 UNEP, District energy in cities unlocking the potential of energy efficiency and renewables, USA 2018.

357 UNEP, Renewable Investment Global Trends Report of 2019, UN NYC 2019.

358 UNEP Finance Initiative (UNEP FI), Global Roundtable on the draft Principles for Responsible Banking, USA 2018.

359 UNFCC, COP26 Outcomes: Market mechanisms and non-market approaches (Article 6), US 2022.

360 UNFCC, China net zero future goals & policy, UN, USA Mar 2021.

361 UNFCC, Biennial Assessment and Overview of Climate, NYC USA 2016.

362 UNFCC, United Nations Framework Convention on Climate Change, Paris Climate Agreement, signed in UN NYC USA, April 2016.

363 UNFCC, Distributed renewable power generation and integration, USA 2015.

364 UNFCC Kyoto Protocol Targets for the first commitment period, USA 2012.

365 UNIPCC, Sixth Global Climate Mitigation Assessment Report, USA Apr 2022.

366 UN IPCC's Sixth Global Climate Assessment Report, Working Group II, USA February 28, 2022,

367 UN IPCC, AR6 Climate Change 2021 Report: The Physical Science Basis, UN US 2021.

368 UNIPCC, Sixth Global Climate Assessment Report WG1, USA Aug 2021.

369 UNIPCC, IPCC special report on the impacts of global warming, UN USA 2018.

370 UNIPCC, Fifth Global Climate Assessment Report, USA 2014.

371 UNIPCC, Evaluation of Climate Models, USA 2013.

372 UNIPCC, Renewable Energy Sources and Climate Change Mitigation Report, UN USA 2012.

373 UNIPCC, Fourth Assessment Report on Climate Change, UN USA 2007.

374 UNIPCC, Summary for Policymakers in Climate Change, Cambridge Univ Press, USA 2007.

375 UN PRI, PRI welcome asset owner signatory in China, UN USA, 4 Sept 2019.

376 UN WMO, State of the Climate Global Report, USA 2019.

377 US EPA, Global Greenhouse Gas Emission Data, USA 2019.

378 US EPA, Overview of Greenhouse Gases in Greenhouse Gas (GHG) Emissions, USA 2018.

379 USA EPA, Climate Change Science, Causes of climate change, USA 2016.

380 US DOE Office of Policy, America's Strategy to Secure the Supply Chain for a Robust Clean Energy Transition, USA FEBRUARY 24, 2022.

381 US National Hurricane Centre, Tropical Hurricane Report, USA 2018.

382 USA Office of the Deputy Assistant Secretary of the Army (Research & Technology), Emerging Science and Tech Trends for 2017–2047, USA Nov 2017.

383 US PNAS Proceedings of the US National Academy of Sciences, Climate-change–driven accelerated sea-level rises, USA 2018.

384 US EPA. Global Mitigation of Non-CO2 Greenhouse Gases, Washington, D.C., USA. 2012.

385 USA Oak Ridge National Lab, Boden, T.A., G. Marland, and R.J. Andres, "Global, Regional, and National Fossil-Fuel CO2 Emissions", Carbon Dioxide Information Analysis Center, U.S. Department of Energy, Oak Ridge, Tenn., U.S.A. 2013.

386 Vattenfall, Our Road to Fossil Freedom, Sweden 2019.

387 Wang, Henry, Growth Leaders Podcast Speech, "Ukraine Conflict Impacts on World Energy & Climate", Hong Kong June 2022.

388 Wang, Henry, HK Green Council Speech, "Decarbonization Strategy', Hong Kong Sept 2022.

389 Wang, Henry, RCHKIE VRE Speech, "Ulkraine Conflict Impacts on Energy, Climate & Rotary" HK May 2022.

390 Wang, Henry, RI ESRAG Speech, "International Climate Youth Summit" HK May 2022.

391 Wang, Henry, RCHKS Speech, "Climate Change Action Plan' HK April 2022.

392 Wang, Henry, ESG Global Forum Panels Speeches, "ESG Global 2022 Forum" UK 8 March 2022.

393 Wang, Henry, B20 Indonesia Women in Business Action Council Speech, "Global Platform International Cooperations" Bali, February 2022.

394 Wang, Henry, East West Growth Leaders Climate Change Podcast, Ireland January 2022.

395 Wang, Henry, HE Ambassador Terry Nichols G20 Climate interview, USA, January 2021.

396 Wang, Henry, China Low Carbon Green Development Forum Speech, "Climate Change Outlooks" Beijing, December 2021.

397 Wang, Henry, Rotary Club of Taipo & Makati san Lorenzo Global Climate Youth Summit Speech, "Climate Change Outlooks" Manila, 25 November 2021.

398 Wang, Henry, SOAS SCI blog paper, "China Climate & Net Zero Outlooks" UK, November 2021.

399 Wang, Henry, Rotary Club of Kowloon East Speech, "Climate Change Outlooks" Hong Kong, 2 November 2021.

400 Wang, Henry, Philippine University Chancellor Speech, "Climate Change & Energy Transition Developments" Manila 20 October 2021.

401 Wang, Henry, Lord Howell led Windsor Energy Group COP Paper 2021, UK October 2021.

402 Wang, Henry, MAP PMAP presentation, "Digital Leadership" Manila September 2021.

403 Wang, Henry, Hong Kong Business Award Speech, "Ethnics" Hong Kong August 2021.

404 Wang, Henry, US Radio Leadership Interview, "Renewable Book" USA June 2021.

405 Wang, Henry, Ekonomiaz paper, "Basque Spain Climate Letter" Spain April 2021.

406 Wang, Henry, Lord Howell chaired Windsor Energy Group Hydrogen Roundtable speech, "China Climate and Energy Transition Plans" London 4 March 2021.

407 Wang, Henry, London School of Economics LSE SU China Britain Business Forum Speech, "Climate Change and Sustainable Finance" London 27 February 2021.

408 Wang, Henry, UK Climate Change Committee Advisory Group Briefing note, "G20 Climate Change, Energy and Sustainability Policy Paper" London February 2021.

409 Wang, Henry, China Bogu Investment Forum Speech, "Climate Change and Clean Energy Investments" Beijing China, February 2021.

410 Wang, Henry, Rotary Club of Hong Kong Island East Speech, "Climate Change, Hong Kong and Sustainable Developments" Hong Kong 3 February 2021.

411 Wang, Henry & Simon Haigh, SDCF Paper, "East West International Collaborations" Hong Kong, February 2021.

412 Wang Henry, Ekonomiaz Policy Letter for Basque Spain titled Climate Change, Energy Transition and Carbon Neutrality Policy Recommendations, Spain Dec 2020.

413 Wang, Henry, B20 Energy, Sustainability and Climate Taskforce Policy Recommendation Paper to G20 Global Leaders, Riyadh, Saudi Arabia, Nov 2020.

414 Wang, Henry, Lord Howell chaired Windsor Energy Group Hydrogen Roundtable speech, "China Hydrogen Plans" London Nov 2020.

415 Wang, Henry, Simon Haigh Global Growth Leadership Interview, "Climate Change & Clean Energy Outlooks" Ireland, July 2020.

416 Wang, Henry, Rotary Connect the World Forum Speech, "Build Back Better Post Covid" Hong Kong 27 June 2020.

417 Wang, Henry, Lord Howell chaired Windsor Energy Group South China Sea Roundtable speech, "South China Sea Strategic Outlooks from China and Global Perspectives" London June 2020.

418 Wang, Henry, Darrell Gunter US Radio Interview "Climate Change and Clean Energy Transition", USA February 2020.

419 Wang, Henry, UK Climate Change Committee Working Group teleconference meeting comments on B20/G20 & COP, London UK 19 February 2020.

420 Wang, Henry, B20/G20 Energy Sustainability Climate Taskforce policy paper teleconference & comments, Riyadh 18 February 2020.

421 Wang, Henry, London School of Economics Negotiation Summit speech, "Business & Climate Change Negotiations" LSE, London 12 February 2020.

422 Wang, Henry, Imperial College Business School London speech, "Climate Change & Clean Energy Management" ICL, London 17 January 2020.

423 Wang, Henry, Hong Kong City University speech, "Environment, Energy & Business Sustainability Management", Hong Kong, 20 November 2019.

424 Wang, Henry, Rotary Club Taipo Hong Kong speech, "Climate Change & Clean Energy Management" Hong Kong, November 2019.

425 Wang, Henry, Oil and Money Conference Geopolitic Panel Speech, London UK, 9 October 2019.

426 Wang, Henry, Management Association Philippines CEO Conference Speech on Business Sustainability, Impacts and Future, Manila 10 September 2019.

427 Wang, Henry, Asia Investment & Banking Conference AIBC Sustainable Finance panel speech, Hong Kong 29 August 2019.

428 Wang, Henry, HKUST Business School Skolkovo EMBA Lectures, Doing Business in China and Business Dealings in Asia, Hong Kong, 10 July 2019.

429 Wang, Henry, Hong Kong Green Council Climate Forum "Global & Hong Kong Climate & Decarbonisation Challenges" Hong Kong 9 May 2019.

430 Wang, Henry, UK House of Lords Westminister Energy Group Windsor Summit "China Climate & Energy Challenges", Windsor Castle UK 2 March 2019.

431 Wang, Henry, HK City University Colloquium "China & Hong Kong Climate & Decarbonisation Challenges" Hong Kong, 21 February 2019.

432 Wang, Henry, HKUST Post COP24 Forum "Hong Kong Climate & Decarbonisation Challenges" Hong Kong, 21 January 2019.

433 Wang, Henry, UK House of Lords Energy Panel Paper "China Fossil & Renewables Energy Transformations", London UK, 5 December 2018.

434 Wang, Henry, FT Asia Climate Finance Summit "Renewables Growth, Challenges and Opportunities" Hong Kong, 21 November 2018.

435 Wang, Henry, India Institute of Director Global Convention London Paper "Climate Change & Green Finance Governance Growths" in London UK, 25 October 2018.

436 Wang, Henry, Imperial College Business School MSc. Climate Finance Lecture "Climate Change & Green Finance Growths" in London UK 24 October 2017.

437 Wang, Henry, London School of Economics Negotiation Society Lecture, "Business Negotiations in China" LSE London UK, 17 October 2018.

438 Wang, Henry, Hong Kong Dragon Foundation Youth Leaders speech "International & China Business Negotiations" in Hong Kong City University, Hong Kong, 25 August 2018.

439 Wang, Henry, India Institute of Director Global Convention Proceedings Paper "Climate Change & Climate Finance TCFD Reporting", Mumbai India, July 2018.

440 Wang, Henry, University College London HK Alumni Association Speech, "Business Negotiations", Hong Kong June 2018.

441 Wang, Henry, HK Rotary Peninsula Club speech "Climate Change & Climate Action Plan HK", Hong Kong, May 2018.

442 Wang, Henry, HK Rotary Taipo Club speech "International & China Business Negotiations" in Hong Kong Kowloon Cricket Club, Hong Kong, 14 May 2018.

443 Wang, Henry, ICIS Global Base Oil Conference Speech, "China Belt & Road Initiative Growths" in London UK, January 2018.

444 Wang H, Sino-British Summit Paper, China NDRC Renewables and Smart City Plans, UK 2017.

445 Wang, Henry, Liechtenstein International Economic Forum Speech "China Economic Growths", Liechtenstein June 2017.

446 Wang, Henry, Hong Kong Science Tech Association speech "Energy, Environment and Climate Change Innovations", Hong Kong, 21 April 2017.

447 Wang, Henry, Hong Kong University speech, "Energy, Environment and Climate Change Action Plans" HKU, Hong Kong 9 April 2017.

448 Wang, Henry, Chinese University of Hong Kong "Energy, Environment and Climate Change", Hong Kong March 2017.

449 Wang, Henry, Imperial College London "Energy and Environment Growth Strategies" in in London UK, February 2017.

450 Wang, Henry, Kings College London "International Energy and Environment Growth Strategies" in London UK, January 2017.

451 Wang, Henry, China Academy of Science Dalin Institute "Energy Growth Strategies" in Dalin PRC, November 2016.

452 Wang, Henry, EU Chamber of Commerce China Energy Panel "Energy Markets in Emerging Economies" in August 2016 in Beijing PRC, 2016.

453 Wang, Henry, *Energy Markets in Emerging Economies: Strategies for Growth*, Abingdon and New York: Routledge, UK 2016.

454 Wang, Henry, Transparency International SOE Integrity Forum paper "Global SOE Management and Governance Improvements" in Berlin Germany, June 2016.

455 Wang, Henry, OECD Integrity Forum paper "Global and MENA SOE Governance and Integrity" in Paris, France, April 2016.

456 Wang, Henry, UK Chartered Management Institute Top Five Management Paper of Year 2015 titled "China Business Negotiation Strategy", CMI London, UK, February 2016.

457 Wang, Henry, Singapore Energy Week Asia Downstream Conference keynote speech and presentation on "Global Supply Chain Management, Risk Minimisation, Resource and Cost Optimisation Strategies", Singapore 28 October 2015.

458 Wang, Henry, ICIS 9th Asia Base Oil & Lubricant Conference keynote speech on "China Demand Growth & Sustainable Growth Strategies", Singapore, 10 June 2015 in Singapore.

459 Wang Henry, OPEC IEA IEF Energy Conference & IEF KAPSARC Energy Roundtable 23–24 March 2015 discussion inputs, IEF Riyadh Saudi Arabia, March 2015.

460 Wang, Henry, UK Chartered Management Institute Management Paper of Year 2014 Submission titled " Business Negotiation Strategy & Planning in China", CMI London, UK, 2014.

461 Wang, Henry, UK CBI White Paper on Business Energy and Climate Change Priorities for the 2015–2020 UK Parliament consultation inputs, UK CBI, London, UK, August 2014.

462 Wang, Henry, OECD BIAC China Task Force Presentation to OECD China Reflection Group & OECD Ambassadors consultation inputs, OECD BIAC, Paris, France, 23 & 24 June 2014.

463 Wang, Henry, Japan Ministry Economic Trade Industry METI Presentation on Saudi Arabia Downstream Industrial Cluster Development Program, SABIC, Riyadh, Saudi Arabia, June 2014.

464 Wang, Henry, KAPSARC Paper on Energy Productivity Aligning Global Agenda Peer Review comments, KAPSARC HQ, Riyadh, Saudi Arabia, April 2014.

465 Wang, Henry, Presentation on Sustainable Petrochemical & Chemicals Outlooks to 2nd IEA Unconventional Gas Forum on 26 March 2014, Calgary, Canada, March 2014.

466 Wang, Henry, King Abdullah Petroleum Studies & Research Centre KAPSARC First International Seminar on China keynote speech & presentation on "Sustainable Growth Scenarios & Strategies" KAPSARC HQ in Riyadh, Saudi Arabia, March 2014.

467 Wang, Henry, Presentation on Sustainable Petrochemical & Chemicals Outlooks to OECD Energy & Environmental Committee Meetings, OECD Paris France, 26 February 2014.

468 Wang, Henry, Fourth International Energy Forum & International Energy Authority & OPEC Symposium on Energy Outlooks speech on "Petrochemicals & Chemicals Growth Outlooks & Strategic Developments" in IEF HQ in Riyadh, Saudi Arabia, 22 January 2014.

469 Wang, Henry, International Energy Agency World Energy Outlook (IEA WEO) Peer Review Panel Global Energy & Petrochemical Investment Cost Reviews commentaries to the IEA WEO Team in IEA HQ in January 2014, IEA HQ, Paris, France, 2014.

470 Wang, Henry, *Successful Business Dealings and Management with China Oil, Gas and Chemical Giants*. Routledge Studies in the Modern World Economy, Abingdon and New York: Routledge, UK 2013.

471 Wang, Henry, International Energy Agency IEA Energy Efficiency EE Manual review commentary to OECD BIAC and IEA EE Team in August 2013, IEA, Paris, France, 2013.

472 Wang, Henry, Presentation to China Ministry of Commerce & China National Oil Companies Delegation visit to Saudi Arabia in May 2013, SABIC, Riyadh, Saudi Arabia, 2013.

473 Wang, Henry, International Energy Agency World Energy Outlook Peer Review Panel – Global Energy Competitiveness inputs to the IEA WEO Team in April 2013, IEA, Paris, France, 2013.

474 Wang, Henry, IEA, OPEC and IEF International Energy Conference presentation at IEF HQ in Riyadh Saudi Arabia, January 2013.

475 Wang, Henry, China Market Developments & Marketing Lecture in April 2012 to EMBA class at University of Colorado Denver Business School, Denver, USA, 2012.

476 Wang, Henry, International Energy & Renewables Strategic Co-Development Lecture in April 2012 at University of Colorado Denver Business School, Denver, USA, 2012.

477 Wang, Henry, Global & Middle East Petrochemical Growth & Developments at University of Colorado Energy Conference, Boulder, Colorado USA, 2012.

478 Wang, Henry, India Oil IOC Chairman Petrochemical Conclave presentation "Opportunities & Challenges in Industries Winning Strategies", IOC, Delhi, India, March 2012.

479 Wang, Henry, Keynote speech to First International Four Kingdom Carbon International Conference organised by Saudi Ministry of Petroleum in Saudi Arabia, 2011.

480 Wang, Henry, Speech & Presentation on Shale Gas Business Growth, Commercialisation & Developments in China, to the First China International Shale Gas Conference on 26–27 October 2010 in Shanghai organised by IBC Asia, China, 2010.

481 Wang, Henry, Deep-water Drilling Outlook Summit in Singapore in July 2010 Paper on China Upstream Offshore Developments, Singapore, 2010.

482 Wang, Henry, Asia Pacific Offshore Support Forum in Singapore in April 2010 Paper on China Offshore Support Industry Developments, Singapore, 2010.

483 Wang, Henry, China International & Beijing State Radio interview in Beijing on International Earth Day in April 2010 on Green Energy, Renewables, Chemicals, Coal Gasification, Energy Efficiency & Sustainable Developments, China Radio, Beijing, 2010.

484 Wang, Henry, China International Radio interview in Beijing China in April 2010 on World Bank Six Asia Country Energy Report, China Radio, Beijing, 2009.

485 Wang, Henry, Argus Carbon Report Interview in London UK in Oct 2009 on China Carbon & Climate Change Trends by Henry Wang with Argus Carbon Editor, Argus, London UK, 2009.

486 Wang, Henry, Bloomberg News interview in Singapore in Oct 2009 on China Climate Change Policies Outlooks by Bloomberg Asia Editor, Bloomberg, Singapore, 2009.

487 Wang, Henry, Carbon Forum Asia in Singapore in Oct 2009 keynote speech & Paper on China Climate Change & Sustainable Development Policies, Singapore, 2009.

488 Wang, Henry (2009) Carbon Forum Asia in Singapore in Oct 2009 Paper on China Carbon Market Management & Outlooks, Singapore, 2009.

489 Wang, Henry, UK China Chemicals CEO Working Group Forum in Shanghai in Nov 2009, Paper & Presentation on Integrated Energy Management, Clean Energy Technologies & Sustainable Developments in China, UK Embassy, Shanghai China, 2009.

490 Wang, Henry, UK Embassy China in Beijing in 2009 presentation on China Clean Energy & Sustainable Development by Henry Wang, UK Embassy, Beijing, 2009.

491 Wang, Henry, China Carbon Forum Government Round Table keynote speech on China Clean Energy & Carbon Developments, Remin University, Beijing, June 2009.

492 Wang, Henry, China State Council Development Research Council Presentation on Clean Energy & Coal Developments in China & Globally, DRC Beijing PRC Nov 2008.

493 Wang, Henry, Remin University and China Carbon Forum Conference in 2008, speech & paper on Clean Coal Developments and Copenhagen Negotiations, Remin University, Beijing, 2008.

494 Wang, Henry, UCL Distinguished Speaker lecture on China Advanced Coal Technology & Successful Project Developments at University College London UK 2008.

495 Wang, Henry, China Netherlands Prime Ministerial Energy Summit at Tsinghua University in Beijing in Nov 2008, paper on Integrated Energy Management, Clean Energy & Sustainable Development, Tsinghua University, Beijing, 2008.

496 Wang, Henry, EU Chamber of Commerce China in Beijing in 2007 Presentation on Clean Energy Developments & Opportunities, EUCCC, Beijing, 2007.

497 Wang, Henry, China Daily CEO Climate Change Round Table in Beijing in 2006 interview on Climate Change Outlooks by Henry Wang, China Daily, Beijing, 2006.

498 Wang, Henry (2006) Energy Seminar for PRC Government Top Officials at Joint Tsinghua Harvard MPA Course presentation & paper on Global Energy Planning, Advanced Technologies & Management to Vice Ministers/Governors, Tsinghua University, Beijing, PRC 2006.

499 Wang, Henry, Climate Change & Sustainable Development Seminar for PRC Government Senior Officials presentation & paper on International Sustainable Development, Climate Change, Carbon technologies & management, Tsinghua University Beijing, 2006.

500 Wang, Henry, China Advanced Management Seminar in Beijing China for top international executives, presentations & papers on China Business Issues, China Energy Planning & China Business Developments, Shell Beijing PRC 2006.

501 Wang, Henry et al, UK China Bilateral Energy Strategic Cooperations Paper with UK China Bilateral Energy Work Group, UK Embassy Beijing, PRC 2005.

502 Wang, Henry, International Advanced Management Seminar papers on Global & China Business Issues, Energy Planning in China, Government structures in China & New Business Development in China, New York Bar Association HQ, New York USA, 2005.

503 Wang, Henry, China Daily CEO Corporate Social Responsibilities Round Table in Beijing in 2005 interview on CSR, China Daily, Beijing, 2005.

504 Wang, Henry, China Global Economic & Leadership Summit, Speech on Energy Economic Developments by Henry Wang with USA Nobel Economists at the Grand Hyatt Hotel in Beijing organised by China Cajing Economic Publishing Group, Beijing PRC, 2005.

505 Wang, Henry, China State Council Development Research Council [DRC] in Beijing in 2005 Presentation on Global & China Energy Scenarios, DRC Beijing, 2005.

506 Wang, Henry, China Ministry of Foreign & Economic Cooperation [MOFCOM] Summit in China in 2005, speech & paper on Multinational Co Co-operations & Sustainable Developments in China, MOFCOM, Beijing, 2005.

507 Wang, Henry, China Economic Summit at Great Hall of People in Beijing in 2005, paper on China Energy Outlooks & Scenarios by Henry Wang, China Cajing Economic Magazine, Beijing, 2005.

508 Wang, Henry, Netherlands Energy Minister Meeting in Beijing in 2005, Presentation on China Energy Developments, Netherlands Embassy, Beijing, 2005.

509 Wang, Henry, Tsinghua University Lecture in Beijing China in 2005, Lecture & paper on Multinational Cos Operations in China, Tsinghua University Beijing, 2005.

510 Wang, Henry, Board Meeting of a leading International Chemical Company & a top Middle East Company Joint Venture in Singapore in 2005, presentation on China Economic & Energy Outlooks, Singapore, 2005.

511 Wang, Henry, China Energy & Strategy Seminar for a leading Asia Government Prime Minister Office PMO & key Ministries presentations & papers on China Energy Planning & Developments, Market Access & Cooperation Strategies & Challenges, Shell Asia 2005.

512 Wang, Henry, Wharton Shell Group Business Leadership Program Business Case paper, Wharton Business School, Pennsylvania, USA, 2004.

513 Wang, Henry, China SASAC Minister Meeting in Beijing China in 2004, speech & paper on China Energy Scenarios & Challenges, SASAC, Beijing, 2004.

514 Wang, Henry, UK Prime Minister Climate Change Adviser & DEFRA Director General Ministerial Meeting in London UK in 2004, presentation & paper on China Energy & Climate Change Outlooks, DEFRA, London, UK, 2004.

515 Wang, Henry, China Ministry of Foreign Affairs & Institute of International Cooperation Meeting in Beijing in 2004, speech & paper on China Energy Business Outlooks & International Co-operations, MOFCOM, Beijing, 2004.

516 Wang, Henry, USA & UK Counsel Generals Meetings in Shanghai China in 2004, presentation & paper on China Energy Outlooks, UK Embassy, Shanghai, China 2004.

517 Wang, Henry, London School of Economics Lecture & paper on China Outlooks & Opportunities, London School of Economics LSE, UK 2004.

518 Wang, Henry, China Economics Round Table in Beijing speech & paper on China Clean Energy Sustainable Developments, China Economics Roundtable, Beijing, PRC 2004.

519 Wang, Henry, China Ministry of Commerce & Foreign Trade MOFCOM Transnational Company Forum Speech on New Development Strategy of Transnational Companies in China, MOFCOM, Beijing, PRC, 2003.

520 Wang, Henry, China National Development Reform Commission NDRC Energy Research Institute ERI Report on China Medium & Long Term Energy & Carbon Scenarios Report in 2003 jointly by China Energy Research Institute of the PRC Government National Development Reform Commission with USA Lawrence Berkley Lab of USA Government Department of Energy & Shell Group Planning, NDRC ERI, Beijing PRC, 2003.

521 Wang, Henry, China Daily 2003 news interview report in Beijing on EU Work Group Energy Proposals to Government with Henry Wang, Chairman of EU Energy, Petrochemicals, Oil & Gas Committee, China Daily, Beijing, China, 2003.

522 Wang, Henry, Singapore Prime Minister Office high level China Strategy Meeting Speech & Presentation on China Social, Economic and Industrial developments & China Strategy Developments, Singapore, 2001.

523 Wang, Henry with Mobil USA & Raytheon USA Authors, Oil & Gas Journal OGJ Paper on UK Refinery Successful Demonstrations of New Ethyl Benzene Process, Oil Gas Journal OGJ, USA, 1995.

524 Wang, Henry University of Leeds, Visiting Lecturer on the "Successful Chemical Plant Start-up & Commissioning" Course at the University of Leeds in UK from 1993 to 1996, Lectures on the "Major Ethyl Benzene Chemical Plant Start-up & Commissioning at Shell UK Stanlow Refinery", University of Leeds, UK, 1993.

525 Wang, Henry, Canada Patent CA2008347 "Removing Hydrogen Cyanide and Carbon Oxy-Sulphide from a Syngas Mixture", Shell Internationale, Canada 1990.

526 Wang Henry, Imperial College of Science & Technology MSc DIC Thesis on Bubble Flow Biological Reactor Research & Developments, Imperial College London, UK, 1997.

527 Washington Post, The United States already has a carbon tax, USA 2019.

528 WECF Fact Sheet Dangerous Health Effects of Home Burning of Plastics and Waste, USA 2005.

529 WEF, Global Risks Perception Survey, Switzerland Jan 2022.

530 WEF, What is sustainable finance, WEF Switzerland Jan 2022.

531 WEF, How to address sustainable investment backlash and improve ESG reporting, WEF Switzerland, Dec 2021.

532 Wharton Business School, How the Pandemic can lead to a more sustainable future, US June 2020.

533 Wiseman Ed, Everything you need to know about the new UK Emission Rules, UK July 2017.

534 Wood Mckenzie Greentech Media GTM, GE and BlackRock Launch Distributed Solar and Storage Business, US 2019.

535 Wood Mackenzie Greentech Media GTM, Shell New Energies Director on Investing in Clean Energy, USA April 2019.

536 World Meteorological Organisation WMO, State of the Climate Report, Switzerland 2019.

537 World Bank, Refugee by Country Data, USA 2018.

538 World Bank report, Groundswell: Preparing for Internal Climate Migration, USA March 2018.

539 World Bank, State and Trends of Carbon Pricing, USA 2015.

540 World Bank, Developing East Asia Pacific Growth in 2015, USA 13 April 2015.

541 World Bank, World Development Report 2010, USA 2010.

542 World City summit, Innovative Cities of Opportunity, Singapore 2016.

543 World Economic Forum WEF, Fourth Industrial Revolution for the Earth series, How technology is leading us to new climate change solutions, Switzerland 2018.

544 World Economic Forum, The Global Competitiveness Report 2010–2011, Switzerland 2010.

545 World Ocean Review, Climate change and methane hydrates, USA 2010.

546 WRI, Safer, More Sustainable Transport in a Post-COVID-19 World, USA April 2020.

547 World Resources Institute, WRI, Designing and Communicating Net-Zero Targets, USA July 2020.

548 World Resources Institute, WRI, How COVID-19 Can Drive Transformational Change in Cities, USA Apr 2020.

549 World Resources Institute WRI, Safer, More Sustainable Transport in a Post-COVID-19 World, USA April 2020.

550 World Resources Institute, WRI, COVID-19 Could Affect Cities for Years. Here Are 4 Ways They're Coping Now, USA March 2020.

551 World Science, Industrial Map of China Energy, USA 2013.

552 World Wildlife Fund, WWF, Climate change, Coral Reefs and the Coral Triangle, USA 2019.

553 World Wind Energy Association WWEA, Small Wind World Report, Bonn Germany 2017.

554 Xi Jinping PRC President, Speech to 75th UN General Assembly, Beijing 22 September 2020.

555 Xiaowen Tian, Managing International Businesses in China, Cambridge University Press, UK 2007.

556 Xinhua, China to create Xiongan New Area in Hebei, Beijing 2017.

557 Xinhua News Agency. China to reduce coal consumption for better air, Beijing 2015.

558 Xinhua News Agency. Chinese carbon emissions to peak in 2030, Beijing 2014.

559 Xinhua China, PRC President Xi Jinping Joint Written Interview to the Media of Trinidad and Tobago, Costa Rica and Mexico on 31 May 2013, Xinhua News Agency, Beijing, China, 2013.

560 Xinhua News Agency, China M&A 2012 highlights, 22 May 2013, Beijing, China, 2013.

561 Yale Environment, China Waste to Energy Incineration, USA 2017.

562 Yuen Linda, China Growth, Oxford University Press, UK, 2013.

563 Yuen Linda, Enterprising China, Oxford University Press, UK, 2011.

564 Zhang & He, MIT Joint Report Series, Carbon emissions in China: How far can new efforts bend the curve?, MIT USA 2014.

Index